Word and World

Practice and the Foundations of Language

This important book proposes a new account of the nature of language, founded on an original interpretation of Wittgenstein. The authors deny the existence of a direct referential relationship between words and things. Rather, the link between language and world is a two-stage one, in which words are related to practices, and only practices relate to the world. Arguing against the philosophical mainstream descending from Frege and Russell to Quine, Davidson, Dummett, McDowell, Evans, Putnam, Kripke, and others, the authors demonstrate that discarding the notion of reference does not entail relativism or semantic nihilism.

A provocative reexamination of the interrelations of language and social practice, this book will interest not only philosophers of language but also literary theorists, linguists, psycholinguists, students of communication, and all those concerned with the nature and acquisition of human linguistic capacities.

Patricia Hanna is Professor of Philosophy and Linguistics at the University of Utah.

Bernard Harrison is Emeritus E. E. Ericksen Professor of Philosophy at the University of Utah and Honorary Professor of Philosophy at the University of Sussex.

For Dot and Dudley

Word and World

Practice and the Foundations of Language

PATRICIA HANNA

University of Utah

BERNARD HARRISON

University of Utah

University of Sussex

CAMBRIDGE
UNIVERSITY PRESS

PUBLISHED BY THE PRESS SYNDICATE OF THE UNIVERSITY OF CAMBRIDGE
The Pitt Building, Trumpington Street, Cambridge, United Kingdom

CAMBRIDGE UNIVERSITY PRESS
The Edinburgh Building, Cambridge CB2 2RU, UK
40 West 20th Street, New York, NY 10011-4211, USA
477 Williamstown Road, Port Melbourne, VIC 3207, Australia
Ruiz de Alarcón 13, 28014 Madrid, Spain
Dock House, The Waterfront, Cape Town 8001, South Africa

http://www.cambridge.org

First published 2004

Printed in the United States of America

Typeface ITC New Baskerville 10/12 pt.   *System* LaTeX 2$_\varepsilon$ [TB]

A catalog record for this book is available from the British Library.

Library of Congress Cataloging in Publication Data
Hanna, Patricia.
Word and world : practice and the foundations of language /
by Patricia Hanna and Bernard Harrison.
p. cm.
Includes bibliographical references and index.
ISBN 0-521-82287-4 (hard.) – ISBN 0-521-53744-4 (pbk.)
1. Language and languages – Philosophy.   2. Reference (Linguistics)
I. Harrison, Bernard, 1933– II. Title.
P107.H36 2003
401–dc21   2003051542

ISBN 0 521 82287 4 hardback
ISBN 0 521 53744 4 paperback

Contents

EPILOGUE

Preface

This book is the product of a transatlantic cross-fertilisation. The authors found themselves from 1991 onwards members of the same department, at the University of Utah, to which Harrison had moved from a British university (Sussex). At that time, Hanna was nourishing some doubts about various forms of meaning-scepticism, mainly in Quine and Kripke. Harrison had a number of projects on hand, one of which was an absurdly ambitious attempt to rethink the philosophy of language since Frege from the standpoint of an idiosyncratic reinterpretation of Wittgenstein. Some of the component parts of this enterprise, including a series of exegetical studies of middle-period Wittgenstein, had seen or were about to see print, but the project as a whole was, to put it bluntly, stalled, and had been stalled, except on its exegetical front, since the early 1980s. Conversation between us at first revealed some points of contact between our two projects. Then we began to see the possibility of certain large structural moves that would get Harrison's project moving again, in directions that would provide a framework for Hanna's ideas. At first we thought the work might yield a joint paper. Later we realised that it would have to be a series of papers. Finally we resigned ourselves to producing a joint book. By this time so many changes had occurred in each of our minds, stemming from objections or suggestions by the other, that we would have been at a loss to say which of us "owned" which parts of the project. So far as the actual writing of the book is concerned, responsibility for Parts I–III and the Epilogue has fallen mainly to Harrison, for Part IV mainly to Hanna. But much of the other lurks in the work of each. We have made no attempt to paper over the differences in style between the parts of the book produced by one or the other of us, preferring authenticity to smoothness of surface.

Some of the material in the book has been aired at various graduate seminars at Utah, at a series of seminars on Wittgenstein by Harrison at Brigham Young University, and by Hanna at a series of lectures in 2000 and 2001 at Universität Rostock. We are grateful to the many colleagues and students who, on these occasions, by formulating objections, or in other ways, have helped us to think it through. We owe a heavy debt of gratitude also to the many colleagues and friends who have undertaken the task of reading and criticising earlier drafts of the book, including James Anderson, Marianna DiPaolo, Randall Eggert, Gabriel Josipovici, Don Garrett, John Gibson, Donald Gustafson, Michael Krausz, Diego Marconi, Susan Miller, Anthony Palmer, Guy Robinson, Guy Stock and Samuel C. Wheeler III, not forgetting the anonymous Cambridge readers, and Dorothy Harrison, who proofread the entire manuscript. It goes without saying that, while many improvements must be credited to them, any errors that remain are entirely our own responsibility.

Patricia Hanna   Salt Lake City/Lewes, Sussex
Bernard Harrison   November 2002

Introduction

Philosophy, as Gilbert Ryle[1] noted long ago, deals characteristically in dilemmas: their exploration and (sometimes) their resolution. Ryle was clearly right. Philosophical puzzlement very often originates in a question – which for some reason seems to us momentous – either answer to which commits us to unpalatable or implausible consequences.

So it is with the question whether "language" in the abstract, language taken as a semantic order, a system of meanings, "mirrors the world": whether the categories, concepts, structures with which it furnishes us, far from being inventions of the human mind, simply transcribe categories and structures already inscribed in Nature, or Reality. If we answer "yes," we surely discount, or at least minimise to an implausible degree, the part played by human ingenuity in the constitution of meaning in actual languages. If we answer "no," by contrast, we seem to be denying the possibility of truth and objectivity. For how are we to describe anything truly, if the terms in which language forces us to frame all that can be said are set, not by the nature of what is to be described, but by linguistic or social convention?

The dilemma is a characteristically philosophical one; one, certainly, which has occasioned the spilling of much ink by philosophers. But its implications transcend the bounds of philosophy, at least philosophy narrowly considered as what goes on in philosophy departments. In linguistics, literary studies and the social sciences, many of the debates of the past thirty years have turned on the issue of the "referentiality," or otherwise, of language. A range of influential writers, including Derrida, Saussure, Lévi-Strauss, Roland Barthes, Julia Kristeva, among many others, have argued that the constitution of meaning within a language is neither constrained nor validated by anything external to language. Those opposed to these developments have tended to see them as promoting forms of relativism hostile to the very possibility of objective truth.

In this book we shall opt for neither wing of this ramifying and occasionally acerbic debate. Instead we shall argue that the debate itself is misconceived, because the choice, between relativism and referentiality, which appears to most of its participants to exhaust the available options, does not in fact exhaust them. There is, we shall show, a way of understanding the constitution of meaning in natural language that will allow one both to deny the existence of any extralinguistic correlate of meaning and yet, perfectly consistently, to affirm the possibility of objective truth.

The path we shall pursue falls half within and half outside the familiar terrain explored by analytic philosophy since Frege. Because our conclusions are, if correct, rather surprising ones, it is perhaps hardly surprising that the argument should be not only long and complex, but at times quite unfamiliar, not only in a number of its crucial moves, but even in much of its detail. We have tried to address the difficulty by dividing the stages of the argument between short, numbered and subheaded, and we hope reasonably clearly related, sections of text, easily relocatable by reference to an unusually detailed table of contents. A preliminary map of the stages of the argument, with some indication, however rough and preliminary, of their content and interrelationships, may nevertheless prove helpful. To that we now turn, with the proviso that what is offered in the next few pages is a bare and highly schematic outline of the argument, leaving out, along with most of its detail, most of what might make it – we trust – persuasive.

The argument of the book has a main thread running from beginning to end, to which are attached, at various points, a number of essential but subordinate discussions. The business of the main argument is the refutation, and replacement, of the doctrine introduced in Chapter 2 under the label *Referential Realism*. The Referential Realist holds that meaning is introduced into a language by the association of some class of meaning-bearing elements of the language with some class of real-world entities whose existence and nature owe nothing to linguistic convention. The case for Referential Realism, a powerful and enduring one, is developed in Chapters 1–2 and §i of Chapter 4. It rests essentially with the thought that unless the members of some class of elements of language derive their meaning simply from association with the members of some class of elements of "the world," language becomes hermetically self-referential, a prison made for itself by the mind, rather than the means of articulating thoughts concerning a mind-independent reality.

In Chapter 4 §i, we develop what is in effect a *reductio* argument against Referential Realism. It follows from Referential Realism, we argue, that, in general, we can know whether a string of words expresses a thought, in the Fregean sense of a content capable of being assessed for its truth or falsity, only if we know some other proposition to be true: for example, the proposition that each of the names in the proposition possesses, "out there in the world," a bearer. But we cannot set about assessing the truth of any proposition until we know what it asserts, as until we know that, to put it bluntly, there is nothing to submit to such assessment. It follows that all questions concerning the assertoric content of propositions must be settled in advance of raising the question whether any proposition is true or not, because in advance of those questions being settled, there is nothing about which to raise the question. And from that it follows that Referential Realism, as it entails the contrary, must be false.

This argument can be exhumed, with minimal exegetical effort, from discussions between Russell and Wittgenstein during the period from Wittgenstein's first meeting with Russell in 1911 to the composition of what was to become the *Tractatus Logico-Philosophicus*. It is, we suggest, the argument that gives force to a remark of Wittgenstein's that we label *Wittgenstein's Slogan* and that constitutes the leitmotiv of the *Tractatus* and the *Notebooks 1914–16:* "Logic must take care of itself" (*Die Logic muss für sich selber sorgen*). Coming at the argument by this route, given that a majority of philosophers now regard the *Tractatus* and its arguments as of purely historical interest, will to many eyes give Chapter 4 a quaint air of philosophical palaeontology. Can these antique speculations have much bearing on more recent writers, such as Kripke, Davidson, Dummett, or Gareth Evans?

One answer is that introducing the argument in its historical context renders not only its provenance but also its motivation and implications considerably clearer. Another is that contemporary philosophy of language is sufficiently Russellian in its assumptions, and even in much of its content, for Wittgenstein's early dissenting voice to have, as we shall see as the argument develops in detail, a sharper resonance today than might at first sight seem likely.

At first sight Wittgenstein's argument might seem indeed to lead into a dead end. On the one hand, it seems perfectly sound. On the other, it is difficult to see how its conclusion can be correct. If the constitution of linguistic meaning must logically precede the establishment of any contingent truth about the world, even the truth that a given name has a bearer, it is hard to see how language can get off the ground. Without some connection with reality, it would seem, language can be nothing but an hermetic game played with contentless counters; but how could reality enter the process of meaning-constitution, except by way of our grasp of some body of contingent truths, if only the truth that the noise "Mama" designates Mama?

The goal of the book is, in effect, to answer this question: to construct an account of meaning in natural language in tune with the implications of Wittgenstein's Slogan. This enterprise proceeds in three stages, the first roughly coextensive with Chapter 3, the second with Chapters 5–7, the third with Chapters 9–12. The first of these sections proposes an outline solution. It is, in effect, that we stop attempting to represent "the relationship between language and the world" as a relationship between *meaning-bearing elements of language and some class of entities envisaged as corresponding elements of the world.* The alternative proposed is that we think of the relationship as a two-stage one, in which world and meaning-bearing elements of language are related

to one another not directly, but only via their relationship to the third constituent of the relationship: practices. This move, in effect, separates two
questions commonly supposed conterminous: "How is language related to
the world?," and "How do linguistic expressions acquire meaning?" Once
these questions are seen in this way to be distinct, we are in a position to
avoid much philosophical muddle arising from the attempt to answer them
as if they merely expressed different aspects or versions of one and the same
question. The answer to the second, we suggest, is that linguistic expressions acquire meaning through their involvement in a wide variety of practices. The answer to the first is that the practices through which linguistic
expressions acquire meaning are not, for the most part, practices of symbol-
manipulation (although some, card-games for instance, are). For the most
part their point, and their utility in our lives, stems from the fact that they
involve (as, for instance, the practices of measurement, or the recording of
music in terms of the tonic scale involve) the manipulation of things not
constituted by human convention: actually existing elements of the sensory
field. It follows that the meaning-bearing elements of a natural language
cannot be said, in their content and structure, to "mirror the world." If their
content and structure "mirror" anything, it is the content and structure of
the practices through involvement in which they have acquired whatever
meaning we have bestowed on them. But it does not follow from that, that
language is an hermetic play of signs, for the practices in which linguistic
signs participate are not (or not all), as Locke would say, themselves "occupied about" signs, but about real things: things "real" in the sense of things
existing prior to, and independently of, human convention.

For this outline solution to stand as a tenable account of meaning in
the spirit of Wittgenstein's Slogan, however, it needs to be shown in detail
how it can be developed to account for "meaning" of at least the following
two kinds: on the one hand, the kind that consists in the relationship of a
proper name to its bearer, and, on the other, the kind ("sentential meaning,"
"assertoric content") that renders at least some sentential signs fit to be
assessed for truth or falsity. The first of these issues occupies Chapters 5–7,
the second Chapters 9–12.

Philosophical dispute about proper names has addressed two closely connected questions. The first concerns the issue of what it is for a proper name
to possess a meaning. Are we to say that a proper name has a Fregean sense,
usually equated with an identifying description, or are we to say that it is
a purely – or "directly" – referring expression, whose meaning (Fregean
Bedeutung) is to be identified with its bearer? The second question concerns
the conditions that have to be met in order that a speaker may be said to be
in a position to refer by means of a proper name. To both we offer answers
that fall outside the range of options offered by contemporary debate.

On the second question, there is agreement that a speaker cannot be
in a position to refer by means of a proper name unless he or she stands

in some special relationship to its bearer. Opinions differ, however, as to the nature of the required relationship. One body of opinion holds the necessary relationship to be forged internally to the mind, and to consist in the possession by each competent speaker of an identifying description, or something of the sort. Another holds, with Kripke, that the connection is forged externally to the mind, and consists in the existence of a causal chain linking present uses of the name to past ones, and ultimately back to an original baptism.

The view presented in Chapters 5–7 might be seen from one perspective as a version of externalism, but one that appeals not to a causal history, but to the integrity of a system of practices, namely all those practices that involve the painstaking recording of proper names for an indefinite variety of purposes from registers of birth and deaths to library catalogues, records of shipping, maps, legal documents, and so on. Such practices, we suggest, make up an intricately crossed-referencing matrix through which individuals of many kinds, including human beings, ships, townships, farms, and so on, may be traced or tracked by the traces left by recorded uses of their names. We call this matrix, created by the observance of a multitude of social practices involving names, the *Name-Tracking Network*. The path from a name to its bearer is traced through this network, much as, in Kripke's account, it is traced back down a causal chain of uses to an original baptism; and as either route proceeds externally to the mind of any individual speaker, our view could well be seen as, in a similar sense to Kripke's, "externalist" in character.

But in another way, however, we might be supposed to hold a version of internalism. A speaker's knowledge of his own language will include, it is to be supposed, familiarity with some large subset of the practices that enter into the constitution and maintenance of the Name-Tracking Network. So he will be in a position to infer, merely from the occurrence of a name in a context appropriate to one or more of them, to the actual existence of a bearer of that name, even though he or she not only lacks an *identifying* description of that individual but also any description *of that individual* whatsoever! At the same time, a description of the circumstances of occurrence of a name is a *description*, even if it isn't a description of the individual denoted by the name! So we are proposing, it might appear, an account of the conditions for successful reference by means of a proper name that is, absurdly, both "internalist" and "externalist" in character, albeit in odd senses of those terms!

In fact, our position is neither "externalist" nor "internalist" in the usual senses attached to these terms in current theorizing, as the introduction of the notion of a Name-Tracking Network brings about a crucial shift in the terms of the discussion. It does so by allowing us to dispense with the founding assumption of current discussion, noted earlier, namely, the assumption that a speaker cannot be in a position to refer by means of a proper name unless he stands in some relationship (whose precise characterisation provides the main matter of subsequent debate) to its bearer. According to us, the conditions for reference can be met just in case a speaker stands in the sort of relationship to the Name-Tracking Network that consists in familiarity with some large subset of its practices, augmented by knowledge of some set of circumstances of occurrence of the name in question. He or she does not need to stand in any relationship to the bearer of the name, either via a description or via a causal chain, because the task of locating the bearer of the name is performed, relative to a given set of circumstances of name-use, by the Name-Tracking Network (and so, *a fortiori*, by a means external to the mind of the speaker).

Settling the question of the conditions for successful reference in this way allows us to take a related line on the question of the meaning of a proper name. Here also current debate rests on a shared assumption, namely, that for a name to have a meaning is also for it to stand in a certain relationship to its bearer, in this case the relationship of *reference*, in one sense of that term. Our counterclaim can, once again, be viewed from two aspects. On the one hand, we propose that a name has meaning, not because of an occult relationship linking it to some individual, but because it is *in use* as one of the verbal counters deployed in the process of conducting one or more of the practices that make up the Name-Tracking Network. On the other hand, this move fails to sever the link between name and bearer, because it merely transforms it from a *direct* link (one whose very directness renders it occult because *sui generis*) into an indirect (and hence naturalistically explicable) one, established as the resultant of the distinct and very different relationships in which, respectively, name and bearer stand to a fabric of practices. Of course the name is introduced to its role *as a name* through being *associated*, baptismally or otherwise, with some individual. But (and this is the essential point) the act of so associating it would not confer on it the status of a name – would be a mere empty ceremony – if it were not for the "background" provided by the web of socially instituted and maintained practices within which it will subsequently find a use. Absent those practices indeed, no sense could be attached to the notion of *the bearer of a name*, because it is only by reference to those practices that we can make clear what it is to *be* the bearer of a name. To what, then, can we say that a name such as "Odysseus" or "Saul Kripke" *refers? Of what*, exactly, is it the name? It is, we shall suggest, the name of a *name-bearership*: a role or status as defined relative to a set of practices. That role is, of course, occupied in the case of those and other names, by particular persons, but there is in each such case no *single* "relationship of reference" that *both* links a phonemic string to a person *and*, by so doing, constitutes it *as a name*. Rather, there is a double, or two-stage relationship: on the one hand, the conferring on the phonemic string of the status of a name through its involvement as a counter in some set of practices, on the other, the accession of an individual to the role of bearer-of-a-name through the bestowal on him, in the context of those same practices, of that string *as* his name.

We thus have a theory of naming consistent with the demands of Wittgenstein's Slogan. It follows from it, contrary to the requirements of Referential Realism, that, in order to attach a meaning to a statement, it is not necessary to know any contingent fact concerning the bearers of the names that figure in it. All that is necessary is familiarity with some reasonably large subset of the practices making up the Name-Tracking Network. It follows also, consistently with the outline solution proposed in Chapter 3, that there is no relationship of name-reference, conceived as a relationship between a meaning-bearing element of language and some corresponding element of the world, but rather a two-stage relationship, linking both language-element and world-element to practice, and only through those links relating them to one another, of exactly the sort proposed in Chapter 3. Finally, Chapters 5–7 introduce a further claim central to the argument, namely that insofar as a language-element can be said to possess a referent, its referent is invariably some object constituted in part relative to linguistic convention, or as we put it (Chapter 5 §i) a *nomothetic object*. Among the various extraordinary doctrines recommended in this book, this is the one most likely to stick firmly in the craw of anyone of decently Realist philosophical predilections. It will therefore give us particular pleasure to show it, in due course, to be consistent with every variety of Realism to which a decent Realist should wish to subscribe.

We now come to the third and final stage of the main spine of argument in the book; the one mentioned earlier as occupying Chapters 9–12. Here, what centrally concerns us (once again this outline summary of the argument excludes much detail) is the genesis of assertoric content, or to put it nongenetically, what it is that makes certain strings of words ("This table is a metre long") susceptible or truth or falsity, whereas others ("James Peter John") are not thus susceptible. It is characteristic of Referential Realism to hold that the capacity for truth and falsity is not *intrinsically* conferred on linguistic expressions in consequence of the operation of any set of linguistic conventions, although the explanation of the truth-conditions of particular sentences may often require reference to such conventions. On the contrary, according to the Referential Realist, it is in principle possible for the truth-conditions of an utterance, an utterance, that is, taken merely as a semantically unmarked phonemic string, to be explained simply by associating it with some perceptually salient set of environmental conditions. Most Referential Realists also have held that this is precisely the way in which the simplest sentences in a language, those having a purely sensory content and reference, are in fact explained.

In Chapter 10 §§i–v, we deploy against these claims a second *reductio* argument that, although it will strike most readers as wholly unfamiliar, is in fact to be found in Wittgenstein, notably in the early sections of the *Philosophical*

Grammar and the *Philosophical Remarks*. The argument comes in two parts, or stages. Stage 1 runs as follows. Referential Realism implies the in-principle possibility of communicating a grasp of the truth-conditions of a phonemic string S, simply by indicating environmental circumstances in which S takes the value "true," together with circumstances in which it takes the value "false." But that will be possible only if there is some criterion by appeal to which aspects of environmental circumstance relevant to the truth or falsity of S *in virtue of what S means, or asserts,* can be distinguished from aspects that either have no bearing on the truth or falsity of S, or the kind of purely contingent bearing dependent, as Quine would put it, on "collateral information." And, manifestly, no such criterion is, or could be, furnished by the environmental circumstances themselves. Stage 2 of the argument addresses the question what could furnish such a criterion. We suggest, again following Wittgenstein, that possessing the required criterion is equivalent to seeing an intrinsic connection of some sort between the natural circumstances that, according to native speakers, justify the assertion of S and those that, according to native speakers, justify its denial. For to be unable to see any such connection is, precisely, to lack any means of distinguishing between natural circumstances that the native speaker takes as excluding the value "true" for S merely in virtue of the meaning (the assertoric force) of S, and natural circumstances that either have no bearing on the truth or falsity of S, or some connection apparent to the native speaker, but unguessable to the learner because merely contingent in character. Finally, if we now ask what could supply the required intrinsic connection between what is asserted by S and what is asserted by its denial (by "S is false"), the only possible answer (one given by Wittgenstein) appears to be that the assertoric contents in question are related to one another as alternative possible outcomes of the application of some practice. Thus to grasp what aspects of an indicated object are relevant to the truth of S when S is "O is 3 cm. long," it is essential to know what would be asserted by the denial of S, namely that O is *some other length in centimeters*. And grasping this is – can only be – a matter of grasping that statements of length are intrinsically related to one another as expressing alternative outcomes of applying a measuring stick according to the terms of some native system of measurement.

It follows that what makes certain phonemic strings rather than others apt for truth and falsity cannot be the mapping of those strings on to anything assertoric "out there" in the world: anything, that is, in the nature of Russell's "facts." There *is* nothing assertoric in the world external to language. On the contrary, aptitude for truth can only be conferred internally to language, by the manner in which we choose to position sentences as the verbal markers of alternative outcomes in the operation of one or another kind of practice.

We thus see, conformably to the spirit of Wittgenstein's Slogan, how meaning in the sense of aptitude for truth or falsity can be determined prior to the affirmation of any contingent truth. It is determined in determining the place occupied by specific sentences relative to the conduct of one or more of the multiplicity of practices, from measuring to sorting colour-samples relative to one another, or classifying animals or plants with respect to some chosen principle of classification, which underlie language. Meaning, in conformity with the outline solution proposed in Chapter 3, is a relationship between language-elements and practices, whereas the relationship between language and reality is reconstrued as a relationship between those practices and the aspects and elements of the extralinguistic world on which they operate.

So much, then, by way of a very bare sketch of the main articulations of the book's central argument. The remaining sections and chapters are designed to counter possible lines of objection, to demonstrate the power of the argument to dissolve certain varieties of meaning-scepticism, and to draw out its implications for various phases of the evergreen dispute between relativists and Realists.

The reception of Wittgenstein's thought has long been bedevilled by the accusation that his position in the later work amounts to a version of verificationalism or operationalism, distinguished from others only by the tedious length and obscurity of its exposition. That reading has been helped on its way by the overt verificationism of a good deal of would-be "Wittgensteinian" writing in the field, particularly in the era of so-called Ordinary Language Philosophy. Be that as it may, one of our aims in this book has been to demonstrate, at least in outline, the possibility of a reading of Wittgenstein that reveals the true extent of the gulf separating him from Vienna Circle Positivism, thus incidentally making sense of his own claim never at any time to have subscribed to a verificationist account of meaning. This phase of the argument comes to a head in §§xii–xiii of Chapter 10.

A second line, or rather two opposed lines, of objection to the views proposed here concern the notion of a rule. As will now be apparent, the theory of meaning proposed here relies heavily on the notion of a practice. It might reasonably be assumed that practices are – have to be regarded as – systems of conduct governed by rules. But that thought would seem to expose us to two objections, of equal destructive power, although of diametrically opposed and mutually inconsistent purport, coming from opposite poles of current philosophical debate. On the one hand, stand philosophers such as Dummett, who defend the possibility of a theory of meaning making explicit the rules, a grasp of which, according to them, constitutes mastery of a language. It is an essential part of Dummett's position that a theory of meaning must represent mastery of a language as a species of theoretical knowledge. If this is correct, it must follow that the position recommended here is internally incoherent, as we claim both that meaning is a matter of the involvement of linguistic expressions in practices, and also, in the spirit of Wittgenstein's Slogan, that mastery of language is logically prior to knowledge of any contingent truth, and thus intrinsically nonepistemic. On the other hand, there are all those philosophers who argue, with Kripke, that there is no sense to be made of the notion of a rule. Kripke holds, with Dummett and most of the recent writers on rules, that the notion of obedience to a rule is essentially epistemic in character. An agent is applying a rule correctly on a given occasion if, and only if, his conduct is *guided* by what he did on past occasions when he applied the rule. But his conduct on those past occasions always can be reinterpreted in such a way as to certify *anything* he may do on the present occasion as obedience to the rule. It follows that there can be no fact about the agent's mental life capable of guaranteeing the correctness of his interpretation of the rule, and hence that the required guidance can only come from the willingness of the language-community in general to accept what he does on each occasion as correct. We – the holders of the view recommended in these pages – thus seem to be left with an unappetising choice between a Dummettian cognitivism that leaves us holding an incoherent theory, and a Kripkean anti-cognitivism that commits any theory of meaning based on the notion of a practice to relativism and meaning-scepticism in their most radical forms.

These issues are addressed in Chapter 8. The reason for placing them here, at the end of the discussion of naming but before the opening of Part III, is, of course, that the questions they raise are pivotal, and cannot be left hanging once the general drift of our proposals has become clear. Answering them requires us to offer some suitable account of what it is to understand and participate in a practice, and this we do in Chapter 8 §vi. According to that account, a speaker is participating in a practice if, and only if, he shares a certain pattern of habits of response and initiation of behaviour with other members of the linguistic community, and exercises those habitual patterns of conduct in such a way as to indicate that he is aware of what advantages are to be gained by doing so, and proposes to gain those advantages. The advantage of such an account is that it allows us to dispense with the notion that conduct can be understood as intelligent only if it is "guided" by appeal to some piece of knowledge, either knowledge of a "rule," or knowledge of some "fact" about past conduct. It opens the way to a *nonepistemic* account of linguistic competence. It enables us to acknowledge the force of the argument underlying Wittgenstein's Slogan, in other words, while avoiding the Kripkean interpretation of Wittgenstein, together with its terminus in a combination of meaning-scepticism and social relativism. The quasi-Humean problem perceived by Kripke, of stating the grounds that justify a speaker's belief that his conduct of a practice, such as counting, is "correct," fails to arise if no such justification is required. And no such justification is required. The competent speaker simply activates learned habits of response that mesh with those of other speakers. Nor, according to us, could there be "grounds" external to the practice to which appeal could be made, to establish the "correctness" of its implementation by an individual speaker. No "fact" about an individual speaker could serve this function, because linguistic practices are essentially social in character. But nor could an appeal to the approval or disapproval of other members of the linguistic community establish "correctness," either. Either the individual speaker who participates in a practice has access to criteria of correctness internal to it, given its nature and the practical purposes it serves, or the supposed "practice" has no criteria of correctness at all: is, in other words, not a practice at all, but a pointless charade.

Chapter 8 begins the work of drawing out the anti-sceptical implications of the view of meaning presented here. That work is completed in Part IV, which deals with two further versions of meaning-scepticism that have bulked large in recent debate, namely, Quine's thesis of the Indeterminacy of Meaning and Kripke's paradox of belief. We argue, in effect, that both arguments succeed. Neither can be refuted; each marks an important advance in philosophy. What each reveals, however, is not some hitherto quite unsuspected paradox that genuinely confronts us, but rather a hitherto quite unsuspected paradox that would confront us if Referential Realism were really the only option open to us in our deepest thinking about the relationship between language and the world. Quine is right that meaning of an expression is empirically underdetermined. But meaning of an expression is not "empirically" determined. It is not, that is, determined by its relationship to some set of sensory items, but by its relationship to a practice. Kripke is right that, if we allow the translation of "Londres" as "London" in translating a sentence sincerely assented to by a speaker in one language into a sentence of contrary purpose sincerely assented to by the same speaker in another language, we shall find ourselve unable to say which of the mutually inconsistent claims made by means of the sentences in question the speaker actually believes. But what that shows is that the meaning of a name is not to be identified with its bearer – that is, with something external to either language – but, rather, with something internal to each language in play in the example; namely, a name-bearership. A name-bearership is a nomothetic status that may be borne by more than one entity, and in the mind of a speaker who sees no inconsistency in affirming both that London is ugly and *que Londres est jolie*, is borne by more than one entity. The power of Kripke's paradox stems, in short, precisely from the fact that it is *not* a paradox "about belief" but, rather, one "about" a theory of meaning to which the philosophical world has hitherto failed to perceive any alternative.

Talk of nomothetic entities, entities forged in the furnace of linguistically marked practice, returns us, finally, to our beginnings in the issue of realism versus linguistic and other kinds of relativism. In the text we defer these issues to an Epilogue, mainly becase an adequate discussion requires the entire course of the argument to be present to the mind of the reader. But it will do no harm to offer a brief outline of our conclusions here. Four kinds of Realism concern us: Realism about concepts, Realism about the existence of a world external to language, Realism about meaning, and Realism about truth. The theory of meaning outlined here is relativist on the first of these, Realist on the others: hence relatively Realist.

The first is roughly conterminous with what philosophers used to call the Problem of Universals, the theoretically possible solutions to which are said to comprise Realism, Conceptualism, and Nominalism. Realism about Universals says, in effect, that concepts mirror nature, and in that sense are Real. This we deny: according to us, what concepts a language honours is relative, not to the presence in Nature of extralinguistic entities of the required metaphysical kind (Ideas, Universals, Kantian categories), but to the nature of the practices on which that language happens to be founded. The force of this denial in our case is not, however, caught by either of the traditional alternatives to Realism, Conceptualism, and Nominalism. We hold, that is, neither that concepts are "the work of the mind," nor that we are free to choose which individuals we rank under a concept. What we hold is that we assign sense, and truth-conditions, to linguistic expressions by the manner in which we choose to employ them relative to practices; but that in devising practices we are forced to interact with a world external to language; a world that is in no way pliant to arbitrary caprice. We establish truth-conditions for a range of sentences precisely by locating them relative to a practice in such a way that different outcomes of operating that practice assign the value "true" to one member of the range and "false" to the others. But no decision of ours can determine the outcome of operating a practice. Only the world can do that. The practice, as it were, gives speech to the world, by conferring on natural circumstances the status of truth-conditions (in our terms another kind of nomothetic status), and we devise the practice. But, having devised it, we are powerless to determine what the world so rendered articulate will say. In the same way, we establish a family of general names by devising priciples of classification that will serve to sort individuals into named sets. But even though it is we who are responsible for devising the notion of, say, a species, it is the world that must determine whether a given population of Papuan snails comprises one species or two, or whether, given that the principles of classification we devise are never without fuzzy edges, which become crucially determining in a minority of contexts, the question is unanswerable on the terms we have chosen.

It might be objected[2] that we have no right to allow ourselves the concept of an objective, extralinguistic, "Nature," or "Natural World," as our theory appears to make it impossible to grasp the nature of that world except in the terms dictated by a specific language. Are we not committed to the view that the world as it exists outside language is ineffable – intellectually inaccessible, except, perhaps, in the purely theoretical guise of something along the lines of the Kantian Thing-in-Itself – because nothing can be said about it except in terms fatally tainted by linguistic convention?

The answer is that such terms as "grasp" or "render accessible" are not uni-vocal. There is a way of grasping the nature of things that consists in making true statements, and a way that consists in the sensory-cum-physical manipulation of the world. When we engage in the latter, we not only engage with a world external to, and prior to, language; our own bodily-cum-sensory activity is itself external to, and prior to, "language," if one takes that to consist in the manipulation of words representative of already formed concepts. The enlightenment, the grasp of "the nature of things," which consists in the discovery that certain procedures have, in nature, certain possible outcomes, is a type of enlightenment wholly unmediated by language. Language begins only at the point at which we introduce verbal markers for alternative outcomes, and with them the notions of reference, truth, and falsity. In this way, we give the extralinguistic world we encounter in prelinguistic practice as it were the means of expressing itself. We give it the means of answering questions in terms we can understand because the terms in which we ask them are creatures of the practices in which we have chosen to confront the extralinguistic. But the answers given by the extralinguistic world to those questions belong to it alone: *they* are not the product of linguistic convention.

The argument presented here thus supports what one might call commonsense Realism about the extralinguistic. It allows us both to claim access to a world untouched by language because encountered through practices that are prelinguistic because foundational to language; and assert also the status of the majority of commonplace and scientific truths as truths *about that world.* We are in that sense scientific Realists. There is another way of envisaging scientific realism, however, which the argument presented here will not support. We have in mind the reductionist account that rests on the assumed possibility of something along the lines of Russell's "logically perfect language": one that in its concepts and structure correctly represents the constitution of Reality itself. That ideal is, if we are right, not merely unattainable but vacuous. Its possibility requires the truth of Referential Realism, and Referential Realism is, if we are right, not merely false but internally incoherent. Language cannot transcend practice, and hence, although what we truly say about the world is in a quite unproblematic sense true of *it,* as spoken *by* it, discourse can never emancipate itself from the possibility that the devising of a new practice will enable the world to speak its nature in altogether new and unexpected terms. There cannot be a Final Language. There are truths, but (for reasons of principle) no Final Truth.

In terms of the present argument, however, there is no obstacle to Realism both about truth and about meaning. This is because anti-Realism on each of these topics is the fruit of the consensus in current philosophy that sees both concepts as profoundly epistemic in character. It is that consensus that this book, following a route marked out in our opinion by Wittgenstein, is intended to weaken.

PART I

SCEPTICISM AND LANGUAGE

1

The Prison-House of Language

i. Scepticism and the content of "commonsense"

We think, and we speak our thoughts. Necessarily we speak them, even to ourselves, in some language, either in a so-called natural one – French, English, Hebrew, Greek – or in one of the so-called artificial languages of mathematics or formal logic. Whatever language we choose to speak, or must speak, however, we take ourselves often enough, most often perhaps, to be speaking in it of real things: things "real" in the sense, a sense introduced to philosophy by Descartes, and the source of much enduring intellectual anguish since, of being "outside the mind."

But are not words themselves creatures of language? Is language itself not a creation of the human mind? If so, what assurance have we that, when we speak, we speak of the furniture of the universe, of Reality itself, rather than merely of the homely, and home-made, furniture of our own minds?

In raising such doubts we envisage the possibility that language, although it may seem the house of the mind, with windows opening on an extramental, extralinguistic world, may in fact be a prison, with none. The image of language as a prison no doubt owes something, historically, to Plato's myth of the Cave. But those immured in the Prison-House of Language, as philosophers since Locke have conceived it, are rather worse off than those chained facing the back wall of Plato's Cave. For the shadows that flicker on the wall of the Cave are at least shadows cast by real things borne on the heads of those who pass before the fire closer to the entrance; whereas those in the Prison-House of Language may be (and perhaps are, if some of Derrida's admirers are to be believed) condemned to converse solely with conceptual fictions fabricated entirely within language, shadows lacking even the tenuous contact with Reality enjoyed by the ones in Plato's myth.

Worries of this kind belong to the category of what is called "philosophical" or "sceptical" doubt. A good deal of philosophy has consisted in the

17

attempt to resolve or allay such doubts. When engaged as philosophers in such enterprises, we are apt to assume a sharp division between the doubts themselves and our efforts to think our way out of them. It seldom occurs to us that patterns of thinking motivated by the desire to put an end to such doubts might be conditioned in their nature by the nature of the very doubts they are designed to eliminate. We think of scepticism, as it were, by analogy with the enemy in trench warfare: separated from us by no-man's land and two sets of barbed wire entanglements. We are insufficiently alive to the possibility that the enemy might be all the time behind the lines, indeed in charge of GHQ, and actually directing the eternally ineffectual artillery barrages we lay down against his supposed positions. Yet in reality the power of philosophical scepticism often lies not so much in the threat it poses to "reason" or "commonsense," as in its power to direct the very patterns of thought that seem to us most essential to what, under the impetus of the effort to evade it, we are led to admit as reasonable or commonsenical.

The mechanism of this curious, and for the most part covert, transformation of the sceptic into Director of Anti-Sceptical Operations is simple enough. Bradley is perhaps the most obvious example of a philosopher who defends his views not so much by offering positive grounds for accepting them, but instead by arguing that there is no possible alternative to them that cannot be shown to be inconsistent with itself. But argument of that kind, argument *à rebours*, is universal in philosophy. Philosophers constantly defend their opinions by arguing that to take any other view is to court conclusions that, for one reason or another, by reason of incoherence, or absurdity, or simply because many or most of us find them "intolerable," are to be avoided at all costs. But "intolerable" positions in philosophy are very often felt to be intolerable precisely because, from the perspective that they open up, questions – riddles – can be posed that we have no clear idea how to answer, yet that we feel we must answer if we are to avoid accepting the "intolerable" stance from within which they appear to pose themselves. Such questions inevitably possess a form and a content that influence, if they do not entirely determine, the form and content of our attempts to answer them. To set about formulating a direct, head-on, answer to the sceptic's question is generally to accept, that is, as part of the unexamined groundwork of subsequent argument, the terms in which the sceptic has chosen to formulate it, and thus, to a degree, the sceptic's "intolerable" point of view. Thus it is that Sphinx and Oedipus, Rameau's nephew and *Monsieur le Philosophe*, bewilderingly change places; the responses of the Man of Reason, or those of his English-speaking counterpart the Man of Commonsense, coming in the process to seem curiously infected with the accents of the very scepticism both are trying so hard to avoid.

Such is the case with doubt concerning the supposed capacity of language to transform itself from the vehicle of the converse of thought with reality into a prison in whose hermetically sealed rooms the mind in its wanderings encounters only a shadow-play of conceptual fictions of its own devising. This potent image, or rather the earnest attempt to show why, exactly, it misrepresents our situation, has, as we shall try to show, motivated a great deal of the best theorising, from Russell to Quine and from Michael Dummett to Saul Kripke, which has been produced in Analytic circles this century under the rubric of "Philosophy of Language." Many of these theories are of sublime subtlety and ingenuity. Nevertheless, we shall do our best to combat the attractions of such theorising, and to do so in part by showing how much of it is not merely haunted by, but infected with, the image of language as prison. For our part we shall argue, in the footsteps of Wittgenstein, that the construction of philosophical theory is the wrong response to scepticism, here as elsewhere. There is no need to construct philosophical theories, of whatever degree of subtlety, to refute the sceptical conclusions supposedly implicit in the picture of language as the prison-house of the mind. That picture could no more correctly describe our condition than a real physical object could be as depicted in one of the drawings of M. C. Escher. Just as there is no way of coherently mapping an Escher drawing on to a real three-dimensional object, so there is no way of coherently mapping the 'picture' of language as prison on to our actual situation as speakers; and for the same reason: both drawing and picture are, though in different ways, internally incoherent. It is in one way perfectly correct to say that, as Merleau-Ponty puts it, "in a sense language never has anything to do with anything but itself."[1] But the sense in which that remark is true is, as we shall try to show, not that suggested by the image of the prison-house, and not one which carries any threat to the unimpeded converse of the mind with Reality.

ii. "Tree" and "demonic possession"

There are many ways, as we shall see, of articulating the fear that the need to use language in conversing with Reality might render that converse illusory. One intuitively persuasive way of giving body to such doubts exploits the evident difference between notions like *tree* or *blue*, which possess innumerable exemplars in experience, and ones, like *phlogiston* or *demonic possession*, which possess none. When we use concepts like the latter two, we want to say, although we may think that our discourse is engaged with reality, in reality it is not: it is moving only within the ambit of our own imaginings. Something has gone wrong.

But what, exactly, *has* "gone wrong"? Is the fault to be traced to the failure of such concepts to meet whatever criteria of adequacy govern concept formation, or to the epistemic grounding of the claims in whose articulation we employ them? Is it, in other words, *language* that has imprisoned our minds in the circuit of their own fancies, or simply superstition, or bad physical theory?

At least two benign philosophical consequences would result from giving an answer of the latter kind. To begin with it would, by liberating us from the need to locate the defect in some malfunction of language, make it possible to entertain the thought that *phlogiston, demonic possession,* and so on, might be perfectly well-formed concepts; notions, that is, having a clear meaning, a clear sense. And such a move would have distinct philosophical advantages. It would, for one thing, be in line with Frege's rather telling argument for the publicity of sense. The sense of a sentence (a Thought, in Frege's terminology), is what shows us how to set about determining the truth or falsity of the sentence, and for that reason it must be "public" – available in common to all speakers of the language – as otherwise the common pursuit of truth would be impossible.

> ... it must be possible to put a question to which the true answer is negative. The content of such a question is, in my terminology, a thought. It must be possible for several people who hear the same interrogative sentence to grasp the same sense and recognise the falsity of it. Trial by jury would assuredly be a silly arrangement if it could not be assumed that each of the jurymen could understand the question at issue in the same sense. So the sense of an interrogative sentence, even when the question has to be answered in the negative, is something that can be grasped by several people.[2]

The sense of a predicate expression (a "concept," for Frege) contributes to the senses (the Thoughts) expressed by the sentences in which it occurs. So we can say, extending, but only slightly, Frege's thoughts on the matter, that such an expression has a clear sense (corresponds to a well-formed concept), just in case grasping the sense of a sentence employing it allows us to see how to set about attaching a truth-value to that sentence. And that is clearly the case where *phlogiston* and *demonic possession* are concerned. It is far from being the case, in other words, that we can *make no sense* of these notions. On the contrary, we can make quite sufficiently good sense of them for it to be clear that there is no such thing as phlogiston and no evidence whatsoever for the existence of demonic possession. Equally plainly, if they were not well-formed concepts, no such conclusions could have been established.

iii. The Correspondence Theory of Meaning

The second advantage of locating bad theorising, rather than some defect of language, as the source of the perennial tendency of the human mind to take for realities phantoms of its own devising, is that it would allow us to make do with one, rather than two, ways in which language may be said to "correspond to," or "be adequate to," Reality.

In philosophy, talk of "correspondence" between language and the world has been most in evidence, and most at home in, versions of what is known as "the Correspondence Theory of Truth." Most versions of the Correspondence Theory make at least the following three claims:

1. The assessment of truth and falsity is made possible by the existence of semantically mediated correlations between the members of some class of linguistic entities possessing assertoric force (in some versions of the Correspondence Theory propositions, in others sentences, or bodies of sentences), and the members of some class of extralinguistic entities: "states of affairs," or "facts," or bodies of truth-conditions, or of assertion-warranting circumstances.

2. The subsisting in nature of the real-world correlate of an assertion is what *legitimates*, in the sense of rendering true, the assertion in question.

3. The power to legitimate an assertion, in the sense of determining its truth, belongs to nature, not to thought. Truths – at least truths concerning the world given to us in experience – are *discovered*: they are not stipulated, or "constituted by convention," or in any other way "the work of the mind."

As a theory of truth, even for the most banal statements of fact, the correspondence theory is notoriously less clear and less simple than it might seem at first sight. Familiar difficulties arise when, for instance, we try to make clear exactly what entities stand to one another in the required relationship of correspondence, and how, exactly, that relationship itself is to be envisaged. But, granting all that, there does nevertheless seem to be something harmlessly truistic about the thought that what makes truth possible in the first place is some form of semantically mediated correlation between an assertion and a state of affairs, that the obtaining of a state of affairs legitimates the corresponding assertion, and that only a discovery about how things stand in the world can legitimate an utterance aiming at factual truth.

Since Plato, however, philosophers of a Realist persuasion have often talked as if they believed, or would like to believe, not merely in a correspondence theory of truth, but also in something in the nature of a Correspondence Theory of Meaning, committed to analogues of (1)–(3). An outline, or schematic, form of Correspondence Theory of Meaning, that is, would hold:

1'. that there is a distinction of some sort to be drawn between legitimate and illegitimate concepts, analogous to the distinction between legitimate (true) and illegitimate (false) assertions;

2'. that concepts, like assertions, are rendered legitimate by the fact of standing in a relationship of correspondence of some sort to something actually subsisting "in the world"; and

3'. that whether or not a concept is, in the required sense, legitimate, is not something that can be established by stipulation, or by any species of thought that remains internal to the mind, but only by the *discovery*, "out in the world," of an actually existing entity of the right kind to stand in the right sort of correspondence to the concept in question. (3'), of course, entails as a corollary

4'. that it is as possible to be mistaken about what concepts correspond to reality as it is to be mistaken about what judgments correspond to the facts.

The holder of the Correspondence Theory of Meaning, in other words, does not regard the phlogiston theory as an erroneous theory of combustion framed in terms of a well-formed concept, *phlogiston*. For him what is wrong with the theory is not merely that its judgments fail to match up to reality; the concepts, or some of them, in terms of which that theory is formulated, fail to match up to reality as well.

Put baldly, without benefit of philosophical scene-setting, the Correspondence Theory of Meaning might not appear very attractive. It is one of those philosophical claims, indeed, which it is rather difficult to imagine anyone holding if he or she were not in the grip of some independently compelling doctrine that appeared to entail it as a consequence. Things in that respect might not seem at first sight quite as bad as they are, because there is at least one intuitively plausible, albeit abstract, line of argument that might be thought to establish the Correspondence Theory of Meaning independently of any supplementary philosophical commitment. Its initial steps run roughly as follows:

i. A language L offers its speakers only certain possible ways of formulating sentences capable of serving as the vehicle of intelligible assertions.

ii. Whatever assertions can be formulated in L must, therefore, be conveyed by means of sentences capable of being formulated according to the canons of intelligibility proper to that language.

iii. It would not be possible to utter truths by means of those sentences unless there existed some prior relationship between the world and the canons of intelligibility of L, which fits sentences constructed according to them to serve as the vehicle of truth.

But, plausible as (i)–(iii) may be as premises, they will not, unsupplemented, yield as their conclusion any version of the Correspondence Theory of Meaning. They do indeed suggest a possible way of distinguishing between legitimate and illegitimate sentences, and so, derivatively, perhaps, between legitimate and illegitimate concepts, by appeal to the existence, or absence, of the right sort of relationship between the world and the canons of intelligibility proper to the language. But it offers no reason why the relationship in question should be conceived as one of *correspondence*, between, on the one hand, elements of the language or their semantic contents, and, on the other, some class of real-world *entities*.

Something more, then, some further and more intrinsically compelling philosophical commitment, is required to motivate the understanding of meaning in terms of correspondence. That something falls within our grasp the moment we decide to make language bear the onus of explaining what has gone wrong with our thinking when it revolves around such concepts as *phlogiston* or *demonic possession*. Very early in the development of modern philosophy, Locke takes what amounts to this step in drawing the distinction, in Book III of the *Essay*, between names of substances and names belonging to the category he calls "mixed modes," of which he gives "procession" as an instance, which stand for what he terms "creatures of the understanding." Such notions are, he says

... not only made by the mind, but made very arbitrarily, made without patterns, or reference to any real existence; wherein they differ from those of substances, which carry with them the supposition of some real being from which they are taken, and to which they are conformable.[3]

Locke is here formulating the beginnings of a distinction between legitimate and illegitimate concepts of just the kind required by the Correspondence Theory of Meaning. A concept is legitimate – of use in the scientific study of Nature – when there is "some real being" to which it is "conformable." When there is no such "real being" standing over against the concept, it is a mere "arbitrary" fabrication of the mind, to be studied as an object, perhaps, by those interested in investigating the anatomy and causes of the inexhaustible human capacity to invent such "creatures of the understanding," but of no use in fabricating any truth concerning the real nature of things, including whatever truths may ultimately turn out to capture the basis in Nature of that capacity.

To formulate the distinction between scientifically useful and scientifically useless concepts in this way is at once to raise the spectre of the Prison-House of Language. For it makes it appear that the main obstacle to the achievement of a language capable of representing accurately how things stand in Reality is the creative fertility of the mind in the elaboration of concepts. And that in turn raises the possibility that that very fertility might shut the mind off from Reality, blinding it, to employ a graphic phrase of Berkeley's,[4] with a "false imaginary glare"; not, in this case, the glare of sensory experience, of which Philonous was speaking, but the deceptive radiance of seeming illumination shed by concepts having no basis in nature.

Locke's account, of course, raises that spectre only to exorcise it in the same breath. For Locke's account of concept-formation offers us a way of avoiding being blinded by the glare of our own conceptual fictions. We shall be freed from that danger just to the extent that we confine ourselves to concepts the content of which owes nothing to the inventive ingenuity of the human mind, because they are modelled on the template of "some real being from which they are taken."

The point to which we wish to draw attention, now, is that *spectre and exorcism are part and parcel of one another.* Locke is offering what must be one of the earliest versions of the Correspondence Theory of Meaning in modern philosophy. Freed from the specific concerns and terminology of Locke's philosophy, it commits one to versions of the analogues of (1)–(3) we mentioned earlier. These might be stated as follows:

1″. What makes conceptual thought about reality possible is a correspondence between a linguistic expression, or some suitably envisaged mental correlate, and an item or aspect of reality;

2″. What legitimates a linguistic expression, or any putative mental correlate that we may suppose it to possess, in the sense of rendering it useful in the description of reality, is the actual existence of the real-world entity to which it corresponds;

3″. Whether a linguistic expression or its putative mental correlate is or is not legitimate in that sense can be established only by a discovery – the discovery that the putative real-world correlate does actually exist – not by stipulation, or any other form of activity wholly internal to the mind.

The main arguments in favour of accepting the position sketched by (1″)–(3″) are, first, that, if sound, it really does exorcise the spectre of the Prison-House of Language, and secondly, that, as long as one takes that spectre to pose a real threat, it is very hard to think of any other set of philosophical moves that would exorcise it. For if the problem with *procession,* and for that matter *phlogiston* and *demonic possession,* is that they are fabrications of the mind, then that problem could only fail to arise in the case of concepts *in the fabrication of whose content the mind has played no part.*

We are faced, in short, with an instance of precisely the type of covert relationship, between scepticism and philosophical theory ostensibly designed to rebut it, which engaged our attention in §i. Locke's mind is, as Wittgenstein would put it, "held captive by a picture." The picture is of a man speaking or writing. He takes what he is saying or writing down to be a description of his world. But in fact the terms that express the whole content of his discourse bear no more relationship to what exists in, or is the case concerning, the world in which he finds himself, than the concept *demonic possession* does to our world. Notice that this picture is common both to the sceptic and to his adversary in the shape of Locke and his philosophical successors. The sceptic is fascinated by it because he wishes to suggest that there may be a terrible price to be paid for the inventiveness, the conceptual fertility of the mind, displayed in the conceptual constitution of language, that price being that it may place us, unawares, in the position of the man in the picture. The sceptic's adversary, himself fascinated by that picture, and blinded by its power to constrain the mind, accepts without further ado the sceptic's suggestion that what accounts for the position of the man in the picture is the conceptual fertility of the mind, or of language. Accepting that, the anti-sceptic concludes, reasonably enough in his terms, that there can be only one way of evading such a fate: namely, to confine ourselves to concepts in the constitution of whose content the treacherous inventiveness of the mind has played no part, because they are merely casts, or rubbings, of templates found in nature. The sceptic's adversary thinks that in taking this step he has defeated the sceptic. But in fact, by the time this step is taken, the sceptic has won; has won, that is, if not the battle to make a fellow-sceptic of his adversary, at least the battle to make scepticism a dominant force in the adversary's thinking. He won that second battle when his adversary advanced blindly from mere contemplation of the situation of the man in the picture to the acceptance, without argument, of a substantial philosophical thesis: that what is to be blamed for the situation of the man in the picture is the conceptual fertility, in the absence of logical or scientific regimentation, of the natural languages we ordinarily speak.

2

Referential Realism

i. From correspondence to realism

When once adopted on those grounds, especially by minds that, like that of the early Russell, happen to be sympathetic to empiricism, while at the same time repelled by any form of Idealism, the Correspondence Theory can very easily be reworked to provide the basis of a form of Realism – call it Referential Realism – definable by its opposition to two opposing views: Conventionalism and Relativism. The Referential Realist shares Locke's conviction that what we say has a bearing on reality only if its content is "conformable" to "some real being." The Referential Realist need not, of course, commit himself to any view concerning the identity of the ultimate content-bearing elements of a language. It is indifferent to him, for instance, whether he sets up his position in terms of names and predicate-expressions, or in terms of sentences, or in terms of theoretically articulated collections of sentences. His claim is, simply, that only if some semantic contents, whatever linguistic entities they may attach to, in some way correspond to, or mirror, actually existing elements of Reality, will it be possible, in the language concerned, to construct propositions having a bearing on reality. Conventionalism, from the Referential Realist's point of view, is the claim that *all* the entities picked out by the content-bearing expressions of a natural language might be linguistic constructs: entities wholly constituted by linguistic convention. Referential Realism is not, of course, incompatible with the claim that some may be. The Referential Realist can grant without damage to his position, for instance, that "parenthesis," "the ampersand," "alpha," indeed all merely syncategorematic expressions, pick out entities that owe their existence and nature purely to linguistic convention. What he must resist is the idea that all the content-bearing expressions of a natural language might pick out such entities. For if he were to grant that, then, as he sees it, the gates of the Prison-House of Language would close on him. He would be granting, again as he sees it, that language is no more than an hermetic play of conventions, with no opening on Reality.

For the Referential Realist, the requirement that whatever content-bearing elements may be semantically primary in a language pick out entities whose existence and nature owe nothing to linguistic convention is, as he sees it, the main constraint exercised by Reality on the content of our conceptual vocabulary. Such a Realist is struck by the fact that different languages, the languages of Western science and of Azande magic for instance, represent Reality in quite different lights. How are we to adjudicate between such differing views of how things stand in the world? The Referential Realist's preferred answer, like Locke's, is, in effect, that the entities picked out by the terms that occur most basically in scientific explanation are really existing entities, whereas those picked out by the terms basic to Azande explanations of things are, to reapply Davidson's celebrated phrase concerning metaphor, the "dreamwork of language." The result of denying the truth of Referential Realism, in the opinion of the Referential Realist, can only be, therefore, a relapse into Relativism, because, if the entities picked out by the names and predicate-expressions of natural languages must all, without exception, be regarded as mere constructs of linguistic convention, there can remain, as he sees it, no way of adjudicating rationally between the differing visions of Reality offered by the differing systems of thought and explanation corresponding to different languages.

ii. Semantic foundationalism

There are, as we shall see, a wide variety of ways of articulating Referential Realism as one element of a wider philosophical stance. In this and the next two sections we shall offer a rough survey of three such ways, which together span much of the literature of analytic philosophy of language since Russell. Any embodiment of Referential Realism must, of course, identify the content-bearing elements of a language, and the real-world entities to which they correspond, or in Locke's words, "are conformable." How are we to do this? A natural course would be to identify the primary content-bearing expressions of a language as proper names and predicate-expressions, the items picked out by names as really existing individuals, and those picked out by predicate-expressions as recurrent aspects or qualities (*qualia*) of sensory experience. That is the option explored, for instance, by Russell in his early, Realistic phase. It encounters the immediate objection that very many predicates, "is constitutional" or "has a pH of 3.1," for instance, have no very obvious correlates in the immediate content of sensation. But some, such as "is red" or "is hard," do, and it seems plausible to suggest that in such cases the meaning of the predicate-expression can be explained simply by indicating, or as the early Russell would have said, by becoming *acquainted* with, its sensory correlate. "The word 'red' can only be understood through

acquaintance with the object,"[1] says Russell, espousing just such a view, in
Lecture II of the Monist lectures of 1918. The attraction, for Russell, of the
acquaintance-based account of meaning that appears to receive the support
of such cases, is precisely that it suggests, to a Realist of Russell's stamp at
the time, a way of circumventing the presumed power of thought, or language, to shut off the mind from the world behind the screen interposed
by the false imaginary glare of its own conceptual constructions. With terms
such as "red," which appear to pick out simple aspects of the world given
to sensation, the mind appears actually to "reach out and touch" objects
wholly outside itself. What appears in such cases to guarantee the unmediated directness, prized by the Realist, of the contact between Mind and
the Extramental, is, of course, the fact that, just as in Locke's account of
names of substances, the constitutive activity of Mind (or Language) in the
fabrication of "concepts" or "meanings" has been reduced to a minimum.
All that mental activity contributes to the provision of a meaning for "red,"
on Russell's account, is the stipulation of a particular phonemic string as
the one to be definitionally associated, by the English language, with the
sensory content apprehended through acquaintance with tomatoes and pil-
larboxes. The *content* of the *concept* "red," by contrast, is entirely contributed
by the sensory content of a given act of acquaintance, because, on Russell's
view, it is *identical with* the latter content. Conceptual content and linguistic
convention, in other words, are neatly partitioned-off from one another,
with the latter occupied solely with such evidently intralinguistic matters as
phonemics, or morphology, in which its intervention presents no threat to
unimpeded intercourse between Mind and the Extramental.

What, now, is to be done about predicates whose content does not appear
to be identifiable with any directly given sensory content? Russell's answer
appeals to one of the several conceptions of reductive analysis that dominated one phase or another of English-speaking philosophy throughout the
past century. Dependence on reductive analysis as a philosophical technique
is sometimes taken to be exclusively linked with the phenomenalism and
anti-Realism characteristic of 1930s Logical Positivism, and vice versa. This
is an error. Michael Dummett has argued persuasively that "anti-Realism
need not take the form of reductionism."[2] It can as easily be shown that
reductionism is entirely compatible with Realism, provided we are talking
about a reductionism advanced on semantic rather than epistemic grounds.
Epistemic reductionism addresses the *hauptfrage* of epistemology: "How far
can we be said to possess knowledge?" The answer it offers is that what we
know concerning the immediate content of experience, because it is immune to doubt, can serve as a secure epistemic grounding for those kinds
of knowledge that turn out to be reducible to it. Semantic reductionism, by
contrast, addresses the rather different question that has so far concerned us
here: not "Is our knowledge real?," but "Are the concepts in terms of which
language invites us to conceive of reality merely fabrications of the mind?"

The answer it offers is that some, "basic," concepts are not merely fabrications of the mind, and that other, "nonbasic" ones escape this description to the extent that they can be reductively defined in terms of members of the first set. A successful programme of epistemic reductionism would tend, therefore, to work in favour of some version of phenomenalism, and thus of anti-Realism; whereas a successful programme of semantic reductionism would tend to demonstrate the conclusions of Referential Realism: that it is, after all, possible for the mind to enter directly, in a way unmediated, that is, by processes inherent in either thought or language, into relationship with a mind-independent Reality.

Semantic reductionism enters the thought of the early Russell as a by-product of the doctrine of Acquaintance and Description. Acquaintance and Description are admittedly introduced, in Chapter 5 of *The Problems of Philosophy*, as types of knowledge. Knowledge "by acquaintance" is "knowledge of things." "Knowledge by description," by contrast, "always involves . . . some knowledge of truths." But the choice of those as the grounds on which the two types of knowledge are discriminated is sufficient in itself to show that the distinction with which we are dealing here is not, fundamentally, epistemic but rather semantic. Knowing "truths" manifestly entails knowing language: knowing, by Acquaintance, "things," equally manifestly does not. The mind that "knows by Description" is thus, in effect, a mind shut within the walls of language, while the mind that "knows by Acquaintance" is one that has passed beyond those walls to stand in the unmediated presence of the world.

The semantic character of the distinction becomes clearer still when it is set to work to define a version of reductionism. Again Russell uses the language of epistemic foundationalism:

All our knowledge, both knowledge of things and knowledge of truths, rests upon acquaintance as its foundation.[3]

Later in the chapter, however, it becomes clear that, for Russell, the considerations that compel us to regard Acquaintance as foundational are, primarily at least, semantic ones. It is by appeal to Acquaintance that we learn, in other words, not what, when it comes down to it, our claims to knowledge amount to; but what, when it comes down to it, we are talking about: what *our words*, "ultimately," *mean.*

We must attach *some* meaning to the words we use, if we are to speak significantly and not utter mere noise; and the meaning we attach to our words must be something with which we are acquainted. Thus when, for example, we make a statement about Julius Caesar, it is plain that Julius Caesar himself is not before our minds, since we are not acquainted with him. We have in mind some *description* of Julius Caesar: "the man who was assassinated on the Ides of March", "the founder of the Roman Empire", or, perhaps, merely, "the man whose name was *Julius Caesar*". Thus our statement does not mean quite what it seems to mean, but means something involving, instead of

Julius Caesar, some description of him which is composed wholly of particulars and universals with which we are acquainted.[4]

Why is it, exactly, that our words would lapse into meaninglessness, would not even possess "*some* meaning," if the possibility of associating at least some, "basic" words with objects of acquaintance were to be denied us? Why is it philosophically futile to respond with the obvious thought that we can, and frequently do, make clear our meaning in a perfectly satisfactory way by means of a definition or a description? Russell's reply, which he was still prepared to give thirty years later, in *An Inquiry into Meaning and Truth* (and not surprisingly, because the point is a powerfully persuasive one), is that the explication of verbal formulae in terms of other verbal formulae can only be futile, unless at some point we can escape the circle of the merely verbal by relating words directly to things.

In later life, when we learn the meaning of a new word, we usually do so through the dictionary, that is to say, by a definition in terms of words of which we already know the meaning. But since the dictionary defines words by means of other words, there must be some words of which we know the meaning without a verbal definition.[5]

In the *Inquiry* "the immense majority" of these words belong to a part of language which Russell terms "primary or object language." Primary language consists wholly of "object-words," defined

logically, as words having meaning in isolation, and, psychologically, as words which have been learnt without its being necessary to have previously learnt any other words.[6]

We shall label *semantic foundationalism* this view that language contains two categories of words, "basic" and "nonbasic"; and that a "basic" word is categorisable as such because it is capable of being given a meaning without the necessity of relating it to any other expression of the language to which it belongs; simply, as Russell puts it, "by hearing it frequently pronounced in the presence of the object." Semantic foundationalism is a version, although by no means the only possible one, of Referential Realism, motivated, like other versions, by the perceived need to avoid being forced to concede that the mind never encounters a reality lying beyond the circuit of its own conceptual or linguistic constructions.

iii. Spontaneity and receptivity

We have now to consider, briefly, two further embodiments of Referential Realism. One of these is platonism, in the modified version offered by John McDowell in a recent set of lectures; the other a collection of twentieth-century views, originating in the work of W. V. Quine, which, for reasons that will become apparent, we shall lump together under the label "Hyperempiricism."

First, McDowell. The argument that leads McDowell to a version of platonism takes its rise in a puzzle suggested by Kant. The puzzle is this: Kant distinguishes between the understanding, considered as the source of the array of concepts in terms of which we interpret our experience, as a faculty of freedom, or *spontaneity*; to be contrasted, as such, with the mere *receptivity* of sensory experience (*intuition*). The latter "can never be other than sensible; that is, it contains only the mode in which we are affected by objects." It is the understanding, a faculty of active thought, as distinct from the merely passive reception of sensory impressions or "representations" contributed by intuition, "which enables us to *think* the object of sensible intuition": to grasp sensory representations as representations *of physical things*, for instance. Hence Kant's celebrated remark, "Thoughts without content are empty, intuitions without concepts are blind."[7]

McDowell's response to this passage in the first *Critique* is interesting as exemplifying the pervasiveness in analytic philosophy of the type of sceptical worry we have been examining. McDowell sees Kant's distinction, in other words, as raising in a particularly sharp form the possibility that the price of the spontaneity of conceptual thought may be the opening of a gulf between thought and the reality it endeavours to comprehend.

When Kant describes the understanding as a faculty of spontaneity, that reflects his view of the relation between reason and freedom: rational necessitation is not just compatible with freedom but constitutive of it. In a slogan, the space of reasons is a space of freedom.

But if our freedom in empirical thinking is total, in particular if it is not constrained from outside the conceptual sphere, that can seem to threaten the very possibility that judgements of experience might be grounded in a way that related them to a reality external to thought. And surely there must be such grounding if experience is to be a source of knowledge, and more generally, if the bearing of empirical judgements on reality is to be intelligibly in place in our picture at all. The more we play up the connection between reason and freedom, the more we risk losing our grip on how exercises of concepts can constitute warranted judgements about the world. What we wanted to conceive as exercises of concepts threaten to degenerate into moves in a self-contained game. And that deprives us of the very idea that they are exercises of concepts. Suiting empirical beliefs to the reasons for them is not a self-contained game.[8]

This is the problem to which, for Russell, semantic foundationalism provided the solution. That solution, stigmatised as "the Myth of the Given," McDowell rejects, for sound reasons. One set of these derives from the attack on abstractionism mounted forty years ago by Peter Geach in an influential little book.[9] Semantic foundationalism claims that conceptual capacities can be derived from simple confrontation with what is given in sensory experience. But what sensation offers us is always complex: is "manifold" as McDowell and Kemp Smith's Kant put it. So, "in order to form an observational concept, a subject would have to abstract out the right element in a presented multiplicity."[10] It is the possibility of forming any concept in this way which, in McDowell's words, "has been trenchantly criticised, in a Wittgensteinian spirit, by P. T. Geach."[11]

Geach's strategy on this point is to argue, not that abstractionism as a theory of concept formation is empirically refutable, but that it is devoid of explanatory force. His argument offers powerful reasons for concluding not merely that abstractionism is incapable of explaining the acquisition of relational concepts such as "big" or "to the left," but that it is incapable of explaining the acquisition of precisely the type of simple sensory concept, *red*, or *chromatic colour*, for instance, generally supposed to provide the most favourable cases for the theory.

Abstractionism as a theory of concept-formation has played too central a part, over the past three centuries, in empiricist philosophy and psychology, for there to be no deeper conclusions to be drawn from its failure on grounds of explanatory nullity. But what conclusions, exactly? Here Geach and McDowell part company. Geach concludes that concepts are "made in the mind," not found in the world.

Having a concept never means being able to recognise some feature we have found in direct experience; the mind *makes concepts*, and this concept-formation and the subsequent use of the concepts formed never is a mere recognition or finding; but this does not in the least prevent us from applying concepts in our sense-experience and knowing sometimes that we apply them rightly. In all cases it is a matter of fitting a concept to my experience, not of picking out the feature I am interested in from among other features given simultaneously.[12]

We shall argue in the following chapters that this conclusion is substantially correct. But it is clear why it could not be accepted by someone as conscious of the threat posed by prison-house scepticism as McDowell. If the mind "*makes concepts*" what is it that secures the title of such *makings* to represent reality? If concepts are not picked from reality but "fitted to" it, what secures adequacy of fit? Geach's 1957 discussion does in one way, it seems to us, respond in advance to this point, by way of a remark that, in effect, gestures towards the Fregean thought that we canvassed a few pages ago in §ii. That thought is, precisely, that it cannot be necessary, in order for a concept to play its part in the articulation of truths, that the concept in question *should* "fit" or "correspond to" reality.

Suppose I look at a lot of billiard balls on a table, and form the judgment that some of them are red and some are not. If I state this judgment in words, "red" may plausibly be taken to report a feature of what I see, but "some" and "not" certainly cannot. But it would be perverse to infer that my distorting conceptual thought represents the reality as exhibiting features, somehood and nottishness, which are not really there; and no less perverse to argue that, since my judgment is correct, there must be somehood and nottishness *in rebus*. We must resist the perennial philosophical temptation to think that if a thought is to be true of reality, then it must copy it feature by feature, like a map.[13]

Attractive as such Fregean (or, equally, Wittgensteinian) common sense may be, however, we have already noted the power of prison-house scepticism to override it. In any event, McDowell's assessment of the consequences to be drawn from the failure of abstractionism differs sharply from Geach's. McDowell agrees that concepts are "made by the mind" to the extent of taking the Kantian distinction between conceptual "spontaneity" and sensory passivity to be persuasive. But why is this distinction so persuasive? Why should it seem so "appropriate to describe the understanding, whose contribution to this co-operation [between thought and sensory content] is its command of concepts, in terms of spontaneity?"[14]

McDowell answers this latter question by appeal to Wilfrid Sellars's idea of a "space of reasons."

A schematic but suggestive answer is that the topography of the conceptual sphere is constituted by rational relations. The space of concepts is at least part of what Wilfrid Sellars calls "the space of reasons."[15]

To possess a concept, in other words, is to know what warrants, grounds, gives reason for, judgments in which a grasp of that concept is exercised. This is a reasonable enough suggestion on the face of it; but it is one that raises the spectre of the Prison-House of Language (or of concepts), in just the form that McDowell finds so threatening. The reasons, the warrants we accept as justifying our judgments are, ultimately *our* reasons, *our* warrants. Surely then, our everyday presumption that the judgments such reasons warrant accurately reflect the nature of reality must itself require some grounding, some warrant.

McDowell's fundamental objection to "the Myth of the Given" is, now, that appeal to the sensory Given fails to provide that second-order warrant. The difficulty is that the notion of the Given is, precisely, that of an array of mere sensory impacts; and a sensory impact is not a reason: ". . . we cannot really understand the relations in virtue of which a judgment is warranted except as relations within the space of concepts: relations such as implication or probabilification, which hold between exercises of conceptual capacities." Thus, even if we take a sensory impact as "probabilifying" a certain judgment, we do so on grounds that spring from within the conceptual sphere, conceived as a "space of reasons," and the deeper problem McDowell takes himself to have identified, of grounding, warranting, our belief that that space is so constituted as to ensure the conformity to Reality of judgments assessed in terms of it remains unaddressed.

We see now why McDowell could not rest content with Geach's conclusion that abstractionism fails because concepts, being made by the mind, are not to be found in nature. For McDowell, the thought that concepts are made by the mind does not resolve the problem of the relationship of Mind and World: rather, it raises that problem in a sharper form. McDowell's conclusion, in effect, is that abstractionism fails because, like all versions of "the Myth of the Given," it fails to address that sharper version of the problem. It fails to see that the "space" constituted by the qualitative character of sensory contents – "innate quality space," to employ a phrase of Quine's – is not, and could not, be a space of reasons.

McDowell's solution to the problem takes the form of what he calls a "naturalised" platonism, to distinguish it from the "rampant" platonism espoused by many platonists, and possibly by Plato. Naturalised platonism is reached by way of the thought, common, as McDowell sees it, to Aristotle and to a suitably interpreted Wittgenstein, that the attainment of conceptual capacities involves not merely a passive attention to the content of sensory experience, but active involvement in the world: the progressive education, or *Bildung*, of a being whose animal nature already, in multifarious ways, involves it in the world whose nature it comes, through *Bildung*, to explore. The concepts – or to put it in McDowell's terms, the grasp of the "space" of logical relationships in which judgments arrange themselves relative to the reasons that warrant them – which it acquires in this process are not to be regarded as in any sense constructions of the human mind. They are, as much as any matter-of-fact truth we may articulate in terms of them, forced on the mind by the world. But they are accessible to the human mind only by a process of *Bildung* that – and this is the important point – cannot be scrutinised or described from a standpoint outside the system of concepts, the "space of reasons" that it makes available.

This naturalised platonism is quite distinct from rampant platonism. In rampant platonism, the rational structure within which meaning comes into view is independent of anything merely human, so that the capacity of our minds to resonate with it looks occult or magical. Naturalised platonism is platonistic in that the structure of the space of reasons has a sort of autonomy; it is not derivative from, or reflective of, truths about human beings that are capturable independently of the structure in view. But this platonism is not rampant: the structure of the space of reasons is not constituted in splendid isolation from anything merely human. The demands of reason are essentially such that a human upbringing can open a human being's eyes to them.[16]

The nature of the naturalised platonism McDowell proposes is brought out even more clearly by the remarks concerning Wittgenstein that immediately follow the above passage. McDowell's platonism, as we have noted, develops out of a proposed merging of Wittgensteinian with Aristotelian themes. McDowell grants the difficulty created for such a strategy of argument by the widespread impression that Wittgenstein, far from being in any sense a platonist, was in fact a constructivist of a rather extreme type.

...rampant platonism figures as a pitfall to avoid in Wittgenstein's later writings about meaning and understanding. And I think naturalised platonism is a good way to understand what Wittgenstein is driving at here.

I want to stress how different this is from many readings of Wittgenstein. Many readers implicitly attribute to Wittgenstein a philosophical stance...in which one finds a spookiness in the very idea that requirements of reason are there for subjects to have their eyes opened to them, unless the idea can be reconstructed out of independent facts. This poses a philosophical task, and the thought is that Wittgenstein points to a way of executing it by appealing to social interactions, described in a way that does not presuppose the material to be reconstructed.

If we try to construct something that can pass for possession of meaning, the kind of intelligibility that is constituted by placement in the space of reasons, in this communitarian or "social pragmatist" style, we cannot see meaning as autonomous. Indeed, that is the point of this kind of reading: the sense of spookiness reflects the conviction that any platonism about meaning, any position that credits meaning with autonomy, must be a rampant platonism, with its characteristic trafficking in the occult.[17]

McDowell argues further that decisive textual support for his view of Wittgenstein as a naturalised platonist is to be found in Wittgenstein's "'quietism', his rejection of any constructive or doctrinal ambitions."[18] That, for McDowell, chimes in with the naturalised platonist's conviction that no view of the genesis of our conceptual scheme in *Bildung* is accessible from a standpoint outside that conceptual scheme.

A "social pragmatist" account of meaning, McDowell reasonably suggests, is one according to which "there is nothing to the normative structure within which meaning comes into view except, say, acceptances and rejections by the community at large."[19] That type of social relativism about meaning has been so decisively criticised, for instance by J. Zalabardo,[20] that if the only alternative to such a reading of Wittgenstein were McDowell's, one would certainly opt for the latter. We shall argue that it is not. But, be that as it may, McDowell's assessment of the options confronting us in the interpretation of Wittgenstein certainly makes clearer the status of his "naturalised platonism" as a version of Referential Realism. Naturalised platonism assents to all the tenets of the Correspondence Theory of Meaning, as set out in Chapter 1 §iii. For the naturalised platonist, "the requirements of reason are there for subjects to have their eyes opened to them." The naturalised platonist, like his unnaturalised counterpart, in other words, is committed to the doctrine that concepts are not made but discovered, with its corollary that it is as possible to be in error concerning the conformity of one's concepts to reality as it is to be in error concerning the conformity of one's beliefs to the facts. Some concepts are legitimate, others not, and what legitimates the members of the former set is that it is possible, via a process of *Bildung*, to encounter them in nature. The naturalism of the naturalised platonist consists simply in his contention, following a platonised version of Wittgenstein, that we have no means of viewing the world independently of the "space of reasons" acquired through participation in *Bildung*, with the result that the conceptual structure of reality is, for us, inherently bound up with aspects of our humanness, rather than, as McDowell's "rampant" platonist would have it, utterly inhuman in character.

We can now return, in conclusion, to the Kant-inspired version of prison-house scepticism from which McDowell sets out. In that version, as in others, what causes the problem is the conceptual fertility of the mind, or of language, here seen in Kantian style as opening a gap between the "spontaneity" of conceptual thought, constituted as a space of reasons, and the passivity of sensory experience, or as Kant would say, of Receptivity. Locke and Russell accept the sceptic's diagnosis; agree, in other words, that it is the spontaneity of conceptual thought that threatens to cut the mind off from the world it endeavours to understand. Locke and Russell propose, however, each in his own way, to resolve the problem, not, quite, by denying the spontaneity of thought, but, as it were, by representing *spontaneous* thought as *pathological;* pathological, that is, in contrast to a mode of thinking and speaking which escapes the sceptic's net because the contents of the concepts it honours are identical with the contents of aspects or elements of experience. McDowell's objection to this is, in effect, that concepts can only be grasped as such relative to a space of reasons, and that sensory experience ("Receptivity," "the Given") offers no such space to direct, conceptually unmediated inspection: to Russellian "Acquaintance," for instance.

McDowell's solution, by contrast, is the centrally Romantic one (S. T. Coleridge would have embraced McDowell as a brother-in-arms) of denying the accessibility to us of a Nature unimbued with the spontaneity of the mind. This indeed foils the prison-house sceptic by making it impossible to open up a gap between Spontaneity and Receptivity. This way of closing the sceptic's gap between Mind (or Language) and World stands in one way at the opposite extreme from Locke's or Russell's way of closing it. Where they abase the spontaneity of the mind before the iron face of Nature viewed as a system of bare quiddities, McDowell infuses that spontaneity into a Nature that can no longer be viewed as a wholly independent entity standing over against the human modes of activity and engagement through which we gain access to it. But from another point of view, McDowell's thinking, just as much as Locke's or Russell's, acts out the founding moves of Referential Realism. The first of these moves, the crucial one, is acceptance of the sceptic's suggestion that what creates the possibility that Thought (or Language) might become a prison-house is the conceptual fertility of Thought (or Language). The second is acceptance, as the only way of closing the supposed gap between Thought (or Language) and World thus apparently opened up, of some form of Correspondence Theory of Meaning. From this point onwards it matters little whether we interpret the required correspondence as subsisting between Thought (or Language) and the Given, or between Thought (or Language) and a Nature that, in Kantian style, cannot be encountered except as a space of reasons. Either way, from this point onwards, we shall be committed, like McDowell, Locke, or Russell, to the three main tenets of the Correspondence Theory; and our acceptance of those tenets will seem to us justified as the only means of preventing the sceptic's supposed gap from reopening.

iv. Hyperempiricism

A third, and very influential, version of Referential Realism is to be found in the work of Quine. At first sight the identification will seem implausible, to say the least. The Referential Realist, as we put it in Chapter 2 §i, nails his colours to the claim that "whatever content-bearing elements may be semantically primary in a language pick out entities whose existence and nature owe nothing to linguistic convention." That way of putting things suggests at first sight a fairly tight connection between Referential Realism and Semantic Foundationalism. And Quine is generally, and rightly, taken to have devised powerful arguments against Semantic Foundationalism. But we have already seen in the case of McDowell that Referential Realism can survive the rejection of Semantic Foundationalism. All that is required for a philosophical theory to manifest Referential Realism is that it should make the ascription of assertoric content to sentences dependent on the recognition of an associative relationship of some type between some class of linguistic expressions – the "semantically primary content-bearing elements" of the above definition – and some class of natural features of the world: features "natural," that is, in the sense of owing nothing to linguistic convention. As we shall see, Quine's views are as fully answerable to this requirement as are those of McDowell or the Semantic Foundationalists.

Quine is often seen as an opponent of Vienna Circle Positivism. Up to a point this is correct. Quine's attack, moreover, focuses on the Semantic Foundationalist doctrine of analysis that the Positivists took over from Russell, among others. Positivist theory of meaning initially pursued the project of explicating meaning in terms of verification: hence the slogan "the meaning of a statement is its method of verification." By the mid-1930s, however, this enterprise had foundered on the difficulty of defining what is to count as a "verifiable" statement. As a result, by the late 1930s, positivism had come to be identified with the project, carried furthest in Carnap's *Logische Aufbau der Welt*, of determining whether, for any given sentence, a synonymous, or "analytically equivalent" sentence couched in purely observational terms can be found. Quine argues, in effect, that any such project is *in principle* doomed to failure. His arguments on this point were presented in 1951, in a celebrated paper,[21] but their significance is perhaps best understood by setting them in the context of the following remark from an essay published fifteen years later.

It was sad for epistemologists, Hume and others, to have to acquiesce in the impossibility of strictly deriving the science of the external world from sensory evidence. Two cardinal tenets of empiricism remained unassailable, however, and so remain to this day. One is that whatever evidence there *is* for science *is* sensory evidence. The other... is that all inculcation of meanings must rest ultimately on sensory evidence.[22]

These remarks position Quine, not as an enemy of *empiricism*, not even of empiricism in its Logical Positivist incarnation, but on the contrary as what one might term a *hyperempiricist*: someone, that is, who insists that *no exemption can be made, on behalf of the technical terminology of empiricist theory*, to the principle, dear not only to Quine, but equally to Russell and to the Positivists, that unless an expression is mere verbiage, the explanation of its meaning must at some point conclude in the demonstrative indication of some feature of experience. It is quite possible to miss the truly radical nature of what is being proposed in this passage. The second "tenet," connecting meaning with "sensory evidence" might appear at first sight to align Quine with the Semantic Foundationalism of Locke or Russell, against the anti-foundationalism of someone like McDowell. That would be a mistake: Quine's views are no more friendly towards Semantic Foundationalism than they are towards the platonism of someone like McDowell. What Quine is claiming is precisely *not* that the assertoric content of specific sentences *is* to be identified with the experiential content *of* specific pieces of "sensory evidence," but merely that judgments concerning meaning must be capable of being grounded in experience. As we shall see, the implications of Quine's second "tenet," which is not foundationalist but merely empiricist in character, take us as far from Locke's or Russell's theory of meaning as they do from McDowell's.

That journey begins, in "Two Dogmas of Empiricism," with an attack on the credentials of the two concepts, *synonymy* and *analyticity,* central to the Russellian-cum-Positivist conception of analysis. It is important to see that it is the *empiricist* credentials of these two notions central to the "logical empiricism" of the previous generation, their own claim to be independently explicable in terms of experience, that Quine is attacking. The strategy of Quine's argument in "Two Dogmas" – its details are too familiar to need spelling out here – is to show that neither term can be defined, except either in terms of the other or in terms of third terms such as "necessarily," which covertly presuppose the original two. It is worth noticing also how very Russellian in spirit such a strategy is. A central argument of Russell's for semantic foundationalism was, as we noted earlier, that the meaning of words cannot, without circularity, be endlessly explained in terms of other words. Unless language is to be an hermetic game, or an uninterpreted formal calculus, there must come a point at which its basic terms are equipped with extralinguistic reference: in the familiar and graphic phrase of William James, "assigned a cash-value at the Bank of Experience." Quine's argument is, precisely, that that condition cannot be met for "synonymy" or "analyticity." Such terms, along with their cognates, compose an hermeneutic circle, operating inside language. The terms composing that circle can be defined endlessly in terms of one another, but as there never comes a point at which any can be equipped independently of the others with a respectable empirical content, the whole circle remains shut off from extralinguistic reality.

Quine's choice of strategy in attacking the Logical Positivist account of analysis thus already, in effect, presupposes a Referential Realist account of what it is for discourse to have a bearing on reality. According to that account, discourse has a bearing on reality just in case the expressions it employs, or some of them, are such that their content can be sufficiently explained by demonstratively indicating items belonging to some class of constituents of reality. Something along those lines is in any case written into Quine's generally empiricist requirement that "all inculcation of meanings must rest ultimately on sensory evidence." Russell and the Logical Positivists shared Quine's respect for that requirement. Their way of honouring it, however, committed them to the theory of analysis undermined by Quine's hyperempiricist assault on the credentials of the concepts of synonymy and analyticity. According to that theory, analysis of the required type should yield as its outcome a list of sentences employing "nonbasic" expressions, each matched to a sentence employing only "basic" ones. Quine invites us, on the one hand, to think of this list, reasonably enough, as a translation manual, and, on the other, to investigate with him the actual empirical constraints bearing on the construction of such a manual. That enquiry forms the bridge between Quine's critique of Russell and the Positivists and his own neo-Pragmatism.

Quine makes the issues more open to inspection by choosing to marshal his arguments around the problem of constructing a translation manual for two languages, English and a "native" language sharing none of the former's roots. The arguments apply equally, however, to programmes of translation within one language, including the Positivist programme of translating epistemically and semantically nonbasic English into epistemically and semantically basic English. The problem for the would-be translator committed to empiricist principles is the same in either case. Lacking the notions of analyticity and synonymy, now, what grounds has the translator for justifying any given pairing of entries in the manual he is attempting to construct? Quine argues that the sole empirical grounds available to the translator are those to be derived from observation of the environmental scene, or those aspects of it accessible to observation, in which natives are inclined to assent to, or to dissent from, the assertion made by uttering a given Native sentence. Quine introduces the term *stimulus-meaning* to designate the ordered pair of sets of stimulus-conditions prompting, on the one hand, native assent, and, on the other, native dissent, to assertions made by means of a Native's sentence S_N.[23] The translator's problem, now, is to decide which English sentence, S_E, he is to write alongside S_N in his manual. All he can do, given the limitations of the evidence on which he must base his decision, is to choose an English sentence whose stimulus-meaning roughly matches the stimulus-meaning of S_N. To the extent to which they do match, S_E and S_N may be said to be "stimulus-synonymous." Stimulus-synonymy is manifestly, however, a far weaker relationship than synonymy; and important philosophical consequences hang on this.

In particular, three further assumptions of Semantic Foundationalism, in addition to the assumption that the notions of synonymy and analyticity are unproblematic, come under threat. Semantic Foundationalists have traditionally assumed, first, that it is possible to make an absolute distinction between observational and nonobservational sentences, an observational sentence being one whose assertoric content can be equated with the experiential content of a given observation or series of observations ("Red here now" is the war-horse example). Second, they have assumed that each nonobservational sentence can be shown to be equivalent in meaning to some specific collection of observational sentences. And, third, some, in particular Russell, have assumed it to be empirically determinate what type of entity (e.g., a universal, a particular, a relation) a given name picks out.

If the evidence on which the would-be translator (*any* translator, remember) must base his translation manual amounts to no more than knowledge of the stimulus-meanings of native sentences, all three assumptions become groundless. For a start, observationality becomes a relative notion. All that can now be empirically grounded is a concept of relative observationality: one relative, that is, to consistency of the native responses that constitute stimulus meaning. "We have defined observationality for occasion sentences somewhat vaguely, as degree of consistency of stimulus meaning from speaker to speaker."[24] No doubt by this criterion most of the sentences presumed by Russell and the Positivists to be observation sentences will still come out high in relative observationality. But that does not affect the fact that observationality now amounts to no more than a high level of consistency in the stimulus meanings recorded from speaker to speaker. And that consistency may result as much from the sharing of collateral information among speakers as from the sharing of common intuitions concerning meaning. As Quine slyly puts it, "I suspect that no systematic experimental sense is to be made of a distinction between usage due to meaning and usage due to generally shared collateral information."[25]

This last difficulty entails that the would-be translator's judgment in deciding which English sentence to set down in his manual against a given S_N cannot but be influenced by what he believes concerning Native beliefs and intentions. Each choice he makes will, of course, have consequences for other choices; but equally those consequences can be softened or eliminated by further adjustments to the manual. But this means that the construction of the translation manual is not the mere sum of a series of choices affecting individual lines of the manual. Rather, the construction of the manual rests on a single act of choice, in which the translator balances out the entire array of English sentences against the entire array of Native sentences in such a way as to maximise agreement in stimulus-meaning.

Nothing, now, requires that the criterion of maximal agreement in stimulus-meaning should single out a single translation manual. There is not only no reason to suppose such a thing, but every reason to suppose the contrary: that for any given pair of languages alternative translation manuals are possible. Given that each manual would, *ex hypothesi*, maximise agreement in stimulus-meaning, there would be no way of discriminating empirically between them; and thus no way of discriminating between the ways in which each handles questions involving synonymy between sentences or the manner in which a given term divides its reference. On the one hand, it becomes, as Quine puts it, following Duhem, "misleading to speak of the empirical content of an individual statement."[26] The statements of the natural sciences face the bar of experience as a collective body, no individual item of which has any specific set of experiential warrants to call its own. On the other hand, as Quine has never ceased to delight in reminding us, the question whether a Native term "Gavagai" is to be interpreted as dividing its reference over, say, individual whole rabbits, things satisfying the universal *Rabbithood*, collections of undetached rabbit parts, or spatio-temporal slices of rabbits, also becomes empirically undecidable. The Semantic Foundationalist's final two assumptions turn out to be baseless, not because the fact of the matter as regards the analysis of a given sentence or the reference of a given term cannot be established, but because in neither case is there any "fact of the matter" to be established.

Remote though the position to which Quine's arguments lead may seem from the two versions of Referential Realism that we have examined so far, the fact remains that what Quine offers is a version of Referential Realism. As we are using the expression, Referential Realism is defined by commitment to the Correspondence Theory of Meaning in the form outlined in Chapter 1 §ii: as embodied, that is, in tenets (1′)–(3′). By this criterion, Quine is a Referential Realist. In holding that meaning, so far as it is empirically determinable, consists in a relationship between, on the one hand, the entire body of sentences composing a theory and, on the other, a body of stimuli, Quine clearly subscribes to a version of (1′). In holding that what *both* (a) renders a theory scientifically useful, and (b) informs its sentences, taken collectively, with meaning in the sense of cognitive content, are the "experiential implications" of the theory – those implications, that is, whose realisation in nature counts in favour of the truth of the theory and whose failure to be realised counts in favour of its falsehood – Quine is committed to a version of (2'). And, finally, Quine is committed to (3') by his contention that the issue of what meaning is to be assigned to any sentence in a language, so far as it can be settled at all, is settled, not by appeal to rules, or stipulations, or conventions, but, rather, by appeal to processes of observation and induction continuous with those governing the conduct of empirical enquiry in general.

There is, however, a deeper sense in which Quine is a Referential Realist; one constituted by the profound sympathy evident in his work with the empiricist, anti-metaphysical strain in European thought, of which the version of Referential Realism represented by one form or another of Semantic Foundationalism has traditionally been regarded as an essential component. It is arguable that rational metaphysics has always found its central impulse and justification in the thought that, as Spinoza puts it (*Ethics*, Part II prop. vii), "The order and connection of ideas is the same as the order and connection of things." Reason, on this view, determines equally how things occur in nature and how the ideas of things order themselves in the mind: that is why Reason alone, conducting its enquiries internally to the mind, can yield important insights concerning the ordering of nature. Empiricism, on the contrary, has drawn much of its vitality from a profound suspicion of that thought. The empiricist sees no reason at all why the "order and connection of ideas" in the mind should bear the slightest relationship to the order and connection of things in the world. That is why, as we have been arguing here, prison-house scepticism has been felt by empiricists, as well as others, of course, but perhaps more than others, to pose such a worrying threat. If the mind is operative in constituting the very terms in which we conceive of the world, how can we ever free ourselves from its trammels sufficiently to apprehend the world as it is in itself, independently of our mind-spawned notions concerning it?

One of the main attractions of Quine's view lies in the clarity and simplicity of the answer it offers to this question. The facts that constitute the world, the "fact of the matter" on which both our judgments concerning meaning and our judgments concerning the adequacy of scientific theory rest equally, are the facts constituted by observable natural phenomena. Semantic Foundationalism addresses the problem of prison-house scepticism by attempting to distinguish between those linguistic expressions that correctly reflect the nature of the extralinguistic world, and those that do not. Thus we find Russell attempting to distinguish between terms such as "Bismarck" or "red," which pick out existing individuals or kinds, and terms such as "Odysseus" or "manna," which do not; or the Vienna Circle attempting to distinguish "verifiable" sentences, which admit of analysis in observational terms from "metaphysical" ones, which do not.

Quine's objection to these ways of sorting sheep from goats, of partitioning "concepts," or "meanings," or "assertoric contents" between the categories of the viciously inventive and the innocuously representative, is in effect that they themselves involve us in empirically ungrounded metaphysical commitments. Russell's atomism demands an "ontology," a classification of the contents of nature into types of entity: individuals, properties, relations. The Positivist programme of analysis requires the support of intuitively persuasive but empirically ungrounded notions of synonymy and analyticity. Quine's version of logical empiricism dispenses with all such metaphysical excrescences, in effect by denying empirical bearing, and thus empirical content, to any question concerning such semantic entities as *meanings, concepts, propositions, assertoric contents,* and so on. For Quine, the meaning of an expression is the meaning it receives relative to a given translation manual. One cannot ask whether that manual accurately represents its "real" meaning, because there is simply no "fact of the matter" to be pursued by such a question. In this way Quine escapes the threat of prison-house scepticism. The prison-house sceptic can get his form of scepticism off the ground only if he is allowed the possibility that one language may represent Reality in a way that differs from the representation of Reality offered by another. If Quine is right, this possibility lapses into vacuity. All languages represent Reality in the same way, by means of a collection of sentences, with truth-conditions assessable collectively in terms of stimulus-meaning, theoretically linked in such a way as to distribute the ascription of truth and falsity in such a way as, ideally, to maximise success and minimise error in predicting natural phenomena. Different speakers, it is true, may intuitively perceive certain sentences rather than others to be synonymous, and certain terms to distribute their reference in one way rather than another. But it is only if these intuitive distinctions can be shown to have some grounding in experience that they can be taken to have any bearing on the way in which a language represents Reality. And they can be shown to have no such grounding.

v. Meaning and Prima Philosophia

To conclude, all three of the versions of Referential Realism we have examined so far have as a central goal the removal of any potentially delusive "mental" intermediary standing between knowledge and its objects. Like Locke or Russell, but also, in an odd and less obvious way like McDowell, Quine wants a direct and unmediated contact between thought and the world it endeavours to represent and understand. All three positions have as their goal the closing of the prison-house sceptic's putative gap between Thought and World. Locke and Russell do it, as we have seen, by identifying the content of thought with that of the Given. McDowell does it by assimilating to the side of Nature – through the processes of *Bildung*, so that they can be thought of as issuing indifferently both from Spontaneity, and from the nature of things – conceptual structures that, if they were left to be credited solely to the side of Spontaneity, might appear worryingly arbitrary. Quine agrees with McDowell in dismissing the possibility of connecting Thought with the Given in the manner envisaged by semantic foundationalism. By contrast, Quine's scientism is incompatible with any form of platonism. What Quine is after is a form of naturalism according to which we dispose of no ways of investigating reality other than those comprised in the methodological armoury of the natural sciences. He is thus opposed to any view, whether Platonic, Cartesian, or Kantian in character, according to which the methods of science need to be grounded in a *prima philosophia*: a prior philosophical theory concerning the relationship of Thought and World. Talk of "meanings" for Quine, is inseparable from *prima philosophia*. Each must be dispensed with if we wish to dispense with the other. Quine's answer to the sceptic who would set up meanings as a stratum of – possibly deceptive – mental structures mediating between natural science and the world it reveals to us, is, in effect, to dispense with both simultaneously. His strategy is to deny that there is any way of distinguishing the constitution of meaning from the constitution of theories concerning the nature of things, on the grounds that there is no way of partitioning up the bodies of sensory evidence on which a theory of the latter sort rests, into collections of truth-conditions, each attaching to a single sentence of the theory. There is, however, a price to be paid for this summary elimination of assumptions and enterprises that have constituted, historically, a great part of the content of philosophy. That price is the acceptance of what has recently come to be called "meaning-scepticism": the thesis that judgments about meaning are indeterminate, not just in the sense that it is difficult to establish what linguistic expressions mean, but in the sense that there simply is "no fact of the matter" concerning what they mean. Many have found this price too heavy. It could be argued, indeed, that while one can at a pinch live with prison-house scepticism, as in a sense Hume did, it is not possible to live with meaning-scepticism. Among other things it is unclear, as Jane Heal[27] has argued, whether anti-Realism about meanings, of the type advanced by Quine and his school, is ultimately compatible with any form of Realism, including scientific Realism. We shall return to these issues in later chapters.

3

Out of the Prison-House

To say that self-sufficient thought always refers to a thought enmeshed in language is not to say that thought is alienated or that language cuts thought off from truth and certainty. We must understand that language is not an impediment to consciousness...

– Maurice Merleau-Ponty

i. Reference, Meaning, and Intention

The three forms of Referential Realism we have so far distinguished, albeit in a fairly brisk and sketchy way, account for a considerable part of what has taken place in analytic philosophy of language since 1900. They exhibit numerous incompatibilities, and the discussion of their relative merits has achieved considerable heights of complexity and acuity. We shall not, except occasionally and indirectly, enter into those discussions. Our object in this book is not to argue for or against any particular version of Referential Realism but to attack Referential Realism root and branch.

In opposition to the Referential Realist we shall contend that the entities "picked out by," or "referred to," or "designated by" all of the content-bearing expressions of a natural language are without exception linguistic constructs: things "constituted by linguistic convention," in the sense of being things having no existence in nature prior to the constitution of language. At the same time we shall argue that such a claim yields neither of the absurd consequences it is generally supposed to yield. It does not entail, on the one hand, that a language of which it is true must function to imprison the mind within the circuit of its own constructions. Nor, on the other hand, we shall suggest, does it entail any vicious form of relativism. In particular, it does not commit us to the view that there is no way of adjudicating rationally between the claims of natural science, and those of Azande magic or the *Malleus Maleficorum*, to inform us about the workings of nature.

The attempt to undermine Referential Realism in something like the manner just outlined is not entirely unprecedented in recent philosophy. Something of the sort is to be found in Maurice Merleau-Ponty's *La Prose du Monde*. And it is possible to argue that that such a strategy is central to the later work of Wittgenstein. But *La Prose du Monde* was abandoned in a fragmentary state by its author, and remains an obscure work, the more so in English translation; while the interpretation of Wittgenstein remains controversial.

What we shall have to say in this book is strongly influenced by both writers, although very much more so by Wittgenstein. We trust, however, that it will not strike the reader as a mere rehash of any of the sorts of argument commonly associated, since Wittgenstein's death, with the epithet "Wittgensteinian." It is true that much of what we have to say here will tend to suggest a certain, rather unfamiliar, way of reading Wittgenstein; one that has been to a certain extent elaborated in a series of explicitly exegetical studies published elsewhere.[1] But no argument to be presented here depends for its credit on the correctness of that or any other exegesis of Wittgenstein. Respecting Wittgenstein, we have tried to take to heart the remark "I should not like my work to spare other people the trouble of thinking."[2] Although he is present in the book, it is as its presiding genius, not as the means of preserving its authors from the pains of mental activity. Although certain aspects of the grand strategy of the argument are, as we happen to think, Wittgensteinian in provenance, relatively little of its detail is. We shall do our best, in short, to turn the strategy outlined in the preceding paragraph into a structure of detailed discussion and argument sufficiently strong, by the common standards of analytic philosophy, to be capable of standing on its own feet without the dubious support afforded by the intellectual hagiography rather too common in the academic writing of the present day.

That said, the strategy we have just outlined might still seem to present the reader with a blank cheque for a fairly staggering sum. But, although it will require a good many pages of detailed argument to meet that sum in full, it is nevertheless possible to outline in comparatively few words, at this point, how we propose to meet it, and this we shall do in the remaining three sections of this chapter. Before that, however, there is a preliminary objection to be met.

The objection is this. Surely, to say that all the content-bearing expressions of a language refer to entities having no existence in nature prior to the constitution of language, must entail, trivially, that it is impossible to refer by means of language to any entity whose existence is prior to, and independent of, language. And that is simply absurd.

The supposed entailment rests on an equivocation, the conveniently ambiguous expressions in the case being "refers" and "reference." Talk of the reference of expressions occurs standardly in everyday English in two quite different types of context. In the first, what is to be explained is someone's intention in using a certain expression. The following would be examples:

1. "In speaking of 'The Islets of Langerhans,' John was referring to those fuzzy pink blotches you see to the left of the sample on the slide."
2. "In referring to 'Baxter's Piece,' John was talking about that scrubby bit of ground between the angle of the A37 and the B234, backed by that old, half-demolished barbed-wire fence."
3. "When John says 'red' he means to refer to something like the colour of that tomato, not that sickly pinkish shade you have there."

In these cases, there can be no question but that the fuzzy pink blotches, the scrubby bit of ground, and what you see when you look at *that* tomato, are things that exist prior to, and that are quite unaffected by, let alone constituted by, any conventional machinations that may or may not enter into the constitution of language.

There is, however, another everyday type of context in which we habitually use the verb "to refer." Here what is at stake is not the intentions of a speaker, but the reference of an expression, where that phrase itself bears something like the sense assigned by Frege to his term *Bedeutung*: "the object itself which we designate by its means."[3] The following are examples:

1. "The phrase 'the Islets of Langerhans' refers to (designates, is the name of) a histological structure."
2. "'Baxter's Piece' refers to (designates, is the name of) a field."
3. "'Red' refers to (designates, is the name of) a colour."

It is reference in this second category of uses that interests the Referential Realist. His argument – the argument we are considering – is that unless it were the case that some at least of the content-bearing expressions of a language "referred" in *this* sense to entities that can plausibly be thought of as existing in nature prior to the institution of any linguistic practice or convention, then it would be impossible to refer, by means of language to any such entity. Once the two senses of "refer" deployed in stating this argument are distinguished, its weakness becomes readily apparent. It is implausible on the face of it, perhaps, that *fields* could have existed prior to the institution of agriculture, or that *histological structures* could have existed prior to the development of the scientific means, practical and theoretical, necessary to the study of cells; and equally, although less obviously, implausible that *colours* could have existed prior to the institution of colour vocabulary, given that what a colour *is*, is (roughly speaking) a set of specific colour shades, of membership varying from language to language, united under one colour-name by a specific natural language. It would seem, in short, that the artificiality, the constructed character, of the concepts we use in speaking of the world in no way prevents us from speaking of things – patches of land, the appearance of collections of cells treated with a given stain, what one sees when one looks at a tomato, and so on – whose existence owes nothing to language.

ii. Word and practice, practice and world

But can such things be? How can the argument we have just sketched, for instance, be made convincing as well as – perhaps – persuasive? How, if the concepts in terms of which we claim to describe the world are creatures of language, that is of human convention, can language not be, essentially and *per se*, the prison-house of the mind?

The answer we shall pursue in this book is one that, *inter alia*, takes up and develops the hints, on the part of Frege and Geach, noted in Chapter 1 §ii and in Chapter 2 §ii. Although requiring complex and lengthy discussion at the level of detail, it can be stated quite simply in general terms. The Referential Realist envisages just one kind of link between language and world: a conventional association between some element of language (a proper name, a general name, a sentence, a collection of theoretically linked sentences) and some aspect or element of Reality (an individual, a universal, a feature, a set of truth-conditions, a collection of "stimuli"), the existence of which is prior to and independent of language. According to the Referential Realist, it is the setting up of such an associative linkage that transforms what, before the association was set up, was a mere phonemic string or set of marks, into a meaningful expression in a language.

We propose that, in thinking about the relation between discourse and what it concerns, we replace this one-level model, with just two component elements, word (or, more accurately, linguistic expression) and world, with a two-level model of three elements, word, world, and practice.

According to this model, there is no associative link between any member of any category of linguistic expressions and any extralinguistic entity, whether metaphysically or naturalistically conceived. More generally, the kind of relationship between language and the world that does obtain cannot, without the risk of serious misunderstanding, be described as any kind of "linkage" connecting "items" drawn respectively from two "realms," on the one hand, that of language, and, on the other, that of the extralinguistic. What actually relates language to reality, we shall argue, is better conceived as a two-level process of engagement, or embedding: at the first level the engagement, or embedding, of linguistic expressions in practices; at the second level the engagement, or embedding, of practices in the matrix of natural conditions and circumstances, in and with respect to which they are carried on. For the purposes of the argument at its present stage, counting, measuring length, weighing, arranging colour-samples in qualitative series, will serve as examples of practices; we shall encounter many more as the argument proceeds.

Evidently we are committed to advocating a version of the doctrine that "meaning is use." That doctrine, or slogan, has, unfortunately for us, a good title to be regarded as one of the more threadbare and overworked philosophical clichés of the twentieth century. It has figured, after all, and always somewhat less than persuasively, in such a diversity of mutually incompatible philosophical enterprises, from Heidegger to Wittgenstein, from Austin to Strawson, from Searle to Grice, that one might reasonably despair of attaching to it any clear unitary sense at all, let alone a useful one. The least that can be asked, therefore, of anyone who wishes at this point to claim any explanatory value for the slogan, is that they make clear at the outset what is to be understood by "use."

When philosophers speak of the "use" of an expression, they very often have in mind either its use in framing sentences – in another not uncommon phrase, its privileges of sentential occurrence – or its use in performing speech-acts: in asserting, referring, sentencing, marrying, and the like.

Neither of these uses of "use" will be very central to the argument here. In contexts in which the term is so employed we shall therefore in general avoid it, speaking instead of "employments," "functions," or the like.

When we speak of "use" we shall in most cases have in mind one or other of two sorts of thing, for the most part clearly distinguishable by context. On the one hand, when we speak of the "use" of a linguistic expression, we shall understand by that the mode of engagement of the expression in some practice. And when, on the other hand, we speak of the "use" of a practice, we shall understand by that the manner, consequent on its mode of engagement with reality, in which it serves the purposes of language-users. For convenience we shall on occasion distinguish these two uses of "use" by means of subscripts, viz.: "use$_E$," "use$_P$."

As we noted in the preceding section, when we speak of what expressions "designate" or "refer to," it is natural enough to take such locutions as invoking a range of *entities* that constitute the *meanings*, or *referents* of the expressions in question. It seems natural, that is, to regard "red" as designating a *colour*, "five grammes" as designating a *weight*, and so on; and natural, also, to proceed on the basis of that presumption to argue that unless each such entity actually exists, no remark phrased in terms of any expression designating it can possibly have any bearing on reality.

But suppose it could be shown, as we shall endeavour to show, that all talk of what an expression "designates" or refers to" is in the end merely a shorthand way of talking about the manner in which that expression engages with, or is involved in, some practice or other: of its use$_E$, in short. The supposed *entities* in the case would then dissolve, not quite into thin air, but into modes of engagement. The mode of engagement of an expression with a practice, now, is clearly not part of the furniture of the natural, extralinguistic world. On the contrary, it is quintessentially a work of human invention, as much a fabrication of ingenuity in the forging of convention as, say, the Petrarchan sonnet form or the rules of golf. It would follow, in other words, that when we speak of the entities referred to or designated by expressions, we speak, so far as we speak of anything at all, of fabrications of the mind.

But how, even if we can find a way of making such a claim plausible, do we avoid the conclusion, which has haunted us for three chapters, that all discourse bears only on the creatures of our own maggoty minds, and none of it on the furniture of nature? We avoid it because the bearing of language on the world, according to us, or more precisely, according to the two-stage model we have just outlined, is a function, not of the modes of engagement of linguistic expressions with practices but of the modes of engagement of practices with the world. A practice just *is* a mode of engaging with the contents of reality, as they present themselves to creatures with the physical constitution and perceptual powers of human beings. For a word to be en-meshed in a practice therefore, is for it to acquire a use$_E$ with respect to a system of procedures, responses, and results of one sort or another, which is always *already* "connected to the world," and that would not otherwise be of the slightest value or interest to those who make use$_P$ of it. Colour words, for example, find their use$_E$ in the context of the practice of sorting and arrang-ing shades of colour, by appeal to several different dimensions of relative similarity, into verbally labelled collections. Correlatively that practice is of use$_P$ to us in a variety of ways, as by presenting a verbal label of this sort we can enable others, in the absence of an object, to predict into which verbally labelled collection of colour-samples the object would sort according to the conventions of the language. The fact that the constitution of the collec-tions of specific colour presentations grouped under given colour-names is, to a degree, determined by conventions that can vary in certain ways from language to language, in no way impedes the utility of the practice. That is the reason why, when one says that a certain tomato is red, one can be referring to something entirely real and "extralinguistic," namely, the way the tomato looks to a human observer in a good light, even though *what "red" refers to*, namely *a colour*, is a fabrication of the human mind, or rather of human ingenuity in the constitution of practices. In general, if a name or a predicate-expression has a use$_E$ in connection with a practice having a use$_P$ it has a meaning, and hence an application to Reality, irrespective of whether anything we choose to say in terms of it turns out true or false. And, *per contra*, if it has no use$_E$, it is neither a predicate expression nor a name, but an empty vocable, a mere *flatus vocis*. There is no *further* question whether a name or a predicate (or concept) *is or is not, as such, "adequate to Reality."* Its business with Reality was already concluded when it entered the language. It was concluded in, and by, its acquiring a use$_E$ in connection with some practice that speakers find or have found, perhaps only temporarily, useful$_P$.

The idea that language could ever constitute, by its nature, a prison-house for the mind was always, in other words, an illusion: an illusion fostered by philosophers' persistent, not to say ingrained, habit of looking in just the wrong place for an answer to the question how language is related to reality: at the supposed unique relationship between words and things, rather than at the multifarious relationships between words, practices, and the world. That could, in one way, stand as the closing sentence of this book. But, of course, the real work of making plausible the two-level model still lies before us. All we have done in this section is to sketch in the barest outline a strategy for squaring the denial of Referential Realism with a corresponding denial of the possibility that language could, by its nature as a system of conventions, constitute a prison-house for the mind. In Part II we shall begin the work of developing that strategy by returning to the roots of analytic philosophy to examine a dispute, or rather, less a dispute than a profound difference of outlook, which came to divide Wittgenstein and Bertrand Russell during the 1920s. It remains in these introductory chapters to outline a little more fully some of the larger implications of the strategy we have sketched, and to address one or two of the more general objections to it.

iii. Truth, reference, and "language games"

The account we propose to give of the relationship of language to reality manifestly has its roots in what Wittgenstein has to say about what he calls language games (*Sprachspiele*). Interpreters of Wittgenstein have not, on the whole, found that notion very perspicuous. Two major difficulties are worth raising here. The first was raised by Sir Peter Strawson, and still lacks a clear response. Strawson notes that in Wittgenstein talk of "use" is supposed "to get us away from our fascination with the dubious relation of naming, of meaning," and that talk of different "uses" shades easily into talk of different linguistic activities or practices. But what differentiates one "practice," one "language game," from another? Difference of use, presumably. But difference of use is, as we have just noted, a broad category. Is copying a story out a different "use" from reading it aloud? And isn't there "the special use involved in sending an old man to sleep by reading aloud from a translation of a play?" "Surely," says Strawson, reasonably enough, "distinctions are needed here to save the whole notion from sliding into absurdity."[4]

The second objection, very widely held, is that the analogy Wittgenstein draws between language and games such as chess, or systems of tools or controls (the various kinds of control in the cab of the locomotive in paragraph 12 of Part I of the *Investigations*, for instance), misses precisely those features that crucially distinguish language from "games" or "practices" of other kinds: namely the fact that in language, and only in language, it is possible to refer to things, to formulate propositions concerning those things, and to establish, affirm or deny the truth or falsity of those propositions. To see Wittgenstein's later work as offering no answer to this objection is to see it, as many do, as inexplicably turning away from the effort to explicate the connection between meaning and truth, an enterprise, begun by Frege, which formed a central concern of his own early work, the *Tractatus Logico-Philosophicus*, and has continued to be the central concern of most subsequent analytic philosophy of language; choosing instead to play around with the idea of a putative connection between meaning and "use," a notion that, as we have just noted, many consider not merely ill-defined, but entirely and hopelessly obscure.

In what follows we shall take both these bulls by the horns. For every philosophical tradition, there are certain notions to which the duty of the philosopher to subject concepts to searching analytic scrutiny is held not to extend. In recent analytic philosophy the concepts of truth and reference have enjoyed just such a status. They are held, that is, to be concepts lacking which we should lack a conception of language *per se*, but which themselves admit of no analysis or explication in terms of other concepts. We shall argue, on the contrary, that neither the concept of truth nor that of reference would be accessible to us if the experience of using language had not familiarised us with practices, the utility of which to us essentially depends on the engagement in them, or the enmeshing with them, of linguistic expressions. It is commonly supposed that the conditions under which a statement is true or false can be defined by correlating statements, at any rate simple, "highly observational," ones, with observable natural conditions. We shall argue that this is false. Truth-conditions, like concepts, are not to be encountered in nature. The truth-conditions of an utterance U, and thus the status of U as (not merely a cry or a rumbling sort of groan, but) the kind of utterance with respect to which it is intelligible to raise the issue of truth or falsity, can only be determined relative to some means of singling out, among the infinity of features and aspects presented by what Quine felicitously dubs "the passing show," those that are truth-relevant to U; and that means can only be provided by the enmeshing of U in some practice, some "language game." And, because grasping the reference of an expression is in part a matter of grasping the truth-conditions attaching to sentences in which it can occur, the concept of reference also will turn out, if we are correct, to be dependent on, and derivative from, the prior notion of a practice.

Such arguments require development at length if their merits are to be seriously assessed. We shall return to them with that in mind at the commencement of Part II. They are arguments with, we believe, a firm basis in the later work of Wittgenstein, and in that connection we have already developed them to some degree elsewhere.[5] Their presence in the later work suggests that that work, far from constituting an abandonment of the Fregean doctrine of a conceptual relationship between truth and meaning, represents, on the contrary, a continued effort, after Wittgenstein's recognition of what he considered the failure of the *Tractatus*, to illuminate that relationship from a new direction. This in turn suggests an answer to Strawson's worry about how we are to construe the function, and thus the identity-conditions, of the language game. The function – or one central function – of language games, we shall argue, is neither to send old men to sleep on windy nights, nor to reproduce a story by copying it out, but to fix the conditions of truth and reference for the expressions, sentential and otherwise, which find a use$_E$ in them.

iv. Resisting reductionism

Referential Realism enshrines, in many of its forms, the doctrine that unless a proper name or general term corresponds to some entity whose existence owes nothing to language, no thought articulated in terms of it can have any bearing on any reality external to the mind. It is a very short step from this to the ideal of a Universal Language: a language, that is, in which it would be impossible even to articulate error or fantasy, because it would contain no content-bearing expressions save ones whose meaningfulness consisted simply in their serving as labels for just such entities. That ideal has been persistent in philosophy since the Renaissance, and has taken various forms, from Leibniz's *Characteristica Universalis*[6] or Wilkins' "Real Character,"[7] to Russell's conception of a "logically perfect language."[8] It is an ideal necessarily linked to the enterprise of semantic reduction. The thought implicit in the ideal of a Universal Language is that only in such a language could one articulate what is *objectively* – independently of human wishes or fantasies – *the case*. That seems to entail, because there is only one natural world, that there can be only *one* language capable of articulating what is the case concerning that world; and hence that everything that is the case must be capable of articulation in a single language, namely, that one. Insofar, therefore, as it is possible, in the mutinously conceptually inventive languages we actually speak, to speak truly of what, objectively, is, it can be so only because those languages encapsulate within themselves disjointed fragments of the One Universal Language, the meanings of whose words owe nothing to human conceptual inventiveness. One has, of course, various choices when it comes to identifying the parts of our everyday language that do, in fact, approximate most nearly to the demands of Universal Language. Philosophers of empiricist leanings tend to identify them as those of which we tend to avail ourselves when we attempt to give as bare a description as possible of the content of sensory experience. Others, of a more scientistic bent, identify them with the languages of the natural sciences. It is fairly common for philosophers of the latter persuasion to take it for granted that the "folk" languages we ordinarily speak are capable of conveying truths only insofar as what we say in them is capable of being rephrased in some "scientific" language, and that the languages of science, actually at present rather a diverse and motley collection, must in time prove capable of reductive regimentation into a single, all-embracing language capable of comprehending all truth.

Every mind forms a picture, a representation of its world. That there are few minds, and no societies, whose world-picture is not at some points, and often at many points, adrift from reality, is evident, at any rate to the disabused scrutiny of our maturity. The Referential Realist is not committed, however, just to the affirmation of the philosophically harmless truism that received ideas are often not only false but absurd. He is committed, in addition, to a philosophical, and philosophically far from harmless, way of accounting for that depressing fact. According to the Referential Realist, as we have seen, what accounts for the fact that received ideas often bear little relation to reality is that the sentences in which those ideas are phrased are not ones that could be satisfactorily replaced by sentences in a Universal Language, either the language of basic, or "brute," sensory description, or the language of unified science.

The ideal of a Universal Language is, as we have seen, the ideal of a language whose content-bearing expressions owe their meaning to their status as associative labels for entities existing independently of language. It is just because of this feature that the ideal of such a language – a language which, as Merleau-Ponty put it, "would deliver us from language by delivering us to things" – has obtained such a firm grip on the intellectual imagination of the past four centuries. But, because few of the concepts required to describe the life of human individuals or cultures are plausible candidates for inclusion in the conceptual vocabulary of the Universal Language, must not such a deliverance deliver us equally from our humanity? The idea that "objective" reality attaches only to what can be mentioned in some plausible fragment of the Universal Language carries with it the suggestion that the entire human world is a parade of phantoms projected by the mind, or by "language," on a reality that is not only in itself profoundly inhuman, but that offers no foothold to the human. There is no place in the resulting vision for any notion of symbiosis between the human and the natural. It offers no foothold to any conception of human activity as creating, through the elaboration of materials and possibilities afforded by nature, an order of beings in whose constitution the natural and the human can no longer be distinguished as separable components, and whose union cannot therefore be dissolved or made to fall apart by any form of reductive analysis. On the contrary, it forces us to think of any human activity constitutive of concepts having no prior instantiation in nature as a departure from, a turning of the back on, the natural. On such an estimate of the relationship between thought, or language, and the world, to allow any place in one's life to any of the grander constructions of the human spirit, to literature, art, religion, say, is to prefer illusion to disillusionment, the comforts of dream to the dispiriting recognition of a reality which offers no consolation save the consciousness, dear to Stoics and puritans, of being terminally undeceived.

The effect of this vision on the modern mind has for the last few centuries been progressive and profound. It shows, for instance, in the pervasive attachment of educated opinion in the West to the belief that unless moral principles can be shown to be "objective," which is to say, somehow or other inherent in a "Nature" untouched by human hands, we have no option but to embrace a noncognitivism according to which morality is a tissue of subjective "feelings" or "commitments," and as such immune from rational criticism. In another way it shows in the conviction, widespread in literary studies, that there is ultimately no distinction of value to be drawn between great literature and the most trivial piece of kitsch, as literature *per se* is a fantasy; a further layer of coloured illusion that we interpose between ourselves and the realities of which we would be glumly confined to speaking, did we but speak a language as hostile to fantasy as the Universal Language would be, and as such putative fragments of it as, say, the languages of the physical sciences already are.

And yet this vision of our place in Nature, powerful as it is, blurs distinctions that, when not under its spell, we feel it natural enough to draw. Instead of contrasting *tree* and *demonic possession*, as we did earlier, let us try contrasting *tune* and *demonic possession*. Tunes cannot be regarded by any stretch of the imagination as numbered among the things capable of existing independently of human activity in the elaboration of practices and conventions. The existence of tunes requires the existence of the kind of musical tradition in which such things can be composed, can be recognised, can be whistled, can prompt nostalgia. And such traditions are the fruit of heaped-up centuries of tradition in multiplying and interweaving human practices of all kinds, from the diatonic scale to the traditions of grand opera or music-hall kitsch. It is deeply implausible that an account of these matters could ever be given in any of the candidate Universal Languages promoted this century by philosophers. And yet, we want to say, tunes, objectively speaking, exist, are items included amongst the furniture of reality.

In this respect, tunes seem to most of us things not at all on all fours with demons. Tunes, after all, are things encountered every day; demons are not. It is, in a certain obvious sense, just a mistake to suppose that demons exist. There seems to be no very obvious parallel sense in which it is, or could be, "just a mistake" to suppose that tunes exist.

The Referential Realist's position allows him only two ways of addressing such commonplace, or as he sometimes likes to say, "folk" convictions. He can grasp the nettle and maintain that some people's conviction that they hear tunes is just as much a delusion as some other people's conviction that, in dreams, magical ceremonies, and the like, they see and converse with demons. Or he can argue that sentences mentioning tunes are susceptible of reductive elimination in favour of sentences drawn from some preferred fragment, psychological, neurological, or information-technological, of a putative Universal Language.

Although some minds find this choice natural and unconstraining, others find it decidedly unappetising, not least because they find dubious the claims of programmatic philosophical reductionism of the types generally proposed in such contexts to be "scientific," at least if that is supposed to mean continuous with the practice of actual scientists. As Gaston Bachelard[9] has argued, real science, although it may offer compelling explanations of the phenomenal, rarely does so by way of a reductive elimination of the terms in which the phenomena to be explained are described, for the very good reason that the latter course would yield not an explanation of the phenomena in question but a denial of their reality. To such minds it will be of interest that the two-level account of the relation of language to the world that we propose to defend here offers a way of distinguishing between reality and fantasy that, unlike the Referential Realist's way of doing that, does not group *tune* with *demonic possession* over against *tree*, but on the contrary groups *tree* with *tune* over against *demonic possession*.[10]

It does this because, as we shall see, it construes the contrast between terms that pick out realities and those that pick out maggots of the mind, not as a contrast between the types of entity to which those terms putatively refer, nor even as a contrast between the modes of engagement of those terms in practices (a move that yields, among other things, what used at one time to be termed "Wittgensteinian Fideism"), but as a contrast between the modes of engagement with reality exhibited by the practices in which the terms in question find a use$_E$. Tunes are genuine constituents of reality, that is, because the musical practices in which talk of them finds a home are so rooted in, and elaborated on the basis of, the phenomenology and physics of sound, as to leave in the tissue of our musical life no fissure capable of admitting even the philosophers' slender blade, that antique weapon patented by Locke and much improved by Berkeley and Hume, which since 1688 has been ceaselessly at work dividing what is "really there" from what is "mere interpretation." Demons, by contrast, are not bona fide constituents of Reality because the practices in which talk of them finds a use, although richly enough enmeshed with other aspects of social and religious usage to satisfy a Wittgensteinian Fideist, and possibly the James of "The Will to Believe," are not enmeshed at all with the kind of aspects of the world with which, if what believers in demons say about them is to be taken seriously, one would expect to find them enmeshed.

v. Adequating (or not adequating) concepts

As indicated in Chapter 3 §ii, we shall be arguing that if we wish to think of names as "designating" or "picking out" *entities* – such entities as *Napoleon Bonaparte*, or *redness*, or the modulus *one metre*, or *England*, or *tigerhood*, say – then the entities in question are best thought of as, one and all, linguistic constructs; but that such ways of speaking offer at best a muddled and misleading way of talking about the modes of insertion of linguistic expressions into practices. We have further suggested – also, as yet, entirely programmatically – that there can be no question whether one name – or to fall back into the first way of speaking, one concept – is in itself more "adequate to Reality" than another. There can be no question, in other words, of dismissing an expression as "meaningless," in the manner dear to the Logical Positivists, on the ground that it fails to stand in some putatively required relationship to Reality. A name, simply *qua* name, has a meaning if it has a use$_E$, and it has a use$_E$ just in case the practice with which it is engaged affords it one.

That, however, suggests the following possibility. Suppose two languages, L_1 and L_2, enshrine different practices, P_1 and P_2, which in turn give sense to a pair of names, N_1 and N_2, expressing concepts, C_1 and C_2, which purport to address the same phenomenon P, but which, as it happens, given that L_1 and L_2 are the vehicles, respectively, of two physical theories that cannot both be true, cannot both figure in a correct description of P. It looks, on the one hand, as if one or other of the two concepts is the correct one for purposes of scientific description, and the other, when it comes down to it, just vacuous, in the sense of corresponding to nothing in nature; and, on the other hand, as if the account programmatically outlined above is going to leave us with no way of representing this state of affairs. For it appears that, on the above view, any concept is, *qua* concept, an adequate concept, just in case the name that expresses it has a use$_E$ relative to some practice. So, as both N_1 and N_2 have uses$_E$ relative to, respectively, P_1 and P_2, there seems to be no way, within our account, in which we can express what it is that constitutes the relative inadequacy of either C_1 or C_2, and grounds, correspondingly, the relative adequacy of its fellow.

The short answer to this, already hinted at in the small print of Chapter 1 §iii, and in the previous section,[11] is that what gets "adequated," or the reverse, through the progress of scientific enquiry (among other things), are not concepts but, rather, practices – and that practices do not so much get "adequated," or the reverse, so much as adopted or discarded for many kinds of good reason, including scientific ones. The term "phlogiston," for instance, has a perfectly good sense relative to certain practices (we shall begin to get clearer soon about how the content of the relevant notion of a practice is to be spelled out in detail), which in turn contribute to rendering intelligible a certain physical theory concerning the chemical nature of combustion. That theory, as we know, turned out to be false; it was therefore discarded. The practices within which the term "phlogiston" found a use$_E$ being discarded with it, that term ceased to figure in up-to-date books on physical chemistry. It ceased to do so, in other words, not because of a discovery concerning the relation (or lack of one) to Reality of the concept it expresses (what, after all, *pace* the millennial influence of conceptual Realism on the philosophical mind, could such a "discovery" conceivably consist in?), but because of discoveries concerning the nature of combustion.

To put it in another way, this time in the terminology in which the question was posed, the adequation of one system of concepts relative to another comes about, in general, through processes operating *internally* to the total system of sense-bestowing practices, taken together with their multifarious modes of insertion into the world. What robs the word "internally," taken in this context, of its power to generate the threat of our being cut off from a just apprehension of the nature of Reality through the entanglement of the mind in the web of its own practices, with the associated array of terms and concepts upon which they bestow sense? Simply the fact that those of our practices that possess cognitive relevance possess it because of the nature of their modes of insertion into – Reality! We think, are endlessly tempted to think, that we need an *external* criterion of adequacy – external, that is to the fate of "practices," or of any other creation of Kantian "spontaneity" – to allow us to adjudicate between competing systems of concepts. In fact, we need no such thing. We can manage perfectly well with an internal criterion – "internal," that is, to the total system of practices taken together with their modes of insertion in the world – because the fate of our practices, the issue of whether we shall find it useful to adopt, to elaborate or to discard them, *already* hinges on the nature of Reality in quite sufficiently many ways to ensure a dynamic and progressive relationship between our cognitive structures and the way things stand in the world.

vi. Relative Realism

The Realism of the Referential Realist does not, or at least need not, go very deep. Referential Realism asserts, after all, merely that it is possible to speak of the real world only in a language at least some of whose content-bearing elements refer to members of some class of constituents of that world. That claim is modest enough to be equally compatible, at one, Realistic, extreme, with the naturalised platonism of McDowell, and at the opposite extreme with Quine's thesis of the indeterminacy of translation, or for that matter with the anti-Realism about truth of Dummett and his school.

By contrast, the denial of Referential Realism is widely supposed to entail the acceptance of some fairly radical version of Relativism. Certainly the account of the relationship between language and reality that we shall defend here is in one respect relativistic in character. It holds that concepts are relative to practices: that what concepts a natural language honours is determined not by the nature of things, but by the specific range of practices that enter into the constitution of that particular natural language. So contending, it contends also that, as no limit can be set in principle either to human purposes or to the practices that human inventiveness may devise in their service, so no limit can be set to the invention of new concepts. Plato was familiar neither with the modern concept of valency in chemistry, nor with Gerard Manley Hopkins's concept of *inscape*, nor does there seem any intelligible sense in which either concept could be said to be "discovered in the world." Both are constructions, on the one hand, of chemical theory, on the other, of a certain writer's theory of poetry; but that need not, and does not, prevent either from having a use in the description of reality.

Conceptual Relativism of this kind, however, whereas it is incompatible with McDowell's or any other version of Conceptual Realism, is not only not incompatible with, but positively helpful to, Realism of several other kinds. It is, for instance, as we shall see, hostile to most forms (e.g., Quinean, Kripkean) of meaning-scepticism. Certainly it shares "the important negative thesis which is in common between Quine and Wittgenstein, namely that to hold that an utterance means so and so is not to take it that some item lies behind or causally explains that utterance – rather it is to take it that the item has a certain place in a pattern of items."[12] It shares, that is to say, Quine's, or Davidson's, or Putnam's disbelief in the existence of a class of *entities* called "senses" or "meanings." According to it there are no meanings, only linguistic expressions strewn across the fabric of the practices in which they acquire a use$_E$. But, by contrast, because it takes the acquisition of a grasp of the meanings of linguistic expressions to consist in the acquisition of the ability to operate practices, it holds, against Quine, or Davidson, or Kripke, that the meaning of a linguistic expression is by no means empirically underdetermined. For, on the one hand, neither Quine's nor anybody else's arguments show why we should suppose it impossible for a participant in a practice to teach that practice to someone else. And, on the other, for a language to be teachable, it must be possible to have sufficient empirical grounds for the belief that a given practice is the one that a given participant is operating: that Mikhail Tal, say, is playing chess and not ludo. We accept, that is, Michael Dummett's "Manifestation Principle."[13] But we differ from Dummett, as will become apparent, in holding a radically nonepistemic view of language. Thus, whereas, for Dummett, what has to manifest itself if language learning is to take place is to some quite large extent the conditions that warrant assertion, for us what has to be manifested is the procedures and uses$_P$ of practices. As we shall see in what follows, that shift in the identification of what needs to be "manifested" for a language to be learnable offers the basis for an entirely Realistic account of truth. Finally, even if what we say here is hostile to all versions of platonism, it is not at all hostile to McDowell's or Sellars's Kantian talk of the conceptual realm as a "space of reasons." Such talk is reminiscent of Wittgenstein's talk of "logical space" in the *Tractatus* and elsewhere. We shall argue, however, both against McDowell, and in another context against Kripke, that the structure and content of the canons of rationality composing such spaces can be fully understood in terms of the modes of engagement of practices with reality, without invoking any further "grounding" or "justification" external to the practice and its mode of engagement with the world.

We shall be defending, then, a view that, while it offers from one point of view, a version of Relativism, offers from many other points of view a defence of rather robust kinds of Realism. A relatively Realistic view, then, and one whose Realism depends, in important respects, on its Relativism. What better name for it, accordingly, than *Relative Realism*?

PART II

NAMES AND THEIR BEARERS

A name means an object. The object is its meaning.
– *Wittgenstein, Tractatus* 3.203

4

Russell's Principle and Wittgenstein's Slogan

i. Understanding Algernon

"Bunbury," as all lovers of Wilde are aware, is the name of a mythical friend and chronic invalid invented by Mr. Algernon Moncrieff to justify his absence from London dinner-tables during the summer months. To those not in on the secret, Algernon is unwillingly responding to the voice of conscience urging him as a sacred duty to spend time at the bedside of his sick friend. Those in on the secret are aware that he is doing nothing so improbable as his duty. He is simply off enjoying himself in the country: "going Bunburying." There is no Bunbury.

In what sense, then, can those not in the secret be said to *understand* the remark "Bunbury is ill again"? Those in the unphilosophical and rather numerous majority whose bookshelves are innocent of the works of Gottlob Frege, seeing no problem, may be inclined to respond that they understand it as well as, and in the same way as, any other English sentence employing a proper name. For analytic philosophers since Frege, by contrast, the issue has been a loaded one; one that, almost more than any other, brings into focus a nest of problems concerning the question that has been occupying us: how and to what extent are the spontaneities of language constrained by reality?

It will do no harm to rehearse some of the reasons for this, well-known as they are. Let us briefly abandon Moncrieff and Bunbury for a rapid tour of a part of Frege's philosophy of language. Central to that philosophy is the extremely persuasive suggestion that to understand an assertoric sentence is to know how to assess the truth or falsity of assertions made by means of it. That plausible thought is, in turn, articulated in terms of Frege's technical notions of sense (*Sinn*) and reference (*Bedeutung*). The *reference* of a proper name, Frege says, "is the object itself which we designate by its means."[1] The *sense* of the name, by contrast, is the "mode of presentation" of that object.[2] In terms of Frege's famous example of the evening and the morning star, the reference of "evening star" would be the same as that of "morning star," but not the sense.

According to Frege, assertoric sentences, such as "Bunbury is ill" or "Napoleon lost the Battle of Waterloo" also have senses. Frege calls them *thoughts*: " . . . We need a short term for what can be the sense of an indicative sentence. I call this a thought."[3] It is not uncommon to distinguish Frege's special sense of "thought" by a capital letter: we shall do the same, because we shall also wish to speak of thought, and thoughts, in a more common-place sense. A Thought differs from the sense of a proper name or other denoting expression in that it can form the content of a judgment. The first stage in the passage from merely grasping a Thought to judging by means of it is to make it the content of a question. Thus we pass from merely grasping the sense of "Bunbury is ill" to raising the question "Is Bunbury ill?" To answer this question in the affirmative is to judge that Bunbury is ill; in the negative, that Bunbury is not ill.[4]

In the philosophy of language of seventeenth- and eighteenth-century British Empiricism, the meaning of a name is an *idea,* or a complex of ideas. By "idea," those writers most commonly have in mind a sensation, or the memory of a sensation, or a mental image: things, in other words, essentially private to the mind of one person. Frege insists that the *sense* of a linguistic expression is not, in any of those senses, an idea, but is something to which all competent speakers of the language have access. We have touched on his argument already, in Chapter 1 §ii, but it will bear citing once more.

. . . it must be possible to put a question to which the true answer is negative. The content of such a question is, in my terminology, a thought. It must be possible for several people who hear the same interrogative sentence to grasp the same sense and recognise the falsity of it. Trial by jury would assuredly be a silly arrangement if it could not be assumed that each of the jurymen could understand the question at issue in the same sense. So the sense of an interrogative sentence, even when the question has to be answered in the negative, is something that can be grasped by several people.[5]

Thoughts, according to Frege, are neither mental states nor constituents of the world revealed to sensory experience.

A thought belongs neither to my inner world as an idea, nor yet to the external world, the world of things perceptible to the senses.[6]

But, Frege contends, it is only because we have access to these abstract, "third-world," entities that we can engage in a common pursuit of truth.

Not everything is an idea. Thus I can also acknowledge thoughts as independent of me; other men can grasp them just as much as I; I can acknowledge a science in which many can be engaged in research. We are not owners of thoughts as we are owners of our ideas.[7]

Access to senses, including Thoughts, then, liberates us into a common world of discourse; permits two or more investigators to address the question of whether a given propositional content corresponds to reality with the assurance that the propositional content under consideration is the same for all of them.

But does access to a common world of discourse necessarily come to the same thing as access to the real world? Referential Realists will answer in the negative. So would Frege have done. Frege, like the early Russell, is concerned to deny the central thesis of Idealism: that what we are in the first instance acquainted with is not extramental reality but some mental state, a sensation or an "idea," which represents reality only in the sense that it "coheres" with other mental states. For Frege, indeed, the point of insisting on a sharp distinction between Thoughts and ideas is precisely to combat the notion that truth is, or could be, a property of mental states. Truth, Frege argues, is to be sharply distinguished from qualities such as "'red,' 'bitter,' 'lilac-smelling'"[8] that can characterise sensations. "... Anything the senses can perceive is excluded from the realm of things for which the question of truth arises."[9] Thoughts are what populate the latter realm: "I mean by 'a thought' something for which the question of truth can arise at all."[10]

To arrive at truth, Frege thinks, we must advance from merely entertaining (or "grasping") a Thought to making it the content of a judgment. To judge is, precisely, to attribute a truth-value, either True or False to a Thought. One can think of the sense of an indicative sentence, the Thought it expresses, as locating a truth-value, either the True or the False. The passage from grasping the sense of an indicative sentence (a Thought) to judging it to be true or false is complicated, however, in the case of sentences involving a proper name, by the possibility that the proper name may lack a bearer. Only if there is an object of some sort bearing that name, of which the remark is asserted, can it be either true or false. For if there is no such object there is nothing for the remark to be "about," and the question of its truth or falsity does not arise.

Frege, in a celebrated passage, offers as an instance the sentence "Odysseus was set ashore at Ithaca while fast asleep":

... anyone who seriously took the sentence to be true or false would ascribe to the name "Odysseus" a reference, not merely a sense; for it is of the reference of the name that the predicate is affirmed or denied. Whoever does not admit the name has reference can neither apply nor withhold the predicate.[11]

An interest in knowing what individual a name picks out thus argues an interest in discovering whether the sentence in which it occurs is true or false. If we were merely aesthetically interested in the above sentence, the absence of a bearer of the name "Odysseus" would be of no concern to us.

In hearing an epic poem, for instance, apart from the euphony of the language we are interested only in the sense of the sentences and the images and feelings thereby aroused . . . it is a matter of no concern to us whether the name "Odysseus," for instance, has reference, so long as we accept the poem as a work of art. It is the striving for truth that drives us always to advance from the sense to the reference.[12]

From that concluding thought, that "it is the striving for truth that drives us always to advance from the sense to the reference," Frege concludes, notoriously, that "We are therefore driven to accepting the *truth value* of a sentence as constituting its reference."[13] Few commentators have found that assimilation anything but confused and a source of confusion.

Frege's queer proposal that sentences should be regarded as names of truth-values need not detain us, however. Let us consider instead the equally characteristically Fregean thought that led Frege to it: the thought that it is through access to the bearer of a proper name that we advance from mere contemplation of the sense of a sentence in which it occurs, to the judgment that it is true or false, with the converse that in the absence of a bearer that advance is frustrated and cannot take place.[14]

Back now, with that thought in mind, to Bunbury. Suppose some acquaintance A of Moncrieff's, one not in the secret, says, believing it to be true,

1. Bunbury is ill this weekend.

It would be natural to say of A,

2. A thinks that Bunbury is ill this weekend

Nor does A himself take himself to be merely "entertaining" or "grasping" the Fregean sense of this sentence (the Thought it expresses). He takes himself to be making a judgment that has that sense as its content. That judgment, evidently, concerns the bearer of the name "Bunbury." But "Bunbury" has no bearer. The Fregean path from merely grasping, or entertaining, the sense of (1) to judging (1) to express a truth is thus blocked. But in that case, can (2) be correct? Can A be said, not in Frege's technical sense of "Thought," but in the commonplace sense exploited by (2), to "think" anything at all? If he were thinking anything, it would be something about the bearer of the name "Bunbury." But there is no such entity for any such putative thought to be about. Can A, for that matter, be said to be referring to anything in asserting (1)? Once again, if he were referring to anything at all, it would be to the bearer of "Bunbury." But there is no such entity.

We seem forced to say, therefore, that in uttering (1), A, although he does not know it, is neither expressing a thought (even though, if we allow Frege his technical sense of "Thought," he may be said to be "grasping" or "entertaining" one) nor referring: he is merely uttering some words. These are no doubt words that he, and we, "understand" in the sense of grasping their meaning (the Thought they express). But there is, in this context, no "thought" in the commonplace sense, no propositional content, which these words, used in the present context, may be understood as expressing.

In A, in other words, we encounter a new version of the deluded occupant of the Prison-House of Language. A, convinced as he is that he is both referring to an individual and asserting a proposition concerning that individual, is in fact doing neither; he is merely manipulating words. What, now, can save us from the risk of falling into this plight whenever we employ a proper name? What can assure us, when we make use of such a name, that we are (a) in a position to refer by means of it, and (b) in a position to formulate genuine judgments – judgments, that is, capable of proving true or false – by means of sentences employing it? Only, it would seem, the assurance that the name in question possesses a bearer.

As we shall see, the overwhelming tendency of philosophers since Russell has been to assume that the latter assurance must be epistemic in character, and that it must involve either acquaintance with, or some other form of epistemically guaranteed access to, *that very individual*. To accept this assumption is, as we shall see shortly, to forge an intimate link between meaning and the epistemic. In this and the following two chapters we shall find reason to question both the necessity of those assumptions and the existence of any such link.

ii. Russell's Principle

The early, Realist, Russell had little time for Frege's distinction between the sense and reference of a proper name. Certainly Russell agreed with Frege that ordinary proper names such as "Bismarck" or "Wittgenstein" were to be understood as shorthand for such descriptions as "The First German Chancellor" or "The author of the *Tractatus*." But this cannot be taken as tantamount to the admission that all names have both a sense and a reference, because Russell also held, famously, that definite descriptions are analytically dispensable.

What Russell seems to have disliked about Frege's doctrine that every expression has both a sense and a reference is its suggestion that there is always more to knowing the meaning of a name than simply being acquainted with its reference. Russell, for his part, thought that it had to be possible for bare acquaintance with an object (an individual or a feature) N, denoted by a name "N," to bestow a complete grasp of the meaning of "N," without the need for any mediating intervention on the part of Fregean *Sinn*, or for that matter any other mental state or linguistic construct. Russell had two main grounds for this view. The first was the argument, already noted in Chapter 2 §ii, that, while it clearly is possible to explain the meaning of an expression by means of a verbal definition or description, it is possible only because there exists a layer of "basic" or "atomic" expressions, the meanings of which do not need to be so explained, but can be apprehended directly,

through confrontation, in acquaintance, with the individuals or features
that they pick out. The second argument addresses the issue of bearerless
proper names, which Russell generalises to involve general names as well.
How are we to know that a name of either kind denotes something that
actually exists? The fact that it is definable is no help, for definition merely
replaces one verbal formula by another. Only in the case of a name "N"
whose meaning can be wholly explicated by placing it in correlation with an
object of acquaintance, do we have cast-iron assurance that "N" possesses a
bearer. Only such expressions, therefore, Russell thought, can be regarded
as genuine proper names, "logically proper names," as he called them. For
ordinary proper names, the meaning of which can at best be explicated by
appeal to descriptions, the issue of whether they possess bearers can only be
settled in the affirmative if the sentences in which they occur can be shown to
be analytically equivalent to sentences in which only logically proper names
occur. The following passage nicely catches the flavour of Russell's thinking
at this point.

At any given moment there are certain things of which a man is "aware," certain things
which are "before his mind." Now, though it is very difficult to define "awareness,"
it is not at all difficult to say that I am aware of such and such things. If I am asked,
I can reply that I am aware of this, and that, and the other, and so on through
a heterogeneous collection of objects. If I describe these objects, I may of course
describe them wrongly; hence I cannot with certainty communicate to another what
are the things of which I am aware. But if I speak to myself, and denote them by
what may be called "proper names," rather than by descriptive words, I cannot be
in error. So long as the names which I use really are names at the moment, i.e., are
naming things to me, so long the things must be objects of which I am aware, since
otherwise the words would be meaningless sounds, not names of things. There is
thus at any given moment a certain assemblage of objects to which I could, if I chose,
give proper names; these are the objects of my "awareness," the objects "before my
mind" or the objects that are within my present "experience."[15]

At this, "basic," level of language, at which there is nothing equivalent
to Frege's notion of *Sinn*, the meaning of a proper name just *is* its bearer.
Frege's philosophy of language, as we have seen, in effect leaves room for
two senses of "understand." One can be said to "understand" an expression,
a name or a sentence, whose sense one grasps; or, equally, one can be said to
"understand" what someone who advances a judgment is judging to be the
case. In the latter case, understanding involves knowing of which individual
the content of the judgment is predicated. On the level of Russell's genuine,
or "logically" proper names, only the second sense is available. Hence, unless
one knows which individual a proper name picks out, one is not, after all,
dealing with a name at all, but only with a "meaningless sound." That is
why the bearers of logically proper names must be objects of Russellian
"acquaintance."

It is equally the case, in Russell's scheme of things, that it is *only* on the level of logically proper names that understanding in the second sense is available; for it is only to the extent that "complex" denoting expressions can be analytically eliminated in favour of logically proper names that any certainty concerning the issue of whether the names in our sentences actually possess denotata can be arrived at. We are thus led ineluctably to Russell's famous observation in *The Problems of Philosophy*:

Every proposition which we can understand must be composed wholly of constituents with which we are acquainted.[16]

To many philosophers this claim has seemed, even when stripped of Russell's logico-psychological apparatus of "acquaintance" and "logically proper names," to embody a deeply intuitively plausible thought, namely, the thought that, after all, someone cannot be said to be saying anything unless he knows what he is saying it about. A judgment couched in a sentence containing a bearerless proper name, for instance "Bunbury is ill," says nothing because there is no one for it to say anything about. There is thus no sense in which either the speaker or a hearer could be said to "understand" the content of the supposed judgment, as distinct from the meaning of the words in English. The late Gareth Evans formulates precisely that thought, dignified with the title *Russell's Principle*, as follows:

RP: It is not possible for a person to have a thought about something unless he knows which particular individual in the world he is thinking about.[17]

At the start of Chapter 3 of *The Varieties of Reference*, Evans has this to say concerning the pervasiveness of such intuitions.

Many philosophers today look at the theory of reference through essentially Russellian eyes. They have the idea that fundamental differences in the ways in which referring expressions of ordinary language function ultimately rest upon fundamental differences in the ways in which it is open to us to *think* about particular objects. Like Russell, they recognise the possibility, perhaps as a limiting case, of thinking of an object by description: as when one thinks of a man, some African warrior, perhaps, when one thinks that the tallest man in the world is thus and so. But, again like Russell, they cherish the idea of a more "intimate," more "direct" relation in which a subject may stand to an object (a situation in which the subject would be "*en rapport* with" the object), and the idea that when a subject and his audience are both situated *vis-à-vis* an object in this way, there exists the possibility of using singular terms to refer to, and to talk about, that object in a quite different way – expressing thoughts which would not have been available to be thought and expressed if the object had not existed. They have even taken over from Russell the idea that the central case of a situation which gives rise to the possibility of this "more direct" way of thinking and talking about an object arises when we can perceive the object concerned.[18]

This expresses admirably what it is to think about reference in the spirit of Russell's Principle, and at the same time makes evident the way in which such

thinking derives its force from its claim to represent the only way of defeating
the sceptical threat represented by the image of language as prison-house.
Evans grants that the purport of Russell's Principle, as just stated, is not
altogether clear.

The difficulty with Russell's Principle has always been to explain what it means.[19]

Yet, however obscure Russell's Principle may be, the alternatives to something of the sort's being true seem from the perspective of prison-house
scepticism intolerable. To deny Russell's Principle, it seems (at any rate at
first sight) is to steer very close indeed to the twin bugbears of Referential
Realism: on the one hand, Relativism; on the other, what one might call *Linguistic Idealism*, the thesis that the mind never passes beyond the circuit of
its own, linguistically forged, conceptions to encounter a reality that existed
before language, and is independent of it.

Let us take the latter first. Suppose Russell's Principle to be false. Then,
whenever we refer, our act of referring, that act by which we single out
the object concerning which, as subject (to adopt Evans's terminology) we
propose to articulate what Frege would have called a Thought, will in a
certain sense both begin and terminate *within language*. For the object that
that act fastens on, reaches out to, and so singles out, will be in a certain
sense a linguistically *constituted* object. By a linguistically constituted object
of reference we have in mind precisely such an object as *the tallest man*, or
as *Shakespeare*, if by "Shakespeare" we mean, as we normally do, the nominal
common author of a certain small collection of texts. There is a sense in
which, when one has a thought about a linguistically constituted object,
one "knows which particular individual" one is thinking about. But all that
that seems to mean is that one knows how a given referring expression is
to be used relative to a certain system of linguistic rules or conventions,
in this case rules for replacing one linguistic expression with another. And
that leaves hanging in the air the crucial issue, for anyone of even vaguely
Realist leanings, of whether, in picking out such an object, one is picking
out something that genuinely belongs to the real world that we affect to
describe by means of language: the sort of thing that the early Russell liked
to call a "constituent of Reality." And it looks, as it looked to Russell, as
if the only way of resolving this issue in a reasonably Realistic way is to
insist that some of our acts of reference focus on, or connect with, objects
that are not linguistically constituted; and as if the only way of grasping
how *that* could come about must be to think of at least some referring
expressions as directly, that is, associatively, linked to genuine constituents
of Reality. And it further looks, from this point of view, as though the mark of
a genuine constituent of Reality would have to be that our access to it should
be "direct" in the sense of not being essentially mediated by prior access to
any system of linguistic practices, rules or conventions. No doubt, having
taken these steps, it will seem natural to take the further step, common,

as Evans notes above, to Russell and to many of his latter-day disciples, of identifying sensory experience as the main arena in which such direct access can occur. Unless, however, some of our acts of reference connect in some way or other with nonlinguistically constituted objects, we shall have no option (so the Russellian will argue) but to grant that all our attempts to refer end, as well as begin, within language, and that we never escape from the hermetically enclosed circuit of linguistically forged entities to confront the question whether any of these entities enjoy any ontic status outside language. In short, we shall have embraced Linguistic Idealism. And from Linguistic Idealism so defined it seems a very short step to the second of the Realist's twin bugbears: that is, to Relativism, taken full-bloodedly as the thesis that speakers of different languages might, on the one hand, be committed to incompatible accounts of the world, and, on the other, lack any point of common reference from which the adequacy of their various visions of things could, even in principle, be assessed relative to one another or to any third language. For if it is conceivable that all the objects referred to by speakers of each language might be objects linguistically constituted relative to that language, it is surely conceivable that the speakers of one such language might share no object of reference with the speakers of another, with the result that the "worlds" confronted by speakers of the two languages would simply have no ontological element in common.

The consequences of denying Russell's Principle may appear, in these respects, unappetising. But the consequences of affirming it are not much less so. To begin with, it seems flatly contrary to common sense, at least to the common sense of the unphilosophical reader we encountered in Chapter 4 §i, to suppose that one cannot have a thought involving a proper name without the ability to single out the bearer of the name. If an acquaintance, one Moncrieff, tells me that he is going this weekend to visit his friend Bunbury, who is ill, I do not, it would seem, need to know that there is such a person (or even to presume it, since I may take everything Moncrieff says with a large pinch of salt) in order to grasp *what Moncrieff is telling me*. Nor, if I pass on this putative "information," by way of apology and explanation from Moncrieff to his would-be hostess Lady Bracknell, do I need to be in a position to deliver an authoritative verdict on the issue of Bunbury's existence or nonexistence, let alone to single out the bearer of the name "Bunbury," in order to grasp *what putative piece of information it is* that I am passing on. And even if someone were to say to me, "Who exactly is this Bunbury?" the reply, "Some pal of Moncrieff's, according to him," would in most cases be deemed sufficient to qualify me as a person abreast of affairs to a degree sufficient to entitle me both to refer to Bunbury and to pass on information concerning him. In ordinary life, one's right to issue verbal warrants, and to claim that one understands what one is saying in issuing them, can be sustained by the issuing of further verbal warrants to a degree shocking to the philosopher of Realistic predilections.

iii. Knowing-how and knowing-that

Perhaps, however, the Realist is right to be shocked. The process of eluci-
dating the reference of a name by way of supplementary verbal explications
("Who is Moncrieff, anyway?" "Some pal of Jack Worthing's") cannot, surely,
continue for ever. At some point, unless Bunbury, the man himself, can actually be produced, suspicion must begin to grow that "Bunbury" is not a
genuine proper name at all but merely an empty vocable. This, of course, is
the intuition behind Russell's talk of "logically proper names" and Evans's
more cautious talk of "a more 'intimate,' more 'direct' way in which a subject
may stand to an object."

But suppose we grant the force of this intuition? What we are granting,
in granting that, is that what turns "Bunbury" from an empty vocable into
a proper name is the truth of an existential proposition, one to the effect
that a certain item figures among the constituents of reality.

Gilbert Ryle, long ago, distinguished between two types of cognitive state,
"knowing-how" and "knowing-that."[20] Knowing-that is a matter of possessing knowledge of truths, the sort of knowledge that can be expressed in
propositions. Epistemology, as that has been understood since Descartes, has
occupied itself, as Ryle observes, exclusively with establishing the grounds,
credentials, conditions of adequacy, of such knowledge. Knowing-how, by
contrast, is essentially practical. It is knowledge of how *to do* something. One
may know how to play chess, how to pug clay and use it to throw a bowl on
a wheel, how to play cards or how to count, without ever formulating any
proposition concerning the skill one is exercising, which may have become
automatic. In the case of such a skill, although one may be able to give someone a verbal account of how one does it, or at least verbal hints to someone
attempting to acquire the skill, it is not necessary that one should be able to
do those things in order to exercise the skill oneself. Epistemic predicates,
moreover, are inappropriate in cases of knowing-how.

...we never speak of a person believing or opining *how*, and though it is proper
to ask for the grounds or reasons for someone's acceptance of a proposition, this
question cannot be asked of someone's skill at cards or prudence in investments.[21]

Is knowing a language a matter of knowing-that or knowing-how? No
doubt neither answer is exclusively correct. Ryle, for instance, offers knowing
"that the German for 'knife' is '*Messer*'" as one of his examples of knowing-
that. But this case is not typical. More often than not, we shall argue, linguistic competence is a matter of knowledge how, with the result that the
greater part of what is known in knowing a language is nonepistemic in
character, a circumstance on which, as we shall see, hangs much of philosophical importance.

The import of Russell's Principle, on the contrary, is that linguistic competence is for the most part, and certainly at the most fundamental levels,

epistemic in character: a matter of knowing-that. It is not simply that Russell's Principle requires, as a condition of attaching meaning to a proper name, that one be in a position to single out the individual who bears it; nor even that, because Russellian logically proper names name not only individuals but features of the experienced world, the same is true of any "object of awareness." The link between meaning and the epistemic introduced by Russell's Principle runs still deeper. The motivation of the principle lies in the thought that the meanings of names must in some fashion be determined by the nature of things, rather than by human decision or convention, if we are to have any guarantee of the applicability to reality of thoughts formulated in terms of them. The claim of Russell's Principle is that the required guarantee is provided by a simple identity between the meaning of a name and the object "meant," intended by that name. Hence the dictum, common to the early Russell and the Wittgenstein of the *Tractatus*, that, in Wittgenstein's words, "a name means an object. The object is its meaning." Knowing the meaning of a name thus comes, in the last analysis, to knowing, by direct acquaintance with it, that there is such an object.

iv. Names and propositions

It is not just a matter of names, however. We describe reality not by naming it but by asserting propositions to be true or false of it. A proposition is the purport, the assertoric content, of a sentence. Merely to name reality is neither to assert nor deny anything concerning it: names lack assertoric content. Sentences, then, "mean" in a different way from names. Once again it seems compelling to argue that the nature of things, as well as human spontaneity, must somehow or other enter into the determination of the meanings of indicative sentences, if we are to have any guarantee that our propositions have any bearing on reality. Even if we could be confident, that is, that all the names in our language picked out genuine features of reality, nevertheless, if the nature of things exercised no constraint *at the further level* of the assembly of names into sentences, we should still lack any guarantee that our situation differed in any way from that of the occupant of the Prison-House of Language.

The task of furnishing that guarantee, both for the early Russell and for the Wittgenstein of the *Tractatus*, rests with the notion of *fact*. Facts make their appearance in this role in, for instance, the opening lecture of Russell's *Philosophy of Logical Atomism.*

When I speak of a fact – I do not propose to attempt an exact definition, but an explanation, so that you will know what I am talking about – I mean the kind of thing that makes a proposition true or false. . . . It is important to observe that facts belong to the objective world. They are not created by our thoughts or beliefs, except in special cases. . . . The first thing I want to emphasize is that the outer world – the world, so to speak, that knowledge is aiming at knowing – is not completely described by a lot of "particulars," but that you must also take account of these things that I call facts, which are the sort of things that you express by a sentence, and that these, just as much as particular chairs and tables, are part of the real world. Except in psychology, most of our statements are not intended merely to express our condition of mind, though that is often all they succeed in doing. They are intended to express facts which (except when they are psychological facts) will be about the outer world.[22]

Russell claims, at this point in the *Monist* lectures, to be enunciating "truisms":

I propose . . . always to begin any argument that I have to make by appealing to data which will be quite ludicrously obvious.[23]

The existence of facts as well as particulars is billed as the first and most obvious of these truisms.

The first truism to which I wish to draw your attention – and I hope you will agree with me that these things that I call truisms are so obvious that it is almost laughable to mention them – is that the world contains *facts*, which are what they are whatever we may choose to think about them.[24]

Unless one is altogether seduced by Russell's breezy, open-air tone of voice, like a rather matey army instructor introducing the men to the more obvious elements of map-reading, however, it is hard to resist the thought that, actually, it is a good deal easier to see why one should believe in the existence of chairs and tables than to see why one should believe in the existence of "facts." Chairs and tables force themselves on one's attention irrespective of the blandishments of philosophers. "Facts" do not. We need to have it explained to us why we should postulate the existence of such entities. And, in fact, Russell supplies those reasons, even though, as befits one dwelling on a "truism," he skips rather lightly over them.

A fact is "what makes a proposition true or false." A philosopher with a greater tolerance than Russell for Idealist, or "anti-Realist," styles of thinking might translate this as "what brings it about that we regard a proposition as true or false." But such a translation, precisely because of its anti-Realist flavour, would not capture Russell's thought. A fact, for Russell, is not just any old natural occurrence or state of affairs the obtaining of which would induce us to regard some proposition as true. It is the *obtaining in the world of just that state of affairs that the proposition asserts to obtain*. Thus, for instance, the fact that Gandhi died, although it might bring an admirer to assent with a peculiar, sad, emphasis to the assertion that all men are mortal, is not the fact that makes the assertion true: *that* fact is the fact that all men are mortal. That is why, or one reason why, for the Russell of the *Monist* lectures, there have to be general facts as well as particular ones. A fact, in short, as Russell tells us, is not merely "what makes a proposition true or false," but what a statement expresses. A fact, for Russell, has a certain structure;

is put together in a certain way out of "constituents" or "components" that, like the fact that they compose, are "part of the real world." Moreover, the components of the fact are the meanings of the signs that compose the sentence that expresses the proposition that the fact obtains. "We may lay down," says Russell, "the following provisional definitions:"

That the components of a proposition are the symbols we must understand in order to understand the proposition;

That the components of the fact which makes a proposition true or false, as the case may be, are the *meanings* of the symbols which we must understand in order to understand the proposition.[25]

Even though, as Russell warns us, they are "not absolutely correct," because they do not "apply to words which, like 'or' or 'not,' are parts of propositions without corresponding to any part of the corresponding facts," these definitions sketch an initially highly persuasive way of explaining how sentence-meaning, the meaning of groups of words possessing assertoric force and so capable of expressing propositions, can be understood as something constrained by the nature of reality, rather than as something that rests at the beck and call of what Kant and McDowell call "spontaneity." Components of facts, Russell's "logical atoms," are, according to Russell, of different types. They include, for instance, individuals, such as Socrates and Plato, and two-term relations, such as the one picked out by the English word "loves." Different types of logical atom display different properties of possibility of combination into facts. Thus, a two-term relation such as *loves* can combine with a pair of individuals, *Socrates* and *Plato*, to form the fact symbolised by the sentence "Socrates loves Plato." The three components of the fact are the meanings of the names that make up the sentence. So what those signs express when put together in that way is the proposition *Socrates loves Plato*. What proposition a string of names expresses, in short, is a function of the ways in which the objects picked out by those names combine into facts. In genuinely factual discourse, no "spontaneity," no human inventiveness, enters into the relationship between a proposition and what it expresses. It enters, presumably, and only, in the case of the would-be statements Russell mentions, which, although they are "intended to express facts," succeed only in expressing "our condition of mind."

It follows that the complexity of the sentential sign is in no way a product of the inventiveness or "spontaneity" of the mind. It is, on the contrary, a reflection of a complexity obtaining in nature antecedently to the invention of the means of representing it linguistically: namely, the complexity of the fact. Here is Russell again:

It might be suggested that complexity is essentially to do with symbols, or that it is essentially psychological. I do not think it would be possible seriously to maintain either of these views, but they are the sort of thing that will occur to one, the sort of thing that one would try, to see whether it would work. I do not think they will do at all. . . . I shall try to persuade you that in a logically correct symbolism there will always be a certain fundamental identity of structure between a fact and the symbol for it; and that the complexity of the symbol corresponds very closely with the complexity of the facts symbolised by it. Also, as I said before, it is quite directly evident that the fact, for example, that two things stand in a certain relation to one another – e.g., that this is to the left of that – is itself objectively complex, and not merely that the apprehension of it is complex. The fact that two things stand in a certain relation to each other, or any statement of that sort, has a complexity all of its own. I shall therefore in future assume that there is an objective complexity in the world, and that it is mirrored by the complexity of propositions.[26]

The thought that facts have an objective complexity that is mirrored in the complexity of the sentential sign leads him immediately to the version of the ideal of a Universal Language, which we mentioned in Chapter 3 §v.

A moment ago I was speaking about the great advantages that we derive from the logical imperfections of language, from the fact that our words are all ambiguous. I propose now to consider what sort of language a logically perfect language would be. In a logically perfect language the words in a proposition would correspond one by one with the components of the corresponding fact, with the exception of such words as "or," "not," "if," "then," which have a different function. In a logically perfect language, there will be one word and no more for every simple object, and everything that is not simple will be expressed by a combination of words, by a combination derived, of course, from the words for the simple things that enter in, one word for each simple component. A language of that sort will be completely analytic, and will show at a glance the structure of the facts asserted or denied. [27]

We do, of course, possess systems of symbols the purpose of which is to represent naturally occurring structural relationships. The representation of molecular structure by means of the familiar symbols for the elements of the Periodic Table offers an obvious example. But it is a feature of such systems that whether a particular combination of symbols makes sense, means anything at all, depends on whether or not the relationship represented by the combination occurs in nature. Thus the molecular formula "NaCl" means something, because there exists a compound of sodium and chlorine. "NaHe," by contrast, means nothing because sodium and helium do not enter into molecular combination with one another.

The issue of which putative molecular formulae make sense, "mean something," is not, therefore, something which can be settled internally to the system of representation, as part of the business of laying down the rules for the use of chemical symbolism. It is evidently a matter of contingent fact that, whereas sodium and chlorine enter into molecular combination, sodium and helium do not. So, in effect, in the case of chemical notation, the question of whether a particular combination of signs makes sense reduces to a question of contingent fact concerning the existence or nonexistence of a particular type of structure in nature. The logical and the epistemic here blend into one another.

To suggest, with Russell, that language *per se* is such a system, or can at any rate be reduced to such a structure by analytically purging the "ambiguities" of the everyday language we actually speak, is thus to suggest that the same relationship between meaning (or meaningfulness) and the epistemic prevails throughout language. To know that a sentential sign is meaningful, expresses a genuine proposition capable of truth and falsity, in other words, is to possess a piece of knowledge concerning the world; a piece of knowledge exactly analogous, in its contingency and independence of linguistic convention, to knowledge of the facts concerning the formation of molecular compounds by chemical substances: namely the knowledge that a certain, corresponding, type of "fact" exists "in nature."

Russell's Referential Realism thus forges, at the level of sentence-meaning, as tight a connection between meaning and the epistemic as the one it forges at the level of proper names. The connection makes itself felt, for instance, in Russell's concern to determine what types of fact actually do exist.

There are a great many different kinds of fact, and we shall be concerned in later lectures with a certain amount of classification of facts. I will just point out a few kinds of fact to begin with. . . . There are *particular facts*, such as "This is white"; then there are *general facts*, such as "All men are mortal."[28]

Russell writes here, and in similar passages, very much in the spirit of a naturalist cataloguing the varieties of snail to be found in a Papuan valley, or minerals in Nevada. The philosophy of language, or of "logic," as both Russell and Wittgenstein called it at that time, has metamorphosed into the study of certain features of the natural world, with the happy result, for the Referential Realist, that the supposed power of language to interpose itself as a veil of illusion between the mind and the world it is "aiming at knowing" has been decisively circumvented.

v. Wittgenstein's reservations

Wittgenstein began in philosophy between 1911 and 1914 as Russell's protégé, first as pupil, then as collaborator. "I love him," wrote Russell to Ottoline Morell, "& feel he will solve the problems I am too old to solve – all kinds of problems are raised by my work, but want a fresh mind and the vigour of youth. He is *the* young man one hopes for."[29] By 1913, however, their minds had ceased to be at one. Wittgenstein began to articulate objections to Russell's ideas. These seemed first to concern primarily the latter's Theory of Judgment, and to be answerable, but it soon began to appear that the differences were not only more fundamental but also fundamental in ways that Wittgenstein was finding it hard to articulate and Russell to fathom. In a letter, Russell records what seems to have been an exasperating discussion thus:

We were both cross from the heat – I showed him a crucial part of what I had been writing. He said it was all wrong, not realising the difficulties – that he had tried my view and knew it couldn't work. I couldn't understand his objection – in fact he was very inarticulate – but I feel in my bones he must be right, and that he has seen something I have missed.[30]

What was it Wittgenstein had seen and Russell, rightly or wrongly, thought he might have missed? We can perhaps find a clue in the opening pages of the *Notebooks 1914–16*, which contains the contents of the notebooks, pre-liminary to the *Tractatus*, which were saved from the destruction in 1950, on Wittgenstein's orders, of many other notebooks containing preliminary work, by the accident of having been left in the house of his youngest sister at Gmunden, rather than in Vienna.[31] Here, in the opening pages, we find Wittgenstein wrestling with a paradox: one that appears to arise from Russell's account of the relationships among sentential signs, propositions, and facts. The paradox might be stated as follows. If Russell is right, we cannot know that a sentential sign expresses a proposition, an assertoric content capable of being characterised as true or false, unless we know that there *exist* facts of a certain type. But we clearly cannot even raise the contingent existential question of whether there *are* facts of the type sketched out by a given sentential sign, unless we know already, merely from the constitution of the sentential sign, what type of fact the sentential sign in question *does* sketch out; because if that sentential sign sketched out no fact that *might* exist in the world, the question of whether that type of fact either *did* or *did not* exist would not arise (nor, for that matter, would the sign in question be recognisable as a *sentential* sign!). But if we can know, merely from the constitution of the sentential sign, what type of fact it sketches out, then we can know, merely from the constitution of the sign, how things would have to stand in the world in order for it to be true, or false. And in that case the sign expresses a proposition after all, because, as Frege taught us, for a sentential sign to express a proposition is simply for it to be clear how things would have to stand in the world for it to express a truth, or a falsehood.

Right at the outset of the *Notebooks*, on page 2e, we find a telegraphic evocation of just this paradox.

How is it reconcilable with the task of philosophy that logic should take care of itself? If, for example, we ask: Is such and such a fact of the subject-predicate form?, we must surely know what we mean by "subject-predicate form." We must know *whether* there is such a form at all. How can we know this? "From the signs." But how? For we haven't got any *signs* of this form.[32]

Suppose, that is, we confront the Russellian question, "Do facts of the subject-predicate form exist?" In order to answer this question in the affirmative, we should have to be in a position to affirm of some fact F, "F is of the subject-predicate form." In order to be in a position to do *that*, we should have to know what we meant by "subject-predicate form." How could we know such a thing? One possible answer, indeed the only one that comes readily to mind, is: "From the (form of, constitution of the) signs." But if Russell is right, and it is necessary to know that facts of a given form exist, before we can attach meaning to sentential signs of the type whose meaning consists in expressing facts of that form, then as yet we are in a position to deploy no such sentential signs.

Wittgenstein proceeds to ask the obvious question: does it then make any sense to talk of establishing the meanings of signs by making discoveries concerning the contents of reality?

Then can we ask ourselves: Does the subject-predicate form exist? Does the relational form exist? Do any of the forms exist at all that Russell and I were always talking about? (Russell would say: "Yes! that's self-evident." *Well!*)

What is the justification for that contemptuous "*Well!*" supposed to be? Presumably that something unintelligible cannot be self-evident, however strongly one feels it to be so. In the same short run of three or four notebook pages, Wittgenstein makes it clear that it is for him, from the perspective opened up by the above argument, indeed unintelligible that the question of the meaning of a sentential sign, of what proposition it expresses, or whether it expresses any proposition at all, might depend on the contingent truth or falsity of some further, existential, proposition.

Then: if *everything* that needs to be shewn is shewn by the existence of subject-predicate SENTENCES etc., the task of philosophy is different from what I originally supposed. But if that is not how it is, then what is lacking would have to be shewn by means of some kind of experience, and that I regard as out of the question.[33]

And, a little further on:

If the existence of the subject-predicate *sentence* does not show everything needful, then it could surely only be shewn by the existence of some particular fact of that form. And acquaintance with such a fact cannot be essential for logic.[34]

"Acquaintance with such a fact" would be "essential for logic," of course, if one could give a sense to a sentential sign – make clear what proposition it was supposed to express, by correlating it with a fact. In that case, one could elucidate the sense of a sentential sign much as one elucidates the reference of a proper name by producing or indicating its bearer. The trouble with this proposal is that, applied literally, it would transform the putative sentential sign to which it was applied from a *sentential* sign into a name.

Wittgenstein, following Frege, makes a sharp distinction, in the *Tractatus* and other writings of the period, between the sentential (or propositional) sign, which possesses assertoric force, and names, which do not.

3.14 What constitutes a propositional sign is that in it its elements (the words) stand in a determinate relation to one another.

A propositional sign is a fact.

3.141 A proposition is not a medley of words. – (Just as a theme in music is not a medley of notes.)

A proposition is articulated.

3.142 Only facts can express a sense, a set of names cannot.

Wittgenstein's thought, an important one, to which we shall recur, now seems to be that, although it is possible to explicate the meaning of a name by indicating the bearer of the name, that is because the individual we thus indicate actually *is the meaning of* that name. Here Wittgenstein is in entire agreement with Russell: the point is spelled out at *Tractatus* 3.203: "A name means an object. The object is its meaning." If, now, it were possible to explicate the meaning of a sentential sign in this way, then, as what is essential to the meaning, or sense, of a propositional sign is assertoric force, whatever natural existent was indicated as constituting *the meaning of* the propositional sign also would have to possess assertoric force. And that would entail that something in nature, "some kind of experience," perhaps, could possess assertoric force. But (and this is the important point, the one to which we shall find ourselves recurring) nothing in nature does, or can, possess assertoric force. If, for instance, we were to attempt to explain the sense of the English sentence "It's raining" by indicating the falling rain, all that would be achieved at best would be the establishment of "It's raining" as a synonym for the English noun "rain." There being nothing assertoric about falling rain, we should have succeeded, not, as we intended, in explicating the sense of a propositional sign, but only in explicating the sense of a (rather odd) name. This, we take it is the sense of Wittgenstein's remark at *Tractatus* 4.064:

4.064 Every proposition must *already* possess a sense: it cannot be given a sense by affirmation. Indeed its sense is just what is affirmed. And the same applies to negation, etc.

One can make an assertion by uttering a sentential sign only if both speaker and hearers already attach an assertoric content to that sign. Moreover, they must be able to read off that assertoric content *from the sentential sign itself*, because, as Wittgenstein says,

4.027 It belongs to the essence of a proposition that it should be able to communicate a *new* sense to us.

4.03 A proposition must use old expressions to communicate a new sense.

If we do not know the meaning of a name, that is, it can be indicated by pointing out something in the world, for there are things in the world, namely individuals, which Wittgenstein, like Russell, is prepared to identify with the meanings of names. With propositional signs it is different. Here it must be immediately apparent, from the way in which a new propositional sign recombines the "old expressions" of which it consists, what assertoric content it expresses; and if it is not, no amount of gesturing towards "the world" will help, for "the world," nature, contains nothing possessing assertoric content; nothing, therefore, capable of being identified with "the meaning" of such a sign.

These arguments all point towards the unnerving conclusion, from Russell's point of view, that the meanings of propositional signs are in our own hands, and not, after all, in those of "Reality" or "the world." That is part of the force of *Tractatus* 4.026:

4.026 The meanings of simple signs (words) must be explained to us if we are to understand them.

With propositions, however, *we make ourselves* understood. [emphasis added]

The same tendency appears in Wittgenstein's fiercely terse critique of Russell's Theory of Judgment:

5.5422 The correct explanation of the form of the proposition, "*A* makes the judgement *p*," must show that it is impossible for a judgement to be a piece of nonsense. (Russell's theory does not satisfy this requirement)

Russell's Theory of Judgment says, apparently innocuously, that judgment is a relationship between the judging mind and whatever it is that the judgment concerns. The issue that chiefly concerns Russell is that of identifying the terms between which this relationship holds. Take Russell's example, "Desdemona loves Cassio." Are we to say that the judging relationship subsists between the mind and *the fact that* Desdemona loves Cassio? Clearly not, for if the judgment happens to be false there will exist no such fact. Russell's suggestion is that the relationship holds between the mind and the constituents of the fact, in this case, Desdemona, Cassio, and the relationship of loving. The mind, Russell says, distinguishes the proposition that Desdemona loves Cassio from the proposition that Cassio loves Desdemona, "because the relation of judging places the constituents in a different order in the two cases."[35] The judgment is true if there is "a complex unity, 'Desdemona's love for Cassio,' which is composed exclusively of the *objects* of the belief, in the same order as they had in the belief, with the relation that was one of the objects occurring now as the cement that binds together the objects of the belief."[36]

Wittgenstein's objection at *Tractatus* 5.5422 fastens on the intuitively plausible thought that, whereas one can speak or write a piece of nonsense, one cannot judge it to be the case. There is a plain difference in this respect between

1. Socrates loves wine

   and

2. Wine loves Socrates,

unless one takes the latter to be an oblique way of saying that Socrates can drink a great deal without suffering the penalties that overtake lesser men, or something of the sort.

What makes the difference between (1) and (2)? An obvious reply would be that while (1) articulates a possible state of affairs, which might either obtain or fail to obtain, (2) does not. Socrates might turn out to be abstemious, or his love-affair with the grape might be all too apparent. By contrast, wine could neither turn out to be nor fail to turn out to be, in love with Socrates.

Are we to say, now, that in noting this difference – that Socrates can love or fail to love wine, while wine cannot either love or fail to love Socrates – we have made a discovery about the world, or to put it more grandly, about the Nature of Things? Plainly not, for any discovery about the world can be stated, can be given propositional expression; but any would-be proposition aimed at articulating the content of this supposed "discovery" would turn in our hands and dissolve into a new piece of nonsense, as incapable of either truth or falsity as (2). The explanation of why certain grammatically possible sentences turn out to be nonsense, since it cannot lie with the Nature of Things, must lie with our own dealings with language. This insight, from which Wittgenstein never subsequently deviates, is already clear to him in the opening entry of the *Notebooks 1914–16:*

Let us remember the explanation why "Socrates is Plato" is nonsense. That is, because *we* have not made an arbitrary specification, NOT because a sign is, shall we say, illegitimate in itself![37]

It might be objected that, if "Cicero is Tully" is not nonsense, then neither is "Socrates is Plato." "Socrates is Plato" is simply false. But this misses the point, which is that it is *only* where such a sentence *merely* asserts the common reference of two signs that it has a sense, because otherwise the "is" of identity has been assigned no sense appropriate to the context. The point is more clearly made in the version inserted at *Tractatus* 5.473:

If a sign is possible, then it is also capable of signifying. Whatever is possible in logic is also permitted. (The reason why "Socrates is identical" means nothing is that there is no property called "identical." The proposition is nonsensical because we have failed to make an arbitrary determination, and not because the symbol, in itself, would be illegitimate.)

What is and is not nonsense, then, is for Wittgenstein a matter decided within language, at the level of the sentential sign. But Russell's Theory of Judgment is designed precisely to emancipate judgment and belief from any intrinsic dependence on language. The function of the sentential sign, for Russell, has been reduced to that of representing the contents and structures of "facts," which, as Russell never tires of telling us, are real existents; part of the contents of reality, entities to which questions of existence and nonexistence, whose resolution either way is a matter of contingent fact, are as applicable as they are in the case of chemical compounds or species of animal. But the distinction between sense and nonsense – this is Wittgenstein's point – cannot be drawn at the level of the kind of natural phenomena about which such existential questions can be raised. There are species of animal that exist, and there are species of animal that fail to exist, but there are no nonsensical species of animal. There is, of course, such a thing as a form of nonsense based on natural impossibility – or, at least, there might be thought to be. Thus it will doubtless be the case that, because of certain facts about valency, atomic structure, and so forth, certain combinations of chemical symbols fail to represent possible chemical compounds. But there is a clear distinction to be drawn between natural impossibility and the "nonsense" represented by (2) or by "Socrates is Plato." The difference is that in the former case reasons "in the nature of things" can be given why there are no compounds corresponding to the chemical formulae in question. But just for that reason a statement along the lines of "There exist compounds of the form XYZ," where "XYZ" is such a formula, is not nonsensical at all, but simply false. In short, it is because Russell's theory of judgment reduces judgment to a natural relation between one putative natural existent, the mind, and a relational complex of other such existents, offering a picture of judgment from which language and the sentential sign have been deleted as allegedly irrelevant, that the resources of the theory can supply no answer to Wittgenstein's question why it should be impossible to judge a piece of nonsense. On the face of it, for all Russell's theory has to say to the contrary, the mind is as free to "pass over" or "hold before it" the "constituents" *wine*, *loving*, and *Socrates* in the manner characteristic of judgment, as it is to do the same with any other complex of relations and terms.

vi. "Logic must take care of itself"

The *Notebooks 1914–16* open with the gnomic assertion, or slogan, "Logic must take care of itself." (*Die Logik muss für sich selber sorgen.*) As we shall need to refer to it a number of times in what follows, let us give it a label: Wittgenstein's Slogan. The Slogan, Wittgenstein tells us, a little way down the page, expresses an "extremely profound and important insight." The same thought is reaffirmed – in slightly different words ("Logic must look after itself") in the translation, but in identical ones in the German – at *Tractatus* 5.473. But what does it mean?

Wittgenstein's use of the term "logic" here manifestly stands in need of explanation. *Tractatus* 5.473 offers two supplementary, though in themselves equally obscure *obiter dicta*: "Whatever is possible in logic is also permitted," and "In a certain sense we cannot make mistakes in logic." The gap between these two remarks is bridged by the thought that a nonsensical proposition is so "because we have failed to make an arbitrary determination, and not because the symbol, in itself, would be illegitimate." More elucidation is clearly needed, but more is available. At *Notebooks 1914–16* (entry of 29.10.14), we find:

In order for a proposition to be true it must first and foremost be capable of truth, *and that is all that concerns logic.* [emphasis added]

We think it is fairly evident that these remarks all, in one way or another, invoke the two lines of argument outlined in the foregoing section, against Russell's attempt to sketch the relationships subsisting between language, judgment and reality. From the entry of 29.10.14, it appears that by the term "logic," at this period, Wittgenstein understands whatever has to do with, or with establishing, the *capacity for truth* of a sentential sign. If indeed it is the case, as the first argument we considered seems to show, that "in order for a proposition to be true it must be capable of truth," then its capacity for truth must be established prior to the establishment of its truth or falsity, and *a fortiori,* given the absolute generality of the argument in question, of the truth or falsity of any other proposition (cf., in its application to Russell, *Tractatus* 2.0211: If the world had no substance, then whether a proposition had sense would depend upon whether another proposition was true).

It follows that the distinction between sense and nonsense also must be prior to the establishment of the truth or falsity of any proposition whatsoever. Nonsense must result from a failure on our part to bestow sense. Refusal to adopt such an explanation, Wittgenstein suggests, would force us to say that "the symbol in itself would be illegitimate." In what sense "illegitimate"? Not, clearly, in the sense that it fails to conform to *our* requirements for the use of symbols, for that is the account of nonsense that Wittgenstein himself is advancing. Presumably, then, illegitimate in the sense that it fails to conform to Reality. This is the situation with "NaHe": you can put the symbols for the elements together in that way, but you won't succeed in designating anything by means of such a sign, because there is no such chemical compound. Russell would like, in effect, to make that situation the model for our understanding of the relationship among sentential signs, judgments, and facts: you can if you wish say, or judge, that Desdemona is the square root of Cassio, but such sayings and judgings are illegitimate because the "constituents" in question do not, as a matter of fact, combine in that way.

A major weakness of the analogy is that it blurs the distinction between a system of nomenclature and a language. Chemical symbolism is a nomenclature. Its sign-combinations possess no assertoric force: it merely offers a systematic, chemically informative method of constructing names for chemical compounds. Clearly such a method will deliver a result, in the shape of a name possessing a bearer, only if there exists a compound which, by the application to it of the rules of the method, generates that name. Whether a chemical symbol "XYZ" has a meaning, therefore, will depend on whether there exists a chemical compound XYZ.

The problem with extending such an analogy to the sentential sign is that sentential signs do possess assertoric force; indeed, it is their whole point as signs to do so. And though there are chemical compounds in nature, there is nothing in nature possessing assertoric force. This, as we have seen, is Wittgenstein's basic point against Russell at the period of the *Tractatus* and its preliminary notebooks: "Every proposition must *already* have a sense: it cannot be given a sense by affirmation. Indeed its sense is just what is affirmed." So the issue of whether an expression has a meaning cannot depend on whether or not some corresponding element of reality exists. The point about nonsense, as has just been shown, follows from this.

In short, everything that has to do with the sense of a sentential sign, meaning by that its assertoric force, that which makes it "capable of truth," must be established prior to the establishment of the actual truth or falsity of either the proposition it expresses, or the proposition expressed by any other such sign. If "logic" then, is concerned not with the truth or falsity of propositions but with whatever it is that renders propositions capable of truth, it follows that "logic" must be, in its entirety, pre- or extrapropositional. That is the "extremely profound and important insight," derived in order of exposition if not in order of discovery from the arguments against Russell that we traced out in Chapter 4 §v, and fundamental to the entire outlook of the *Tractatus*, which Wittgenstein captures in the slogan *Die Logik muss für sich selber sorgen.*

In passing, we can now elucidate the two *obiter dicta* of 5.473. "NaHe" is a possible combination of signs. It is not "permitted" only because nothing in Reality corresponds to it. Such a possibility cannot arise for a sentential sign whose capacity for truth is governed by the demands of "logic," whatever those may turn out to be. If "logic" does not make it clear merely from the constitution of a sign S what state of affairs it asserts to obtain, then S has no assertoric force and so is not a sentential sign at all, but represents merely an unsuccessful attempt to construct such a sign, vitiated by our having failed to specify a sense for one or more of its constituent signs. Hence, "whatever is possible in logic," – whatever is assigned sense by adequate acts of sense-giving – "is also permitted." Logic, because it is prior to the establishment of truth and falsity, is beyond the reach of any critique founded on considerations of what is empirically the case. What *can* be said, logically, *may* be said. Much the same considerations elucidate "In a certain sense we cannot make mistakes in logic." What would a "mistake" in logic consist in? Lack of fidelity to our own practice in bestowing sense is one kind of mistake, surely, but not a mistake *in* logic. The only other possibility would arise if in logic, as in natural science, it were possible to be wrong about the nature of reality, as the promoters of the phlogiston hypothesis were wrong. But if the arguments considered in Chapter 4 §v go through, there must be some mode of sense-bestowal for sentential signs – that something that Wittgenstein, no doubt out of the habit of his conversations with Russell, and for want of a better term, calls "logic" – for which this is not a real possibility.

vii. Meeting the demands of the Slogan

Russell's Theory of Judgment, and beyond that Russell's Principle, clearly enshrine versions of the Correspondence Theory of Meaning. Both, if true, entail that meanings, of names in the one case, of sentences in the other, are discovered in the world. Both equate senselessness of linguistic expressions with failure to match reality; in the case of names, failure to pick out any existing individual; in the case of sentences, failure to match the structure of any existing category of "facts." Equally clearly, both Wittgenstein's Slogan, and the arguments that support it, are hostile to Correspondence, at least in the case of sentences. The drift of the Slogan is, after all, that remarks about sense are to be sharply differentiated from statements expressing contingent truths concerning the contents of Reality, or "the world."

At the same time, the Wittgenstein of the *Tractatus* accepted a doctrine very close to, if not indistinguishable from, Russell's Principle: the doctrine that "A name means an object. The object is its meaning." The theory of meaning adopted by Wittgenstein in the *Tractatus* results largely from the interaction of the conflicting influences exerted, on the one hand, by this quasi-Russellian doctrine, and, on the other, by the Slogan and its supporting arguments.

What the Slogan excludes is any account of what it is for a sentence to possess an assertoric content that, like Russell's, makes its *capacity for truth* depend on a natural, that is to say a contingent, relationship between it and the contents of Reality. What Wittgenstein attempts to do in the *Tractatus* is to meet the demands of the Slogan by making the relationship between a sentence and its real-world correlate an internal, or as he puts it a "logical one." The dawning realisation that such a move might do the trick can be traced in the early pages of the *Notebooks 1914–16*.

In the entry of 8.9.14, Wittgenstein returns to his worry that there is something vacuous about Russell's belief that it is possible to raise questions concerning the "existence" of such – in Wittgenstein's view purely "logical" – entities as "facts" having the subject-predicate form, and that, on occasion, the existence of such entities may be regarded as "self-evident."

The "self-evidence" of which Russell has talked so much can only be dispensed with in logic if language itself prevents any logical mistake. And it is clear that "self-evidence" is and always was wholly deceptive.

But what is the term "language" supposed to comprehend here? And if it comprehends simply some symbols taken together with some rules laid down for their use, how can Wittgenstein counter the objection that "language" so understood can offer no more than an hermetic game of signs, without any bearing on the world its sentences are supposed to describe? That objection is one that, at any rate, Wittgenstein recognises, and proposes to deal with.

The difficulty of my theory of logical portrayal was that of finding a connection between the signs on paper and a situation outside in the world. I always said that truth is a relation between the proposition and the situation, but could never pick out such a relation.[38]

The wording of this last remark suggests that the difficulty of finding a connection between a situation and "the signs on paper" is one that has now been resolved. But how, exactly?

What Wittgenstein seems to take himself to have seen at this point, the cleaving stroke, as one might say, is that he has been looking in the wrong place. He has been assuming that the relationship between the written or spoken signs that compose a proposition, and the "situation" (*Sachverhalt*, the Tractarian term commonly translated "state of affairs"), which that proposition picks out, will be what, following Hume, we have been calling a *natural* relation: one whose detection adds to the description of Reality. What he has now realised is that there are relations brought into being by what he terms *methods of symbolising*, which, in virtue of having been brought into being in this way, do not figure among those constitutive of reality: are not among those recorded by the "facts" [*Tatsache*] of the *Tractatus* which go to make up the world, collectively constituting "what is the case" (*was der Fall ist*). In Wittgenstein's notebook entry for 21.9.14 we find,

Now it suddenly seems to me in some sense clear that the property of a situation must always be internal.

And a little later, at 26.10.14,

So it looks as if the logical *identity* between sign and things signified were not necessary, but only *an* internal, *logical*, relation between the two. (The holding of such a relation incorporates in a certain sense the holding of a kind of fundamental – internal – identity.)

The point is only that the logical part of what is signified should be completely determined just by the logical part of the sign and the method of symbolizing: sign and method of symbolizing *together* must be logically identical with what is signified.

The sense of a proposition is what it images.[39]

How does this address Wittgenstein's problem of "finding a connection between the signs on paper and a situation outside in the world?" The thought is that both sign and signified possess a "logical part." On the one hand, the *possibility* of a "situation" must be guaranteed internally, by the nature of its constituents, because otherwise it would have, absurdly, as Wittgenstein sees it, to be established by empirical inquiry. It may help us to grasp what kind of thing Wittgenstein has in mind here if one reflects that it is in a sense internal to blue and green, inseparable from their nature as colours, that each may characterise the other. That it is possible for one shade of green to be bluer than another would on this account belong to the "logical part" of the situation of a given shade of green's being bluer than another; while the actual hue, saturation, and so on, of the shades in question would constitute the "empirical part" of the situation. The relationship "bluer than" would thus be, for Wittgenstein a "logical one." And at 30.9.14

... it looks as if all relations must be logical in order for their existence to be guaranteed by that of the sign.

On the other, the relationship between the "logical part" of the sentential sign and the "logical part" of the situation it represents or expresses must also be internal and capable of being "read off" from the sign, given a grasp of the "method of symbolising" appropriate to it, as otherwise it would be, again absurdly, an empirical question what assertoric content a sentential sign possessed, or whether it possessed any. If these conditions can be met, then clearly "logic," that is to say, all questions concerning the "capacity for truth" of the sentential sign, will "take care of itself" in the sense of being satisfactorily insulated from the empirical and the contingent. Once we have given meaning to the basic names of the language by linking them to the basic "objects" that enter into the constitution of "situations" (*Sachverhalten*), and established "methods of signification" allowing the internal structures of the sentential sign to represent the internal possibilities of combination into "situations" inherent in the nature of "objects," it will be possible simply to read off from the constituent signs of a sentential sign, together with their method of signification, what situation that sign asserts to obtain in the world. Crucially, there will be no contingent claims to be made concerning the senses of sentential signs, or more generally concerning the relationship of language to the world, because the relationship of language to the world will be wholly a matter of internal relations, relations, that is, which, unlike external ones, add nothing to the description of the world.

viii. The *Tractatus* and its failure

We are, clearly, on the verge of the account given in the *Tractatus* of the relationship between a sentential sign and the situation it asserts to obtain. In the *Tractatus* Russell's "logical atoms," the "constituents" equally of Russellian "facts" and Russellian "judgments," are metamorphosed into what Wittgenstein variously terms "objects" (*Gegenständen*) and "things" (*Dingen*). A fact, for Wittgenstein as for Russell, consists in the obtaining of a relationship R between objects, x, y, ... n. For Russell, as we have seen, R is an external relationship, one that can hold or fail to hold between the objects in question. Moreover, Russell makes no distinction between the relationship's holding between a set of objects and the *possibility* of its holding between the members of that set. That is why, in order to know whether a sentential sign of a given logical form makes sense, in the sense of expressing a *possible* fact, we need to know whether or not facts of that type exist.

Wittgenstein's suggestion is that, on the contrary, the *possibility* of a relation R's relating a member of a set of objects is written into the nature of the objects in question. Hinted at in the string of notebook entries cited above, it is made fully explicit at *Tractatus* 2.011–2.0121:

2.011 It is essential to things that they should be possible constituents of states of affairs.

2.012 In logic nothing is accidental: if a thing *can* occur in a state of affairs, the possibility of the state of affairs must be written into the thing itself.

2.0121 It would seem to be a sort of accident, if it turned out that a situation would fit a thing that could already exist entirely on its own.

But if possibility of occurrence in states of affairs is internal to objects, it follows that the possibility of a fact, and thus of a proposition, of the form R $(x, y \ldots n)$ will be evident merely from acquaintance with $x, y, \ldots n$. All that will then be necessary, in order to introduce a sentential sign capable of expressing a proposition of that form, will be, first, to correlate simple signs $s_1, \ldots s_n$ with the objects $x, y, \ldots n$, and, second, to introduce some conventional way of representing the relation R between $x, y, \ldots n$ as a relation between $s_1, \ldots s_n$.

This is the so-called Picture Theory of Meaning. According to the Picture Theory a sentential sign s functions, in effect, as a diagram of a possible state of affairs S. That it diagrams a *possible* state of affairs is guaranteed by the internality of the relationship between the logical form of s, as derivable from its "method of symbolising" (or, at *Tractatus* 3.327, its "logico-syntactic employment"), and the specific possibilities of combination into states of affairs that internally characterise the objects designated by the component signs (the names) that enter into the composition of s. The internality of the relationship between the possibility of combination actualised by S and the logical form of s (given the "logico-syntactic employment" of the component signs of s), allows s to function as a "logical picture" of S. And, as to be acquainted with an object is to be acquainted with all its possibilities of combination into states of affairs, we can, given that we know which basic names in our language pick out which objects, sketch possible facts, by constructing new sentential signs, without ever needing to check whether these constructions match reality; whether, in other words, the types of fact they adumbrate "exist." If a sentential sign has a sense at all it sketches a *possible* fact, and if it does not sketch a *possible* fact; if, that is, its truth and falsity conditions are not evident from the sign itself, then it is senseless.

The requirements of Wittgenstein's Slogan are thus satisfied. Logic is left to "take care of itself" in the sense that all questions of the intelligibility of the sentential sign and the specification of its propositional content are settled on the level of the sentential sign itself, without the need to appeal either to the mental life of sign-users (as, for example, Russell does in explaining the difference between judging that Desdemona loves Cassio and judging that Cassio loves Desdemona), or to the truth of contingent claims concerning the existence of types of fact.

A very sharp, and very un-Russellian, distinction is thus introduced, between "Logic," on the one hand, and the epistemic, on the other. All logical questions are to be settled, merely through the provision of arbitrary rules of use for signs, not only before any assertion concerning "the world" is known to be contingently true, but before any such assertion can be formulated. Introduced in this way, it leads immediately to the further, characteristically Tractarian, claim that there can be no *propositions* about "Logic," because "Logic" is not a matter of contingencies, of things that happen to be so but might be otherwise, but a matter either of internal relationships or of conventions for representing them. Hence, about "Logic" nothing (or nothing propositional) can be "said." *Wovon Mann nicht sprechen kann, darüber muss Mann schweigen*, with the consequence that the entire text of the *Tractatus* itself must be dismissed (at 6.54) as nonsense, although nonsense of a mysteriously philosophically helpful character.

The Picture Theory not only allows Wittgenstein to break the link woven by Russellian Logical Atomism between the logical and the epistemic, it allows him equally to dispense with Fregean *Sinn*, at least considered as a class of entities belonging to a "third realm," distinct both from the material world and the mental realm inhabited by "ideas." Here again, Wittgenstein is emphatic that meaning is a matter of convention, and not of *entities* of any type.

Frege says: Every well-formed sentence must make sense; and I say: Every possible sentence is well-formed, and if it does not make sense that can only come of our not having *given* any meaning to certain of its parts. Even when we believe we have done so.[40]

But in Wittgenstein's account of what makes a sentence *possible* lie the seeds of the downfall of the *Tractatus*. A string of signs composes a possible sentence, possesses a propositional content, according to the Picture Theory, just in case its component simple signs name objects that are internally characterised by the possibility of combining in the way depicted by that sequence of signs when understood in accordance with given conventions of representation: a given "logico-syntactic employment." That possibility of combination may either be realised in the world or fail to be realised. It follows that the possibilities of combination enshrined in the internal relations of objects to one another must be independent of one another, in the sense that the realisation or failure to be realised of any such possibility can offer no bar to another such possibility's being realised, or for that matter failing to be realised. The same truth-functional independence must, *ceteris paribus*, characterise simple sentences (or propositions). The truth or falsity of one simple sentence, that is, can have no implications for the truth or falsity of any other such sentence. Unfortunately, as Wittgenstein was to realise, there are sentences – "a is red" and "a is green" are instances, as are all sentences concerning degree in any system of measurement – which fail to satisfy this requirement, yet can by no stretch of ingenuity be represented as truth-functionally complex.

That seems to have been the difficulty that led Wittgenstein himself to abandon the *Tractatus*. But other problems also beset the Picture Theory. There is the one mentioned above, of accounting for the sentences of the *Tractatus* itself: if they are "nonsense," why are they, if they are, philosophically important? And there is the further problem of what we are to make of Wittgenstein's "objects." Are they naturally occurring constituents of reality, of experience perhaps, or are they in some sense linguistic constructs? Much ink has been spilled over this question with no very conclusive result. If anything is clear, indeed, it is that there seem to be conclusive objections to either construal. In order for their internal relations to one another to be constitutive of the possibility of states of affairs, they must, it seems, belong to the world. But, then, why is it so hard, not to say impossible, to point to concrete examples of such entities? The obvious Wittgensteinian reply, that it is because there can, precisely, be no propositional discourse concerning the relationship between discourse and reality, is hardly satisfying because it is a reply internal, as it were, to the metaphysics of the *Tractatus*. And if "objects" are in some sense internal to language, what saves the Tractarian scheme of things from the conclusion that the "possibilities" revealed by their internal relationships are, after all, possibilities only for the conduct of an hermetic game played with signs? The attempt to implement Wittgenstein's Slogan in the terms proposed by the *Tractatus* appears to have led nowhere.

ix. Russell's Principle and Wittgenstein's Slogan

What moral should one draw from this *débacle*? One response would be to say that the breakdown of the *Tractatus* demonstrates the inherent superiority of Russell's way of looking at things; is part of what accounts for the fact that, as we earlier found Evans observing, "many philosophers today look at the theory of reference through essentially Russellian eyes." Filling in the details of this response, one might go on to point out that the approach of the *Tractatus* to reference is broken-backed from the start, because it enshrines contradictory principles. On the one hand, the Wittgenstein of the *Tractatus* is as much a Referential Realist as the Russell of the *Monist* lectures or *The Problems of Philosophy*. As we defined the term at Chapter 2 §i, Referential Realism asserts that whatever content-bearing expressions may be primary in a language pick out entities whose existence and nature owe nothing to semantic convention. Unless, implausibly, we interpret the objects (*Gegenständen*) of *Tractatus* 2.01 as linguistic constructs, that doctrine is as much a central doctrine of the *Tractatus* as of early Russell. As we have seen, it is a doctrine that commits anyone who holds any version of it to asserting a fairly tight connection of some sort between meaning and the epistemic, in the sense of Ryle's knowledge-that. If the meaning of a proper name is its bearer, and if name-bearers are not linguistically constituted entities but constituents of Reality, then, as Frege thought, I can know that a name has a meaning (*Bedeutung*) only if I know that its putative bearer *exists*. If a sentential sign has a meaning (a propositional content) only if it expresses a possible state of affairs, something that could obtain or fail to obtain, and if what is possible in the way of states of affairs depends, not on what some set of linguistic conventions establishes as a possible combination of *signs*, but on the nature of Reality; then, once again, I can know that a putative sentential sign expresses a propositional content only if I know that states of affairs (Russell's "facts") of the right logical type *exist*. And so on.

On the other hand, as we have seen, the Wittgenstein of the *Tractatus* and the *Notebooks* is committed to the principle enshrined in Wittgenstein's Slogan: the principle that "Logic," which in Wittgenstein's and Russell's usage of the period covers, among other things, all questions of meaning, reference, and assertoric content, must "take care of itself," in the sense of not depending in any way on the knowledge of contingencies; on knowledge of contingent truths. That principle implies, just as emphatically as Referential Realism implies the contrary, that there is a radical separation between "Logic" and the epistemic, as if Wittgenstein's Slogan is to be upheld, all "logical" questions must be settled before the speakers of a language can have access to the notion of propositional content; hence, antecedently to the formulation of, let alone the attachment of a truth-value to, any proposition whatsoever; and, hence, antecedently to the possession of propositional knowledge – Rylian knowledge-that. The thrust of the Slogan, in other words, is towards the conclusion that linguistic knowledge is, in Ryle's terms, a form of knowing-how: to put it specifically, knowing-how to operate with signs. But such a conclusion is incompatible not merely with Russell's Referential Realism, but with the Referential Realism of the *Tractatus* itself.

It would be difficult to dissent from this diagnosis of what has gone wrong. The Wittgenstein of the *Tractatus cannot* have both the Referential Realism enshrined in the doctrine that the meaning of a name is its bearer, and the conventionalism enshrined in Wittgenstein's Slogan. But which is to be abandoned? The Referential Realist will be in no doubt: it is the Slogan that must go. But is that so obvious? The arguments in favour of Wittgenstein's Slogan that we explored in Chapter 4 §v have not been answered, nor is it easy to see how they could be answered from the standpoint of Referential Realism. Moreover, one could as well argue that the failure of the *Tractatus* arises from its residual attachment to the Frege-Russellian doctrine that the meaning of a name is its bearer, as that it arises from its attempt to implement the Slogan. The drift of that argument would be, then, that what is shown by the failure of the *Tractatus* is merely the impossibility of implementing the Slogan in the context of an accompanying commitment to Referential Realism.

That in turn suggests the opposite possibility: dropping Referential Realism, by finding some independent way of implementing Wittgenstein's Slogan. That would, of course, entail, among other things, breaking with the doctrine that the meaning of a name is its bearer.

It is arguable that that was the course taken by Wittgenstein; the step which led to his later work. Part of the textual evidence for such a reading would be the centrality of the polemic, in the opening sections of the *Philosophical Investigations*, against the idea that the meaning of names consists in their being correlated with "simples," which can be named but not described. As we said in Chapter 3 §i, however, our main business here is not the exegesis of Wittgenstein, but the elaboration, although no doubt in a Wittgensteinian spirit, of an alternative to Referential Realism. That, however, is plainly going to involve finding some way of advancing the programme announced by Wittgenstein's Slogan: the programme of showing that, and how, "Logic" (that is, everything that concerns the fitness for truth or falsity of the sentential sign) *can* "take care of itself," and that, in turn, will involve drawing out the implications of some of the arguments in its favour that, in Chapter 4 §v, we found formulated, admittedly in forbiddingly brief and gnomic ways, in the *Tractatus* and the *Notebooks*.

Russell's Principle remains, as Evans notes, one of the most plausible statements of Referential Realism. So we shall begin, in the next two chapters, by attacking it in the spirit of Wittgenstein's Slogan. Its main support is what Wittgenstein would call the "picture" promoted by prison-house scepticism: the picture of the speaker, Moncrieff's deluded acquaintance, say, who imagines himself to be asserting a truth in remarking that Bunbury is ill, but who in fact is not even succeeding in specifying a propositional content, a thought in the commonplace, non-Fregean sense, because, all unknown to him, "Bunbury" lacks a bearer. In the next two chapters we shall show that there is an alternative to this picture. We shall show that the ability to refer by means of a proper name, and the right to claim to understand what one is judging in asserting the truth of propositions expressed by sentences in which it occurs, stem not from knowing which particular individual in the world that name picks out, nor from the possession of any other piece of knowledge-that; but from a grasp of the role played by proper names in a web of linguistic practices; from the possession of some knowledge-how, in other words. We shall argue that what differentiates those of Archibald Moncrieff's friends who are in the know from those who are not, is not a piece of knowledge-that about the world (that none of its constituents is to be identified with the bearer of "Bunbury," or something of the sort), but merely a grasp of how the name "Bunbury" fits into the web of linguistic practices. And we shall argue that it is the relationship between the web of practices and the world, and not a relationship of any sort between name-users and name-bearers, which allows us to describe the world, correctly or incorrectly, by means of assertions couched in terms of sentences employing proper names, and which, in so doing, exorcises the spectre of prison-house scepticism.

5

The Name-Tracking Network

i. Nomothetic objects

Russell's Principle in Russell's version is the dictum that "Every proposition which we can understand must be composed wholly of constituents with which we are acquainted." In Gareth Evans's version, it is the more or less equivalent claim that it is possible for a person to have a thought about something only if he knows which particular individual in the world he is thinking about, with the rider that at some point the phrase "which individual" will have to be spelled out in terms of sensory acquaintance if the demands of the principle are to be met.

It is worth noticing right at the outset, therefore, that there are types of reference and referring expression to which neither version of the Principle appears to have any application whatsoever. Take for instance, the sentence "The King can move one square in any direction."

"The King" is a referring expression. It picks out an object, the chess-King. It would be possible, for that matter, to envisage a chess nomenclature in which, rather than being indicated by means of definite descriptions, "The White King," "The White Queen's Bishop," "The White Queen's Knight's Pawn," and so on, the objects so indicated would be baptised with proper names: "King George," "Queen Mary," "Kaiser Wilhelm," "Bishop Wilberforce," and so on.

The identity of the object picked out by the definite description "The White King," or by an equivalent proper name, however, neither needs to be explained, nor could be explained, "by acquaintance." For what would it be to "show" X a white chess-King? It could only be to present X with a piece of pale boxwood of the requisite size carved, let us say, into the shape that represents the King in the standard playing set. But how is X to interpret this showing as bearing on the *Bedeutung* of the expression "The White King"? Let us suppose that X knows nothing of chess. One possible outcome, in that case, is that X will take "The White King" to be a fanciful name for a small carved figure of a particular shape in his host's possession, possibly valuable, on which his host has bestowed a comically grandiloquent title, much as a tediously whimsical person might refer to a garden statue as The Friendly Lion, or to his car as Miranda. But that would be a misunderstanding, for "The White King" in fact refers to a *chess piece.* Clearly, the only way of correcting the misunderstanding would be to teach X to play chess, or at least to give him an account of the game sufficiently detailed to make clear to him the differing roles of different types of piece. But to have chess explained to him, or to learn to play it, will be sufficient to make clear to X to what the expression "The White King" refers.

It is worth noting that there appear on the face of it to be many contexts in which we find ourselves referring not to "natural" or "real" objects of reference (supposing there to be any such) but to objects in some sense "constituted" by systems of rules or conventions. Although language can be regarded, *pace* Davidson,[1] as one such system, not all such systems are linguistic in character. We need a name for the wider class of such systems. We shall call them *nomothetic*[2] *systems,* and objects constituted by, and relative to, such systems, *nomothetic objects.*

The game of chess, now, is clearly a nomothetic system, although not, except incidentally, in virtue of possessing a special terminology, a linguistic one. Equally clearly, the King in chess is a nomothetic object. When, that is, in specifying a move in chess in some such words as "King takes Bishop's Pawn," we refer to the King, what we are referring to is plainly an entity constituted by the rules of chess, whose essence, whose being, as it were, is determined simply by certain provisions of those rules; as that it is the piece that occupies a certain square at the outset of the game, which disposes of certain powers of displacement from square to square of the board, and that, finally, is the piece whose immobilisation by one of the players constitutes victory in the game. Granted, the King in most actual games of chess is represented by a piece of boxwood or ivory carved in a certain characteristic way. But it is not the material of which it is made, nor the characteristic shape into which it is carved, which makes it a chess-King. Chess-Kings can be carved or moulded out of many materials, and in many styles. What makes a physical object a chess-King is its place in a practice: a practice that is in part a linguistic practice. What makes it a chess-King is that it is one of a set of objects made to serve as chess-pieces, and hence carved in ways that make it possible to distinguish pieces endowed by the rules of chess with conventional properties of one sort or another: different powers of displacement from square to square, for instance.

It is in the nature of names for nomothetic objects that it will not be possible to explain the meaning of such a name by correlating it with any constituent or aspect of the natural world. For nomothetic objects are not natural. They are, precisely, creatures not of *physis,* but of *nomos.* They have no existence in nature because they have no existence prior to the institution of the systems of convention that call them into being. It follows that the intuition that writers such as Evans see as central to Russell's Principle, that thought stands in a "more direct" relation to an object when the entity in question is an object of sensory acquaintance, fails for nomothetic objects. It is possible, as Wittgenstein suggests at *Investigations* I.31, that someone might have learned the rules of chess without ever having been shown an actual piece. But though such a person may not know, yet, what a chess-King *looks like*, it seems evident that he or she nevertheless *already* knows, prior to being shown a sample piece, what a chess-King *is*. For what a chess-King *is*, is a function of the rules of chess, and *ex hypothesi* the learner already knows those. Sensory acquaintance with a chess piece of that type merely supplies the learner with a piece of collateral information *about* the King, namely, that it is represented in a certain way according to a certain (standard) representational convention. But representational conventions governing the appearance of chess-pieces – and there are others, early Mediaeval, Asian, or African, for instance – are clearly external, or at best supplementary, to the rules of chess themselves; and it is the latter that define the concept of the King: define, that is, what one *means by* the expression "chess-King." In this case, then, knowledge of some rules, some conventions, gets thought as close to its object as it can be got. There is no "more direct" relationship in which it could be placed, and certainly none mediated by sensory acquaintance.

The reply of those who, with Evans, "look at the theory of reference through essentially Russellian eyes," will doubtless be that names of nomothetic objects form only a special and limited class of names. It could not be the case, they will argue, that all the names in a natural language L named nomothetic objects, because that would have as a consequence that it would be possible to refer in L only to creatures of *nomos*; in other words, to objects having no existence prior to the institution of systems of convention. We shall argue, on the contrary, that all names not only are, but are necessarily, names for nomothetic objects, and that the supposed consequence does not in fact follow.

The immediate Russellian retort might well be that the proposal is simply and evidently false. Its falsity, it might be thought, is particularly evident in the case of proper names: names such as "Russell," "William Hague," "Manchester," "Titanic." Proper names to all appearances pick out concrete individuals: persons, cities, ships, for instance, and it is surely absurd to suggest that concrete individuals of any of these types, or others, are nomothetic objects. Manchester, Russell, Hague, not to mention the Titanic, that vast mass of metal now mouldering at the bottom of the Atlantic, are surely creatures of *physis*, not *nomos*. It can hardly be denied, that is, that they, unlike their names, and unlike the King in chess, enjoy an existence prior to, and wholly independent of, any system of conventions whatsoever.

Such intuitions are closely connected to two associated doctrines, or themes, which have played a major part in philosophical discussion of proper name reference since Frege. The first is the thought we encountered in Chapter 4 §§i–ii: the thought, central both to Frege's treatment of proper names and to Russell's Principle, that it is only possible to *understand* a sentence employing a proper name – where "understand" means something like "attach an assertoric content to" – if one knows which individual the proper name in question picks out. The second is the thought that what allows one to be sure that he does know which individual a given proper name picks out is the possession of a uniquely identifying description of that individual: "The author of the *Principia*," for instance, or "The Yorkshireman who took over from Major," or "The transatlantic liner that struck an iceberg and sank in 1911." This second contention, often known as "the description theory of proper names," dominated the literature until 1970 when the damaging arguments levelled against it by Saul Kripke in *Naming and Necessity* (1972) were first aired as a series of three lectures at Princeton.

We shall defer discussion of Kripke's arguments to Chapter 6. Here what will engage us is the coherent complex of three mutually supportive doctrines that we have just distinguished: the doctrines

1. that the meaning, or as Frege would say the *Bedeutung*, of a proper name is an individual that it picks out;
2. that one cannot attach any assertoric content to a sentence employing a proper name N unless one knows which individual N picks out;
3. that what assures one that one does know which individual N picks out is one's possession of an identifying description of that individual.

As we shall need to refer back from time to time to this collection of claims in what follows, let us give it a label: *the Orthodox View*. As we shall see, notwithstanding the force of Kripke's attack on the Description Theory, it is these three doctrines that chiefly stand in the way of the conclusion that proper names, like all other names, are names for nomothetic objects. For our purposes, in any case, we shall need to pursue against them a line of attack quite independent of Kripke's. To this task we shall now turn.

ii. Actual and nominal descriptions

Description theorists have in general taken it for granted that nothing distinguishes the descriptions associated with proper names from descriptions formulated for other purposes. A description, for the purposes of the theory, is simply a specification of some set of natural features or properties: "struck an iceberg in 1911," "wrote the *Principia*," "is a Yorkshireman," "was elected Party leader after Major stood down," and so on. What makes a given description of special interest for the theory of proper name reference is merely that the collection of characteristics it specifies happen to be simultaneously satisfied by one individual alone.

It is a strong *prima facie* argument in favour of the Description Theory that when one is asked to explain the reference of a proper name the most natural, and in many cases the most helpful, response is to offer a definite description: "N is the x which is F." In real life we not infrequently say things such as "James is the man over there in the corner with the meerschaum pipe," "When I said 'Epstein' I was thinking of the sculptor, not of our friend Ed," "Tiddles is the Persian cat next door," and so on.

The descriptions, which figure in such explications, fall, however, into two logically distinct types, which we shall call respectively *actual* and *nominal* descriptions.

An actual description directly contributes information concerning the nature of the individual it describes. It tells us something about what G. E. Moore like to call the *natural properties of* the bearer of the associated name. Examples of such descriptions might be:

i. Charles Morgan is the red-haired man in the corner.
ii. The Galveston is the coaster refuelling at the end of Pier 3.
iii. Mendes is a Peruvian mestizo about five feet tall, with a four-inch scar up the left side of his face.
iv. The University of Sussex is on the left four miles out of Brighton on the A27.

The properties ascribed by an actual description, as these examples suggest, are ones that might help someone actually to locate, or single out, the individual thus picked out. The description theorist who, when she speaks of descriptions, has in mind actual descriptions – call her the *actual description theorist* – is thus closely in tune with the Orthodox View (see Chapter 5 §ii). According to the actual description theorist, in other words, someone who understands a proper name, someone who can attach an assertoric content to a sentence in which it occurs, and thus, as it is often put "entertain a thought concerning" the individual it names, is someone who knows *which particular individual* he is thinking about because he is armed with a description that, given only the practical power to instigate investigations of an appropriate kind (the sort of powers that might be conferred by a ticket to Brighton, or by access to Pier 3, or to the closely guarded stronghold of the Colombian drug mafia, for instance – it makes no philosophical difference that the powers in question may be for practical reasons hard to come by) would put him in a position actually to locate or single out the individual in question.

Nominal descriptions, by contrast, identify individuals only via descriptions of the circumstances of occurrence of tokens of proper names. Thus, for instance:

i′. the "Charles Morgan" John referred to yesterday at the Board Meeting,
ii′. the girl whose name I noticed in the class register,
iii′. the ship whose name was painted on the smashed lifeboat the coastguards found washed up on the beach this morning,
iv′. the Volusenus whose name occurs on a Roman tombstone in Chester town museum.

Nominal descriptions, like actual ones, ascribe properties to individuals. It is, after all, as much a property of Charles Morgan that his name was mentioned by John at the Board Meeting this morning, as that he is red-haired or standing over there in the corner. There are nevertheless some important differences between the two types of description.

First, and most obviously, the properties ascribed to an individual by an actual description attach to that individual in virtue of its being the kind of individual, the kind of thing, it is. The property of being red-haired, for instance, attaches to Charles Morgan because of his pigmentation, ultimately because of his biochemistry. The properties ascribed to an individual by a nominal description, however, attach to that individual merely in virtue of his being known by the name in question. They attach to it, one might say, only indirectly, by way of the circumstances of utterance of a token of its name. Nor is it surprising that this should be so, beacuse a nominal description conveys information *only* about the circumstances of occurrence of a token of a name; and none whatsoever about the individual who happens to be that name's bearer. It might be objected that there are some pieces of information about the natural properties of name-bearers that are conveyed merely by the character of the associated name. No bearer of the name "Sarah" is likely to be male, no bearer of the name "Fido" human. The reply to this is that any information of this kind that may happen to be conveyed in offering a nominal description is not conveyed *by the content of the description*. It is just contextually inferred, like the suggestion of a cloud hanging over Charles Morgan's head, which may be inferred from the tone of voice in which someone describes the circumstances of occurrence of a token of his name.

iii. Describing and locating

A second difference between actual and nominal descriptions emerges over the question to what extent a description of either kind permits one to *locate*, to single out from amongst other individuals, the individual it describes. Earlier we said that possession of an actual description may arm a speaker with the means of doing precisely that, on condition only that he or she dispose of relevant practical powers and abilities. If one knows, for instance, that the *Galveston* is the coaster refuelling at the end of Pier 3, then provided he can gain admission to Pier 3, he has all the information he needs to pick her out from the other ships moored in her vicinity.

It seems evident, however, that possession of a merely nominal description places the possessor in no such position. Knowing that the Charles Morgan you have in mind is the one John referred to yesterday at the Board Meeting, not only confers on me no ability to single out the man in question, it does not carry me even a single step towards the possession of such an ability, in the way that the least piece of factual information about Morgan, that he wears a Rolex Oyster, that he fingers his beard obsessively – anything at all – might do. And this, again, need come as no surprise, for to have progressed even one step towards singling out an individual, I need to have acquired some piece, any piece, of information about that individual, and, as we have seen, a nominal description conveys no information about the individual whose name it mentions. It conveys information only about the circumstances of occurrence of a token of that individual's name.

Nevertheless, it is very often the case that all one has, as a basis on which to found conversational reference to a given individual, is a merely nominal description of some sort. Consider, for example, the following conversation, based on (iii′) above:

A: Poor devils, I suppose they must be out there somewhere.
B: Who do you mean?
A: The crew of the *Galveston*.
B: What ship is that, then?
A: The ship whose name was painted on the smashed lifeboat the coastguards found washed up on the beach this morning.

Intuitively, at any rate (we shall examine the intuitions concerned more closely in a moment), it appears that we have here a situation intrinsically inhospitable to the Orthodox View. It is in particular inhospitable to clauses (2) and (3) of that view (Chapter 5 §ii). For while, on the one hand, it seems clear that A is referring to a particular real individual, namely, a particular ship, it seems, on the other hand, equally clear that A has no means of *locating*, or *singling out* that ship, not merely because the ship in question is, presumably, at the bottom of the sea, but because A possesses no *actual* description of the vessel in question. Of course, *in a sense* the demand of (2) is satisfied: A *does* know "which individual ship" he is referring to. He is referring to the ship whose name was painted on the smashed lifeboat. But, in another sense, he does not know to "which individual ship" he is referring. For, possessing only a nominal description of the *Galveston*, A knows no natural property of the *Galveston*, and thus no property that could allow him actually to pick out the *Galveston*. To put it dramatically, if the

Galveston were raised and moored among other wrecked vessels, all, as it happens with their names obliterated, A knows, so far, nothing about her which could in any way help him to single her out from amongst those other vessels.[3] So A does not (3) possess an "identifying description" of the *Galveston*, at least if the phrase "identifying description" is understood as it has traditionally been understood by holders of the Orthodox View. Hence A does not know, again in the sense in which the words have generally been understood by holders of the Orthodox View, "which individual" the name "Galveston" picks out. Yet it seems – intuitively, at any rate – clear that, in the above conversation, A is offering a perfectly precise, perfectly viable account of what he takes to be the reference of the name; and that that account, such as it is, is sufficient (2) to permit B to attach, unproblematically, an assertoric content to each sentence of A's in which the name occurs. But the failure of conditions (2) and (3) in this example brings condition (1) into question. Ought we to be taking it for granted quite as readily as philosophical discussion of the topic has done since Frege, that the meaning of a proper name N is best thought of, wholly or in part, as consisting in its possession of what Frege called *Bedeutung*: that is, in the existence of a conventional linkage of some sort between N and some particular, locatable individual?

iv. The whereabouts of Easthampton

Whatever softening-up may be achieved by the foregoing two sections, however, a set of doctrines that has dominated the philosophy of language for a century is not to be displaced by a single counterexample. A defender of Frege and Russell would no doubt wish to object that the example is too neat, and too cunningly buttressed with queer circumstantial detail, to be readily generalisable. Surely, an objector along these lines will argue, there are plenty of obvious cases in which no one – or at least no one not chiefly animated by what our late friend and colleague Virgil Aldrich engagingly called "philosophical funsterism" – would wish to ascribe understanding of a name, or the ability to refer by means of it, to someone with absolutely no idea of how to locate its bearer. Michael Dummett, in *Frege: Philosophy of Language*, offers the following as a plausible case of this kind for retaining the Orthodox View:

It is not possible that none of those who use a name have any criterion for identifying the bearer of the name, that all of them use it with only a partial criterion in mind, but with the intention of referring to the commonly agreed referent: for there would, in such a case, be no commonly agreed referent. It is conceivable, for example, that a wide circle of people were in the habit of using the word "Easthampton" as the name of a town in England, say with a vague impression that it was somewhere in the East Midlands . . . but if we suppose that there is no single person who knows, and no printed reference-book which supplies, any determinate way of identifying a town as being Easthampton, then the name has no referent and no definite sense.[4]

Dummett here avails himself of an argument that goes to the heart of the Russellian tradition of Referential Realism continued by writers like Evans. The ability to locate, to "reach out and touch" as Russell might have said, the bearer of a name is an essential component of the ability to refer, because without it the name can be assigned no *Bedeutung*, and hence no meaning.

Dummett's version of the argument could be formally summarised as follows:

a. A place-name, such as "Easthampton," has a definite sense only if it possesses a commonly agreed referent.
b. But if no one in the speech-community can actually locate the bearer of a place-name, we have no means of making sense of the idea that the name *has* a commonly agreed referent.
c. So, if no one in the speech-community can actually locate the bearer of "Easthampton," "Easthampton" has no definite sense.

Presumably, "has no definite sense," here, is to be taken as equivalent to something along the lines of "is a mere *flatus vocis*" or "is an empty vocable."

Discussions in which counterexample counters counterexample can be as irritating as ones in which question counters question. Nevertheless, that is the way a response to Dummett's argument must go to begin with, for one reason because it will begin to lay down some necessary foundations for a less forensic, more principled response in Chapter 5 §vi.

Suppose, then, that Easthampton is not a further twentieth-century blot on the blackened landscape of the East Midlands, but one of the many "lost" mediaeval villages of the fourteenth century, deserted as a result of the Black Death, and eventually ploughed over, whose foundation-courses constitute a fairly numerous class of British archaeological sites. A certain number of references to Easthampton in charters and legal documents of the twelfth, thirteenth, and early fourteenth centuries can be shown on internal evidence to concern one and the same village of that name, and these documents also contain sufficient information about the concerns of the village, its inhabitants, and certain noble families between which the feudal rights pertaining to it were contested, for Easthampton to be not infrequently referred to by historians of the period. However, there is no means, short of a miracle, of ascertaining which, out of some eight or nine archaeologically and historically plausible locations, is the true site of Easthampton. We cannot, then, "identify the bearer" of the name "Easthampton" in the sense required by Dummett's example, for we do not know, and have no means of finding out, where exactly Easthampton stood, and where some of its foundation courses perhaps still "stand." And yet despite that we – where by "we" one means the historical community – are able to refer to Easthampton, secure in the knowledge that we have good grounds for supposing, (1) that "Easthampton" picks out a unique village, and (2) that the village one historian refers to as "Easthampton" is the very village habitually referred to by his colleagues under that name. The reader may verify for herself that the features of the *Galveston* example that make that case inhospitable to the Orthodox View recur in the present case. The possibility of reference by means of a proper name, and of attaching a perfectly clear assertoric content, other things being equal, to any sentence in which it occurs, are, in short, preserved in both cases in the absence of any possibility of actually locating, or "picking out", the bearer of the name.

v. Naming practices

Might not analysis of these examples, and related ones, reveal the outlines of an alternative account of proper name reference; alternative, that is, to the Orthodox View? Let us begin with an obvious question. What is it that in practice permits the members of the historical community to credit themselves with the ability to refer to Easthampton, and to attach assertoric content to sentences in which the name occurs, even though no member of that community has the faintest idea which, of a number of areas of early mediaeval architectural vestiges, occupying widely separated sites, are the remains of Easthampton? Given the textual character of historical data, those abilities can only repose on the possession of what we have been calling a *nominal description* of Easthampton, or rather a series of such descriptions. Easthampton is known to historians, let us suppose, as the village of that name referred to successively in the Domesday survey, a sequence of charters, and a range of surviving letters and legal documents relating to disputes of the thirteenth and fourteenth centuries over feudal rights relating to the village. Internal evidence, moreover, is sufficient to establish that all the references in question are references to one and the same village, but not to provide an exact location for that village within a radius of twenty miles, say.

Why, now, should historians take it for granted that such textual evidence is sufficient to establish that a specific village of that name actually existed, with the consequent likelihood that it still exists, if only in the form of a tract of buried foundation-courses? One obvious reply would be that mediaeval people did not create and store legal documents merely to amuse themselves. They were not playing games, except, possibly, language games. Litigation was, as it still is, expensive; so was vellum. The services of scribes capable of engrossing sheets of the latter with quantities of legal Latin were no less costly. It is no doubt possible to imagine bizarre circumstances in which much expensive litigation might occur over the ownership of an imaginary manor, but such imaginings belong to fiction, not to real life. In real life, people dispute over real goods, including real manorial rights, not fictional ones. Hence one can infer with reasonable certainty that where records testify to a lengthy and circumstantial legal dispute over a manor known as "Easthampton" there existed a manor for the litigants in the case to dispute over.

Let us look a little more closely at the reasoning implicit in this reply. Although our use of place-names is sometimes quite loose (where, for instance do "Middle America" or "The Levant" begin and end?), we go to a great deal of trouble to establish and operate far stricter criteria of identity for named "places" falling into a range that includes cities, towns, villages, districts, fields, commons, gardens ("messuages"), estates, and others. We establish the boundaries of such entities with care, marking them with boundary-stones, surveying them in order that they may be accurately delineated on cadastral maps, town plans, estate maps, and so on. We do these things because they serve, are indeed essential to, a wide variety of purposes arising in the context of a wide variety of legal, commercial and governmental transactions; transactions involving inheritance, conveyancing, the areas of responsibility of adjacent local authorities or police forces, feudal rights and duties, planning regulations, and so on. A place-name of this type, a name such as "Easthampton," or "Baxter's Piece," or "Middle Farm," once it gains currency, rapidly begins to acquire what in Chapter 3 §ii we called a use$_E$, or rather a whole fan of related uses$_E$, in a wide variety of practices. It may be inscribed on boundary-stones, as the names of adjacent parishes used to be, one name on one side of the stone, the other on the other side. It may occur on maps of all kinds, having all kinds of specialised uses. It will crop up in letters, conveyancing documents, statutes governing the rights and duties of local authorities; it will occur on banners and war-memorials, public buildings and railway stations; on the destination indicators of buses; on signposts, in ballads, in histories . . . the list has no obvious conclusion. Since all these practices, whatever their uses$_P$ may be, offer a use$_E$ to proper names, let us call them *naming-practices*. It is crucial to the integrity, which is to say, the continued usefulness, of all such practices, that each name be used consistently to pick out one and the same entity of a given type. So if the circumstances of occurrence of a name "N" within the context of a given practice are such as to give reasonable assurance that the interests of those operating the practice were sufficiently bound up with the existing and continued utility of the practice to ensure due regard for the integrity of the practice, then the *circumstances of occurrence of* "N" *alone* warrant us in asserting the existence of a unique bearer of "N."

We can now state more precisely, and conformably to the promissory notes issued in Chapter 3 §§ii–iii, what it is that allows the historical community to refer to Easthampton, even though none of its members can say where Easthampton was, or is. Historians possess reasonable assurance that the name "Easthampton" picked out a unique individual, namely a village, because of the nature of the use$_E$ made of that name in a variety of naming-practices, given the uses$_P$ of those practices. It is entirely beside the point that none of them can locate Easthampton spatially, because they possess perfectly adequate means, to put the matter in a way sympathetic to the spirit of Wittgenstein's Slogan, of locating it logically.

vi. Some further examples

A few more examples, involving other types of naming practices, may help to make clearer both the nature and the generality of the point just made. Consider the conversation between A and B concerning the *Galveston* in Chapter 5 §iii. We claimed that, "intuitively," A is in a position to refer to the *Galveston*, even though A lacks any means of singling her out from among other vessels, even if she were raised. And we promised to say something more about the nature of the intuitions involved. We can now keep that promise. A's ability to refer to the *Galveston*, although unable to locate her or single her out, rests merely on A's acquaintance with the circumstances of occurrence of a token of her name. The name was found painted on a smashed lifeboat. Let us suppose that the inscription reads:

S.S. GALVESTON
Monrovia

Such an inscription, to an informed observer (informed about relevant naming practices, that is to say), instantly locates itself relative to a fabric of conventional observances involving such names. Open boats of the size of the lifeboat do not have ports of registration, certainly not ones on the other side of the Atlantic. By contrast, the name of a ship, with her port of registration, is routinely painted on all manner of items belonging to her, including lifebelts, lifeboats, and so on. These practices, like other naming-practices, would lose their usefulness relative to a wide variety of other practices, involving theft, insurance, and so on, if care were not taken to ensure that each ship is registered under a single name, and known by it thereafter; that the name painted on a ship's lifeboats is her name; that small boat owners do not jokingly put misleading inscriptions on their craft, and so on. So, although it would be possible to invent circumstances in which it would be to someone's advantage to inscribe a lifeboat with the name of a nonexistent ship, such circumstances, if they occur in nature at all, will be of extreme rarity. Hence A is justified in ruling them out of consideration in the present case, and inferring, just on the basis of the circumstances of occurrence of a token of the name "Galveston," that that name has a bearer. What sustains the inference is the nature of the web of practices within which such an occurrence of a token of that sort of name situates itself; that is to say, in terms of the two-level model of naming introduced in Chapter 3 §ii, the mode of insertion of the name into a set of practices, and the modes of insertion of those practices into the world.

Again, take the nominal description,

iv′. The Volusenus whose name occurs on a Roman tombstone in Chester museum.

Someone, A, with a smattering of classical learning, might ask whether the person so commemorated could have been the Volusenus sent ahead by Caesar to scout the south coast of Britain prior to the invasion of 52 B.C. And B, an ancient historian, might reply that it could not be, as the date of the Chester stone is at least 250 years later than the earlier Volusenus's scouting expedition. In so speculating, A has advanced a Thought, in Frege's sense, concerning a specific individual, the Volusenus of the Chester tombstone. Equally, B has, on good grounds, assigned that Thought a truth-value, namely, False. And yet neither A nor B have any means of locating the individual, Volusenus, whom the stone commemorates. They do not, in that sense, know, in Evans's words, "which particular individual in the world" they are referring to and speculating about. Yet they do know that there is a particular individual, part of the furniture of the universe timelessly considered, concerning whom A is raising a speculative possibility, and who is the individual to whom both A and B refer by means of the name "Volusenus." They know this merely because of what they know concerning the conventions surrounding a naming practice, namely, the convention, which has descended from the Romans to ourselves, of commemorating an individual by raising on his grave a tombstone bearing his name. Of course, as with every conventional practice, joke, hoax, or parody deployments of the practice are imaginable. Thus a film company might have a tombstone made bearing the legend "Count Dracula RIP," and this stone might survive and be discovered by a future archaeologist, whose inference to the actual existence of such a person in twentieth-century Beverly Hills would manifestly be ill-founded. But, equally, any such mistake or deception may be unmasked. And even setting that aside, however tediously humorous in its proceedings the present day may be, there are no grounds for supposing Roman Britain to be given to jokery of that sort. So, if we have a Roman Briton's tombstone, we have the man it commemorates: "have" him, that is, in a sense sufficiently strong to sustain reference, even if we know nothing of him beyond the fact that he was so commemorated.

vii. The Name-Tracking Network

Finally, take the description,

> i'. The "Charles Morgan" John referred to yesterday at the Board Meeting.

Manifestly, someone, let us call him A again, who refers to Morgan by means of such a description may, like the historians in the "Easthampton" example, possess no means of locating, or singling out the individual to which he or she intends to refer. For he or she may know nothing about the "Charles Morgan" in question. In fact he or she may refer to him in the context of an enquiry concerning his identity: "Who was the 'Charles Morgan' John referred to yesterday at the Board Meeting, and what has he to do with the Company?," or something of the sort. What, then, sustains A's ability to refer to Morgan?

What is surely sound in Michael Dummett's discussion of the "Easthampton" example is the generally Fregean thought that the use of a proper name by the members of a community requires that the name pick out a "commonly agreed referent." This is plainly right: if A is thinking of one Charles Morgan and B of some quite different person of that name, and there is no way of clearing up the confusion, then enquiry must, clearly, grind to a halt. How is this requirement to be met? A general commitment to Referential Realism would suggest, along the lines of Dummett's suggestion in the Easthampton case, that it can be met only if one or more members of the linguistic community can actually produce, or at least pick out, perhaps at some sort of identity parade, the Charles Morgan intended. But, just as in the Easthampton case, there are grounds for thinking this condition far too strong.

The normal situation in which a man introduces himself as, say, "Charles Morgan" may be compared with the situation, which used to be common in a certain sort of B-movie, in which a highwayman, asked to identify himself, says, "Call me Captain Moonlight." Plainly, this, although it solves the immediate problem of how to address the man, will not satisfy Dummett's Fregean requirement of a commonly agreed referent. For since there may be two, or several, or any number of mysterious masked outlaws going around saying "Call me Captain Moonlight," we have no assurance whatsoever that two speakers who refer in conversation to "Captain Moonlight" are, in fact, referring to one and the same person. "Charles Morgan" is a different matter, precisely because it is not some *nom de guerre* plucked out of the air, but a baptismal name. To give such a name is not merely to indicate how one wishes to be addressed, but to reveal, in the ordinary way of things, a label that has been used for many years, through occurrences of tokens of it in the context of many naming practices, to trace, or track, one's progress though life. Such tracking operates by way of a variety of practices: the keeping of baptismal rolls, school registers, registers of electors; the editing and publishing of works of reference of the *Who's Who* type, the inscribing of names, with attached addresses, in legal documents, certificates of birth, marriage, and death, and so on. Such practices are mutually referring in ways that turn them into a network through which the bearer of a given name may be tracked down by any of dozens of routes. Let us call the web of such mutually referring and cross-indexing practices the *Name-Tracking Network*. In a host of normal cases, access, via a name, to the Name-Tracking Network will allow one to locate the bearer of a name in the sense of putting one in a position to actually confront him. Having established from *Who's Who* that the residence of a certain novelist is such-and-such, one goes there, knocks on the door, and lo and behold, there stands Charles Morgan in the flesh. But it is in principle also possible to have access to an individual only as a trace, as it were, left by that individual in the fabric of the Name-Tracking Network. Suppose, for the sake of an example sharply unfriendly to Referential Realism, that Charles Morgan has vanished, and that, by some extraordinary combination of circumstances, not only has Morgan vanished but also every single person who knew him and could recognise him has vanished also. All that remains to mark his passage through the world, is a series of occurrences of tokens of his name across a range of documents, school, church and electoral registers, marriage certificates and legal records of one sort and another, which all record a Charles Morgan residing over a period of time at a series of addresses linked by overlaps between documents of different types. Under such circumstances, although Dummett's Fregean requirement of common reference from speaker to speaker to a specific individual cannot be satisfied by anyone's disposing of the ability to locate or produce Morgan, it is, nevertheless satisfied. It is satisfied because (1) we have a trace, marked by successive occurrences of the name "Charles Morgan" across a series of documents, and because (2) the conventions governing the construction of documents of those types are such as to assure us that the successive marks that constitute the trace, were left by one and the same individual.

When someone, say John, at the Board Meeting, mentions a person by name, the presumption is, now, that this occurrence of a token of the name in question represents merely an extension of the trace left across time by innumerable previous occurrences of tokens of the name through the fabric of the Name-Tracking Network. By the nature of the conventions governing the practices, institutions, and observances constituting the Name-Tracking Network, such traces are guaranteed each to correspond to a specific individual. So the extension to the Charles Morgan trace constituted by the occurrence of a token of the name in John's remarks to the Board Meeting yesterday is also guaranteed (unlike an *ad hoc* title of convenience such as "Captain Moonlight") to correspond to a specific individual. No doubt Charles Morgan in person will turn out to be traceable through the Name-Tracking Network. But even if he were not, for reasons of the sort sketched above, the mere existence of a suitably cross-indexed trace of occurrences of tokens of the name through the Name-Tracking Network would suffice to meet the requirement, for success in referring by means of the name, that the name pick out a commonly agreed referent.

Now, of course, "Charles Morgan" may turn out after all to be a variant of "Captain Moonlight." The person who introduced himself to John under that name may turn out, having vanished, taking with him a substantial sum of the firm's money, to have been a confidence trickster. Worst of all, it may turn out to be impossible to establish which confidence trickster he was, because, as the police wearily inform John, a number of such characters, none of whose real identities are known, all of them of similar appearance, and known to be distinct individuals only in virtue of their simultaneous presence in widely spaced localities, have been going about their business in the vicinity under the name "Charles Morgan." Does the possibility of such a state of affairs being the case invalidate A's confidence that the nominal description "the Charles Morgan John referred to yesterday at the Board Meeting" possesses a unique, commonly agreed referent? Under those circumstances yes; in general, no. For in general the trace in the fabric of the Name-Tracking Network to which a proffered name gives access does not, in that sort of way, run cold, or come to a full stop. If that were to change; if the condition of society were to become so anarchic, and its members so unwilling to be traced, that people invariably identified themselves only by the adoption, often only for a few days or weeks, of one of a range of popular *noms de guerre*, reference to specific persons by means of proper names would become impossible. But this is, in a way, merely a special case of a familiar observation of Wittgenstein's:

> . . . if anyone believes that certain concepts are absolutely the correct ones, and that having different ones would mean not realising something that we realise – then let him imagine certain general facts of nature to be different from what we are used to, and the formation of concepts different from the usual ones will become intelligible to him.[5]

The logico-linguistic institution of reference to individuals by means of proper names, that is, requires, as an underpinning "fact of nature," the proper observance of all those rules and practices that assure the integrity of the Name-Tracking Network. If the integrity of the network decays to the point at which no name has any more currency than the highwayman's "Captain Moonlight," the possibility of proper name reference decays with it. But equally, to the extent that the integrity of the Name-Tracking Network is preserved, so is the possibility of proper-name reference. To find, under the latter circumstances, that one has miscalculated in the case of a specific transaction involving the proffering of a name, is thus merely to find that one has made a mistake about that transaction, not that the whole edifice of assumptions under which proper name reference proceeds is crumbling, or even under threat.

viii. "Logic must take care of itself"

We are now in a position to redeem, at least partially, the promissory note issued at the end of Chapter 4. We proposed there that Wittgenstein's Slogan may be read as summarising a series of arguments tending to the conclusion that all questions concerning the meaningfulness of linguistic signs must be settled antecedently to the assignment of a truth-value to any proposition. Russell's Principle manifestly entails the contrary, because it asserts that at least some signs, "basic names" or whatever one wishes to call them, can be meaningfully deployed in sentential contexts only by a speaker either acquainted with their bearers, or possessing information concerning them sufficient to allow him or her to locate, to single out, the specific individual picked out by such a name. We suggested that one reason why the *Tractatus* is broken-backed (a verdict shared, after all, by its creator) is that the Tractarian enterprise was vitiated from the start by the internal contradiction created by its commitment, on the one hand, to Wittgenstein's Slogan, and, on the other, to the version of Russell's Principle enshrined in the dictum, equally dear to Wittgenstein's heart at that stage in his development, that "A name means an object. The object is its meaning." One way of resolving the contradiction would be, we suggested, to drop Wittgenstein's Slogan and with it the botched metaphysic of Tractarian atomism, and return, as many philosophers have chosen to do, to the exploration of essentially Russellian ways of thinking. The other would be to make a serious attempt to think consistently in the spirit of Wittgenstein's Slogan. That would entail dropping Russell's Principle, and that move in turn would appear to carry with it the risk of turning language into an hermetic fabric of signs lacking contact with reality. Nevertheless, and however *prima facie* unpromising, that second line of enquiry was the one we proposed to pursue.

The account of proper name reference we have just developed, in terms of naming-practices and the Name-Tracking Network, constitutes at least a first step along that road. Although by no means Wittgensteinian in its detailed machinery, it is very much in the spirit of Wittgenstein's Slogan, and in consequence opposed to that of Russell's Principle. Its central thought is that the conditions required for a speaker, A, to possess the ability to refer by means of a proper name N, and to entertain thoughts expressible by sentences containing N, are much weaker than Russell and Frege supposed. All that is required is:

R_1 – that A grasp the workings of at least some of the naming practices that go to make up the Name-Tracking Network;

R_1 – that A have good grounds for taking N to be one of the names tracked by the Name-Tracking Network.

(R_1) will generally be satisfied by the vast store of general knowledge that anyone has of the systems of conventional arrangements regulating social life in his society. (R_2) will generally be satisfied by the circumstances of occurrence of tokens of N. That N appears engraved on a tombstone, or painted on a lifeboat, or typed in a class register, or that N is mentioned by a CEO addressing a Board Meeting (that is, under circumstances in which the introduction of names invented on the spur of the moment is to say the least unlikely), are considerations sufficient in most cases to establish that N is a real name: that is to say, a name in actual use, and so one tracked by the Name-Tracking Network.

If (R_2) is met, then A has good grounds for supposing that N possesses a bearer, O. But those grounds are not supplied by any epistemic relation in which A may stand to O: in virtue, that is, of A's possessing knowledge of any actual predicates true of O, as distinct from merely nominal predicates. For A may, as we have seen, not be in a position to ascribe any actual predicates whatsoever to O. It may be, as in the cases of the *Galveston*, or the Volusenus of the Chester tombstone, that the only predicate S has any grounds for ascribing to O is the purely nominal predicate "bearer of the name N, a token of which occurs in circumstances xyz." In such a case, as we have seen, the burden of establishing that N has a bearer is borne entirely by S's familiarity with the conventions surrounding the operation of one or another naming practice.

In Chapter 5 §i, we distinguished between natural objects, such as pegs of boxwood, and nomothetic objects such as the King in chess. In the same way one might distinguish natural from nomothetic relationships. Causal relationships, such as that in which a catalyst stands to the chemical reaction whose rate it affects, are natural in the sense that their existence and nature is in no way dependent on the institution of any system of rules or conventions. Equally a relation such as *being adjacent characters in the Roman alphabet* is by the same criterion nomothetic.

To possess knowledge concerning an object is clearly to be causally related to it, and thus, by the above criterion, to stand in a natural relationship to it. No mere juggling with rules or conventions, evidently, can in itself put one in a position to assert any true statement concerning any of the objects which make up the world. To be acquainted with an object, or to possess the kind of information embodied in actual descriptions – to meet, that is, either of the requirements proposed by one or another version of Russell's Principle as conditions for the ability to refer by means of a name, is, plainly, to stand in an epistemic relationship to that object, therefore, in one or another type of causal relation to it, and therefore in a natural relation to it. It follows that, according to the Russellian deliverance, reference also is a natural relationship: one holding between a mind and the objects of its thoughts. Russell's account of reference, indeed, offers a palmary instance of what the Wittgenstein of the *Tractatus* and the *Notebooks 1914–16* found so disquieting about Russell's theory of meaning in general; its tendency to recast purely logical, or as we would say nomothetic, relations as natural ones: to treat logic and the theory of meaning as if they were, or could be, departments or subdivisions of natural science.

On the account proposed here, on the contrary, the distinction between nature and "logic," the natural and the nomothetic, is preserved. The capacity of A to refer by means of a name N requires no epistemic relationship whatsoever between A and the bearer of N. All that is required is a relationship between A and, on the one hand, some body of conventions constitutive of one or another naming-practice, and, on the other, some set of circumstances of occurrence of a token of N. Both these relations, by the criterion outlined above, must be accounted nomothetic ones, that is, ones whose existence and nature is dependent upon the institution of systems of convention. A can stand in the required relationship to a naming-practice only in virtue of the institution and operation of a system of conventions, for a naming practice is, and is no more than, a system of conventions. On the present account, then, reference, understood as a relationship between the speaker who makes use of a proper name N and the bearer of N, is a nomothetic relationship. It is a nomothetic relationship because it is a relationship mediated by, and existing solely in virtue of the existence of, a system of conventions. It is not, that is, as an epistemic relationship is, a natural relationship; one of those that go to constitute extralinguistic reality. There is, or at least so far as the capacity to refer goes there need be, no natural relationship whatsoever between A and the bearer of N.

We have, in effect, abandoned tenet (1) of the Orthodox View: the idea, which Wittgenstein shared at the stage of the *Tractatus* with Russell and Frege, that the meaning of a name is its bearer. To know that "Charles Morgan" is a meaningful expression, and, for that matter, to know what it means, is, according to us, simply to know (a) that it is a proper name of the type used to name persons, and (b) that it is a name in use, that is, one tracked by the Name-Tracking Network. To know (a) and (b) is to know how the name is used, to know that is, something about the workings of the system of linguistic conventions in the context of which such names find a use. But a speaker may know (a) and (b) without knowing anything about Charles Morgan: neither who he is, where he is to be found, nor any natural property possessed by him.

But have we, in abandoning that idea, not perhaps also abandoned the idea that language is a tool for exploring and describing the natural world, in favour of representing it as an hermetic tissue of conventions permitting reference to nothing beyond the web of nomothetic constructs they themselves define? Not at all. We have simply moved from the one-level model of the relationship between language and reality characteristic of Referential Realism to the two-level model of that relationship introduced in Chapter 3 §ii. More specifically, we have abandoned the idea that the meaning of a name N consists in the relationship of N to its bearer for the idea that it consists in the relationship of N to one or more naming-practices. But that leaves us free, within the terms of the two-level model, to understand the relationship between language and reality as a relationship between naming practices and the natural conditions with which we engage in operating those practices. It is over the graves of dead men or women that stones are raised bearing their names; it is tracts of land that we survey for the sake of marking out on maps the boundaries of named fields or named boroughs; it is the names under which ships are registered that we paint, with their port of registration, on equipment belonging to them; and so on. In language the link between the natural and the nomothetic is forged at the level of practices, including naming-practices, not at the level of the linguistic expressions, the phonemic strings or their symbolic representations, which in turn acquire meaning, one sort of meaning or another, through their specific modes of involvement in those practices. In language, "logic" does indeed "look after itself." But far from that interposing a barrier between language and the world, it is, on the contrary, as Merleau-Ponty thought and as we shall see, the indispensable condition for the engagement of language with the world.

ix. "Name-Bearerships" as nomothetic entities

What we have just said, though, looks at first sight as if it must be wrong. For, it will be said, we do not, surely, introduce a proper name into a language by connecting it with, or involving it in, a naming-practice; we do so by connecting it, associating it, with its bearer: through an act of baptism, or something less formal of the same general sort. And surely such an act does create, does bring into being, a direct relationship, of just the sort whose existence we have just denied, between a name and an extralinguistic entity, a constituent of Reality. For what is the bearer of a proper name, of the name "Saul Kripke," for instance, if not the living human individual on whom that name was baptismally bestowed? And what is a living human individual if not a constituent of Reality?

The weight of philosophical tradition in favour of this argument is alone sufficient to make it difficult at first to conceive of any reply. And philosophical tradition here is supported by the sort of "commonsense" that is still frequently supposed to be sufficiently independent of philosophical theorising to serve as some sort of constraint on its wilder flights. On that level, the level of "commonsense intuition," it also can appear at first sight unquestionably evident that baptism must be seen as simultaneously bestowing a name on an individual and a meaning, in the sense of a reference, a *Bedeutung*, on the name. But neither tradition nor commonsense offer a sure guide in philosophy. The idea that a name could, even in principle, be equipped with a reference solely through baptismal association with a bearer, is a prime specimen of that not uncommon thing in philosophy, an absurdity masquerading as a truism.

We need to return briefly to the argument of Chapter 2 §i. There we drew attention to the ambiguity of the terms "reference" and "refer," depending on whether one understands reference as a relationship between a speaker and what he refers to in uttering a given sentence, or as the relationship between a name and its bearer, a denoting expression and what it denotes. We argued that it is perfectly possible to "refer" in the first of these senses to a natural object, a perfectly respectable constituent of extralinguistic Reality, even though one does so by means of a name that "refers" in the second sense to a nomothetic entity. "Baxter's Piece," let us say, is the name of a field. When a farm manager says to a man, "I'd turn those bullocks out into Baxter's Piece this afternoon, Jim," he refers, in the first sense, to a natural object, a muddy tract of English land. To what, now, does "Baxter's Piece" refer? Well, we said, it refers to a field. It is the name of a field. But what is it to "name," to "refer" in the second sense to, "a field"? Could one do it through an act of baptism, of some sort: "I name this field ... and so on." Probably not, because that is not, at any rate, how fields acquire such names. Surely, however, one could explain the reference of the name by indicating the tract of land to which, ostensibly, it refers? But could one? How is it to be done? Presumably one has to be imagined standing at a gate and saying, "This is Baxter's Piece." Or, standing on a nearby hilltop from which the field-pattern can be surveyed and saying "There is Baxter's Piece, just to the left of that wood." But how is one to interpret these remarks? Doesn't that depend on how much background knowledge one's hearer possesses, and of what kinds? Let us suppose him to be familiar enough with language to grasp the concept of a name and of a named sacred site or land-feature but unfamiliar with our concepts of land-tenure. He comes, let us suppose, from a traditional hunter-gatherer society in which land belongs to no one, and is never divided into lots according to ownership, but in which named sites serve certain cultural and religious purposes. He knows, therefore, nothing of the erection of hedges and fences to prevent cattle straying and to mark the limits of pieces of land in particular ownership. He can see that the gate leads on to a place, a site of some sort, called "Baxter's Piece," perhaps a dancing-ground or sacred site of the English, or that the name is supposed to pick out some tract of land visible from the hilltop in the direction indicated. But what are the limits of the named tract? How is it marked out from the countryside in general? That, as he can perfectly well see, will depend on what sort of land-form or ritual entity is putatively being named. Is "Baxter's Piece," in short, the name of a dancing-ground (in which case do those stones jutting out of the middle of the field define its limits?) or a natural bowl (a "bottom," in Sussex terminology), in which case its limits will end at the crest of the embracing hill six hundred feet above, or what? Whatever the answer, the hedges can have nothing to do with it, for whoever heard of land-forms or sacred sites being delimited by whatever vegetation happens to be growing in the vicinity?

It is not difficult to see what is needed to remove the hunter-gatherer's puzzlement. What he needs to have explained to him is, first of all, the fabric of institutions licensing and controlling the ownership, inheritance and transfer of parcels of land, and, second, the further systems of conventions that govern the assignment of names to such parcels of land, and the deployment of such names, in conversation, on estate maps, in legal documents, and so on, as part of the machinery of keeping track of such parcels, both in connection with the operation of the first set of institutions, and in the multifarious other contexts, from farming to planning to the activities of walkers and rambling associations, in which our lives are bound up with land and land-ownership. Finally, it needs mentioning that the boundaries of fields in Europe are often, if not always, marked by hedges or fences.

Now, of course, the hunter-gatherer's face clears. He sees what the pointing gesture, accompanied by the remark "This is Baxter's Piece," is supposed to intend: "Baxter's Piece" is not, after all, the name of a land-form, or of some sort of sacred site, but the name of a *field*. The trouble is, however, that unless that much conceptual "scene-setting," as Wittgenstein called it, is provided, the hunter-gatherer will be at a loss to say what in the world the baptismal gesture *is* supposed to intend: to what constituent or feature of the natural world it is supposed to link the name.

To see this is to see at least part of the force of Wittgenstein's remark that "only someone who already knows how to do something with it can significantly ask a name."[6] But, insofar as we grant that, we grant also that the referent of a name, the entity to which the name is supposed to be linked by the baptismal act, is not simply "given in nature"; is not in fact a linguistically unmediated constituent of natural reality, but a nomothetic entity: one that, like the chess-King of Chapter 5 §i, exists, to be named and referred to, only in virtue of some conventions of our devising. To put it bluntly, without certain conventions of land-tenure and the resulting naming-practices, there are no such things as fields, and so no such things as names for fields. Fields, in short, are as much nomothetic entities as the chess-King.

Well, it will be objected, maybe: but persons are not; cannot be. A person just is a constituent of extralinguistic reality, something "out there," available to be named through a simple baptismal act, without any of the detours by way of convention that can be alleged in the case of fields or types of chess-piece. But what *kind* of name are we thinking of here? "A proper name," comes the obvious reply. But is that quite the homogeneous category it is often taken to be? Is there not a whole range of different types of proper names, and proper-name-like expressions, which can in various senses be said to "belong" to persons and be available for use in referring to them?

Take, for example the Scots custom, well-established in Scots English ("Braid Scots," or "Lallans") and still in use among older people in rural parts of Scotland, such as Galloway or Aberdeenshire,[7] of attaching to a landed proprietor, or even to a farm manager, the name of the estate he owns or manages. A familiar literary example is to be found in R. L. Stevenson's "Unfinished Romance," *Weir of Hermiston*. In the novel, Adam Weir, the Judge-Advocate of Scotland, acquires by marriage the estate of Hermiston, formerly held by a branch of the Rutherford family. He thus becomes "Weir of Hermiston." Now – and this is the point – he can be referred to or addressed simply as "Hermiston." A neighbour, or a senior estate servant might thus say, politely, "Good day to ye, Hermiston," and remarks such as, "Is that not Hermiston standing there outwith the Tollbooth," "Shall I find Hermiston in his chambers today?" are entirely linguistically imaginable. So in these respects "Hermiston" functions exactly like a proper name, sush as "Adam Weir," for instance. By contrast, there are respects in which it does not function like a proper name. It is not baptismally conferred, for instance, but acquired, in this case by marriage, but no doubt in other cases by inheritance or purchase. And if someone were to ask, at a time when the usage was more current and the social and agricultural order more stable than perhaps such things are today, "Where is Hermiston to be found when legal business does not keep him in Edinburgh?" he would no doubt invite a puzzled look and the reply, "Are you asking where *Hermiston* is?"

If one were asked, then, in the spirit of Frege, to specify the *Bedeutung*, the referent, of "Hermiston," one would at first be at rather a loss whether to answer "a person, Adam Weir," or "A Lowland Scottish estate." No doubt one would begin by distinguishing its application to the estate from its application to the Judge-Advocate. In the former application the *Bedeutung* of "Hermiston" might perhaps be satisfactorily identified as a nomothetic entity, the estate. If one wished to capture the way in which the name "Hermiston" relates to Adam Weir, however, one could hardly do so by identifying Adam Weir, in Fregean style, as the *Bedeutung* of "Hermiston." Other people than Adam Weir have been and will be entitled to be addressed and spoken of as "Hermiston." Isn't that, however, just like the situation recorded in the telephone directory, which lists many John Smiths? That there are many people called "John Smith" does not mean the referent of the name in each case is not the living person who bears that name; it merely means that the same name is sometimes used to pick out one person and sometimes another. But that won't do either, for "Hermiston" behaves quite differently from an homonymous proper name such as "John Smith." "Hermiston" belongs, as a term of address or reference, to whomever, of whatever family, happens to be the laird of a certain estate. A move open to a determined Fregean at this point would be to deny that any *Bedeutung* need be sought for "Hermiston," on the grounds that "Hermiston" is not a proper name at all but, rather, a *title*. This is correct as far as it goes, but what needs to be explained is how a title can serve as the means of accomplishing kinds of singular reference otherwise accomplished by proper names. The answer is surely obvious. To be Hermiston is to possess a conventionally defined status of a certain type. Adam Weir, the flesh-and-blood Judge-Advocate, stands to his status as Hermiston, in other words, in exactly the same sort of relationship in which the carved peg of boxwood of Chapter 5 §i stands to its status as a chess-King. One can refer to the Judge-Advocate by means of the expression "Hermiston," just as one can refer to the peg of boxwood by means of the expression "the King," but that does not mean that "Hermiston" functions logically as a name for that particular living person, any more than "the King" functions logically as a name for a particular bit of carved boxwood. "The King" is the name of a piece in chess, "Hermiston" variously functions as the name of an estate and the name of a lairdship. In both cases it picks out a nomothetic entity, in one sense a constituent of reality, certainly (unless one wishes to contend that, just as there are no such things as ghosts, so there are no such things as lairdships or chess-pieces), but equally not a constituent of a Nature un-played-upon by the "intellectual breeze," as Coleridge put it,[8] of linguistic and other forms of constitutive convention.

Now consider another example. A forest Indian appears on a construction site where a new road is being driven though the Ecuadorian rain-forest. He ingratiates himself with the construction workers, and for cigarettes and odd gifts helps them with various tasks. He is clumsy at some of these tasks, and the workers, being, on the one hand, macho, and, on the other hand, not quite sure how safe he is, want to mock and diminish him. They call him "Estupido," "stupid," and give him orders as if it were his name, "Estupido, do that," "Estupido, go there." One morning the Indian is no longer there, having either met with an accident or faded back into the forest.

Was "Estupido," now, a proper name? And if not, why not? It was used in some ways, certainly, as if it were one: to refer (in the first of our two senses of "refer") to a certain individual, to give him orders, and so on. But there also are logical divergences. One is comparatively trivial. Proper names carry in themselves neither pejorative nor laudatory connotations. But even that difference might make one want to say that "Estupido" is not a "real" proper name but a pejorative epithet used as if it were one. There are more serious differences, however. The Indian is not listed on the pay-sheets of the company building the road, or for that matter anywhere else. The name appears on no baptismal or electoral roll. So there is no possibility of tracing the individual the builders call Estupido by following up occurrences of tokens of the name, for the name is used neither sufficiently widely nor sufficiently systematically. Occurrences of its tokens cannot be used to track an individual because it is not connected to the Name-Tracking Network operated by the builders' society. And this means that reference to the Indian by means of the epithet "Estupido" cannot serve many of the functions that proper-name reference normally does serve. To know someone's name is normally to know "who that person is." That is because once one knows the circumstances of occurrence of one token of the name, it is possible to track the bearer through an indefinite series of other occurrences. And although this may not in the end be enough to locate him, because like Easthampton, or the *Galveston*, or some assistant to a Renaissance painter known to us only from a single reference in Vasari, he has passed untraceably from the world of men; nevertheless, very often it will be enough. In the case of the Indian known as Estupido, no one who knows him by that name knows, in the above sense, "who he is." For who is he? – he is just some Indian or other! Once he has vanished, it will be difficult even for the men who knew him, even if they encounter him again, to be sure that he is the same man. To them all forest Indians look rather alike, after all; and suppose he denies it, what then? If the Ecuadorians knew his real – that is, his Indian – name, and if they were in contact with his tribe, the Yanomamis, let's say, *then* they might be said, in virtue of knowing his name to know "who he was"; for *then* they might be in a position to track him by reference to occurrences of tokens of his name. But that is because *that* name would connect them to a different Name-Tracking Network, that is, the one operated by Yanomami society.

Of course, if the Indian were to join Ecuadorian society, and if a version of the name "Estupido" were thus to find its way into the fabric of institutions and customs that compose the Name-Tracking Network, then it would, if only gradually, become possible to track that individual by reference to occurrences of tokens of that name. So perhaps we could class "Estupido" as, if not a proper name in the full sense, at least as an embryonic proper name. But that thought, surely, throws a most un-Fregean and un-Russellian light on the question of what it is to possess a proper name. If what turns "Estupido" into a proper name in the full sense is not Estupido's having been pejoratively baptised with it by some jeering road-worker, but the assimilation of the name into the workings of some Name-Tracking Network, then what makes an expression into a proper name is not the (baptismal) relationship in which it stands to the individual who bears it, but its relation to one or another Name-Tracking Network, in this case either the Ecuadorian or the Yanomami one. It follows that until that assimilation has taken place, Estupido cannot properly be said to be the bearer of a proper name. But then it follows that to be a proper name bearer is to possess a certain, conventionally defined, *status.* The relation between the flesh-and-blood individual who enjoys the status of proper name bearer is exactly analogous to the relationship between the carved peg of boxwood and its status as a chess-King, or between Adam Weir and his status as laird of Hermiston. So, supposing the assimilation to have taken place, and supposing Estupido to have become Señor Raúl Esteban Estudo, the "pi" having been suppressed, naturally, during the rise of the family, what, in Fregean mode, are we to say that that name "picks out," or, in the second of our senses of "refer," "refers to?" What, just *qua* name, is it a name *of,* or *for?* We said that "Hermiston" is the name of a nomothetic entity, a lairdship, which an individual, Adam Weir, happens to possess. Why should we not say, for exactly parallel reasons, that "Raúl Esteban Estudo" picks out a nomothetic entity of the same general type, namely a *name-bearership,* which the flesh-and-blood Estupido has come to possess as a consequence of his assimilation into Ecuadorian society? But if what a proper name is a name of, is a *name-bearership,* then, because a name-bearership is plainly a nomothetic entity constituted in terms of the conventional systems that compose the Name-Tracking Network, it follows that a proper name is the name of a nomothetic entity. Of course, one can equally properly, and no less naturally, say that "Raúl Esteban Estudo" is the name of a certain Indian. But then one could with equal propriety say that "Hermiston" is the name of the Judge-Advocate. The question is *not* how it is most natural to put things but how it is most philosophically enlightening to put them. (One may agree with Russell, in short, that conformity with the locutionary patterns of "Ordinary Language," as it was once called, is not always or necessarily the surest route to understanding in philosophy.)

At one point in the *Philosophical Investigations*, Wittgenstein says, "When we say: 'Every word in language signifies something' we have so far said *nothing whatever*, unless we have explained exactly *what* distinction we wish to make."[9] We have found further reason to agree with this. If names, including ordinary proper names, signify conventionally constituted statuses enjoyed by the individuals to which we refer by means of them, then to say that a name "signifies something" is indeed to say nothing at all – until we distinguish between one type of status and another by saying something about how that particular kind of status is constituted. Thus, the string of examples we have just constructed invites distinctions between the kind of name that picks out a status defined relative to the Scots system of land tenure, one that picks out a status defined relative to one or another Name-Tracking Network, and one defined relative to the temporary, entirely *ad hoc*, but nevertheless conventionally established practices of a group of road-workers; there are, of course, many other such distinctions enshrined in language.

Clearly Wittgenstein was also right to say, in a passage mentioned earlier (n. 6), that one can only significantly ask a name if one "knows how to do something with it." Equally clearly, what one "knows how to do" with a name will differ from case to case. The "something" that one "knows how to do" with a title, such as "Hermiston" is not by any means the same as the "something" one "knows how to do" with an ordinary proper name such as "Adam Weir," or as the "something" one "knows how to do" with a pejorative epithet such as "Estupido" (the question "What do you call him?" need not have either the sense or the implications of "What is his name?").

At one stage, however, Wittgenstein develops this point in a way that may appear, at least in translation, to cede ground unnecessarily to the Russellian contention that a vocal noise can acquire the status of a name merely by being associated with an individual. Towards the end of §26 of Part I of the *Investigations*, we read:

To repeat – naming is something like attaching a label to a thing. One can say that this is preparatory to the use of a word. But *what* is it a preparation *for*?

Wittgenstein does not in fact use the normal German word for a label or tag, *Etikett*; he uses the curious expression *ein Namentäfelchen*. This could be translated, perhaps, "a little nameplate." One imagines a small ceramic or metal plate, with something written or inscribed on it, being solemnly tied to an object or person with a bit of string. In the light of that image, one could take Wittgenstein's point to be that until one knows what is to follow, what is to be done with the cipher on the nameplate, it is by no means clear that it *is* the written form of a name, or even that it is the written form of a word: perhaps it is just a series of squiggles. The translation "label," by contrast, suggests that Wittgenstein is thinking of the *Namentäfelchen* itself as a name. On that interpretation it would be reasonable to reply that, although it may not be settled what *sort* of name has been attached in attaching Wittgenstein's label, it seems evident enough that what has been attached is a *name*, and that calling that name a "label," although it may be a good instance of Wittgensteinian wordplay, alters nothing! One could dispute for some time, no doubt, which translation best captures Wittgenstein's intentions. What is clear, however, is that if the second interpretation is indeed what Wittgenstein had in mind, then at this point he gravely underestimated the potential force of his own arguments. For, to return to our string of examples, imagine someone, call him the Linguistic Ignoramus, who is familiar with no linguistic practice involving names. Not only is he unacquainted with such refinements as the system of territorial honorifics enshrined in traditional Scots discourse; he is unacquainted, also, not merely with the entire sheaf of practices composing the Name-Tracking Network, but even with the practice of using names to address particular individuals in issuing commands, commendations, and so on. Suppose, now, in the presence of the Linguistic Ignoramus, we extend an arm in the direction of another person and utter the phonemic string "Hermiston," or attach to him Wittgenstein's *Namentäfelchen* with its inscribed cipher. Have we by doing so, introduced the Ignoramus to the practice of naming things, establishing in his eyes the phonemic string or the inscribed cipher as *names?* What grounds have we for supposing anything of the sort? Will the Ignoramus be enabled by this pantomime to begin employing the cipher or the string as names? Clearly not: if he does not know antecedently what it is to employ a sound or a mark as a name, the pantomime will not help him. And suppose the Ignoramus learns to perform the pantomime himself, displaying the object and uttering the right phonemic string, or writing down the correct cipher? If he can do that much, and supposing that that is all he can do with the cipher or the phonemic string, are we to say that he understands them as *referring* to the individual, as a name refers to its bearer? For the *reference* of cipher and string was, after all, what the pantomime was supposed to teach him. Again, clearly not, for if that is all he can do with them, he has not begun to grasp what is involved in using words or written signs as names.

But more is at stake here. To set up in an organism the disposition to associate, as the Ignoramus *ex hypothesi* now does, a certain individual with a certain phonemic string or written cipher, is evidently to bring into being a natural, causal relationship of a certain, broadly behavioural, type. If the bringing into being of such a relationship could be identified with the dawning in the mind of the Ignoramus of the concept of reference, then reference would itself be a natural, causal relationship. But such an identification would, as we have seen, be absurd. Reference so envisaged becomes an occult or magical relationship, utterly devoid of explanatory force, and the pantomime that supposedly establishes it a mere obfuscatory waving of hands; a hocus-pocus. The relationship between a name and the individual who bears it thus cannot be a natural or causal one, but must be a "logical" or nomothetic one running by way of that individual's enjoyment of a nomothetic status defined in terms of a wide variety of practices, which in their turn enmesh with reality in a wide variety of ways. The error of the Orthodox View of reference is to misrepresent what is, in fact, a complex diversity of essentially nomothetic relationships in terms of a single, natural, relationship conceived as linking each and every name in the same sort of way to a corresponding individual. The heart of that error consists in not seeing that it is only against the background of a web of nomothetic relationships and the practices that give rise to them, practices from whose existence and importance the Orthodox View systematically distracts our attention, that we can retain any grip on the concepts of a name and of reference, which in abstraction from that background of complex practices simply collapse into vacuity. Here again, Wittgenstein's Slogan, *Die Logik muss für sich selber sorgen*, turns out to point in the right direction.

x. Odysseus and Bunbury

In Chapter 4 §i, we encountered Frege's dictum that a statement containing a name for a fictional character, such as "Odysseus was set ashore at Ithaca while fast asleep," in view of the fact that in the real world there is not and never was such a person as Odysseus, cannot be said to be either true or false. This claim is of more than merely logical interest. For one thing, Frege's dictum, if correct, deprives virtually all literary criticism of serious intellectual content. Suppose, for example, that a critic wishes to advance the view that the Nora Helmer who appears in the first two acts and most of the third act of *A Doll's House* could not have made the ringing defence of the absolute moral primacy of personal self-discovery that Ibsen puts into her mouth in the final ten minutes of the play. As critical claims go, this is a fairly plausibly arguable one, and one that one might easily be persuaded to accept as true. If Frege is right, however, one would be *logically* astray in permitting oneself to be persuaded to accept any such thing. For if Frege is right, a sentence such as "Nora Helmer is inconsistently represented in *A Dolls' House*" cannot be true, or for that matter false either, as the name "Nora Helmer" lacks a bearer. And, although this argument is not likely to impress readers of either criticism or serious literature with its force, to more innocent minds it does have some real power to suggest that neither serious literature nor criticism can really be worth much effort or attention. For it suggests that such activities have nothing to do with truth, but only, as Frege puts it, with "euphony" and with "images and feelings" aroused merely by the "senses" of "sentences" considered without regard to their truth or falsity, and so *in abstracto* from anything that might be asserted or denied by them.

The line of argument we have been pursuing suggests, however, that Frege was simply wrong. On the view we have been developing, what makes it possible to refer by means of a name is not the ability to locate, or produce its bearer but, rather, the knowledge that the name is currently involved in, or possesses a use$_E$ with respect to, some Name-Tracking Network or other. And that is certainly the case with "Odysseus." From a hundred sources, someone who becomes acquainted with the name "Odysseus" by hearing Frege's remark can discover that Odysseus is the chief character in *The Odyssey*. And a brief glance at Book XIII will reveal to him that what the remark asserts is true: Odysseus was indeed sleeping when he was set ashore at Ithaca by the Phaeacians. So it is not the case, after all, either that "Odysseus" lacks a bearer or that no truth-value can be ascribed to a remark about Odysseus, let alone that no such remark expresses an assertoric content, or Thought. It is simply that the Name-Tracking Network in the context of which Odysseus finds a use$_E$ is the one that tracks fictional characters.

J. L. Austin remarks somewhere that to make an important philosophical error, an error of the first water, requires a kind of genius. Frege's error is an error of that kind. It is a response, and by no means an indefensible one, to the threat of Idealism posed by prison-house scepticism. Frege, like Russell, wished to show how the mind could avoid being shut off from contact with reality by the very language in terms of which the investigation of reality must proceed. His solution, like Russell's, was on one level to identify the meanings of proper names with the very individuals to which we refer by means of those names, and to construe the relationship linking name and individual as a natural relationship, itself a constituent of the real, in the sense of extralinguistic, world. That solution, in association with other Fregean doctrines, makes the ascription of truth and falsity themselves depend on relationships between the linguistic and the extralinguistic. Neither, therefore, can characterise sentences concerning entities, such as Odysseus, which manifestly possess no existence external to language. The answer to this line of argument, if we have argued correctly here, is that, by looking fixedly in the wrong place in its attempts to grasp the nature of the intercourse between language and reality, it misrepresents both the *location* and the *nature* of that intercourse. By recognising that language meshes with reality not at the level of a uniform notion of reference, but at the level of the underlying practices in terms of which a wide variety of types of reference need to be distinguished, one frees oneself to treat both reference and truth (as we shall see in more detail later) as purely logical notions, available just as validly to the literary critic as to the scientist or philosopher.

To see reference as a logical relation, in the sense proposed here, is to see also why, as we noted in Chapter 4 §§ii–iii, it is possible more or less indefinitely, even in the case of a fictional name such as "Bunbury," to supplement one verbal explication of the reference of such a name with others, without ever having to justify one's claim to be genuinely referring by means of the name by actually producing or locating a living or dead person as its bearer. The reason is that it does not matter, from the point of view of justifying the claim to refer by means of a proper name, whether or not it has, or ever had, a solid, flesh-and-blood bearer. All that is required is that the name be genuinely in use$_E$; be genuinely one of the names tracked by the Name-Tracking Network. And "Bunbury," in *The Importance of Being Earnest*, is such a name. It matters not a jot that the truth about Bunbury is that he is a fictional character invented by Algernon Moncrieff, and deployed by him in little fictions served up by him as truths to inconvenient would-be hostesses. For some names do just refer to fictional characters. Where is the problem supposed to lie?

But aren't we coming close to saying that there is no such thing as an "empty" proper name? It is, of course, possible to imagine circumstances in which a proper name could be said to be "empty," but such circumstances are much odder than any envisaged by Frege or Russell. One could, for example, go into one of those country churches that display visitors' books beside the postcards and religious tracts, and sign the book with a name invented on the spur of the moment: "Chester B. Zapotinsky, Syracuse NY." But why would anyone do such a thing? And what effect would it have, except perhaps to minutely deform the statistics concerning tourist visits to churches? In any case, what makes the name of Zapotinsky empty is not that Zapotinsky is a fictional character, but that the name is unconnected with any Name-Tracking-Network. That disconnection would equally have been achieved if one had written not "Zapotinsky" but the name of some actual (or "real") fictional character, "Miss Elizabeth Bennett," given that, as all the "real" Miss Bennett's acts must be contained within the covers of *Pride and Prejudice,* the person who signed the visitors' book in that name could not "really" have been her. Either way it is the failure of name-tracking that counts, not the actual or putative absence of a real-world bearer.

xi. Postscript on Russell and Strawson

It may be worth noting some similarities, and also some divergences, between the views defended here and those advanced by Sir Peter Strawson in a celebrated article, "On Referring," attacking Russell's Theory of Descriptions.

Russell's theory famously analyses "The present King of France is bald" as equivalent to the claim that at least one, and only one, thing exists which is both King of France and bald. Strawson accuses Russell of a failure to distinguish between (i) a sentence, (ii) a use of a sentence (e.g., to make an assertion), and (iii) an utterance of a sentence. He argues that the notions of truth and reference are at home only when speaking of some use to which a sentence is put by some utterance of it. Thus, "The present King of France is bald" may be used to make a true assertion at various times prior to 1789, and on those occasions may have a clear reference. Sentences considered in themselves, by contrast, possess no truth-values, nor do referring expressions considered just in themselves, independently of any use, refer, although both may possess meaning, or sense. Russell was thus mistaken, in Strawson's view, to suppose that "The present king of France is bald" is *equivalent in meaning* to any existential statement. The existential claims that Russell wrongly builds into the meaning of "The King of France is bald" are in fact presuppositions of the successful use of the sentence to refer.

The view we have been elaborating here plainly does incorporate certain Strawsonian elements. Our distinction between two uses of "refer" in part echoes Strawson's treatment of reference as a speech-act. Like Strawson, also, we are sceptical of the claim that names or other referring expressions can be said to refer independently of their use. But our use of "use" here differs from Strawson's. For Strawson, the use of an expression is its employment on a definite occasion to perform some speech act. Strawson's paper lies, indeed, somewhere near the inception of the tradition in the philosophy of language, including Austin, Grice, Searle, Jonathan Bennett, Alston, and others, whose goal is the elucidation of the concept of meaning in terms of the notions of intention and "speaker's meaning." That use of "use" has on the whole tended to lead philosophers away from Wittgenstein's use of "use." Our use of "use," in the two senses defined in Chapter 3 §ii, is, we are inclined to think, closer to Wittgenstein's intentions than Strawson's.

In another and deeper respect, also, the argument we have been developing here pursues a different line of criticism of Russell from Strawson's. Strawson, however much he may disagree with Russell concerning the status, as presuppositions of reference or constituents of meaning, of the existential claims that figure in the Theory of Descriptions, in effect agrees with Russell that the possibility of using a designating expression of any kind to refer arises only if certain connected existential propositions come out true. We have been attempting to demonstrate the contrary: that the issue of whether a designating expression has a reference, like the issue of whether a proposition has a sense, must be determined before it is known whether *any proposition whatsoever* comes out true, because only when such matters are decided will it be possible to use a string of words to make an assertion: to say something for which the possibility of truth or falsity arises: that is to say, can intelligibly be entertained.

6

Rigidity

i. From Mill to Kripke

So far we have presented the argument as an attack on the Orthodox View defined in Chapter 5 ii. The Orthodox View, which at any rate until quite recently deserved the name, was there defined as a compendium of three doctrines: (1) the doctrine that the meaning, or *Bedeutung*, of a proper name is the individual it picks out; (2) the doctrine that a speaker can attach no assertoric content to an indicative sentence employing a proper name N unless he or she knows which individual N does, in fact, pick out; (3) the doctrine that what places a speaker in a position to meet the condition spelled out by (2) is the possession of an identifying description of the individual in question. That collection of doctrines would, no doubt, fairly adequately capture the content of philosophical orthodoxy between 1930 and 1970. It does not, however, at least in its entirety, capture the views of a majority of philosophers at present. Doctrines (1) and (2) are still widely held. What has changed is that there is now widespread scepticism concerning doctrine (3).

In order to simplify the exposition of our argument in its early stages, our account has so far ignored the inherent tension between doctrine (1) and doctrine (3). Doctrine (1) contends that the meaning of a proper name "N" is its bearer, N. But if that is so, how can knowing the meaning of a proper name amount to knowing some predicate P which N happens to satisfy, as doctrine (3) contends? Under other circumstances P might cease to characterise N, or never have characterised it. And then "N," with the issue of its applicability or nonapplicability to a given individual tied, logically, to the satisfaction or nonsatisfaction by that individual of P, would no longer "mean" N, no longer have N as its *Bedeutung*, although it might "mean" some other individual altogether. Interposing a predicate between a name and its referent, in other words, appears to introduce the possibility that a mere change in natural circumstances might suffice to tear name and referent asunder. It is worth noticing that such a possibility is in conflict with Wittgenstein's Slogan. "Logic" can be said to "look after itself" only when "logical" questions, including questions of the reference of terms, can be seen to settle themselves independently of any question of how things stand, contingently speaking, in the world, and so of any change in what is found, empirically, to be the case.

The possibility of a name's shifting its reference as a result of a change in the circumstances of its bearer was famously raised, and discounted, by John Stuart Mill in the *System of Logic*. Mill concludes that no predicate can form any part of the meaning of a proper name.

Proper names are not connotative: they denote the individuals who are called by them; but they do not indicate or imply any attributes as belonging to those individuals. When we name a child by the name of Paul, or a dog by the name of Caesar, these names are simply marks used to enable those individuals to be made subjects of discourse. It may be said, indeed, that we must have had some reason for giving them those names rather than any others; and this is true; but the name, once given, is independent of the reason. A man may have been named John, because that was the name of his father; a town may have been named Dartmouth, because it is situated at the mouth of the Dart. But it is no part of the signification of the word John, that the father of the person so-called bore the same name; nor even of the word Dartmouth, to be situated at the mouth of the Dart. If sand should choke up the mouth of the river, or an earthquake change its course, and remove it to a distance from the town, the name of the town would not necessarily be changed. That fact, therefore, can form no part of the signification of the word; for otherwise, when the fact confessedly ceased to be true, no one would any longer think of applying the name. Proper names are attached to the objects themselves, and are not dependent on the continuance of any attribute of the object.[1]

The current lapse from popularity of the Description Theory dates from the revival in the 1970s by Saul Kripke, of this forgotten argument in a new and widely persuasive form involving the fashionable notion of a Possible World. Closely related arguments were advanced around the same time by Hilary Putnam, but as these mainly concern names of kinds, we shall defer discussion of them to Part III.

Kripke's way of developing Mill's point introduces the notion of a *rigid designator*. That idea in turn invokes the notion of a *possible world*. Kripke is at pains, in the transcript of his 1970 lectures, and more especially in the preface that accompanied their publication as a book in 1980,[2] to distance himself from the idea that a possible world should be thought of as any sort of additional department of reality, "something like distant planets, like our own surroundings but somehow existing in a different dimension . . ."[3] He suggests that the terminology of "worlds" that perhaps prompts these misunderstandings might usefully be replaced with " 'possible state (or history) of the world', or 'counterfactual situation.' "[4] He illustrates his use of the term with the example of the thirty-six possible states of a pair of dice. "The thirty-six possible states of the dice are literally thirty-six 'possible worlds,' as long as we (fictively) ignore everything about the world except the two dice and what they show (and ignore the fact that one or both dice might not have existed)."[5]

A (counterfactual) possible world, then, is, for Kripke, just the world as it might be, or might have been, if matters that might in principle go or have gone otherwise than they do, or did, were in fact to go, or have gone, otherwise. Aristotle, for instance, might not have studied with Plato, or not for very long. Repelled by the doctrines and discipline of the Academy, he might have fallen out of love with philosophy altogether, and taken up trading in oil. Such an Aristotle, driven before the winds of commercial success, might have left Athens not for Macedon but for Syracuse, to embark there on a life that, although marked by the innocence associated by Johnson with the making of money, left no trace on subsequent history. At the same time a quite different man, also by a curious chance named "Aristotle," might have entered the Academy, becoming in time Plato's greatest pupil, and elaborating in the course of time, by an even more curious chance, exactly those doctrines that we have come to regard as characteristic of "our" Aristotle.

Now consider the name "Aristotle," as we use it, and the description,

(D₁) the greatest of Plato's pupils.

(D₁) in our world characterises Aristotle. In the alternative possible world that we have just described, it does not. On the contrary, it characterises the man who replaced Aristotle in Plato's favour after the latter decamped, first to his oil-amphorae and then to Syracuse. "Aristotle," by contrast, at least according to the powerful intuition that Kripke shares with Mill, cannot be made to shift its reference by any such trifling with counterfactual possibilities. The name "Aristotle," picking out as it does a certain man in our world, picks out *that very man* in any possible world in which he figures. So in the possible world we just sketched, "Aristotle" picks out the oil-merchant, not the philosopher, for in that world it was *Aristotle* who became that oil-merchant; the philosopher was somebody else.

In Kripke's terminology, the name "Aristotle" *designates rigidly* or is a *rigid designator*. The description "the greatest of Plato's pupils" *designates nonrigidly*, or is a *nonrigid designator*. As Kripke puts it, "Let's call something a *rigid designator* if in every world it designates the same object, a *nonrigid* or *accidental designator* if that is not the case." Plainly, now the argument that shows "Aristotle" to be a rigid designator and (D₁) to be a nonrigid one can be duplicated for any proper name and any description. Proper names in general designate rigidly, descriptions in general designate nonrigidly. So the third component of the Orthodox View must be wrong. Understanding the meaning of a proper name can't be a matter of possessing access to an identifying description, because no description can be any part of the *meaning* of a proper name.

ii. Rigid designation and nominal description

In Chapter 5, we developed a line of attack upon the Orthodox View *in toto*: an attack, that is, which bore simultaneously on all three of its component doctrines, and not merely on the third. The opening move in the argument, from which the whole ensuing strategy of attack developed, was the suggestion (Chapter 5 §ii) that the ability to refer by means of a proper name might not require access to an actual description, but might be conferred by access to a merely nominal one. It will be a contention of this book that Mill and Kripke are correct, as against Russell, Frege, Searle, and other supporters of the Description Theory: proper names *are* rigid designators. That being so, it might be thought odd, to say the least, that we have chosen to rest so much weight on the thought that the ability to refer by means of a proper name may be conferred by access to a nominal description. For isn't that just a further version of the Description Theory? Take, for example, our war-horse example,

> (D_2) The Charles Morgan John referred to yesterday at the Board Meeting.

Granted that (D_2) is satisfied by a given man in this world, what is to prevent its being satisfied, in another possible world, by a different individual of the same name? (D_2) is no more a rigid designator, in other words, than a description of any other type. So how can it, any more than any other description, of whatever logical type, form any part of the meaning of a proper name?[6]

iii. Accounting for rigidity

We need to look more closely at the expression, "the meaning of a proper name." That expression comes heavily laden with Fregean associations. On the question of what it might come to for a proper name to possess a meaning, current discussion perceives two options, and two only, both Fregean in provenance. Either the meaning of a proper name is to be identified with the individual picked out by that name, or else the meaning of a name is some mental content to which a speaker has access, a description or something very like it, which performs the task of identifying the individual in question, or as current parlance has it, "fixing the reference" of the name.

Let us, for the moment, leave on one side Kripke's arguments concerning the status of names as rigid designators. Let us go back a step, and ask what led philosophers to suppose, in the first place, that the task of fixing the reference of a name *could* be performed by a uniquely identifying definite description?

To this question, two quite distinct answers appear to be possible. On the one hand, a uniquely identifying description might be thought to identify the unique individual which *satisfies* the description. The notion of *satisfaction* intended here is not the technical one made familiar by Tarski and Davidson, according to which satisfiers are functions,[7] but the commonplace, everyday usage according to which the police, for instance, speak of a wanted man as "satisfying" some description held in their records. Just as in the Davidsonian usage, however, there is a link between satisfaction and truth. A putatively identifying description is *satisfied by* the individual of which the characterisation offered by the description *is true*. Accordingly, we shall say that the description "the tallest man" is *satisfied by* the tallest man; that the description "the Charles Morgan John referred to yesterday at the Board Meeting" is *satisfied by that* particular Charles Morgan, and so on. To sum up, the explanation offered, in terms of the notion of satisfaction, to the question how a description can identify the referent of a name, is that the individual in question is identified as the one of which the description *is true*.

On the other hand, a description might be supposed to fix the reference of a proper name by serving as the means, at least in principle, of *singling out*, or *locating*, the individual in question. The thought is that by following out the terms of the description one will actually be *led to*, be put in a position, as it were, to *place one's hand on*, the individual in question. Thus, for example, the description "the tallest man" might be thought to identify a particular individual by identifying a procedure, measuring heights, which would, if carried out accurately and with sufficient assiduity, result in the unmasking of that very individual. In Dummett's example of Easthampton (Chapter 5 §iv), again, an identifying description of Easthampton might be – indeed, would have to be, according to Dummett – one that told one *how to get to the town*.

A description may identify an individual, in short, either *as the individual that satisfies it*, or as *the individual that it singles out, or locates*. One reason why these two possibilities are seldom distinguished is, no doubt, that in the case of actual descriptions (Chapter 5 §ii) they are scarcely distinct. In the case of an actual description D_A, the characteristic in virtue of which an individual I satisfies D_A is the very characteristic by reference to which I may be singled out. The tallest man, for instance, satisfies the description "the tallest man" in virtue of the very characteristic that allows us, at least in principle, to single him out from other men. It is in virtue of being the red-headed woman in the corner with a pint of Guinness that that particular woman both satisfies and is singled out by the description, "the red-headed woman in the corner with a pint of Guinness"; and so on.

In the case of nominal descriptions, however, satisfaction and singling-out part company. Consider again,

(D_2) The "Charles Morgan" John referred to yesterday at the Board Meeting.

Trivially, (D_2) is satisfied in our world by a certain individual I_W, namely, the Charles Morgan referred to by John at yesterday's Board Meeting. But can that individual be said to be, in any plausible sense, *singled out* by (D_2)? Plainly not. To know merely that John mentioned some individual or other at the Board Meeting yesterday, and that I_W is that individual, is to know, so far, nothing that might assist in singling out I_W. After all, John might have mentioned just anybody at all. Who is to say who that mysterious individual might have been? Not us, clearly – unless we can learn something further about *him*, rather than about John and his mentionings.

The only further information about I_W offered by (D_2) is his name: I_W is called "Charles Morgan." This will in most cases allow us to make a start on the project of singling out I_W. But it allows us to do that only because of two things. The first is the knowledge we possess, from (D_2), of the circumstances of occurrence of a token of the name. The second is the existence of the web of practices making up the Name-Tracking Network. The natural next move in singling out that particular "Charles Morgan" referred to by John would, that is, be to look up the minutes of the Board Meeting to discover the circumstances in which Morgan's name came up.

Leafing through the files of relevant correspondence might well disclose a telephone number or an address, from which point it would be a short step to contacting Morgan in person. But these ways of proceeding, on the basis of the bare knowledge of a name-token and its circumstances of occurrence, are manifestly only possible because of the rigid maintenance in practical life of certain utterly familiar and banal conventions surrounding the use of proper names: the convention that the name that appears in a letter after the conventional valedictory phrases is that of the signatory, the convention of putting the address and telephone number of the signatory at the head of the letter, the care taken by telephone companies and compilers of directories to keep names correctly matched to titles, addresses, telephone numbers, the correct maintenance of registers of births, marriages and deaths, and so on.

In short, when we are, as we customarily are, able to single out an individual on the basis of a nominal description, it is not *the description itself* that does the work of singling out that individual. That work is done by the Name-Tracking Network.

The role played by nominal descriptions in the structure of the present account is thus rather different from that played by actual descriptions in the structure of the Orthodox View. According to the Orthodox View, the (actual) description generally associated with a name is what *singles out*, as *satisfying it*, the bearer of the name. According to the present view, there *is* no single (nominal) description *generally* or *characteristically* associated with a name. Reference by means of a given name may be sustained, from one occasion to another, by indefinitely many nominal descriptions, depending on the circumstances of the conversation in which the name comes up. None of these descriptions, moreover, single out the bearer of the name as *the individual satisfying the description in question*. When a speaker refers to "the 'Charles Morgan' John referred to at the Board Meeting yesterday," he does not, plainly, mean to refer to *whatever individual might, from time to time, satisfy that description*. He intends, that is, to refer to *a single individual,* not to a (rather strangely specified) *class of individuals*. The individual he intends to refer to is *whichever individual the Charles Morgan referred to by John at the Board Meeting yesterday turns out to be*. And (our suggestion is that) "turns out to be" in this context is to be roughly paraphrased as "would be singled out by the Name-Tracking Network as the bearer of that name."

It is thus true, but beside the point, that a nominal description might, in another possible world W_2, be satisfied by a different individual. If the individual picked out via a nominal description were picked out *as satisfying that description*, then, indeed, a different individual would be picked out in W_2. But that is not how nominal descriptions work. Such a description merely serves to connect speakers, via the circumstances of use of a token of a name, to appropriate parts of the Name-Tracking Network, which in turn matches the name to a bearer.

It does so because the whole purpose of the multitude of conventions and practices that make up the Name-Tracking Network is to establish and maintain a one-to-one correspondence between names and individuals. And because it achieves that end through the medium of a publicly instituted and maintained system of practices, *which* individual it locates is entirely independent of any belief or characterisation entertained regarding that individual by any individual speaker.

So when, in possible world W_1, S refers to "the 'Charles Morgan' John mentioned at the Board meeting yesterday," the Charles Morgan he refers to is the Charles Morgan picked out by the Name-Tracking Network *in W_1*. It follows that when, by envisaging some counterfactual contingency, as that Morgan under other circumstances might not have proved so ready to accede to the Chairman's request to reschedule a loan, S speculates on the acts of Morgan in another possible world W_2, it is on the counterfactually posited acts of *that very Morgan* (i.e., whatever individual is picked out as corresponding to that name by the Name-Tracking Network of W_1) that he speculates. S is able to refer in this way, by means of a given nominal description, to one and the same individual "across possible worlds," because the Morgan to whom he refers is not an individual singled out via some characterisation, which might in W_2 have been otherwise satisfied, built into the description under which X refers to him. The individual to whom X refers is not singled out *via* a *characterisation* – by the *content* of some description he satisfies – at all, but via the Name-Tracking Network.

7

Descriptions and Causes

i. The causal theory

Whether or not one is persuaded by the account of rigidity offered in the preceding chapter, some answer is clearly needed to the question how it can be *possible* for a speaker to refer rigidly by means of a name; that is, to refer to the same individual "across possible worlds."

The answer that has received most attention so far is the one tentatively advanced by Kripke in *Naming and Necessity* in terms of what he there calls "chains of communication," but now generally known as the Causal Theory of Names. Here is Kripke's account of the theory:

Someone, let's say, a baby, is born; his parents call him by a certain name. They talk about him to their friends. Other people meet him. Through various sorts of talk the name is spread from link to link as if by a chain. A speaker who is at the far end of the chain, who has heard about, say, Richard Feynman, in the market place or elsewhere, may be referring to Richard Feynman even though he can't remember from whom he first heard of Feynman or from whom he ever heard of Feynman. He knows that Feynman was a famous physicist. A certain passage of communication reaching ultimately to the man himself does reach the speaker. He then is referring to Feynman even though he can't identify him uniquely. He doesn't know what a Feynman diagram is, he doesn't know what the Feynman theory of pair production and annihilation is. Not only that: he'd have trouble distinguishing between Gell-Mann and Feynman. So he doesn't have to know these things, but, instead, a chain of communication going back to Feynman himself has been established by virtue of his membership in a community which passed the name on from link to link, not by a ceremony that he makes in private in his study: "By 'Feynman' I shall mean the man who did such and such and such and such."[1]

This suggestion works in much the same way as the one presented in Chapter 6. In place of a linkage between the speaker and designated individual mediated by way of the "fit" between the individual and the content of a description known to the speaker, it postulates a linkage set up externally to the speaker's mind. The process of singling out the designated individual is thus divested of any dependence on the beliefs and intentions of the speaker concerning the designated individual. It makes no difference what he believes about Feynman or to whom he supposes himself, on the basis of his beliefs, to be referring under that name. If the chain of causally linked uses, which at one end terminates in his use of the name "Feynman" on a given occasion, terminates at its other end in Feynman's baptism, then it is Feynman he is referring to, and that is the end of the matter. Of course, in another possible world, one or more of those unfunnily humorous slips by nineteenth-century immigration officers that, in Georges Perec's *La Vie Mode d'Emploi*, explain the curious surname of Bartlebooth's valet Smautf, might have led to Feynman's being named something else, Freeman or Finnegan maybe. And in that world there might be a different physicist named "Feynman." But that makes no difference, because it is not under the description "Physicist called Feynman" that Feynman is singled out in this world. What singles him out is just the name, taken together with the causal links connecting its successive uses. In the same sort of way the explanation offered in Chapter 6 discounts both the beliefs, if any, that speakers may entertain concerning Charles Morgan, and any consequent intentions-to-refer founded on such beliefs. Who a speaker is referring to by that name is a matter of who the Name-Tracking Network singles out as its bearer. And the Name-Tracking Network operates just as independently of speakers' beliefs and intentions as Kripke's causal chains of communication. In either case, speakers can envisage a world in which they might be required to entertain *quite different beliefs from those they presently entertain* concerning a named individual N – and that, after all, is all that talk of possible worlds comes to for the purposes of the present argument – because none of the beliefs, if any, which they presently entertain concerning N play any part in singling N out for purposes of reference.

ii. Evans's critique of the causal theory

It has been argued, most notably by Gareth Evans in a frequently cited paper,[2] that no theory which prescinds as completely from speakers' beliefs and intentions as the Causal Theory does, can possibly be correct. Evans rightly distinguishes, as Kripke does not, between two "related but distinguishable questions concerning proper names."[3] The first is the question of "what the name denotes upon a given occasion of use when this is understood as being partly determinative of what the speaker strictly and literally said." Evans introduces "the faintly barbarous coinage: *what the speaker denotes* (upon an occasion) for this notion." The second is the question what a name denotes, or as Evans puts it, "What conditions have to be satisfied by an expression and an item for the first to be a name of the second."

One way of taking the Causal Theory, then, will be as an attempt to state conditions for determining what, on a given occasion, a speaker denotes. Here, up to a point, the Causal Theory works better than the Description Theory; but only up to a point. Suppose somebody, S, hears the name "Louis" used in conversation, and asks "So what did Louis do then?"

There seems to be no question but that S denotes a particular man and asks about him. Or on some subsequent occasion S may use the name to offer some new thought to one of the participants: "Louis was quite right to do that." Again he clearly denotes whoever was the subject of conversation in the pub. This is difficult to reconcile with the Description Theory, since the scraps of information which he picked up during the conversation might involve some distortion and fit someone else much better. Of course he has the description "the man they were talking about," but the theory has no explanation for the impossibility of its being outweighed.[4]

So the Causal Theory gives the right answer in this case. But it has the unfortunate consequence that

at any future time, no matter how remote or forgotten the conversation, no matter how alien the subject matter and confused the speaker, S will denote one particular Frenchman – perhaps Louis XIII – so long as there is a causal connection between his use at the time and the long distant conversation.[5]

Plenty in S's rambling discourse, in other words, might lead us to conclude that although he *means* to refer to the Louis referred to in the pub conversation, he can't intend to refer to *that* Louis; not, that is, to Louis XIII. But, on Kripke's view, provided his use of the word is causally connected back to that conversation, then, because causality trumps belief and intention in these matters, it is *indeed* Louis XIII that he is referring to.

What about the Causal Theory as an account of what it is for an expression to be the name of an item? Here Evans's main argument is that the theory leaves us with no means of accommodating change of denotation. "Madagascar," it seems, is a corrupt form of an African name for part of the mainland, transferred to the island as a result of a misunderstanding by Marco Polo of hearsay reports of Malay or Arab sailors. Are we therefore to suppose, because a causal chain of the type Kripke proposes connects the name with the mainland region it was originally used to designate, that present speakers are deluded in supposing that by "Madagascar" they mean the island and willy-nilly designate by that name some region unknown to them?

A further counterexample of Evans's raises difficulties for Kripke on both fronts. Suppose one inhabitant of a village refers to the little daughter of some holidaymakers as "Goldilocks," and this name becomes current. But now suppose that the little girl is one of a pair of identical twins between whom the villagers, while the holiday-making family remains in the village, altogether fail to distinguish. No doubt there is a causal connection between

present uses and whichever twin gave rise to the original use. But despite
that there seem good *prima facie* grounds to deny that "Goldilocks" is the
name of either child.[6] The existence of the causal connection is insufficient
in itself, that is, to justify us in saying either that the expression is the name
of an item, or that users of the name denote any specific individual by means
of it.

iii. Evans's account

Evans himself offers a sketch of considerable interest designed to accommodate the best aspects of both Causal and Description theories. It might
be termed the *Dominant Cluster Theory.* Evans takes it as truistic that when
speakers refer to an item N they commonly know or believe that there is
such an item in the world, and intend to refer to it. Commonly also there
will be a "cluster or dossier" of information the possession of which by the
speaker "makes it true that he knows of the existence of the item."[7]

Evans's suggestion is that the item that the speaker denotes by "N" is not
the *satisfier* of that dossier of information but, rather, the item that is *causally
responsible* for the speaker's possession of the information in the dossier, or,
if more than one item is responsible, the item that is *dominantly* responsible:
that is, responsible for the *dominant cluster* of information in the dossier.

So much for the conditions which determine "*what the speaker denotes*
(upon an occasion)." What about "what a name denotes," or as Evans expli-
cates that phrase, "what conditions have to be satisfied by an expression and
an item for the first to be a name of the second?" Evans takes the second
set of conditions to be definable in terms of the first set. He thinks, in other
words, that of the two concepts *speaker's denotation in use* and *the denotation
of a name,* the former is logically prior, in the sense that it does most of the
work in explicating the latter, and not vice versa.

Here is Evans's stab at formulating the second set:

"NN" is a name of *x* if there is a community *C*
1. in which it is common knowledge that members of *C* have in their repertoire the
   procedure of using "NN" to refer to *x* (with the intention of referring to *x*)
2. the success in reference in any particular case being intended to rely on common
   knowledge between speaker and hearer that "NN" has been used to refer to *x* by
   members of *C* and not upon common knowledge of the satisfaction by *x* of some
   predicate embedded in "NN."[8]

The crucial notion at work in these definitions is clearly that of causal dominance. Evans gives several examples to indicate how it might work out in
practice, two of which will suffice to indicate the thrust of his thinking on
this point.

Suppose I get to know a man slightly. Suppose then a suitably primed identical twin
takes over his position, and I get to know him fairly well, not noticing the switch.

Immediately after the switch my dossier will still be dominantly of the original man, and I falsely believe, as I would acknowledge if it was pointed out, that *he* is in the room. Then I would pass through a period in which neither was dominant; I had not misidentified one as the other, an asymmetrical relation, but rather confused them. Finally the twin could take over the dominant position; I would not have false beliefs about who is in the room, but false beliefs about, e.g., when I first met the man in the room.[9]

Again, suppose an urn is discovered near the Dead Sea containing papyri inscribed with fascinating mathematical proofs. The sheets are signed "Ibn Khan," and mathematicians come to speak of "Khan's conjecture," and so on. However, Ibn Khan was in fact the scribe who transcribed the proofs: "a small '*id scripsit*'" has been obliterated. Causally speaking, then, "Ibn Khan" is the name of the scribe. On the Dominant Cluster Theory, by contrast, the author of the proofs is the item causally responsible for the dominant cluster of information possessed by scholars regarding the individual they call Ibn Khan. So "Ibn Khan" denotes the author of the proofs.

iv. The Name-Tracking Network versus the Dominant Cluster Theory

Let us assume, for the sake of argument, that Evans's objections to the Causal Theory are conclusive. Earlier, in Chapter 7 §i, we suggested that the theory elaborated in Chapters 5 and 6 functions, so far as the account it offers of rigid designation is concerned, in much the same sort of way as the Causal Theory. Does it follow that it is open to the same objections?

Let us begin with change of denotation. The view we have presented here is that an expression is the name of an item just in case it happens to be the label under which the various practices that go to make up the Name-Tracking Network keep track of that item. The issue of how, causally and historically speaking, a given expression came to serve in that role is irrelevant. So the history of the name "Madagascar" need not be supposed to have any bearing on the present denotation of the name. The same goes for Ibn Khan's proofs. What is crucial in determining which individual the name picks out is that, whatever may have been the name or names by which the author of the proofs may have been known in his own time, and whoever may, at that time, have borne the name "Ibn Khan," "Ibn Khan" is the name under which *our* Name-Tracking Network keeps track of the author of the proofs. Indeed, even if new discoveries of papyri were to reveal new information about him, including his name, reports of the discovery would undoubtedly be headed "New Light on Ibn Khan." Nor, most probably, would the name "Ibn Khan," be dropped, because it would already be recorded in too many parts of the Network for that to be a useful way of proceeding. It would simply be cross-referenced to the original name in the more scholarly sorts of study: "Ibn Khan (Ghazal al-Waziri, 732–c. 800)," or something of the sort.

So far, then, our account seems to elude at least some of Evans's more telling objections to the Causal Theory (we will examine why in a moment). Are there, however, any grounds for choosing our account over the Dominant Cluster Theory as an alternative to the Causal Theory? There are certainly cases in which the two accounts prompt different intuitive responses to specific cases. Take, for example, Evans's "Louis" example. Evans's contention is that a mere causal link between the use of the name in the original pub conversation and some remotely subsequent use of the name by S can't necessitate the conclusion that, on that occasion, the name in S's mouth denotes the person, say Louis XIII of France, it denoted in the conversation. And that seems clearly right. But when it comes to specifying what conditions would have to be met for S still to be referring to Louis XIII, those offered by the Dominant Cluster Theory seem far too strong. S is going to have to know or believe that an item corresponding to the name exists in the world, and to intend to refer to it; and he is going to have to possess a dossier of information that makes it true that he does know (and not just believe?) that; and that item is going to have to be what accounts causally for the presence in the dossier of the dominant cluster of information it contains. This, surely, is asking a lot. When S, a friend of Algernon Moncrieff's, says, "Bunbury? I believe he's some pal of young Moncrieff's – lives in the country – bit of a creaking door, I believe – anyway Moncrieff is always off down there to sit by his bedside," it can hardly be said that he possesses a dossier of information about Bunbury – as distinct from one about the details of Algernon's tall tales – and certainly not that Bunbury is the ultimate causal origin of any of this "information." Very possibly, knowing what he knows about Moncrieff, S does not even seriously suppose that there is any such person as Bunbury. And yet there is a perfectly good sense in which (a) he has told an enquirer perfectly truthfully who people are referring to when they speak of Bunbury, and (b) in so doing, referred to Bunbury himself. This state of affairs is inexplicable in terms of the Dominant Cluster Theory, but entirely explicable in terms of the account defended here. On our account, all that is necessary for a speaker to be in a position to refer by means of a name is that he have in his possession some account of the circumstances of use of a token of the name that connects him to some appropriate segment or segments of the Name-Tracking Network. In the case of "Bunbury," S knows enough, and has told his hearer enough, about the circumstances of use of tokens of the name to enable either of them to track down its bearer: admittedly, a bearer in the shape of a fictional character invented by Moncrieff, but a bearer nonetheless. In the same way, if S takes Louis to be, say "the guy those fellows in the pub were talking about," and intends to refer to that person, then he refers to him; otherwise not. Causality is certainly not sufficient, in other words, to forge the right sort of link between S and Louis XIII, but equally knowledge on S's part of Louis XIII is not necessary. All that is required on S's part is knowledge of the circumstances of use of a token of Louis XIII's name, together with the intention that the token of the name he now employs should have the same reference as that token.

v. Cases involving misapprehension

Finally, let us consider two cases in which one would want, intuitively, to say that a putative proper name fails to qualify as a genuine proper name because of misapprehensions on the part of its users.

First Evans's "Goldilocks" case. On the Causal Theory, implausibly, "Goldilocks" presumably, does qualify as a genuine proper name for whichever of the two little girls is causally implicated in the introduction of the name. Evans finds this "little short of magical," and suggests that the conditions he lays down for a putative proper name to count as a genuine one "are more stringent than Kripke's." But it is not altogether clear that this is so. Evans does not rework the example in terms of the Dominant Cluster Theory, but when one does so it seems, on the face of it, to yield much the same result as the Causal Theory. The villager who introduces the name can, after all, reasonably be said to "know or believe" that there is a certain item in the world, namely the little girl with golden hair he presently observes skipping down the street. Equally, he intends to refer to that item. Certainly, also, he possesses a dossier of information about that item which "makes it true that he knows of the existence of the item." And given that he is looking at the girl and noting her appearance at the very moment when he baptises her "Goldilocks" (we may suppose he has never set eyes on the other twin), there seems no reason not to say that she is the item dominantly responsible for his possession of that information. Suppose again that all the members of the community among which the name subsequently becomes current are gathered around the Originator of the name, outside the church on Sunday, let's say, when he makes the Originating Observation "Look at little Goldilocks there!" It will then be common knowledge that members of that community have in their repertoire the procedure of using "Goldilocks" to refer to the little girl they all saw skipping down the street on that occasion. And it will, seemingly, be possible for each member of the community, in using the name, to rely for the success of the reference on the common knowledge, diffused throughout the community, that the name "Goldilocks" refers to that little girl. It would seem, therefore, that the Dominant Cluster Theory, like the Causal theory, yields the result that "Goldilocks" so used is a genuine proper name.

The problem with this conclusion, of course, is (a) that neither the Originator nor any other member of the community is aware that the little girl is one of a pair of twins, and (b) neither the Originator nor any other community member is in a position, then or subsequently, to distinguish one twin from the other. It remains quite unclear, however, how the Dominant Cluster Theory can take account of these facts. One obvious way would be to build into Evans's conditions some sort of uniqueness requirement. Presumably, as the notion of speaker's denotation in use is primary in Evans's scheme, it would have to be built into the conditions for determining what a speaker denotes on an occasion. That would be achieved if we were to require of the dossier of information in the speaker's possession concerning the item to which he intends to refer, that it contain sufficient information to "make it true" not merely that he knows of the existence of the item to which the dossier relates but also that he knows there to be only one item fitting the descriptions in the dossier. This is, of course, the requirement of *uniquely identifying* description traditionally demanded by the simpler versions of the Description Theory. The trouble with it, as Kripke, Putnam, and others have pointed out, is that it is far too strong to bear any relation to reality. As Kripke observes, how many of those who refer to Feynman could distinguish him from Gell-Mann? If we can disqualify "Goldilocks" as a genuine proper name only by requiring its users to satisfy a uniqueness requirement, then disqualifying it entails disqualifying virtually all putative proper names.

Fortunately there is a simpler way of distinguishing "Goldilocks" from "Feynman." The latter is already a name honoured by the Name-Tracking Network. Any confusion in speakers' minds between Feynman and Gell-Mann, or between Feynman the physicist and Feynman the physician on 42nd Street, can be cleared up by reference to a multitude of documentary and other traces left by each and preserved in the fabric of the multitude of practices making up the Network. The introduction of the term "Goldilocks" by the Originator, now, is an attempt to introduce a new name into the Network. The Originator does not need to intend that that should be so for it to be so. The passage of a proper name into the network of practices through which we keep track of the items such names designate is guaranteed not by any conscious intention on the part of originators of names, but merely by the fact that we conduct such practices: by that being, as Wittgenstein might have said, "What we have been taught to do" with such expressions. The trouble with "Goldilocks" is that it is a flawed, or misfired, attempt at name-introduction. It is essential to the conduct of the Name-Tracking Network that it be possible in the first instance to achieve a unique pairing between a name and an item, for it is the uniqueness of that pairing that the Network exists to transmit through a multitude of subsequent transactions involving the name. In the case of "Goldilocks," that condition is not satisfied, as in the nature of things neither the Originator nor any subsequent user can say, nor is there any means of discovering, which of two distinct individuals the name was first introduced to designate. "Goldilocks" thus fails to qualify as a genuine proper name, whereas "Feynman," for which no such problem arises, does.

Now for one last case. Suppose Charles Morgan is a confidence trickster. Not only that, he is a superb character actor with a talent for informal self-disguise. So he looks, not only to an incautious but even to an ordinarily observant eye, quite different, when he is "being" Morgan, from the way he looks in ordinary life. When he enters the building that contains John's office he "becomes" Morgan; as he leaves it again the appearance drops from him and he "becomes" – either whoever he really is or (again "to all appearances") somebody else.

As "Morgan" he has given John a great deal of information about himself, backing it up with fraudulent documentation of a type not easily exposed as such. All, or almost all, this information is false: there is in reality, as we say, "no such person" as Morgan. To make matters still worse, let's say Morgan is one of a pair of identical twins, whose thespian abilities are also identical, and that, because the particular scam being worked requires Morgan to be in two places at once, John has from the beginning found himself, without realising it, sometimes entertaining one Morgan in his office, sometimes the other.

For Russell, recall, to attach a name to an item it is sufficient to be acquainted with it. At the moment of being originally introduced to "Morgan" John certainly became acquainted, in something like Russell's sense, with an individual designated by that name (just as, in the preceding example, the Originator enjoys Russellian acquaintance with the little girl he dubs "Goldilocks"). From that introduction John also, clearly, derives quite sufficient information to make it true that he knows of the existence of the item to which he proposes to refer by that name. And we can easily so rig the example (by making one of the "Morgan" twins a more frequent visitor to John's office than the other) as to make the original "Morgan" causally responsible for John's possessing the "dominant cluster" of information in his "Morgan" dossier. Of course John doesn't associate a *uniquely identifying* description with the name "Morgan" (but then, how many users of genuine proper names meet that test?). But it does seem that he meets both the conditions proposed by the Causal Theory, and those proposed by the Dominant Cluster Theory, for possession of the ability to refer by means of a proper name. It follows, if either view is correct, that he can transmit that ability, along the lines suggested by Evans, to a community of speakers (the Board of Directors of the firm of which he is CEO, let's say) whose member will then also be in a position to refer by means of it.

Of course this is nonsense. There is no "Morgan," and in consequence, when John employs the name in a putatively referential role, he cannot be said to succeed in referring to any specific item, any more than the Originator of the name "Goldilocks" can. But, once again, there seems no way of explaining what has gone wrong, or what exactly makes John's situation vis-à-vis the name inadequate to sustain the possibility of reference, without reference to the Name-Tracking Network. For what John does not know, and has never known, is *who he is really speaking to* when he is speaking to Morgan.

And it is hard to see how one could give teeth, as it were, to the required notion of the *real identity* of an item, without reference to some public system for keeping track of real, that is, publicly recognised, identities in such a way as to preserve a permanent possibility of distinguishing them from erroneously attributed or assumed ones. The reason why "Morgan" is not, in the circumstances of the example, a name by means of which John, or anybody, can refer to anything at all, is not, in other words, to be sought in the nature of John's cognitive or causal relationship to the item in connection with which the name was introduced, but in the relationship, or lack of one, subsisting between the name and the public systems for recording and tracking names in use on the society at large. John's problem is that his own access to those systems is obstructed by the plausibility of "Morgan's" inventions and forgeries. When the police ultimately become involved, after "Morgan" has vanished, taking with him whatever he wanted from John and his Board, their laboratories will no doubt discern, under ultra-violet light, the inadequacies of Morgan's "United States" passport. Three sets of fingerprints, not two, will be found on the ashtray in John's office touched, over the past month, only by "Morgan" and the office cleaner; two of these sets will correspond to the recorded prints of the Elliot twins, born Gateshead 1952 and wanted for this and that, and the whole scam will stand revealed. John, of course, disposes of neither an ultra-violet scanner nor the police fingerprint database, even had he thought of exposing "Morgan's" identity to that sort of test. So far as John, *or any individual speaker* (of which *caveat* more in a moment) can be expected to judge, that is, "Morgan" is a genuine proper name, a name for a unique individual, an individual moreover with whom he himself enjoys personal acquaintance, in just the sense of acquaintance that Russell considered capable of offering rock-bottom assurance of the character of an expression as a genuine proper name. It is only in the light of the stored cognitive resources accumulated by a faithfully observed practice of recording and tabulating names in a multiplicity of cross-referring contexts that such an illusion on the part of an individual speaker, or for that matter on the part of a community of speakers owing the currency of a name to the credit of an original, deluded, user, could be revealed for what it is.

vi. Causality versus intentionality

Now for some comments on the string of examples considered in the previous two sections. Evans's objections to the Causal Theory concern in the main its failure to allow any role to a speaker's intentions and beliefs, and their interactions with the context of his utterance, in determining to what, and whether, he refers. The objection is that the connection between names, or speakers, and what they denote, forged by causality, appear "magical." If the right sort of causal links were to obtain, it would seem, then one would be forced to say that names, or speakers, might "really" denote items very remote from those they are generally taken to denote, or from those they intend to denote.

The account defended here avoids these consequences not by attempting, as Evans does, to achieve a compromise between Causal and Description accounts, but by replacing causality outright with intention as the link between a name or a speaker, and what either denotes. However, the intentions in question are not, or not primarily, those of speakers. They are intentions, or better, perhaps, "intentionalities" of the sort which characterise not individual speakers but practices. The practices that go to make up the Name-Tracking Network are, after all, like any practices, intentional constructs. They are designed to achieve certain ends, are understood by their users as contributing to the achievement and maintenance of those ends, and are operated accordingly by their users with the full and conscious intention that those ends be achieved and maintained. Hence the matching of a certain island to the name "Madagascar," or the matching of a certain eighth-century Arab mathematician to the name "Ibn Khan" is not, after all, the result of a causally mediated chain of communication linking present users back to an original baptism (which most unfortunately turns out in one case to be that of a portion of the African mainland, and in the other that of a twelfth-century scribe). It results from the intentional operation of a vast system of practices designed, among other things, to preserve and transmit the match between those names and those items.

vii. Speakers' beliefs and intentions

The suggestion that public practices do most of the work of determining both what names denote and what speakers denote on occasions of use might seem to allow an implausibly reduced role to the beliefs and intentions of individual speakers. Do they count for nothing? What the cases dealt with in Chapter 7 §v and others discussed in earlier chapters, tend to show, is that whereas speakers' beliefs concerning the currency of names, if correct, can, and most often do, effectively guarantee the success of intentions to refer founded upon them; speakers' beliefs *concerning the items to which they take themselves to be referring* very often lack the power to do so, *even if true*.

Many philosophers will find this conclusion unacceptable. The British Empiricist conviction that the content of sensory experience must be the ultimate guarantor of every claim we advance dies hard. Evans is surely right to insist, as a rock-bottom condition of the ability of a speaker S to refer to an item x, that S know of the existence of x (call this the *Existence Requirement*). And surely knowledge of the existence of x, although it need not always be founded on sensory acquaintance with x, could not be better founded, and must always ultimately, even in cases in which it does not immediately involve it, fall back on some such foundation. It is at this point in the argument that it begins to seem self-evident, as it clearly did to Russell, that to enjoy sensory acquaintance with an item is to be, in a quite foolproof way, in a position to bestow a name on that item and to refer to it subsequently by means of that name.

And yet, in the cases of Goldilocks and Morgan, the availability of acquaintance in Russell's sense counts for nothing at all when it comes to grounding, or guaranteeing, the ability to refer. John enjoys direct sensory acquaintance, in that sense, with the "Morgan" originally introduced to him. The Originator also, at the moment of introducing the name "Goldilocks," is acquainted in a similar sense with the little girl he intends that it should designate. But these facts have no power whatsoever to establish either that "Morgan" as John uses it functions as a name for Cyril rather than Cecil Elliott (if Cyril happened to be the twin masquerading as "Morgan" when John was "introduced" to the latter), or that users of the name "Goldilocks" succeed in referring to anything at all by means of it.

viii. The requirement of unique discriminability

The reason for this is neither particularly obscure nor particularly paradoxical. What is required, what has to be guaranteed, if S is in future to be in a position to refer to a given item x by means of a name N, whether N is a name in common use or one introduced by S himself, is not merely (R_1) the existence of x, but also (R_2) the possibility of discriminating between x and other items, each of which might otherwise enjoy an equal right to be considered the subject of S's reference. There is not only an Existence Requirement for successful reference, but also a Requirement of Unique Discriminability. Whereas the former can be assured by the simple fact of S's enjoying sensory acquaintance with x, the latter cannot. The Originator, being assured of the existence of Goldilocks, because there she is in front of him, assumes that it will in future be easy to single out this particular child from others, especially given her striking appearance. In that assumption he is mistaken. Similarly, John assumes that having been personally introduced to Morgan it will be no harder to establish which individual he is referring to by that name than it ordinarily is in the case of any other business acquaintance. He is wrong.

But if sensory acquaintance with an item is insufficient to guarantee the satisfaction of the Unique Discriminability Requirement for that item, what possible precaution capable of being taken by an individual speaker could guarantee its satisfaction? And if there is no such precaution, isn't the argument tending towards the sceptical, and absurd, conclusion that it is impossible for an individual speaker to introduce a new proper name?

To this twofold question a twofold answer suggests itself. There is no precaution an individual speaker could take, in bestowing a name on an item, which could guarantee the satisfaction of the Unique Discriminability

Requirement for that item. But there is an in-principle indefinitely large set of types of precaution that *speakers can take in common* to assure the satisfaction of the Unique Discriminability Requirement for the vast majority of items on which they are likely to wish to bestow proper names. The precautions we have in mind are precisely those enshrined in the multitude of practices that go to make up the Name-Tracking Network, from the techniques of fingerprinting used by the police to the practice of identifying an individual car by etching its registration number many times on its windows and chassis.

The position at which we appear to have arrived could be seen as constituting a sort of lemma to Wittgenstein's Private Language Argument: naming is an inherently social, public act. *Pace* Russell, in other words, it makes no sense to envisage an individual speaker *inaugurating language* by the bestowal of a proper name on some item immediately present to him. The introduction of a proper name can only take place against the background of an already existing language, considered as a structure of public, collectively maintained practices, because it is only through access to such a structure that the satisfaction of the Unique Discriminability Requirement can be assured.

It should now be becoming clear why the capacity to refer by means of a name can be conferred merely by the possession of a nominal description. Such a description serves to connect the name in question to a relevant portion of the Name-Tracking Network. And, given the nature and object of the practices making up the Network, the bare information that a name is one tracked by the Network will in most circumstances be sufficient to guarantee that the name possesses an existent and uniquely discriminable bearer (even though that bearer, like Easthampton or the *Galveston*, may not in practice be physically or otherwise locatable); or in other words that both (R_1) and (R_2) are satisfied for that name.

ix. Wittgenstein and Descartes

The Wittgensteinian with any sense of his own mortality must feel, each time he introduces the Master's name into the discussion, the force of the unspoken parallel with Mr. Dick and King Charles's head. So it comes as something of a relief to recollect that the sturdily Russellian Evans also brings Wittgenstein into the discussion. One of the targets of Evans's essay is "a certain Philosophy of Mind" that holds, among other things, that for it to be possible for a speaker S to ascribe a property F to an individual thing *a*, S must know of a property that uniquely individuates *a*. Evans sees Wittgenstein as an ally in resisting that account, and offers the following, exegetically accurate, account of the latter's grounds for dissenting from the Philosophy of Mind in question.

We cannot deal comprehensively with this Philosophy of Mind here. My objections to it are essentially those of Wittgenstein. For an item to be the object of some psychological attitude of yours may be simply for you to be placed in a context which relates you to that thing. What makes it one rather than the other of a pair of identical twins the one you are in love with? Certainly not some specification blueprinted on your mind; it may be no more than this: it was one of them and not the other that you have met. The theorist may gesture to the description "the one I have met" but can give no explanation for the impossibility of its being outweighed by other descriptions which may have been acquired as a result of error and which may in fact happen to fit the other, unmet, twin. If God had looked into your mind, he would not have seen there with whom you were in love, and of whom you were thinking.[10]

The suggestion that context enters into assessing claims to have executed mental acts – for example the act of bestowing a proper name on some item – is one with which we are in wholehearted agreement. Equally clearly Evans is right to see the move from the Description Theory to some version of the Causal Theory, whether Kripke's or his own, as a step in the implementation of that suggestion. If any fact about anything other than a mental state of S's – a fact about who S has and has not met, for instance – is allowed to be relevant to the question of what S denotes by a given name on a given occasion of use, then the latter question ceases to be one that can be settled by "looking into S's mind."

But one may still wonder whether Evans allows sufficient scope to the implications of the remark of Wittgenstein's he paraphrases. The recent writers on the Description Theory, Searle, Gellner, Russell, whom Evans cites as supporters of the Philosophy of Mind he wishes, with Wittgenstein's help, to dislodge, stand in a much longer and wider tradition of thought: a tradition occupied not just with the nature of naming, but with the whole question of the relationship between Mind and World. It was Descartes, after all, who introduced into Western Philosophy the idea that knowledge is first and foremost a transaction between the individual mind and the world presented to its private contemplation either in the deliverances of the senses or through the presence to consciousness of those "clear and distinct perceptions" that yield rational certainty. It is on this, Cartesian, account of the relationship between Mind and World that God must be able to see, if he looks into my mind, what I am thinking, and which individual I am thinking it about; for because on Descartes's view thought is essentially a transaction between the mind and its objects, what I am thinking about must be in some adequately representative way present to my mind, otherwise I could not be thinking about it. Locke, here as so often the British branch of *Ets.* R. Descartes, expresses the essential point succinctly in opening Book II of the *Essay* with the words, "*Idea is the object of thinking.* – Every man being conscious to himself that he thinks, and that which his mind is applied about, whilst thinking, being the ideas that are there . . . "[11]

Cartesianism embraces at this point a version of what one might call *epistemic individualism.* Epistemic individualism is the doctrine that, whatever may be the requirements that must be satisfied in order for a belief to count as knowledge, those requirements will be such that their satisfaction can be established independently by each individual mind, pursuing its enquiries into domains immediately accessible to it, without the need for consultation with others, unless it be to point out errors that a more astute mind could, in principle, have perceived for itself without such aid, and certainly without the need for recourse to collectively maintained institutions. In Descartes, epistemic individualism expresses itself most directly in the doctrine that all knowledge is grounded in "clear and distinct perception."

The thesis central to the Description Theory, that only the possession of an identifying description of the object to which I intend to refer could, as John Searle puts it, "make my intention an intention directed at just *that* object and not at some other,"[12] is a further expression of the doctrine. And certainly Wittgenstein's remark about God's not being able to see, by looking into someone's mind, what that person is thinking about, expresses a contextualism hostile to the Description Theory in Searle's or any other version. But the reverberations of Wittgenstein's remark spread far beyond that topic. It raises a doubt concerning epistemic individualism in any form. The question it raises is whether a whole battery of what are ordinarily classed as "mental acts," including, *inter alia*, knowing, intending, referring, meaning, can be understood solely by reference to proceedings internal to the individual mind.

In the same way, the influence of epistemic individualism spreads far beyond the Description Theory. It is present in any view that makes the possession of cognitive capacities by a community or collectivity derivative from the possession of the same or related capacities by individual members of that community. In recent analytic philosophy of language it manifests itself most obviously in "communication-intention" theories of meaning, like that of H. P. Grice, which make the concept of meaning derivative from that of speaker's intention. Evans's derivation of the concept of *what a name denotes* from that of what a speaker denoted (upon an occasion) is explicitly Gricean in inspiration. For "NN" to be a name of *x*, according to Evans, there must, certainly, exist a body of communally possessed knowledge concerning the use of "NN." But that knowledge, consisting as it does in the "common knowledge that members of C have in their repertoire the procedure of using 'NN' to refer to *x*," is entirely concerned with the linguistic dispositions of the individuals composing the community.

Kripke's original version of the Causal Theory is equally ambiguously situated with respect to epistemic individualism. The remark of Wittgenstein's that Evans cites in support of his view could equally be cited by Kripke in support of his. There is certainly no way, on Kripke's view, in which God could determine, by surveying the contents of S's mind, the denotation of a name used by S. The divine survey would have to take in the entire causal history of the use of the name in S's linguistic community. However, the concept of "linguistic community" invoked by Kripke's account is a curiously bloodless, not to say vacuous, one. The community doesn't *do anything* to determine the denotation of the proper names abroad among its members: it merely provides the passive field across which the causal relationships that actually perform that task propagate themselves. Relative to the community, therefore, it is still the states of individual minds that determine the reference of names: it is simply that it is the causal features of those states, rather than their content, which do the work.

Enough has been done by way of Wittgenstein exegesis over the past half-century to make it reasonable to suggest that an adequate context for Wittgenstein's remark about God and the mind is provided neither by Grice nor by Kripke, and for the same reason: namely, that whereas both Grice's and Kripke's views, each in their own way, enshrine a commitment to epistemic individualism, the doubts insinuated by Wittgenstein's remark concern, precisely, the centrality of the individual mind in the explication of a range of concepts that includes those of reference and meaning.

Moreover, the entire context of the *Philosophical Investigations*, from which the remark is taken, suggests that what Wittgenstein opposed to the individual mind as the realm in which to seek understanding of those concepts was not, or not primarily, natural causality but, rather, social practice. The suggestion advanced here is in that sense entirely Wittgensteinian. In effect it inverts the conceptual dependencies characteristic of epistemic individualism. According to us, what determines the reference of a name is the trace left by that name across the fabric of communally instituted and maintained practices constituting the Name-Tracking Network; something, that is, which is not only not grasped in its entirety by any individual mind but is arguably not graspable in its entirety by any individual mind. The intentions-to-refer of individual minds succeed only insofar as they are founded on adequate access to the Name-Tracking Network.

x. Relativism and social convention

The widespread acceptance, among analytic philosophers, of epistemic individualism in certain of its versions rests to a considerable extent on the equally widespread conviction that it offers the only alternative to certain forms of social relativism. Where questions of meaning and reference are concerned, it has seemed to many compelling that unless individual speakers are in a position to say with certainty what an expression means, or what a name denotes, then neither speakers nor hearers can be in a position to know either what they are saying or what has been said. That way, it has seemed, lies semantic nihilism. As usual in philosophy, voices on what Pope called "the Sceptic side" have not been lacking to argue that that is in fact our situation, and that semantic nihilism is in consequence, whether we like it or not, just true. And the arguments advanced by such sceptics have in the main been arguments aimed at denying responsibility for the determination of meaning and reference to the mental states of the individual speaker, and bestowing it instead either on "language," considered as a structure of conventionally established relationships operating according to laws of its own, laws independent of the conscious states of any of its speakers; or else to the collective judgment of the linguistic community. Leading exemplars of these strategies are, on the one hand, Derrida (or if not Derrida himself, then certainly many of the writers, chiefly in literary studies, associated with the technique of "deconstruction" founded on his work), and, on the other, Quine, or the "meaning-sceptical" Kripke of *Wittgenstein on Rules and Private Language.*

We shall begin to confront these issues in Chapter 8, and shall address them squarely in the Epilogue. Now is a good moment, however, to make a start on the discussion of meaning-scepticism by instilling a few doubts of our own. Is the referral, for settlement, of questions of reference and meaning to "the linguistic community" or to collectively instituted and maintained practices always, and necessarily, a step on the road to semantic nihilism? What the Realist about reference wants is that there should be, as Quine would say, a "fact of the matter" concerning the issues of whether a name denotes and what it denotes. Meaning-sceptics have argued, in effect, that there is no such fact of the matter to be had, because there is no possibility, for any individual speaker, of appealing beyond the collective authority of other speakers' judgments. What is delegated to the community on the present view, however, is not the task of *validating the individual speaker's judgments by establishing their conformity with the judgments of the generality of speakers* but, rather, the task of *keeping a running record of traces left by the item on which a given name has been bestowed,* so that the individual speaker can, at least in principle, *determine for himself whether, and what, a given name denotes.*

Thanks to the maintenance of the Name-Tracking Network, in other words, there *are* "facts of the matter" concerning whether and what names denote. It is, for instance, access to the Network that enables the police to open John's eyes to the fact that the name "Charles Morgan" denotes nothing. In the same sort of way it is the socially instituted conventions governing the ways in which proper names of places are deployed in a multitude of cross-referring contexts that enables historians to conclude that there was once, prior to the Black Death, such a place as Easthampton, even though its site can no longer be determined with certainty. And such objective facts of the matter concerning the denotation of names, although they are made accessible by a fabric of collectively instituted and maintained practices, are made available by that fabric *to each individual user.* The individual user's judgments concerning the denotation of names can claim objective truth, rather than, as one might put it, truth relative to what-is-generally-held-true, because the possibility of grounding such judgments in the deposit of traces recorded in the Name-Tracking Network equips them with a criterion of truth independent of any form of communal *imprimatur*, acceptance, or validation. By a form of paradox inverse in its operation to those we shall discuss in Part IV, the individual user, by ceding to a web of communally maintained practices the final word in matters of denotation, in no way subordinates his judgments in such matters to the rule of communal censure, but precisely emancipates himself from dependence on such censure. It is true, as Aristotle held, that we are social animals. But it is also true – and a truth that the polarisation of social theory between the options of individualism and collectivism has tended throughout the past three centuries to obscure – first, that certain aspects of our life as social beings seem precisely designed to confer on us the possibility of living as autonomous individuals, and, second, that it is only through those aspects of our life as social beings that we can obtain access to that possibility.

xi. Labels and "real names"

In Chapter 5 §ix, we argued that name-bearers are always nomothetic entities. But, someone might object, all the examples of naming offered there are queer, out of the way ones, involving hunter-gatherers, arcane considerations concerning Scots territorial titles, or forest Indians who may at any moment fade back into the green. Arguments founded on such bizarre examples, our objector will protest, although they may serve to disconcert an opponent who, like most of us, takes it as evident to common-sense that a name-bearer is generally a real entity, not a nomothetic one, will never convince him, because they fail to confront the one category of cases in which his contention must, it would seem, go through unopposed: namely, cases involving the introduction of a name through direct baptism of an item.

This is an objection to which we have perhaps responded *ambulando* at various points over the past two chapters, but perhaps still not directly or explicitly enough for our objector. So let us stage the confrontation one last time. Let us consider the following case. A – let's say she has just read a paper by B arguing a case akin to the one argued in Chapter 5 §ix, and has found herself both unimpressed and irritated by it – comes up to B at a conference, bringing with her a woman friend. The following conversation ensues:

A: Here's someone I'd like you to meet, B. Let's call her Dr. X.
B: How do you mean, "Dr. X"? What is this lady's name?
A: What do *you* mean, "What is her name?" You want a name; I have given you a name, "Dr. X." Here, before your very eyes, is an item (excuse me for speaking of you in this way, dear, but B is so dreadfully obtuse!), and I have just baptised it for you with a name. Or isn't that what providing an item with a name comes to?
B: But I mean, what is her *real* name? Who is this lady?

A: Now come, what is this notion of *real* we're getting into here? This really is getting very metaphysical. Surely any other name I gave you would be, just like this one, a mere arbitrary label for the item you see before you. So why won't this one do as well as any other? Or do you believe in Mr. Shandy's Theory of Names, according to which there's an occult link between a particular sort of name and a particular sort of object? And what's with this "who is she?" stuff anyway? You *surely* don't want to say that her *identity* depends on her *name*? "A rose by any other name," you know! All this talk of her "identity," anyway, is just a high-flown way of talking about *her*, as far as I can see. And *she* is standing before you. You can see *who she is* just by looking at her.

B: Well, but...

A: Oh, come along, dear X, this is getting us nowhere. Let's go talk to good old Tom Hobbes over there. You know, "names, though they be the money of fools, are but the counters of wise men." Now *there's* a philosopher!

What, if anything, is to be said against the shrewd, voluble and literate reasoning that has left the unfortunate B floundering, tongue-tied and pulverised, in A's wake? Can it be that "Dr. X," baptismally introduced in the above fashion, really *is* a name, and as good a name as any other, for A's friend? Let us be fair to B: is there not a sense in which he really *has* been left with no idea *who X is*? Maybe he will recognise her subsequently around the conference, so that he can say "Good morning X" with enough bravado to suggest that he did not feel all that flattened by A after all. But maybe he won't. Maybe he will vent this sally on a perfect stranger, whom he mistakes for X, and who may not be pleased to find herself so addressed. "My God that was Ruth Barcan Marcus you addressed as 'X'," someone may say to him, "Who the hell did you think it was?" And what can poor B reply? "I thought it was X"? Even telling the story of A's baptismal introduction of "X," although it may raise a laugh at his expense, will get him no further towards establishing the identity of the mysterious X. For the expression "X" is not associated with any record of anything that has distinguished X's life from that of any other woman of similar age and appearance. She has not published under the name "X." She has not entered herself as "Miss X" on the rolls of any university. Her Social Security number is not listed under "X." And so on. But in that case, *pace* all A's protestations, in what sense can "X," be said to be X's *name*, or even *a* name for X? None of the things people *do* with proper names has been done with "X": in consequence, B cannot *do with* "X" any of the things he could do with X's *real name* if he knew it: look up X's publications in the *Philosopher's Index*, for instance, or her biography in *Who's Who*.

What this shows is that the act of baptism – the association of a verbal expression with an item – is *in itself* insufficient to make that expression into a proper name. What matters is the use – the use$_E$ (Chapter 3 §ii) – which will subsequently be made of the expression so introduced. If the expression will in future be made use of in the multitude of ways in which we make use of proper names, then what took place was, in the ordinary sense, baptism. But if there is not, and never was to be, any such subsequent use of the expression, then it is not a proper name, and what took place was not, after all, baptism.

But if A did not *baptise* X, what did she do? She *labelled X for purposes of current reference.* "Call these trees A and B," someone might, for instance, say. "Now, although it's winter, you can see that the shadow of A will be broader than that of B and will fall across your proposed rose-bed. So, if you're going to cut down either, I'd cut down A." But this is hardly baptism. Perhaps it should be called labelling, as all it does is to affix labels to the two trees for the convenience of present discussion. The function of the labels "A" and "B" is simply to permit two or three speakers to make their suggestions and proposals clear to one another in a specific and temporally limited context of discourse. There is no question of the labels "A" and "B" acquiring any wider status, and certainly no question of their being put to permanent use to track either tree throughout its life in the way that a proper name tracks its bearer.

The ritual of baptism occurs as an element in either practice. But that in itself suffices to show that there is no intrinsic connection between the ritual of baptism and the introduction of a proper name. Baptism may result either in the introduction of a proper name, or merely in the labelling of an item for purposes of current reference, and which it turns out to have resulted in will depend entirely, as Wittgenstein would say, on its consequences in use: on what we subsequently choose to do with the expression that figured in the baptism, with what use$_E$ we put it to. Once again, we see the force of the remark "only someone who knows something to do with it can significantly ask a name."

There is nothing wrong with thinking of baptism as a process which equips an item with a name *of some sort or other*. Where we go wrong is in assuming that because it is an *individual* which is being baptised, the name with which baptism equips it must necessarily be a proper name. It may not be: as in the case of A and her baptism of X, it may be merely a label. It is this distinction, now, as well as every other consideration having to do with the wide differences in use$_E$ which distinguish different types of name-like expression, which is obscured when we identify the bearer of such an expression with the item to which it has been baptismally attached. For such an identification allows us to argue that, because a proper name is one whose bearer is an individual, every name borne by an individual must be a proper name. In view of the actual differences of use$_E$ between name-like expressions, it seems not unreasonable to say that baptism, depending upon the type of name it introduces, confers one or another type of status on the individual it names: either that of a labelled item, or that of the bearer of a proper name. But in that case it is not the natural individual that is dubbed with the name, but that individual *qua* labelled item, or *qua* bearer of a proper name, in either case *qua* possessor of a nomothetically conferred status that transforms it, in each case, into a different type of nomothetic entity. It is *qua* entity of either sort that it bears either type of name. That is why it makes sense to class name-bearers as nomothetic entities, not natural ones.

In the above example, the influence of these considerations, however submerged by A's fluency in argument, shows in two ways. It shows, for one thing, in B's demand to be told X's *real* name. *Pace* A, there is nothing either metaphysical or Shandean about this demand. B simply wants to be given a name for X that will behave, in use$_E$, as proper names behave, and not as a mere label behaves. It shows in a still more significant way in A's apology-in-passing to X for speaking of her as an "item." About this a little more needs to be said.

xii. Proper names and personal identity

In *If This is a Man*, his book about his experiences in Auschwitz, Primo Levi asserts that one of the worst trials a prisoner faced in the camps was the loss of his name, or rather its replacement with a number. According to Levi, the loss of his name obliterates a human being – or threatens to do so, requiring a supreme act of will to counter it.

Nothing belongs to us any more; they have taken away our clothes, our shoes, even our hair; if we speak they will not listen to us, and if they listen they will not understand. They even take away our name, and if we want to keep that, we will have to find in ourselves the strength to do so, to manage somehow, so that behind the name something of us, of us as we were, remains.[13]

Such remarks are commonplace in the writings of survivors both of the Nazi genocide and the Gulag. The difficulty for those who see no difference between baptism and labelling, is to explain why the point is so insisted on: why the mere lapsing from use of a name should be felt as entailing a loss of identity. After all, when he felt these things Levi was still alive. Here he is in the camp: Levi the man. He still has his identity because he *is* his identity. He cannot lose that unless and until he is killed. How, then, can it make any difference to his identity as an individual human being whether that identity is labelled "Primo Levi" or "174517"? Have we not here yet another instance of that fetishism of words, that refusal to recognise that it is things and not names that matter, from which not only Hobbes but many other philosophers associated with the scientific revolution of the seventeenth century strove to free us?

It is perhaps not the least merit of the view recommended here that it offers us an answer to that question; one that makes perfect sense of the remarks of Levi and other survivors on this point. What is at stake in the substitution of a label, in this case a number, for a genuine proper name is not merely the substitution of one phonemic string for another of similar linguistic function but, rather, the replacement of an expression having one sort of role – one collection of uses$_E$ – in human life, with an expression having a radically different role. The name "Primo Levi" was a real name, bestowed in a real baptism. What made it Levi's real name, and the baptism a real baptism, is that it was – would be – the name under which, as the growing Levi acquired, by his acts and achievements, a specific character, an identity, all the acts and achievements of his life would be recorded, in such a multitude of cross-referencing ways as to make them easily recoverable by any inquirer. To be Levi, to possess an identity as Levi, is to be the bearer not only of the name but of the entire life history preserved in the ramifying archive of entries and memories to which that name gives access. That is what a proper name is: a tool of memory, a means of access to a record by which a man or woman can claim the dignity of having existed, of having a memorial and a place in the impersonal record of his society; a record that is impersonal in the sense that, whatever specific purposes, of the police, of booksellers, of the synagogue, of newspaper proprietors, may be served by individual components of the matrix of record, in the end the total matrix, because it is so vast, serves no end more special or sectarian than that of simply recording, of preserving some record of the flood of lives toppling continually into oblivion.

By contrast the number bestowed on Levi by his captors is a mere label. It is a mere label because it is meant to serve temporarily, to keep track of its bearer between capture and final disposal, and because its purpose, even during this time, is to keep track of him as an item to be considered only in relation to the purposes of those in charge of the camps. Just as one does not give a tree a proper name, except whimsically, but only a label or number, which serves to identify it for felling, so one does not give a Jew or a Romani a name but only a number. Once one is known by that number, rather than by a genuine proper name, one's real name, it is not merely that other people will have, through that number, no means of gaining access to one's history, to one's identity as Signore Levi the chemist, or Herr Rotblut the grocer from Wimbergergasse who won all those swimming medals for the town when he was a young man (for the loss of such trivial distinctions is, one imagines, as much as anything what sears the heart). It is that the whole world in which proper names matter, and in which the practices surrounding them, from the keeping of baptismal registers to the erecting of gravestones, are painstakingly observed, has been swept away at a stroke. And it is not just that only in such a world is the living of a human life possible. What destroys the soul is – and this is perhaps the heart of the darkness of Nazism – that it is only in that world that the living of a human life is intelligible: that a man is more than a tree blazed for felling, or a block of stone numbered for transport from the quarry to the harbour works.

xiii. Mind, world and practice

In Chapter 2 §iii we encountered, through John McDowell's restatement of it, the Kantian problem of spontaneity and receptivity; the problem of how we are to reconcile the freedom of the mind in elaborating concepts with the need to retain, as McDowell puts it, a "grip on how exercises of concepts can constitute warranted judgments about the world."

How, and on what, is the spontaneity of the mind supposed to be exercised? Kant conceived it as a faculty of thought: one that "enables us to *think* the object of sensory intuition," as we do, for instance when we represent diverse sensory appearances as belonging to one and the same physical object.[14] Conceived in this way the problem appears intractable, because it appears as the problem of reconciling *mental representations* with the real, in the sense of *extramental*, natures of the things represented. Once matters are put in that way it is not easy to see, from any standpoint save those of Transcendental or Absolute Idealism, how the project of *representing the world in thought* could be rendered compatible with the admission of "spontaneity" of any kind in the constitution of the terms, the conceptual vocabulary, in terms of which that project is to proceed.

What we have begun to develop, in this and the previous two chapters, is a different way of envisaging the spontaneity of the mind, as exercised not in the constitution of mental representations, but in the constitution of practices. There is no problem of how such spontaneity can be conceived as responsive to the nature of the natural, extramental, world, because a practice is, essentially, a pattern of human interaction with the natural world, one that would be not merely useless or unfruitful, but nonexistent as a practice, if it were not responsive to the nature of that world.

Nor is there any particular problem about how such exercises of spontaneity can give rise to "warranted judgments about the world." As we saw earlier (Chapter 7 §v) the possibility of John's discovering his judgments concerning Charles Morgan to be unwarranted exists solely in consequence of the existence of the flights of spontaneity represented by such things as fingerprint libraries and devices for scanning documents under ultra-violet light. And this is more than some accidental feature of some hand-picked example. As we shall see in Chapter 8, and more fully in Part III, it is in general true that we owe not only the concepts in which, as Kant put it, we "*think* the object of sensory intuition," but also the possibility of warranting or exposing as unwarranted judgments framed in terms of them, to the spontaneity of the mind in the elaboration of practices.

xiv. The meaning of a name

Philosophical debate concerning the meaning of proper names has been dominated by the conviction that the answer must lie in one or other of the options introduced by Frege. When we speak of the meaning of a name, we must have in mind either its bearer (*Bedeutung*) or else its sense (*Sinn*), generally understood as what we have termed an actually identifying description.

In common with Kripke, Putnam, and others, we have rejected the Description Theory. But is this, perhaps, premature? Can the puzzles about identity that led Frege to introduce the notion of *Sinn* in the first place be solved in any other way?

There are indications that there may be no replacement that will do the work of the description theory. The puzzles about identity statements, vacuous reference and substitution into opaque contexts, which Frege introduced the description theory to solve, reappear once senses are dispensed with in favor of the view that the reference of proper nouns is direct. How can sentences like "George Orwell is George Orwell" be trifling ones, while ones like "George Orwell is Eric Blair" are not? Or how can a name like "Santa Claus", which has no sense or reference, be meaningful and contribute to the meaning of sentences? How can atheism, if true, even be formulated? Or why is it that someone can believe "George Orwell wrote 1984" but not believe that "Eric Blair wrote 1984"? The answers that today's Millians have given can hardly be hailed as solving these problems once and for all.[15]

It behoves us also to produce answers to these questions. We do so as follows, "George Orwell is Eric Blair," "Hesperus is Phosphorus," "Cicero is Tully," and so on, are informative remarks because they convey information concerning the Name-Tracking Network: information to the effect that the item tracked by the Network under one name is also the item tracked by the Network under another. Such remarks tell us nothing about the mental states of individual name-users; rather, they tell us something about the public practices of record-keeping by means of names current in the linguistic community at large.

This reply (to Frege by way of Katz) is meta-linguistic in the sense that it explains the informativeness of such sentences by identifying the information they provide as information about the use of names, Frege, in "Über Sinn und Bedeutung," offers a general objection to meta-linguistic answers to his question: namely, that they misconstrue the subject-matter of such sentences, which is not the names that occur in them, but the things to which those names refer. To that we reply that the referents of "George Orwell," "Eric Blair," "Hesperus," "Phosphorus," and the rest, are not individuals, but name-bearerships. What the sentence "Hesperus is Phosphorus" tells us, in short, is that two name-bearerships are borne by one and the same individual.

To return to Katz's string of queries, "Santa Claus" is a functioning proper name, despite the fact that we have no compelling reason to suppose that there exists in reality any such person, because there is a possibly fictional character whose adventures in stories and poems are tracked under that name. The same might be said for "God," and even said without blasphemy. Christians have on the whole, since the inception of their religion, managed to be both too vaunting and too nervous about the existence of God; too ready to bank everything on specious "proofs"; too ready to throw up their hands in despair if God cannot be shown to "exist" in the sort of way that Frege considered it necessary for the bearers of genuine, above-board proper names to exist. Why in heaven's name should we expect to be able to "prove the existence" of the Maker of the Universe anyway? Jewish piety, in this respect as in others somewhat more modest and less triumphal in its metaphysical ambitions, is content, after all, to refer to God as "ha-Shem": "the Name."

Finally, opaque contexts. Why isn't "Tom believes that Cicero denounced Catiline" truth-functionally equivalent to "Tom believes that Tully denounced Catiline"? Because, and this is a point on which hang interesting philosophical consequences, as we shall see in Part IV, the content of what a speaker believes is not, in certain limited and specific respects, analytically separable from the language in which he expresses those beliefs. Tom's ability to use the name "Cicero" does not, *pace* Mill and Kripke, put him into a direct relationship with Cicero: it puts him into a direct relationship only with certain segments of the Name-Tracking Network in use in his linguistic community. His beliefs about Cicero include as one component, therefore, beliefs about a name. Hence those beliefs cannot be rephrased as beliefs about Tully without altering their content. A representation of the facts of the situation amenable to the requirements of an extensional logic might be obtained, at the cost of a degree of idealisation no worse than others commonly accepted by logicians, by rephrasing "*a* believes that Cicero denounced Catiline" as "*a* believes that there exists at least one and not more than one item x; and that x is tracked by the name 'Cicero'; and that x denounced Catiline." The reason why it is not possible to generate truth-functional equivalents for sentences obtained by suitable instantiation of this schema by similarly instantiating the schema obtained by substituting "Tully" for "Cicero" is, now, evidently, that the two schemata differ in content.

We conclude that there remains no retaining the Description Theory in any form. But the account defended here is no more hospitable to the doctrine that the meaning of a name is its bearer. The meaning of a proper name is neither a sense nor a reference. For an expression to function as a proper name of a given type, and so to be "meaningful" in the way that such expressions are meaningful, it is necessary, and sufficient, only that it be habitually made use$_E$ of in the context of all those practices which provide roles for proper names of that type. Thus, what makes "Primo Levi" a proper name is that it was baptismally bestowed on a given child *in order that* it might, later, be used to call him to meals, be inscribed in registers designed to keep track of his attendance and progress in school, identify his bank accounts, adorn the title pages of books written by him, and so on. These are banalities, to be sure. But such a pattern of usage and projected usage is all that makes a particular string of letters or sounds a proper name. That is all there is to point to in answer to the question, "What is the meaning of a proper name?" In Austin's celebrated phrase, albeit taken in a sense rather different from the one Austin had in mind, knowledge of meanings, semantic knowledge, comes down in the end to knowing "How to Do Things with Words." In Chapter 8 we shall assess some of the implications of this conclusion.

8

Knowledge of Rules

i. Wittgenstein's Slogan and the later Wittgenstein

In Chapter 3, we outlined a strategy of opposition to Referential Realism. In pursuit of that strategy we committed ourselves in Chapter 4 to a defence of what we there called Wittgenstein's Slogan: "Logic must take care of itself." We took the Slogan to be equivalent to the proposal that all "logical" questions, taking "logical" in a sense broad enough to include all questions of the meaning and reference of terms, must be capable of being settled antecedently to the assignment of truth or falsity to any contingent proposition. And we began our defence by attempting to show, in Chapters 5–7, that the ability to refer by means of a proper name does not depend on a speaker's knowing any contingent truth concerning the entity to which he refers, but only on his knowing-how to participate in some selection of the array of socially instituted practices, maintained with the general object of keeping track of items by means of their names, which we called the Name-Tracking Network.

We have assumed, in short, that what is required to implement Wittgenstein's Slogan, once it is removed from its original context in the phase of Wittgenstein's thought that culminated in the *Tractatus*, is some way of representing what is known in knowing a language as knowledge-how, not knowledge-that: knowledge of the workings of practices, not knowledge of the truth of propositions. In this we have some support from the later work, where a wide range of remarks seem to suggest the same move. One very well-known example is the following, from *On Certainty*:

204. Giving grounds, however, justifying the evidence, comes to an end; – but the end is not certain propositions' striking us immediately as true, i.e. it is not a kind of seeing on our part; it is our *acting*, which lies at the bottom of the language-game.
205. If the true is what is grounded, then the ground is not *true*, nor yet false.[1]

"Justifying the evidence" means, presumably, giving grounds for taking certain things as evidence for the truth of a proposition. The generality of the remark is such as to compel us to take it that Wittgenstein intends any proposition at all, including propositions about the meanings of expressions, to come within its scope. Wittgenstein is sometimes taken to have opposed the whole notion of "grounding" a judgment in anything beyond itself, and *for that reason* to have rejected the foundationalism that constitutes an abiding theme of the empiricist tradition from Descartes to Russell or the Logical Positivists. Dummett, for instance, has argued that in his later philosophy of mathematics, Wittgenstein is a "full-blooded conventionalist" who holds that "if we accept [a] proof, we confer necessity on the theorem proved . . . in doing this, we are making a new decision, and not merely making explicit a decision we had already made implicitly."[2] Nothing like that seems to be at stake in *On Certainty* 204–205. There Wittgenstein's assumption seems to be that talk of "grounding," of "justifying the evidence," of offering grounds for a conclusion, specifically the conclusion that a certain proposition, given the evidence, is true, is all right. It is just that what the justification of such decisions grounds out in is not "certain *propositions* striking is immediately as true" (our italics), but rather something which "is not true, nor yet false," namely, "our acting."

At this very late point in Wittgenstein's development, in short, just as in the *Tractatus*, meaning and truth were still for Wittgenstein, it appears, grounded in something extra-propositional, something having to do with acting, or practice. Even at this late stage, Wittgenstein's thinking is, in effect, dominated by the slogan *Die Logik müss für sich selber sorgen.* All questions of meaning must still be settled antecedently to establishing the truth or falsity of any contingent proposition, by appeal to considerations that are capable of founding the notions of proposition, meaning, and truth because they are themselves nonpropositional in character.

ii. Practices and rules

But there is an objection to be considered to the whole proposal to found the understanding of meaning in competent agency, where competent agency is assumed not to require, or to depend on, any knowledge of the truth of propositions. It derives from a collection of views very widely held among philosophers, and abundantly documented. Because it blocks the path to what we have to say in the remainder of this book, this is a good point at which to confront it head-on.

One way of putting the objection would be to give it the form of a dilemma. The dilemma goes like this. Either the "practices" that allegedly underpin the understanding of meaning are guided by rules, or they are not. If they are guided by rules it will, surely, be possible to give those rules propositional expression. But if they are not guided by rules, then what distinguishes the "practices" concerned as *linguistic* practices? Without the assumption that it is governed by theoretically specifiable rules of a specifically linguistic character, won't the ability to speak a language become indistinguishable from the general ability of human beings to cope practically with their environment, an ability in which propositional and practical knowledge are surely inextricably intermingled?

Many philosophers, faced by this dilemma, opt for the second horn, guided by Quine's powerful arguments for the conclusion that "no systematic experimental sense is to be made of a distinction between usage due to meaning and usage due to generally shared collateral information":[3] that, in other words, there are no observational grounds on which knowledge of meaning could be distinguished from a speaker's empirically based general knowledge of the world. Davidson sums up in the following way the conclusion to which such arguments point:

> ... there is no such thing as a language, not if a language is anything like what many philosophers and linguists have supposed.[4] ... [There is no] learnable common core of consistent behavior, no shared grammar or rules, no portable interpreting machine set to grind out the meaning of an arbitrary utterance, ... [and in general no] boundary between knowing a language and knowing our way around the world generally.[5]

Other philosophers find such a conclusion intolerable. Their objection is this. A practice is, surely, a pattern of activity governed by socially sanctioned rules. To think otherwise, it would seem, would be to interpret what is to be understood by the phrase "our acting" in *On Certainty* 204 as arbitrary, or *gratuitous* action – what the French, having been introduced to the notion first by Gide's 1914 novel *Les Caves du Vatican*, and later by Sartre, call an *acte gratuit*. In the nature of things nothing could intelligibly be said to be grounded in an *acte gratuit*, as the attempt so to ground it would make it part, or a consequence, of the gratuitous act, and so itself gratuitous. To take part in a practice, therefore, is to be aware of, to abide by, and to be guided by, some relevant system of rules.

But choosing this, the first horn of the dilemma, is as fatal as choosing the second to the project implicit in Wittgenstein's Slogan. In order for a speaker to be guided by the rules in question he must, presumably, know (a) their content, and (b) that they are the rules generally accepted and observed within the linguistic community. The fact that the rules have a certain specific content, whatever that may be, as well as the fact that they, and not others are the rules observed within the community, will presumably, now, like other facts, be capable of formulation in some set of true propositions. A speaker who knows the content of the rules and that they are the ones acknowledged in his community will, therefore, in virtue of knowing that, know some propositions to be true (maybe, even, they will "strike him immediately as true"). It follows, that a speaker who knows how to continue, in his own actions, the patterns set by "our act-ing," unless "our acting" is to be construed as a mere tissue of *actes gra-tuits*, does so in virtue of possessing knowledge that is, at least in principle, propositionally formulable. And so, *pace* Wittgenstein, far from the ability to assess the meanings and truth-conditions of propositions grounding out in some kind of prepropositional, and hence nonproposional, knowing-how, it is the supposed knowledge-how in question which in turn grounds out in knowing-that: in knowledge, in other words, of the truth of some propositions.

iii. The theoretical representation of linguistic competence

A leading figure among those who prefer to embrace the first horn of the dilemma, and credit the semantically competent speaker with a grasp of rules capable of being propositionally represented as the content of a "theory of meaning," is Michael Dummett. Dummett, like ourselves, in-vokes Wittgenstein as an ally, in this case against the the Davidsonian view sketched above. But Dummett would not accept our suggestion that Wittgenstein's Slogan, interpreted as we interpret it, stakes out a commit-ment to which Wittgenstein remains as faithful in his latest as in his earliest work. On the contrary, Dummett takes the later Wittgenstein's fundamen-tal proposal to be merely that "a language is a practice in which people engage . . . constituted by rules which it is part of social custom to follow."[6] Dummett takes this claim to be consistent with the possibility that a com-petent speaker may be unable to express the content of his competence in propositional terms, but equally with the possibility that either he, or some more astute and articulate theorist, may be able to do so. Hence, for Dummett, Wittgenstein's suggestion that the notions of meaning and truth ground out in "our acting" not only presents no obstacle to the philosophi-cal enterprise of constructing a theory of meaning, but offers the key to the successful prosecution of that enterprise.

Why, then, is it so compelling to *represent* mastery of a language as if it were theoretical knowledge? Although there is no one who knows what it is to speak Spanish other than those who speak Spanish, it is not strictly true that there is no other way to come to know what speaking Spanish is. Theoretical knowledge, the content of which was a fully explicit description of a practice, would also amount to knowing what the practice was. In the case of a language, such a description would be a theory of meaning for that language, complete with all the linking principles.[7]

Dummett's argument is developed at greater length in his essay "What Do I Know when I Know a Language?," in his 1993 collection *The Seas of Language*.[8] Dummett begins by granting that there is a practical sense of "know" that is applicable in such cases as knowing how to swim or knowing how to ride a bicycle. But, on the one hand, the use of the term "knowledge" in these cases is "a mere manner of speaking, not to be taken seriously."[9] And, on the other, while we should not consider it a miracle if someone, put into the water for the first time, just found himself swimming, it would be "magic" – a *lusus naturae* – if someone who had neither learned nor been brought up to speak Spanish should suddenly find himself speaking it. The difference, Dummett suggests, "lies in the fact that speaking language is a conscious process."[10] Traditionally – by Locke and other seventeenth- and eighteenth-century empiricists, for instance – the difference between a conscious process and a mechanical or habitual one was taken to consist in the presence, in the former case, of an underlying process of thought, conducted in terms of the class of mental entities traditionally termed "ideas" or "concepts." Frege ranks for Dummett as the chief executioner of that "psychologistic" view. Acceptance of a broadly Fregean anti-psychologism might thus seem at first sight to block the way to any theory proposing "the explanation of sense in terms of some inner psychological mechanism."[11] But, Dummett points out, the most telling argument in Frege's anti-psychologistic armoury is to be found in the former's demand that sense be publicly communicable. "The principle which Frege opposes to psychologism is that of the communicability of sense."[12] This principle indeed rules out any account, such as Locke's, which locates the difference between intelligent and mechanical action in the presence of *private*, in the sense of inherently incommunicable, inner states. But it offers no argument against an internal-process account that requires that any internal process postulated by a theory be manifestable in use. The way is thus open for an account of the distinction between what it is to know a language, and what it is to know, say, how to swim, which grants the presence in the former case of something, on Dummett's view, properly to be called "knowledge;" namely, a grasp, either explicitly, or in some "internalised" form not immediately accessible to consciousness, of a structure of linguistic rules and conventions. Far from being opposed to the Fregean deliverance that has dominated analytic philosophy since its inception, Dummett sees such a view, divested of the psychologism of the British Empiricists, as the type of view at which Frege's theory of meaning was aiming.

As I have here presented Frege's ideas, and as, I think, it is natural to conceive the matter from what he said about it, a theory of meaning is not a description from the outside of the practice of using the language, but is thought of as an object of knowledge on the part of speakers. A speaker's mastery of his language consists, on this view, in his knowing a theory of meaning for it; it is this that confers on his utterances the senses they bear, and it is because two speakers take the language as governed by the same, or nearly the same, theory of meaning that they can communicate with one another by means of that language. I shall reserve the phrase "a theory of meaning" for a theory thus conceived as something known by the speakers.[13]

If the contents of such a theory must be manifestable in use, though, why not confine oneself to a description of what is so manifested? Why postulate any underlying structure of knowledge?

...we can represent the objection to the conception of a theory of meaning by means of the following dilemma. If the theory of meaning can be converted into a direct description of actual linguistic practice, then it is better so converted; and we have then eliminated any appeal to the notion of knowledge. If, on the other hand, it cannot be converted into such a description, it ceases to be plausible that, by ascribing an implicit knowledge of that theory to a speaker, we have given an adequate representation of his practical ability in speaking the language. The appeal to the notion of knowledge is therefore either redundant or positively incorrect.[14]

Dummett's reply to this is to deploy "the well-known and often fruitful comparison of a language with a board-game."[15] Imagine a Martian who observes human beings playing chess but does not grasp that playing such games is an intelligent activity. He develops, on purely inductive grounds, "a powerful scientific theory of the game," which allows him to predict moves with considerable accuracy.

He now knows a great deal more than anyone needs in order to be able to play the game. But he also knows *less*, because he cannot say what are the rules of the game or what is its object; he does not so much have the concept of a lawful move or of winning and losing. He could simulate the play of a human player, but, for all the superior intelligence I am attributing to him, he could not play the game better than a human player, because he knows neither what is a lawful move nor what is a good move.[16]

Dummett's fundamental objection to writers such as Davidson or Quine, who view meaning from the viewpoint of what can be inductively established concerning it on the basis of observable behaviour, and in consequence see no way of distinguishing between a speaker's knowledge *of language* and whatever general body of empirical knowledge he may possess, is that they render themselves incapable of distinguishing between the human player and the Martian observer. Only a theory that views linguistic behaviour as guided by some body of internalised knowledge common to all speakers can do that.

Dummett's internalised knowledge will be by definition *theoretical* knowledge, that is, knowledge whose content will be adequately expressible as the content of a body of *propositions*; namely, those that compose an adequate theory of meaning. So, if Dummett is right, the Wittgenstein of *On Certainty* 204 is wrong: what "lies at the bottom of the language game" is not just "our acting," but, after all, "certain propositions' striking us immediately as true." "Giving grounds" for a judgment about meaning is like giving grounds for a certain move in backgammon: one takes down a copy of *Hoyle's Games*, and looks up the rule. Only in the case of language every speaker possesses an internalised copy of *Hoyle's Games*, which he can consult for himself. What makes it possible to transcribe this internal rulebook for the benefit of theory, indeed, is the fact that every speaker can look up independently from this internal process of consultation and either recite the rule that guides his judgment or at the very least recognise and confirm that some proposed formulation of the rule is accurate. As Dummett puts it,

> ...a theory [of meaning] is not open to assessment in the same way as an ordinary empirical theory; it is not to be judged correct merely on the ground that it tallies satisfactorily with objective linguistic behaviour. Rather, the only conclusive criterion for its correctness is that the speakers of the language are, upon reflection, prepared to acknowledge it as correct, that is, as embodying those principles by which they are in fact guided.[17]

iv. Rule-scepticism

Perhaps the most radical doubts concerning the possibility of a Dummett-style theory of meaning are those voiced by Saul Kripke.[18] Kripke agrees with Dummett that, ordinarily, we take the distinction between an intelligent linguistic response and a merely mechanical one, or an *acte gratuit*, to consist in the fact that the former is guided by rules. As Kripke puts it, "Normally, when we consider a mathematical rule such as addition, we think of ourselves as *guided* in our application of it to each new instance. Just this is the difference between someone who computes new values of a function and someone who calls out numbers at random."[19] Kripke differs from Dummett, however, in holding that no sense can be made of the notion of rule-guided performance.

Like Dummett's, Kripke's arguments derive in part from a reading of Wittgenstein. In Kripke's case, the reference is to a celebrated passage in the *Philosophical Investigations*. Wittgenstein has been arguing that, if one wishes to justify a performance as correct by appeal to a rule, one must be able to point to some respect in which the performance "accords with" the rule; and that the problem with this is that there is always some respect in which any performance can be found to accord with any rule one might care to think of. At I.201 he summarises the results of the discussion:

> This was our paradox: no course of action could be determined by a rule, because every course of action can be made out to accord with the rule. The answer was: if everything can be made out to accord with the rule, then it can also be made out to conflict with it. And so there would be neither accord nor conflict here.[20]

Kripke bases his argument on this "paradox," but develops it in an independent way to produce, as he says, a new version of scepticism: scepticism about rules. He takes Wittgenstein to be the originator of this form of scepticism, and the promotion of it one main aim of the *Philosophical Investigations*. Kripke's work in this area thus raises two distinct, although connected, questions, one philosophical, the other exegetical. On the one hand, there is the question whether Kripke's sceptical argument, considered on its own merits, is sound, and if sound, what follows. On the other, there is the question of whether Kripke's interpretation of Wittgenstein is faithful to the latter's intentions.

Kripke sets out his argument in terms of a specific arithmetical example. Suppose "68 + 57" is a computation I have never before performed. I work the sum, obtain the answer 125, and am confident, having checked my work, that it is correct. It is correct not only arithmetically, but meta-linguistically, in the sense that "plus" as I intended to use the term denoted, as it has always done when I used it in the past, a function yielding that value for those arguments.

But now I encounter a "bizarre sceptic." He suggests that, for all I know, the answer to "68 + 57" should have been "5." "Not if '+' means what it meant when I used it on previous occasions," I reply, "and I did mean that '+' on this occasion should denote the function I have always used it to denote." "Hold on," he says. "Your evidence for the supposition that you were, on each occasion, using '+' to denote a given function is simply that every arithmetical computation you have performed so far has instantiated that function. But how many computations have you performed?" I admit that I have never carried out any addition involving numbers larger than 57. "Well then," he says, "mightn't it be that 'plus' for you has always, in the past denoted a function, which we may call 'quus, and symbolise by '$\oplus$', defined thus:

$$x \oplus y = x + y, \text{ if } x,y < 57$$
$$= 5 \text{ otherwise}$$

You always have meant 'quus' by '+', but now, in some strange fit of madness or inadvertency, you have come to misinterpret your own past usage."

Of course, this is craziness. But it is serious craziness. Its seriousness emerges once we begin to ask what might be required to answer such a sceptic. Kripke suggests that any answer to the sceptic will require two components. On the one hand, it must reveal what fact it is about my mental state that constitutes my meaning "plus", not "quus," by "+." On the other, it must show, in some sense, how it comes about that, given the existence of that fact, I am justified in giving the answer "125" to "68 + 57." That is, it must show how the required fact contains, or has built into it, "directions" that determine the answer to be given to any addition sum, the very directions, indeed, which I gave myself for performing the computation "68 + 57," and that determined how I went about performing it.

Kripke devotes a good deal of space to demonstrating rather persuasively why various suggestions for meeting these two requirements fail to do so. One obvious suggestion is that the rule which generates answers to addition sums – to any addition sum – is simply the one we call *counting*.

Many readers, I should suppose, have long been impatient to protest that our problem arises only because of a ridiculous model of the instruction I gave myself regarding "addition." Surely I did not merely give myself some finite number of examples, from which I am supposed to extrapolate the whole table ("Let '+' be the function instantiated by the following examples . . . "). No doubt infinitely many functions are compatible with *that.* Rather I learned – and internalised instructions for – a *rule* which determines how addition is to be continued. What was the rule? Well, say, to take it in its most primitive form: suppose we wish to add x and y. Take a huge bunch of marbles. First count out x marbles in one heap. Then count out y marbles in another. Put the two heaps together and count out the number of marbles in the union thus formed. The result is $x + y$.[21]

But this suggestion is vulnerable to the very same sceptical objection.

Despite the initial plausiblity of this objection, the sceptic's response is all too obvious. True, if "count," as I used the word in the past, referred to the act of counting (and my other past words are correctly interpreted in the standard way) then "plus" must have stood for addition. But I applied "count" like "plus," to only finitely many past cases. Thus the sceptic can question my present interpretation of my past usage of "count" as he did with "plus." In particular, he can claim that by "count" I formerly meant *quount*, where to "quount" a heap is to count it in the ordinary sense, unless the heap was formed as the union of two heaps, one of which has 57 or more items, in which case one must automatically give the answer "5."[22]

Grant, for the sake of argument, that the paradox is real, and that there is no way round it. What does it teach us? Kripke takes the lesson to be learned from it to be a Humean one.[23] It was Hume who, having raised in §IV of the first *Enquiry* some "Sceptical Doubts concerning the Operations of the Understanding," showed us in §V the way to a "Sceptical Solution of these Doubts." Kripke suggests that here also scepticism can best be fought with scepticism. Hume's "sceptical solutions" characteristically involve the inversion of a conditional; or, putting it another way, the exchange of the conditional for its contrapositive. Our ordinary notion of causality presumes the acceptance of conditionals along the lines of "If type A events cause type B events, then if a type A event occurs a type B event must follow." The "must" implies some version of necessity; Hume notoriously denies the accessibility of any notion of necessity capable of filling the bill. How then to read the conditional? By inverting it, so that it is not that antecedent conditions necessitate a regular sequence of types of event, but rather that the failure of a type A event to be followed by a type B event justifies the withdrawal of the hypothesis of a causal connection between them.

Kripke suggests that this is precisely the procedure we should follow in the case of scepticism about knowledge of rules.

It is essential to our conception of a rule that we maintain some such conditional as "If Jones means addition by '+', then if he is asked for '68 + 57' he will reply '125'." (Actually many clauses should be added to the antecedent to make it strictly correct, but for present purposes let us leave it in this rough form.) As in the causal case, the conditional as stated makes it appear that some mental state obtains in Jones that guarantees his performance of particular additions such as "68 + 57" – just what the sceptical argument denies. Wittgenstein's picture of the true situation concentrates on the contrapositive, and on justification conditions. If Jones does not come out with "125" when asked about "68 + 57" we cannot assert that he means addition by "+." Actually, of course, this is not strictly true, because our formulation of the conditional is overly loose; other conditions must be added to the conditional to make it true. As the conditional is stated, not even the possibility of computational error is taken into account, and there are many complications not easily spelled out. The fact remains that if we ascribe to Jones the conventional concept of addition, we do not expect him to exhibit a pattern of bizarre, quus-like behavior. By such a conditional we do not mean, on the Wittgensteinian view, that any state of Jones guarantees his correct behavior. Rather by asserting such a conditional we commit ourselves, if in the future Jones behaves bizarrely enough (and on enough occasions), no longer to persist in our assertion that he is following a conventional rule of addition.

The rough conditional thus expresses a restriction on the community's game of attributing to one of its members the grasping of a certain concept: if the individual in question no longer conforms to what the community would do in these circumstances, the community can no longer attribute the concept to him. Even though, when we play this game and attribute concepts to individuals, we depict no special "state" of their minds, we do something of importance. We take them provisionally into the community, as long as further deviant behavior does not exclude them. In practice, such deviant behavior seldom occurs.

It is then, in such a description of the game of concept attribution that Wittgenstein's sceptical solution consists.[24]

This "sceptical solution" to the Wittgenstein Paradox is clearly quite as hostile to Wittgenstein's Slogan, or to the Slogan-like interpretation we earlier (Chapter 8 §1) placed on *On Certainty* 204–205, as Dummett's optimism concerning the possibility of a theory of meaning. A speaker's understanding of the meaning of "+" is indeed, as Wittgenstein suggests at various points in his discussion of understanding, revealed by "how he goes on" when asked to demonstrate his understanding in practice. And what he does in "going on," how he fills in the incomplete function-schema "57 + 68 = ____" is *guided by something* – is not simply random; not an *acte gratuit*. But what it is guided by is the speaker's estimate of the likely nature of the reception to be accorded his move by other members of the linguistic community. And this estimate in turn must rest on propositionally formulable knowledge derived from past experience. For Kripke as for Davidson there is no "boundary between knowing a language and knowing one's way around the world."

v. Guided or random?

Can anything be said in defense of the Slogan? The best place to start, perhaps, is with the one doctrine which Dummett and Kripke share, namely, the doctrine that an action that is not guided by any piece of knowledge, of rules or of community preferences, an action that an agent "just does," or "just produces, without thinking about it," is *by that token* an arbitrary or random act. This claim is not only one on which Kripke and Dummett agree, it is essential to each of them: for both, an indispensable common element in the otherwise disparate collection of premises on which the two opposed towers of argument rest. It is what allows Dummett to argue that a theory of language must be more than "a direct description of linguistic practice." And it is what, by permitting Kripke to represent the essential characteristic of rule-following to consist in the *successive* application of the *same* principle, allows him to represent as essential the epistemic link between present and past performances that he then finds so little difficulty in snapping.

Is the choice between the options of describing an action as random, or gratuitous, and describing it as epistemically grounded, guided by some piece of knowledge-that, as exhaustive, and so as forced, as both Dummett and Kripke take it to be? The illusion that we are facing a dilemma collapses if it is possible to present even a single case that goes between its horns. And in the present instance it does seem possible to present such a case.

Consider, then, the practice of giving and following directions phrased in terms of the expressions "left" and "right." Linguistic exchanges involving these terms are commonplace between speakers: "Go left at the next junction"; "Look, there's a hot air balloon, to the right of that tree." The success of such exchanges clearly depends on the satisfaction of some background conditions, which are not hard to state, at any rate roughly. The following would seem to offer a reasonable approximation:

(A_1) Each speaker must be in the habit of associating each of the two words "left" and "right" with one side of his own body.

(A_2) The linkage of each term to a given side of the body must be the same from speaker to speaker.

(A_3) Each speaker must see and understand the communicative advantages offered, or better, opened up by what we may as well call for convenience of reference the *"left"/"right" device*. Roughly speaking the device allows speakers to guide, and to be guided, *at a distance*. The giver of advice need not accompany the person he is advising to the next fork in the road and physically propel him on to the leftward path; nor need he take his companion's head in his hands and turn it until the latter is gazing in the direction of the hot-air balloon. He can simply say, "turn left," "look right," and the job is done. The advice is given and it can be left to his interlocutor to act on it, and so receive the profit accruing to him if the advice is good advice. He will take the path opposite the left side of his body, look to the side of the tree which aligns with the right side of his body, and so on.

Is it necessary, in order that a speaker satisfy these conditions, that he or she possess any piece of propositionally formulable knowledge: knowledge in Dummett's sense of the term, that is, Ryle's knowledge-that? It is hard to see that it is. It seems evident, indeed, that the background conditions can be satisfied by a speaker who has simply acquired an appropriate collection of habits. Provided each speaker is in the habit of associating the words "left" and "right" with the same sides of his own body as other speakers, provided he is in the habit of looking right (or left) when someone says "look right" (or "left"), unless he mistrusts the advice or has some other reason for not doing as he is told, and in the habit, subject to the same *caveats*, of turning left when he is told "turn left," there seems no reason why his exchanges with others on this level should not, from a linguistic point of view at least, go swimmingly.

Second, it is unclear what kind of knowledge of the truth of propositions it could be, the possession of which would put the speaker in a position to satisfy the background conditions of the "left"/"right" device. Following Dummett, we might try looking for some internal process by appeal to which we might explain *how he does* what he does. Asking that question will doubtless evoke many different kinds of answer. But it is not obvious that any of them contribute to a *theory of meaning*, as Dummett conceives that. For instance, there will doubtless, in some cases at least, be internal processes by appeal to which a speaker keeps straight which side of his body is the right side and which is the left (more people get this wrong in emergencies than might be supposed). One speaker might think "my right hand is the one I hold my knife with." But there seems no reason to suppose that all speakers employ this particular mnemonic. Another, left-handed speaker might think " 'Right', now, that's my awkward hand: 'left' is the good one." And a third speaker might think nothing at all, employ no mnemonic, but just act: turn left, or right as the case may be, automatically. As Wittgenstein never tired of telling us, the trouble with inner processes is that their presence seems neither necessary nor sufficient to establish that a speaker understands, or to put it in currently fashionable terms, "is linguistically competent" (Putnam was later to discover the force of this unfortunate fact as an objection to functionalism[25]).

At a deeper, neurological level, there will no doubt be processes, involving the bilateral symmetry of the brain, which provide the physical basis for the ability of human beings to distinguish one side of their bodies from the other. And no doubt these processes do help to make possible linguistic performances that presuppose that ability. But there seems no reason to suppose that they do that as a result of being known – even *implicitly* known! – to the speakers who enjoy that ability.

It might be objected that if each user of the "left"/"right" device is to be supposed to act purely out of habit, then he must be supposed to be acting independently of any other user. And this may seem quite to ignore the force of Frege's doctrine of the publicity of sense. That doctrine, central to Dummett's argument, is founded on the thought that language is a common possession of speakers. Ability to speak a language cannot, therefore, be represented as consisting in the possession by each speaker of habits of response that *simply happen to chime in with* those of other speakers. It can only be understood as a *common possession* if *what* speakers are supposed to possess in common is access to a shared system of rules to which each speaker can appeal in justification of his linguistic responses.

The answer to this is that Frege's dictum does not require us to relinquish an account of linguistic capacity in terms of shared habits in favour of one framed in terms of shared access to rules. Its demands can equally well be met by distinguishing between, on the one hand, *purposively co-ordinated habits representing the outcome of training*, and, on the other, mere *idiosyncrasies* that happen to be exhibited by more than one person. Suppose that at precisely 6 P.M. each day, regular as clockwork, Mr. NN takes out his pipe, folds a piece of paper to make a spill that he lights at the fire, uses it to light his pipe and then, and only then, switches on the news. Certainly he may be described as a creature of habit, but equally certainly not as someone who is *following a rule*. Now suppose his old friend Mr. AB exhibits, even when he is on his own, exactly the same ritual pattern of behaviour. In such a case we would indeed not be prepared (and this is the nerve of the objection we are considering) to describe NN and AB as following the same rule, or as participating in the same practice. We should simply say, smiling, "Isn't that typical of the way the two old friends have grown unconsciously to resemble one another over the years?" NN and AB exhibit what would be, if either were alone in exhibiting it, an idiosyncratic pattern of behaviour. But in this case it is a *shared idiosyncrasy*.

Certainly, no adequate account of what it is to understand a language could be based on the notion of a shared idiosyncrasy. But that is not what is at stake in our description of the "left"/"right" device. What makes the difference is what makes it appropriate to use the term "device" in the latter case; namely, that in the latter case we have not merely a collection of people whose habits *resemble* one another, but a collection of people whose habits *mesh with one another in ways so patterned as to serve the purpose of promoting ends common to all and advantageous to all.* A speaker may be acting "habitually" or "automatically" in saying "There's the balloon – right of that tree," in the sense that his performance is not guided by appeal to any inner process whatsoever. He does not, before speaking, have to take out of some inner waistcoat pocket an intangible piece of paper headed "Rules for giving directions in terms of the bilateral symmetry of the human body." Nor would it do him any good if he did, because, as Wittgenstein never tires of pointing out, he would then need a second intangible document to guide his interpretation of the first one. Explanations, as Wittgenstein also was fond of observing, must come to an end somewhere. Similarly the speaker's hearer may equally automatically glance to the right of the indicated tree and reply "Oh yes, I see it now." Habit may be all that is at stake here also. But the habits of different speakers mesh in such a way as to promote the achievement of a certain common advantage; namely the advantage of one speaker's being able to guide another's actions at a distance, merely by uttering a word. That is what allows us to speak of a device here: we are dealing with something serving an end. The habits that qualify individuals to participate in such a device are, certainly, individual possessions. The device constituted by the meshing together of these individually possessed habits is, however, a common possession. And because, according to us, the senses, the meanings, of "left" and "right" are constituted, on the present account, by the use$_E$ we bestow on those expressions in the context of the "left"/"right" device, we are entitled to agree with Frege that the sense of these expressions is something to which speakers have access in common. We differ from Frege only in our account of *what* speakers have in common, and its location. Frege, whose thinking, anti-Cartesian though it is in some respects, is here in tune with the epistemic individualism (Chapter 7 §ix) characteristic of the Cartesian tradition in philosophy, locates what is common to speakers, a grasp of *Sinn*, in the mind of the individual speaker. We, with our bias towards Wittgenstein, locate it outside the mind of the individual speaker, in the structure of the public practice in which the past training, and the resulting habits, of the individual speaker fit him or her to participate.

To summarise, and to give a slightly more formal cast to the position we have been outlining: a speaker S is participating in a linguistic practice iff

1. S shares a certain pattern P of habits of performance with other members of his community;
2. the exercise of P in specific contexts can serve various purposes in an individual's life, and produce various types of satisfaction of need, in ways of which S is aware;
3. P involves the exchange of utterances (verbal or nonverbal) to which the performance of one or another subpattern of P is cued;
4. S, in response to such a cue, exhibits the subpattern of P normally cued to it, and does so in such a way as to suggest that he is aware of what satisfactions of need are to be gained by initiating that subpattern in response to that cue, and intends to gain them.

vi. Kripke and Dummett

Dummett and Kripke are right to argue that there is a distinction to be drawn between intelligent, conscious action and arbitrary action. The mistake both make, according to the view presented here, is to look for the ground of that distinction, consistently with the commitment to epistemic individualism that both share with Frege, within the mind of the individual speaker. There must be some piece of knowledge he possesses, some propositionally formulable rule or principle to which he appeals in justification of a given response, if that response is to be taken to constitute an intelligent manifestation of a grasp of meaning. It might be objected that to accuse Kripke of a commitment to epistemic individualism is unfair, since the whole drift of his thought is, as everyone agrees, towards an "externalism" that represents a speaker's judgments of meaning as grounded, not in a grasp of anything internal to that speaker's mind but in the judgment of the linguistic community. This is sound as far as it goes. But the point stands nevertheless. The assumption of Kripke's that places him in the same camp with Dummett on the issue of epistemic individualism is that if a speaker has access to any basis for his judgments of meaning *other than* the approval of the linguistic community, *that can only be because he has access to some rule or principle internal to his mind.* Show, therefore, as Kripke, following Wittgenstein sets out to show, that no judgment of meaning can be grounded in an "inner process" of any kind, and one is left, as it appears, with the approval of the linguistic community as the only remaining possible basis for such judgments. Dummett and Kripke subscribe, in other words, to the same assessment of the available options for grounding judgments of meaning: either some version of epistemic individualism or – by way of the view that all anyone knows of meaning is what can be gleaned on the basis of inductive assessment of observable behaviour – a rather radical kind of social relativism. We have a new version of the move (Chapter 1 §i) by which the sceptic takes charge of the argument by getting his opponent to accept an account of the available theoretical options that favours the sceptical enterprise.

We, in effect, have chosen to dissent from that assessment of the options. There is, according to us, a way of understanding the difference between random action and action that manifests an intelligent grasp of meaning, which appeals neither to inner process nor to community approval. Our suggestion, like Kripke's, is "externalist" in character. But it is an externalism devoid of social relativism, because it grounds understanding of meaning in a grasp of the way in which habitual responses fit into externally, publicly instituted and maintained practices, and in a further grasp of the point, the goals served and the advantages to be gained, by the operation of those practices in specific contexts. It is by observing the way in which a linguistic performance manifests these two types of understanding that we are enabled to assess it as displaying, or as failing to display, an intelligent grasp of meaning.

We now turn to a more detailed assessment of, first Dummett's, and then Kripke's, arguments in the light of this, at present largely schematic, redrawing of the options.

vii. Martians and chessplayers

Dummett's example (Chapter 8 §iii) of a Martian who sets himself to acquire, by purely inductive means, an understanding of the human game of chess, illustrates Dummett's contention that a grasp of the significance of behaviour that constitutes participation in a practice cannot be acquired through the inductive processing of observations of overt behaviour, as a player's capacity to participate in a practice depends on his knowing the rules of the practice: in effect, that is, in Dummett's terms, on his having access to a theory of meaning.

There are, according to Dummett, two grounds on which the Martian observer is to be distinguished from the human player. On the one hand, the chessplayers have access to the concept of a move's being lawful or unlawful. On the other, the chessplayers know, as the Martian does not, what the object, the point of the game is: they have access to the concepts of winning and losing. It looks at first sight as though these two conditions are not detachable from one another; in fact they are. One can have the latter without the former.

To see this one need only reflect that it is possible to imagine people so good at chess, and so honest in their dealings, that the rules of chess have never been written down. Among them it is with chess as it is with the "left"/"right" device among us. That is to say, chessplayers always make the moves we think of as permitted, and never make any of the moves we think of as prohibited, merely because it is their habit to do certain "done" things and to avoid others that are "not done," just as it is the habit of a competent English speaker to turn left (other things being equal) when someone says "turn left." These habits have, of course been built up by explicit instruction; by a teacher's saying to a child, "Yes, you can do that," and "No, we don't do that," but once the right responses are instilled it is habit, and not an appeal, conscious or unconscious, to propositionally formulated rules, which guides the Virtuous Chessplayers' moves. It never occurs to them to formulate the rule governing, for instance, the Knight's move, because it is just habitual to them to move the Knight that way. They never need to justify so doing by appeal to an explicitly formulated rule because, because everyone learns chess almost at birth, the need to justify moves that have in consequence become second nature to them never arises. So, although it would be possible to represent their habits in terms of a list of rules, they have never produced such a list, as they have no need to do so. And although they would no doubt, if presented with such a list, recognise it as adequately expressing, or as Chomsky would say, generating, their habits, that in itself gives us no reason to suppose that they have really had access to such a list all along, but were unaware of it because (the rules on the list being "internalised" ones) their access to it was unconscious.

The Virtuous Chessplayers thus have no need for the concept of a lawful move because they are never tempted to make an unlawful one. Like ancient Athenian aristocrats before they encounter Socrates, or characters in the quaintly bracing novels of John Buchan, who behave effortlessly like gentlemen without ever agitating the perfect decency and simplicity of their minds with reflection on either the nature or the justification of gentlemanly behaviour, they simply do as one does, among other things moving chesspieces as one moves chesspieces. But they certainly have access to the concept of winning or losing. They know what checkmate is, and they seek it vigorously. Moreover, they assess intervening plays with considerable intelligence according to how far they contribute to that goal. It is open to us, in short, to distinguish the unintelligent, or unconscious, or mechanical chessplayer from his intelligent, or conscious, or rational counterpart in the manner we suggested above: not, that is, on the grounds that the latter justifies his moves as legitimate by appeal to an underlying grasp of rules, while the former does not, but on the grounds that the latter directs his play, in ingenious and effective ways, to maximise the likelihood of his achieving checkmate, while the former simply pushes pieces about, perfectly correctly, perhaps, but at random. And, as it should not be beyond the powers of an intelligent Martian to discover, merely by attending to the overt behaviour of the players, that achieving checkmate is the object of the game – he can see, after all, that certain configurations of pieces occasion relief and jubilation on the part of one player and dejection on the part of the other; and it should require only a modest inductive capacity to work out what those configurations have in common – it should not be beyond his powers to become, merely by paying attention to what the Virtuous Chessplayers observably get up to, himself a chessplayer.

viii. A further example

In the same way we judge whether someone really understands the "left"/"right" device, neither (impossibly) by inspecting his inner life to see whether he is really guiding his performances by reference to "the rules" of the device, nor (possibly but unnecessarily) by seeing whether he can produce, or acknowledge as correct, a statement of the "rules" in question. Rather, as Wittgenstein constantly insists, we decide the issue by reference to whether, when presented with instructions framed in terms of the device he appears to know, as Wittgenstein often puts it, "how to go on." Presuming that he wants to go to Dulverton, does he turn left on to the Dulverton road, or does he hesitate? Is he always in the habit of hesitating in such cases? Does he look to the left of the tree when told to look to the right of it, and then express strong disappointment at not seeing the balloon? When we ask him which his left hand is, does he simply stare from one to the other in hopeless misery? If he does any of these things or others, there will be some doubt whether he grasps the meaning of the words "left" and "right." Further investigations will perhaps show whether the problem lies in his not having been trained in the right habits of association or in his failing to see the point of the "left"/"right" device: the advantages to be gained from operating it (such investigations might open up lines of inquiry into the nature of the brain damage from which he may be suffering). But it is only if such situations arise that we begin to doubt whether someone grasps the meaning of "left" and "right." If he accepts such directions as "turn left for Dulverton" with relief and thanks, and (other things being equal) acts on them unhesitatingly; if he says, correctly "Oh yes, there it is on the right, but it's moving left; yes, there it is now on the left of the tree"; then we take it, reasonably enough, that he has been trained in the right habits of association to allow him to operate the "left"/"right" device accurately and unhesitatingly, and is perfectly well aware of the point of the device and the communicative advantages it brings with it. And that is enough to establish that he knows the meaning of "left" and "right." Nor is it just a matter of no further test being needed. What further test could there be?

ix. Kripke and his critics

Let us now turn back to Kripke and meaning-scepticism. Discussion of Kripke's paradox has tended to pursue two lines of objection, one, broadly speaking, philosophical in character, the other exegetical; which is not to say that the partitions dividing the two topics are not extremely thin and permeable. On the one hand, it has been argued that the consequences of accepting Kripke's sceptical argument are far more radical than Kripke suggests, and that the quasi-Humean sceptical solution he proposes does not improve matters. On the other, it has been argued that not only the "sceptical solution," but the sceptical argument that it supposedly answers, are both equally unfaithful to Wittgenstein's intentions.

The sceptical argument is that *any* course of action can be made out to accord with a given rule. Its conclusion is thus not that we have no grounds for distinguishing between two or more possible interpretations of a rule, any of which might be the correct one, but the more radical one that there no sense to be made of the notion of correctly applying a rule – or, in other words, semantic nihilism. "The real conclusion of the sceptical argument was that no content can be attached to the hypothesis that a determinate meaning attached to a given expression."[26] As Kripke himself puts it, if the argument goes through "there can be no such thing as meaning anything by any word. Each new application we make is a leap in the dark."[27] But if this is correct, as José Zalabardo and Crispin Wight[28] have in different ways pointed out, the sceptical solution fails. According to the sceptical solution, ascriptions of content are "really" claims about the community's "game of concept attribution." On such an account, to ascribe a given content to a given expression would be merely to advance a judgment concerning one's fellow speakers' inclinations to accept such an ascription. But, leaving aside the inherent absurdity of the suggestion that judgments about content reduce to judgments about speakers' inclinations to ascribe content, even if such a judgment were to prove correct, what weight could it have? What the sceptical argument appears to show is that there are no truths, no "facts of the matter," about the assertion conditions that any individual speaker associates with a given sentence. But then, *a fortiori*, there are no truths about the assertion conditions that the community (i.e., the individual speakers considered collectively) associates with sentences either. In other words, the judgment of the community is as worthless as the judgment of the individual. Suppose the community supports the individual in writing "125" rather than "5" as the solution to "68 + 57," what follows? One is tempted to say, "Couldn't the community just be wrong about that?" But this misses the real nerve of the problem, which is that, if the sceptical argument goes through on its own terms, there is nothing for the community to be right or wrong about, any more than there is anything for the individual to be right or wrong about. As Wittgenstein says, "There would be neither accord nor conflict here."

x. Kripke and Wittgenstein

So much for the first line of objection to Kripke. It is clearly not conclusive, as it offers no answer to the sceptic who takes his stand on the Wittgenstein Paradox as Kripke develops it. It satisfies neither of Kripke's two criteria for a successful answer: it neither says what fact it is about a speaker's mental life which constitutes his meaning plus by "+," nor shows what it is about that fact that turns it into a justification for writing down "125" rather than "5" as the answer to "68 + 57 = —?" Can the second line of objection do better?

The second line of objection has two prongs. On the one hand, the claim is that Kripke is wrong to construe Wittgenstein as a sceptic, let alone a Humean one; on the other, that an adequate response to the sceptical argument is to be found in Wittgenstein himself. The first suggestion rests on the continuation of the paragraph (*Investigations* I.201) from which Kripke distils it. The whole passage runs as follows:

201. This was our paradox: no course of action could be determined by a rule, because every course of action can be made out to accord with the rule. The answer was: if everything can be made out to accord with the rule, then it can also be made out to conflict with it. And so there would be neither accord nor conflict here.

It can be seen that there is a misunderstanding here from the mere fact that in the course of our argument we gave one interpretation after another; as if each one contented us for a moment, until we thought of yet another standing behind it. What this shews is that there is a way of grasping a rule which is *not* an *interpretation*, but which is exhibited in what we call "obeying the rule" and "going against it" in actual cases.

202. And hence also "obeying a rule" is a practice. And to *think* one is obeying a rule is not to obey a rule. Hence it is not possible to obey a rule "privately": otherwise thinking one was obeying a rule would be the same thing as obeying it.

Enigmatic though this passage is, there is enough in it to make it reasonably probable that, exegetically speaking at least, Kripke is on the wrong track. What the sceptical argument shows is that *if an individual has to choose between one interpretation of a rule and another,* there is no fact about his present or past mental life that could determine his choice. In the opening paragraph of 201 Wittgenstein grants the force of this paradox. But in the second he says, in effect, that it doesn't matter, because an individual does not in practice have to choose between one interpretation of the rule and another. Obeying a rule is not a matter of first fixing on an interpretation of the rule and then obeying *that,* because "there is a way of grasping a rule which is *not* an *interpretation.*" 202 amplifies this a little. "Obeying a rule" is a practice. And because of that there can be no question of someone's obeying a rule privately: if there could, "thinking one was obeying a rule would be the same thing as obeying it."

Strenuous efforts have been made to distil from these scraps an answer to Kripke's "bizarre sceptic," with at best inconclusive results: a state of affairs no doubt stemming in part from the lack, at present, of an agreed interpretation of very considerable parts of the later thought of Wittgenstein. On some interpretations, indeed, Wittgenstein is very difficult to distinguish from Kripke's sceptic. Thus, for instance, Dummett's influential reading of Wittgenstein's philosophy of mathematics makes of the latter a "full-blooded conventionalist"[29] who holds, just like the Kripkean sceptic, that in Dummett's words "if we accept [a] proof, we confer necessity on the theorem proved . . . in doing this, we are making a new decision, and not merely making explicit a decision we had already made implicitly."[30] Many of those who, discounting this interpretation and others like it, think that there is an anti-sceptical argument to be got out of Wittgenstein, are inclined to pursue it by, in effect, opposing to Kripke's Humean Wittgenstein a kind of Kantian Wittgenstein, armed with a quasi-transcendental notion of "grammar" (of which we shall have more to say in Part III) credited with the power of somehow transmuting contingencies of usage into necessities of rule-following.[31]

xi. On not answering Kripke's sceptic

None of the more familiar ways in which Wittgenstein is currently read, in short, yield a direct answer to Kripke's sceptic. But that is, perhaps, scarcely surprising, given that the sceptic's own arguments are sufficient to show that no answer to the sceptic on his own terms – no answer that involves pointing to some justifying fact about the mental life of the speaker who chooses to write down "125" as the solution to "68 + 57 =" – is possible. Kripke's sceptic, like Hume's, is unanswerable on his own terms. But are those the only terms on which the question what it is to know the meaning of an expression, of "+," for instance, can be posed and answered? We have already found reason to suspect (Chapter 8 §vi) that they are not: that the appearance of inevitability they present to many minds is an artifact of the commitment to epistemic individualism that has pervaded Western Philosophy since Descartes. The sceptic's argument, that the absence of any "mental fact" that could justify writing down "125" leaves the approval of the linguistic community as the sole source of justification for doing so trades, as we have seen, on the concealed, or at any rate not very evident, premise that an act unguided by appeal to knowledge of rules is by that fact an arbitrary or random act. We have found reason to doubt the solidity of that assumption. And that seems to open the way to a different reponse to Kripke's sceptic: one which answers him not by producing the kind of answer he demands, but by showing that and why, that kind of answer is not required, either to underpin the judgment that a certain function takes a certain value for given arguments, or to underpin the judgment that a given speaker correctly understands the meaning of a given expression. Let us now try to develop that suggestion, relying initially on some work by the Australian philosopher Len Goddard.

xii. Goddard on counting

In 1962, in the *Australasian Journal of Philosophy and Psychology*,[32] Goddard published a paper entitled "Counting." It attracted some notice at the time – it was brought at that time to the attention of one of us by no less distinguished a judge than the late Professor Gilbert Ryle – but it appears to have been largely forgotten by the time the debates over Kripke's interpretation of Wittgenstein on rule-following began in earnest a decade and a half later.

Goddard's quarrel in "Counting" is with Russell's conviction that the notion of counting, unlike that of similarity between classes, is irrelevant to the logical foundations of arithmetic. This interest is not ours, at least in the present work, and raises issues that we have no intention of pursuing here. What interests us is the force that Goddard's account of counting appears to possess against Kripke's related contention that the paradox of rule-following, as it applies to the choice between writing "125" or "5" after "68 + 57 =," cannot be resolved by appealing to the notion of counting. Kripke's argument on that point is that the issue of choosing between two "rules," which forms the nub of his discussion of "plus" and "quus," simply arises again in the case of "count" and "quount." It is this contention that Goddard's account appears to have the power to subvert.

Goddard's contention is that an understanding of counting is logically prior to, and founds, the understanding both of the concept of number and of those of such arithmetical operations as addition. His method is to "look at how a child might be taught to learn these things,"[33] and so looks at first sight, as he grants, genetic or psychological rather than philosophical in character. Goddard meets this objection with an early instance of what has now become a rather standard rebuttal: he is investigating not what takes place when a child acquires the concept of number, but what kinds of prior understanding a full or even half-fledged understanding of that concept logically presupposes: "what must be known before we can understand number."[34]

"Understanding number" according to Goddard, and consistently with the central claim of the present chapter, is not a matter of knowledge of the truth of propositions – knowing-that in terms of Ryle's distinction – but a matter of knowing-how: of knowing-how to conduct a certain practice. The practice as a whole consists in the interarticulation of several component practices. The most fundamental of these, because it is indispensable to the others, is what Goddard calls *the counting rhyme*.

It is easy for a child to learn the counting rhyme. By this I mean that a child can be taught to say the numerals "one," "two," "three," . . . , until he catches on to the fact that there are certain key words ("twenty," "thirty," . . . ,"a hundred" . . .) and certain repetitive patterns (after "thirty" you say "thirty-*one*," "thirty-*two*," . . . and so on) It is rather like learning those special kinds of nursery rhyme which are composed of repetitions with minor twists, some of which are such that the last line leads back to the first and the whole thing can be repeated indefinitely. So the child learns an endless routine by catching on to the rather complicated rules about repetitions.

These rules about repetitions are important. For they are such that (when the child has learnt them all) there is never any doubt about what *numeral* comes next. It is always a different numeral and there is always a recipe for its construction. The child who is in doubt about what comes after "one thousand three hundred and twenty-three" has not yet learnt the rules in terms of which the rhyme is constructed. So it is with the child who thinks there is no next numeral, that this is the end.[35]

Two other components of the counting-practice as Goddard describes it are *counting* and *controlled counting*. *Counting* is a game of pointing-and-saying.

We show a child a finite collection of objects, say the following,

x x x x x

and we instruct him to point to (say) the left-hand object and say "one"; next we tell him to move his finger to the adjacent object on the right, point to it and say "two." And we explain that he is to carry on in this way, saying the numerals he has learnt in the rhyme and pointing to the objects in turn. He makes mistakes and we correct him until he has learnt to associate (one-one correlate) his counting rhyme with his moving finger. Each numeral (the spoken word) corresponds to an action (pointing). The numerals go on indefinitely in terms of the fixed pattern which he has learnt (the rules for *saying* the rhyme correctly) and the actions can go on indefinitely even with a finite set of objects. Thus we might say to him: when you get to the end and say "five," start at the beginning again and say "six," and then carry on in the same way. Now he can count; and he can go on counting for ever. His endless verbal routine has been associated with an endless pointing routine.[36]

Controlled counting "controls" the practice thus set up in the sense of giving it a use. And it is in terms of the use we give it that numbers come into the picture.

We say to him [the learner]: if you want to know *how many things there are,* count (point and say, beginning at the beginning) until you come to the end, then stop. What you say then ("five" e.g.) is the number of objects there. That is what we say; and that is what "the number of objects there" *means* for him. Why do we say this? Because the objects are distinct, the numerals are distinct, and the objects are linked to the numerals by the distinct pointing actions. The actions are a mediating device which give the numerals a use. Later, the actions become different. We look at each object in turn instead of pointing to each in turn; but the actions, though no longer overt, are still there. "*Count the objects.*" then, means, "*Count* (point and say) *and stop* (when the objects run out)." The actions never run out and counting need never stop. We have thus added something to counting when we get to numbers. We have controlled it; given it a use. We have shown how it can be used to answer the question "How many?"[37]

... we might teach a child what "plus" and "equals" mean in the following way: We might say: count (point and say) to four, and stop; then start counting again with the next object until you get to three. You have now counted four and three. This is what "four plus three" means. And you can see that this is the same as seven. In this way: first mark the point you reached and then start at the beginning and count to seven. You can see that you get to the same point.

$$
\begin{array}{ll}
\text{x x x x x} & \text{x x x x x} \\
1\ 2\ 3\ 4\ 1 & 1\ 2\ 3\ 4\ 5 \\
\ \ \ \ 2\ 3 & \ \ \ \ \ 6\ 7
\end{array}
$$

This is what "equals" means. So you can see that four and three comes to the same point as seven; or, four plus three equals seven. (Is this an empirical fact or a logical one?) But "four and three" does not mean the same as "seven." "Four and three" means "Control-count to four *and then* control-count to three," while "seven" means "control-count to seven." And doing this we find we get to the same point. We do two different things but get the same result; like two roads which lead to the same village.[38]

There is more to Goddard's paper than this summary conveys. But these extracts bring us to a point sufficiently advanced to allow us to mount a rebuttal of Kripke's sceptic. Goddard's learner, having mastered controlled-counting to the point at which he has a use for such expressions as "four plus three" and "equals," has set his new skills to work by counting items to 68, stopping, counting to 57, then returning and counting through the whole set of items already counted, to obtain the result "125." The bizarre sceptic now steps forward with his familiar question: "Bearing in mind that you have only performed these operations a finite number of times, how can you be sure that the rule which governed your actions in previous cases does not require you to write '5' rather than '125' in the present case? What fact about your mental record of your past proceedings compels you to write down one figure rather than the other?" To this, the Goddardian Counter's reply is evident: "I am not governing my actions on this occasion by appeal to any fact about my mental record of my past proceedings, any more than I was on any previous occasion. I am just doing what I have been trained to do; just carrying out a sequence of steps in a prescribed order, as other Goddardian Counters do; and '125' is the result I get. I need no further reason, therefore, for writing down '125.' The situation is rather that if I were to write down '5' I should need some reason for doing that; and it is entirely opaque in what such a reason could consist, since the act of writing down '5' is simply unintelligible in relation to the practice of Goddardian Counting. It is unintelligible because there is nothing in that practice which could make it intelligible; and what *outside the practice* could make it intelligible?"

If the sceptic amplifies his question by suggesting that the Counter might in the past have taken "+" as a name for a function other than addition – "quus," for instance – and that writing down "5" might be a perfectly intelligible move in the context of quusing, the Counter again has a reply ready. His move is to repeat what he said the first time, namely, that he just does what he has been trained to do, writing down the result he gets by doing so, and that since the result he gets by doing so in the present case is "125" and not "5," he has plainly not been trained to quus, but rather to add.

If the sceptic now tries the familiar Cartesian move of asking what justifies, in the sense of what *epistemically grounds* the move of writing down "125," the Counter again has an answer. That answer is that nothing *epistemically* grounds his writing down of "125." He writes that number down because it is the result obtained by counting. But does he never feel a doubt about whether the number he writes down in such circumstances is the correct one? Certainly, but if such doubts arise, his only recourse is to perform the counting procedure again, but do it more carefully this time. There can be no question of any appeal to justifying considerations *external* to the counting procedure, and certainly no appeal to justifying considerations *internal* to his own mental life, because, as the sceptic's own arguments admirably show, there are no such considerations to be had. As Wittgenstein puts it, "It is not a kind of seeing on our part; it is our acting, which lies at the bottom of the language game."

The sceptic has one last card to play, namely, the one Kripke plays on pp. 15–16 of *Wittgenstein on Rules and Private Language*. Maybe as the Goddardian Counter used "count" in the past, it referred not to counting, but to a different practice, quounting, in accordance with which what the Counter should now write down is "5." The Counter's counter to this is simply to repeat once more what he has already said *ad nauseam*: that what he does now when he counts is not guided by anything, but is just what one does when one counts: what he has been trained to do. In particular, what he does is not, and never was, now or in the past, guided by any understanding of "the meaning of" the word "count," in which a "meaning" is to be understood as some kind of mental template or rule embodied in his past actions. Rather, it is the other way about: "count" has a meaning only as a general label for a certain collection of habits, namely, the collection some of whose components he manifested in doing what he just did to obtain the result "125."

xiii. The meaning of "signpost"

Kripke's argument about rule-following is not, of course, supposed to have a bearing only on mathematics. It is supposed to be an argument of magisterial generality, applying to all cases of rule-following whatsoever; which is why it has been supposed to have as its conclusion a form of scepticism, or nihilism, concerning meaning in general. So we need perhaps to look at other cases of rule following, to see whether, and how far, the answer to Kripke which we have distilled out of Goddard's paper, and what in detail about it, might prove more generally applicable.

Let us take a very prosaic example. How would one teach someone the meaning of, say, the term "signpost," and how would one set about assessing whether the teaching had been successful; whether he "understood the term correctly," "knew its meaning," or not?

It is imaginable that people might invent the practice of constructing signposts, installing them, and using them to direct their journeys, without having a term for these contraptions. Then one is introduced: "signpost." Now suppose someone asks, "What is the meaning of 'signpost'?" What are we to answer? We might begin, in a spirit of Referential Realism, "'signpost' is the name we give to ... " But to what do we give that name? To signposts, presumably, but such an answer will hardly be helpful. Its unhelpfulness is, philosophically at least, puzzling. The type of reply that we here began to construct is based on the, at least initially, reasonable presumption that the world, *along with all the things that are in it*, is equally accessible to ourselves and to the inquirer, and that a name acquires a meaning simply by being bestowed upon one of these commonly accessible things. Signposts are certainly among these mutually perceptually accessible things: here is one; it stands before us. So what is the problem? What has gone wrong?

Let us try bulldozing. We point to the signpost before us, which the inquirer can, for heaven's sake, see as well as we can. In a louder voice, tinged a little with irritation, we say, "'Signpost' is the name we give to *things like this*!" "To things like what, exactly?" replies the inquirer, timid but persistent. "For example, is that tree stump over there with three projecting branches a 'signpost'"? And there is the problem. To know the meaning of "signpost" it is not enough to know that this thing before us counts as one. One needs to be put in a position to tell which other things count as signposts, and which are to be excluded from the class of entities covered by the word. That demand, of course, raises serious, deep and much-discussed problems, some of which we shall address in Part III. For the moment, a simple, if *ad hoc*, solution suggests itself to the problem of how best to satisfy the inquirer's demand to be told the meaning of "signpost." There is a practice, of constructing and erecting wooden markers bearing place-names, to guide travellers in choosing their direction where roads or paths divide. We needed a name for the wooden constructions that figure in that practice. We chose to call them "signposts." That is what we need to explain to him. Once he grasps that, he grasps the meaning of "signpost" in a way which confers upon him substantial autonomy in his subsequent use of the term. Grasping that, he grasps, for one thing, why the tree stump with gesturing branches, however much it may physically resemble a signpost, is not one.

Explaining the meaning of "signpost" is not, in short, a matter either of associating the term with some element in a commonly accessible perceptual field, or of substituting for it another verbal expression, by matching it with a synonym, or translation, or dictionary definition. It is a matter of inducting the learner into a certain practice, which at present we alone operate, and he knows nothing of, but in which he can easily be made a full participant.

Being a full participant will, of course, still leave him open to many kinds of epistemic doubt *about signposts*. He may doubt whether what he sees in the gloom ahead is a signpost or an old stump, or whether something which looks for all the world like a signpost is really one, or a counterfeit left by a retreating army to confuse the invaders. But is it intelligible to envisage him entertaining epistemic doubts concerning *the meaning of the word* "signpost"? The question posed by the "bizarre sceptic" would have, presumably, to run along along the following lines. "You have never been asked whether this tree stump here is a signpost. And in the past you have employed the word 'signpost' only upon a finite number of occasions. How can you be sure that, on those occasions, you were not using the term in a sense – according to rules – which require you to answer 'yes' rather than 'no,' on the present occasion, to the question 'Is that tree stump a signpost?'" The answer to this, surely, is that one's use of such a term on a given occasion is not guided by past usage, because it is not "guided" by anything, and so not "guided" by a grasp of *senses*, or *rules*, construed as mental entities or "inner processes" of some sort. The term has meaning only in the context of a practice, which in itself is no more than a collection of generally shared habits, which mesh with one another to produce various advantages, various ways of satisfying needs, the achievement of which is served in various ways, in the context of the practice, by various sorts of utterance, to which the *ratio* of the practice makes various kinds of response intelligible. Hence it is the speaker's present, or better timeless, relationship to *the practice* that confers intelligibility on an utterance employing the term "signpost," not his relationship to a rule supposedly enshrined *in his own past uses of the term.* To reply "yes" to the question "Is that tree stump a signpost?" is not "wrong" or "incorrect" because ruled out by *the speaker's prior understanding of the meaning of "signpost."* What rules it out is not, for that matter, best understood as its "wrongness" or "incorrectness" in the first place. What rules it out is its *unintelligibility* as a move in the practice of making and using signposts. In short, the bizarre sceptic's question requires no answer, because the possibility he raises is not itself – at least so far – an intelligible one. To give his question some point the sceptic needs to sketch some possible relationship between calling that tree stump a signpost and the general practice of making and using signposts. And maybe there is such a connection. Maybe tree stumps are used as signposts by fairies, with the various fungal growths on the projecting stumps of branches serving (having by supernatural means been carefully cultivated to that end) to designate the various fairy mounds in the district. Now we have an intelligible sense for the sceptic's question – and a suitably "bizarre" one! But, by that very token, the question has ceased to be, in the philosophical sense, sceptical in its implications. It has become a straightforward (although queer) question with a straightforward answer: "Give us some hard evidence for the existence of fairies and of their magical biotechnologies, and we might begin to take you seriously."

We can now see what it is that makes Goddard's account of counting capable of delivering an answer to the Kripkean meaning-sceptic. It is what Goddard's account has in common with the signpost example. In both, questions of *what a sign means* go to ground not in some epistemically flawless piece of knowledge-that, but simply in a piece of knowledge-how: in a mere *habitus* resulting from training. It is not our superiority to the beasts in knowledge, in knowledge of the truth of propositions, which, initially at least, raises us above them. What initially raises us above them is our ability collectively to devise, and individually to make use of, the practices through which sense is bestowed on our words. If apes, say, could create signposts, or by cries indicate to one another whether to go left or right; if they could call one another by name, or name the parts of the body for such purposes as directing succour; then they would be on the way to language.

xiv. Devitt and Sterelny on knowing-how

We claim that a speaker's knowledge of his own language is knowledge-how, not knowlededge-that or propositional knowledge. Similar claims by

Michael Devitt and Kim Sterelny have attracted attention in recent years. Competence in a language, they say, "does not consist in the speaker's semantic propositional knowledge, or of representation of rules. It is a set of skills or abilities, some of them grounded in the external world. It consists in the speaker being able to do things with a language, not in his having thoughts about it."[39] Like us, also, they are sceptical about "the Cartesian assumption . . . that a person's linguistic competence gives her some privileged access to facts about meaning . . . that she exemplifies in her intuitive judgments."[40] Here, however, the resemblances between their view and the present one cease. They propose, contrary to the whole drift of the present work, "A 'representationalist' view of meaning,"[41] and they take the power of symbols to represent to depend upon their reference, taking reference in the usual sense; a sense, that is, whose hold on the mind we have been trying sedulously throughout this work to loosen. Finally, following Fodor and others, they conjecture that there may be such a thing as a "language of thought," or "Mentalese," and they suggest that linguistic competence may consist in "the ability to translate sentences back and forth between Mentalese and the sounds of the language."[42] Whatever be the merit of the two views, it seems clear that we are barking up altogether different gum-trees.

xv. Objectivity, the individual and society

In Chapter 7 §x, we began to question the common presumption that access to an "objective fact of the matter," on any topic whatsoever, must depend on a *direct* relationship between the individual mind and the world; "direct" in the sense of being unmediated by social convention, and that, therefore, any theory which interposes a mediating structure of social convention between the individual mind and the objects of its supposed knowledge must represent a dilution of the concept of knowledge: a step in the direction of some version of social relativism.

This presumption has its roots in the Cartesian tradition of epistemic individualism, which we have also begun to find grounds to question. But its consequences for our thinking ramify far beyond the – to some minds rather abstruse and overly "academic" – knot of issues with which we have ostensibly been occupied here. It is central to the Romantic contrast between a corrupt Society, and a pure, because at least potentially Rational, Individual: the latter conceived as a being capable, in principle at least, of rising above the clouds of socially fabricated delusion generated by a convention-ridden *ancien régime*; and, by so doing, of acquiring the capacity to remake life in the image of a Universal Truth accessible to any individual mind once it has ascended into the universally bestowed and shadowless sunlight of Reason. That tradition can be traced from Rousseau onwards through Kant and Hegel, by way of the French Revolution, the Marxist theory of ideology and the inchoate revolutionary enthusiasms of the 1960's, to our own manifest inability to reconcile an economic and social individualism over whose disquieting consequences we feel ourselves to have less and less control with each succeeding year, with some of the most elementary demands of social organisation and social justice. On the one hand, we fear the fragmenting and dissipating forces of an unbridled individualism; on the other, we feel, living as we do still in the shadow of the Romantic wing of the Enlightenment, that social organisation is *in its essential nature* hostile to individuality: and that to abandon a stance of virtually asocial Individualism is thus tantamount to abandoning oneself to a dark tide of tyranny and socially generated illusion in which objectivity and reason will be drowned. Some minds wish to maintain at all costs a Reason and Objectivity which they think of as virtues accessible to the individual mind only to the extent that it can divorce itself from, or raise itself above, all considerations having to do with the social. Others, holding such individualism to be either politically suspect or illusory or both, wish to advance the cause of a social order in which the notions of Reason and Objectivity, along with that of the Individual himself, will be abandoned as shibboleths of an outworn Liberalism. All that both sides agree on is the ingrained and absolute character of the opposition between Individual and Society.

When our thinking becomes as impacted as this, it is sometimes helpful to return to questions that seem "academic" only because their fundamental character locates them far below the excitingly agitated surface on which the disputes which seem so urgent to us take place. The importance of Reason to the individual has been held to consist largely in its power to secure him or her in the possession of an objective truth, a truth independent of the convenience of powerful interests, including those of churches or political parties or movements. What we have been arguing is that the notion of objectivity itself depends on the availability to the individual of socially instituted and maintained practices of various sorts, and that to the extent that he isolates himself, or we conceive of an ideal individuality as isolated, from these resources, his grip on any working concept of objectivity loosens. In the case of proper names, the accessibility of an objective anwer to the question, "Who is (was) that person?" depends on the maintenance of the multitude of practices that compose the Name-Tracking Network. In the case of simple arithmetic, access to an objective answer to the question "What do 68 and 57 come to?," an answer independent of the approval or disapproval of the linguistic community, depends on the public availability of the procedures of counting, as Goddard describes them.

The insight that there is a rigid linkage between, on the one hand, the availability to the individual of objective knowledge and, on the other, the availability to him, or her, of "criteria" rooted in public social practice, and that scepticism is the result of attempting to break that linkage, is

Wittgenstein's. It is the thought at the heart of the Private Language Argument. It is what is at stake in *Investigations* I.202:

> 202. And hence also "obeying a rule" is a practice. And to *think* one is obeying a rule is not to obey a rule. Hence it is not possible to obey a rule "privately": otherwise thinking one was obeying a rule would be the same thing as obeying it.

Such complicities between the deep structures of social organisation and the power they confer upon individuals to question, in the name of objective knowledge, the dealings of more superficial structures, are striking, not least in the hope they offer, that further reflection on them might reveal to us ways of construing the relationship between individual and society that might lead beyond the impacted oppositions of our present perplexities.

xvi. The difference between swimming and speaking Spanish

Wittgenstein's Slogan, in the interpretation we have given it in associating it with such passages in the later work as *On Certainty* 204–5, is thus vindicated. What knowing a language comes down to is not knowledge of rules, or of the truth of propositions, but knowledge of how to participate in publicly instituted and maintained practices. That in turn is a matter, on the one hand, of grasping the point of the practice, and, on the other, of having the right habits of performance: habits that mesh in the right sort of ways with those of other speakers. That is why knowing Spanish is not like knowing how to swim. Swimming is a matter between the swimmer and himself. Provided someone can keep his head above water, it does not matter whether he or she does so by means of some orthodox stroke, or by some clumsy dog-paddle of his or her own devising. So it is by no means unintelligible or surprising that someone, a baby for instance, might find himself able to swim when first thrown into water, simply by making instinctive paddling movements with his limbs, as a young dog may do. In order to understand language, or to make oneself understood in it, on the other hand, one must learn habits that will mesh in highly complex ways with those of other speakers. But from that thought it does not follow that the kind of conformity with others that needs to be learnt is conformity in obedience to commonly apprehended rules. The meshing of acquired habits, together with a grasp of the benefits, in enhanced ease of communication, to be derived from such meshing, will generally produce, in a native speaker who knows nothing either of grammar books or of dictionary definitions, better results than those produced in a nonnative speaker by the most sedulous efforts to adhere to propositionally formulated rules.

There is one further objection that needs to be if not answered at least noticed at this point. Chomsky, among others, has made it a generally received notion that there is an essential difference between a language and a repertoire of conditioned habits. And it may look at first sight as if the account of meaning that we have developed in this chapter commits us to denying this. This is not so, but the reader will have to wait until Part III for an adequate explanation of why it is not so. For the moment it must suffice to note that Chomsky's arguments are sound against the suggestion, by B. F. Skinner and other experimental psychologists of an earlier generation, that the acquisition of linguistic capacities could be the outcome of conditioning. It should be sufficiently evident that the sense in which the term "habit" has been used in this chapter is not that in which a "habit" is a conditioned and so automatic response to a given stimulus. But fuller discussion of the point will have to wait.

xvii. Wittgenstein and "full-blooded conventionalism"

Finally, there is an objection of a more exegetical character to consider: one, that is, not to the arguments advanced here, but to their claim to offer, in some sense, a vindication of certain views of Wittgenstein's. Wittgenstein's account of mathematical necessity is widely supposed to be an unusually radical (and implausible) version of conventionalism, according to which necessity is not discovered but conferred by linguistic decision. To quote Dummett again, "Whenever we accept a proof we are conferring a necessity on the connection between premise and conclusion, and . . . are making a decision, and not making explicit a decision we had already made implicitly." The Goddardian Counter, on this account, looks to be a very un-Wittgensteinian character. For one thing he *decides* nothing; he just counts: carries out the steps of the counting procedure as he has been trained to do, nothing more. For another it does seem to be necessary that he gets the result "125," at least in the sense that there seems to be no way in which his procedure could yield any other result, unless he were to make some mistake in executing it. So does Goddard's analysis of counting have anything at all to do with Wittgenstein?

As we have said before, it is at bottom of no consequence to us if no argument presented here has anything to do with Wittgenstein, provided it works. At the same time it is seriously questionable whether the radical conventionalism some writers find in Wittgenstein is actually there in the texts. Much hinges, here as elsewhere, on the vexed term "rule." As Guy Robinson suggests in an excellent recent book,[43] although saying that it is a matter of "choice" how we interpret a rule does involve saying that our procedure in writing down a mathematical result cannot be described as making explicit what was implicit *in a verbal or symbolic formula*, as any such formula will on such a view be variously interpretable, it does not follow that what we *do* in performing mathematical operations cannot *in any sense* be described as "making explicit" what was "implicit." For, if what we write down is the only result that could issue from carrying out a certain procedure in a certain way, then in a perfectly good sense the result may be said to have been implicit in the procedure. The difference between Wittgenstein and some other philosophers of mathematics is not that decision enters into the conduct of a mathematical procedure such as counting, but rather that, for Wittgenstein, *nothing validates the procedure.* The procedure is not, that is, validated by its success in aiding us to discover mathematical truths; rather, mathematical truth is what issues from the procedure. The logical possibility of decision that, according to Wittgenstein, insinuates itself between premise and conclusion, is thus merely the possibility of adopting a different procedure: the sort of possibility realised, for instance, when one transfers plane geometry to the surface of a sphere, with consequent shifts in what follows from the axioms so reinterpreted.

PART III

PROPOSITIONS

If you prise the statements off the world you prise the facts off it too; but the world would be none poorer. (You don't also prise off the world what the statements are about – for that you would need a different kind of lever.)

Sir Peter Strawson, "Truth"

9

Meaning and Truth

i. Sense and truth-conditions

It has been a commonplace of philosophy since Frege that "the sense of a sentence is determined by its truth-conditions."[1] But that, as it stands, is a dark utterance. We need for a start to distinguish between the sentence and its sense. A sentence is just a string of words. Different sentential strings may have the same sense: "express," as is often said, "the same proposition." Both (some) sentences and the propositions they express may be said to be assertoric in form, in the sense that what each expresses is the content of an assertion. It is this that makes "The cat is on the mat" an altogether different sort of logical entity from a mere string of names: "James Peter John." So one could say that both sentences and propositions *aim at truth*. What one means by that, roughly speaking, is that only in the case of the kinds of sentence that express the content of a possible assertion does the question of truth arise. As Frege put it, "The only thing that raises the question of truth at all is the sense of sentences."[2] But to *raise the question of* truth and falsity is not necessarily to be *susceptible of* truth or falsity. Even an assertoric sentence, such as "The cat is on the mat," cannot be said to be *in its own right* true or false. The reason for that is that it is perfectly possible for someone to utter such a sentence without its being clear, merely from the words he has uttered, *what he is asserting, or stating*, in uttering it. Before we can attach a truth-value to what he has said we need to know which cat he is referring to, and perhaps other things as well. Only if answers to these questions are forthcoming can we move on to the stage of determining whether he has spoken truly or falsely; but even then, what we determine to be true or false is not the sentence he uttered, nor even its propositional – assertoric – content but, rather, the statement, the assertion he made *in* uttering a sentence expressing that content.

Taking these preliminary distinctions on board, it looks as if Frege's dictum, to be rendered plausible, needs reformulating along something like the following lines: to know the sense, the propositional content, of a sentence is to know, in some sense yet to be determined, under what conditions a statement made by means of it would be true or false.

There is a more to be said yet, however, even at this preliminary level. Frege's dictum is generally taken to embody a wider claim concerning the relationship between the concepts of *sense* and *truth*. That claim is, roughly speaking, that the first is to be explicated in terms of the second. The relationship is commonly supposed to be that the sense of any expression E in a language is, roughly speaking, the contribution that it makes to the determination of the truth-conditions of statements made by means of sentences in which E occurs.

Such a suggestion invites the obvious objection that not all sentences do "raise the question of truth." Commands do not; nor do gerundives ("delenda est Carthago"), nor wishes ("O that this too, too, solid flesh would melt"), nor exclamations ("O ye heavens!"), nor invitations ("Let's talk a little about truth"), nor performatives ("I sentence you to five years' imprisonment"). And there are lots of other kinds ("Beware of the Bull," "Down with Sanchez Mendoza!," etc., etc.). Such sentences possess no *assertoric content* because they do not *aim at truth*. They cannot, therefore, serve as the vehicles of statements, and the issue of truth and falsity does not arise in their case. Nevertheless, there seems no denying that they possess senses.

This thought, among others, has been widely held to provide grounds for dissociating the concept of sense from that of truth, associating it instead with some notion of "use." The development, over the half-century since 1950, of extensive, and in practice to some considerable degree independent, bodies of literature concerned with "use" and "truth-conditional" theories of meaning, has led many philosophers to take it for granted that the notions of *truth* and *use* (whichever of several current senses is attached to the latter) themselves are *conceptually* independent of one another.

One of the main aims of this and the next two chapters will be to question this latter assumption. On the one hand, we shall argue that in one way Frege was right. The notion of sense, or meaning is indeed ultimately to be understood in terms of the relationship between an assertoric sentence and the truth-conditions of statements made by using it. On the other hand, we shall argue, the question what truth *is*, or what "true" *means*: what sort of relationship, in other words, subsists between a true statement and the circumstances which make it true, is to be answered in terms of "use," in the sense, or rather the pair of senses, in which that term has been employed so far in these pages.

ii. What is it to know the truth-conditions of a statement?

To grasp the propositional content of a statement is to know what would make it true and what would make it false. But what is it to know that?

One possible answer is offered by what used to be called the Verifiability Theory of Meaning. For the verificationist, the truth-conditions of a statement S are to be identified with the members of whatever set of observation-statements it is whose truth would warrant us in concluding to the truth of S. A variant of this suggestion, known as operationalism, holds that the meaning of a contingent statement is to be defined in terms of whatever operations, of measurement, observation, and so on, are involved in determining its truth or falsity.

Verificationism and operationalism have declined in popularity; a development partly due to the influence of Quine, and in particular to Quine's arguments in favour of holism: in his hands the thesis that the "totality of our so-called knowledge or beliefs . . . is a man-made fabric which impinges on experience only along the edges."[3] If, as Quine argues, we are as dependent on experience for our grasp of meaning as we are for our grasp of the causal workings of nature, it follows that no sense can be made of the idea that a single sentence, taken independently of its theoretical links with other sentences, can be associated with any specific set of observations or verification procedures.

Many philosophers, including Donald Davidson, have taken Quinean holism to entail the further conclusion that there is no way of stating the truth-conditions of a statement except in terms of further statements. There is, in other words, no footing or standpoint outside language from which one could display, as it were "from the side," the relationship of statements to reality. A recent writer on Davidson puts the point, with admirable concision, thus:

Davidson's concept of truth-conditions has nothing to do with verification-procedures or the possibility of determining truth-values. (In fact Frege's conception did not either – the verificationist idea seems to be an importation of the logical positivists into a Fregean format.) For Davidson, all there is to giving truth-conditions is (systematically) giving a sentence of one's own which has the same truth-conditions. So, the truth-conditions of "His mind is a magpie's nest" are given by the formula, " 'His mind is a magpie's nest' is true if and only if his mind is a magpie's nest." Davidson explicitly denies facts, correspondence and adequation to anything else as a condition of truth-conditions, except in the trivial formulaic sense above.

The detachment of truth-conditions from verification-conditions is related to Quine's insistence that languages are explicated in (assumed to be OK) languages, his "regress to and acquiescence in a background language." For Davidson, interpretation can be in no medium better or more transparent than language, because there is no such medium.[4]

iii. Translation and interpretation

This conception of what it is to specify truth-conditions is nowhere better exemplified than in Davidson's conception of a theory of truth. A

Davidsonian truth-theory displays the logical relationships through which the truth-values of simple sentences map systematically on to those of complex ones. Davidson's claim, which accords with Frege's dictum that knowledge of meaning is knowledge of truth-conditions, is that such a theory gives the meanings of sentences by giving their truth-conditions. "A theory of truth for a language does, in a minimal but important respect, do what we want, that is, give the meanings of all independently meaningful expressions on the basis of an analysis of their structure." It does so by giving "a precise, profound and testable answer to the question how finite resources suffice to explain the infinite semantic capacities of language."[5]

To anyone who grants the fundamental plausibility of Russell's Principle (Chapter 2 §ii), such an account of meaning will seem at best incomplete. For one implication of Russell's Principle is that one cannot wholly specify the meaning of an expression in terms of its structural relationships, including its truth-theoretic relationships, to other expressions. Unless language is an hermetic play of signs, there must come a point at which it is put into connection with something outside language. Davidson encounters that problem,[6] in effect, as the problem of connecting the formal structures of a truth-theory with the sentences of an actual natural language. A speaker of a language utters some sounds: we interpret them as equivalent in meaning to a sentence in our language, or perhaps in the formal reconstruction of our language offered by a Davidsonian truth theory. What enables us to do that? – or to put it in another way, what are we doing when we do that? On the one hand, there stand the linguistic goings-on of a speaker, on the other, there is an interpretation of those goings-on. There is a gap. How is it bridged? A considerable merit of Davidson's discussion is that it brings out rather clearly the weaknesses of a number of traditional philosophical theories of meaning when faced with this question. Could we, for instance, bridge the gap by appeal to the existence of the same "concepts" or "meanings" in the mind of the alien speaker? How could we know, except by way of an interpretation of his utterances, what concepts he honours in discourse? Could we bridge it by showing his utterances, like ours, to be linked in the same sort of way to corresponding extralinguistic entities, to "facts," or "properties," or "individuals," for instance? Once again, how could we establish what types of entity, what ontology his utterances presuppose without first interpreting them? Causal theories, such as those of Charles Morris, or Ogden and Richards, which attempt behavioural analyses of sentences taken one by one, are unpersuasive even for the simplest sentences, and do not "touch the problem of extending the method to sentences of greater complexity and abstractness."[7]

These weaknesses emerge because of Davidson's entirely proper insistence on demanding what evidence we have for interpretation: "given a theory that would make interpretation possible, what evidence plausibly available to a potential interpreter would support the theory to a reasonable degree?"[8] Davidson's answer to this question owes a good deal to Quine, who confronts it in the celebrated Chapter 2 of *Word and Object*, in the essay "Ontological Relativity" and at numerous other points in his extensive *oeuvre*. Quine's commitment to empiricism makes him suspicious of "meanings" on grounds of the empirical inaccessibility of such objects conceived as mental entities. What better way of pursuing such doubts than to shelve talk of meanings in favour of an investigation into the empirical grounds sustaining judgments of the type in which reference to such supposed entities most fundamentally occurs: namely, judgments concerning the sameness or equivalence in meaning of two linguistic expressions? One standard context in which we make such judgments is offered by translation between different languages. But Quine argues that the empirical considerations available for grounding interlinguistic judgments of equivalence of meaning are no different from those available for grounding intralinguistic ones. In interpreting what speakers of my own language say, in other words, I rely on kinds of evidence no different from, and no more extensive than, the ones I rely on in interpreting utterances in a foreign language.

Quine, like Davidson, and in another way like Dummett, rests his argument on the entirely sound principle that "all inculcation of the meanings of words must rest ultimately on sensory evidence."[9] What is the nature, and the extent, of that evidence? In most actual cases in which we interpret the utterances of another speaker, we are entitled to assume a general conformity of linguistic structure between the language he speaks and our own, either because they are the same language or because they are historically closely related, as closely related, say, as English and French or English and German. In such a situation what the interpreter confronts is, plainly, not the sensory evidence for meaning ultimately available to him, but that evidence heavily supplemented by assumptions derived from his own language. If we are to focus on the nature of the bare empirical warrants underpinning judgments of sameness of meaning, therefore, we need, Quine suggests, to consider the situation of an interpreter confronted by speakers of a language, call it *Native*, with no historical links to his own: a "radically" alien language, as Quine puts it.

Where, then, is the radical translator to make a start in matching Native sentences to English ones? What is to warrant any such matching? Quine's answer is that the only warrant possible is conformity between the observable circumstances Native speakers take as warranting assent to or dissent from the assertion made by uttering a native sentence S_N, and the observable circumstances that English speakers would take as warranting assent to or dissent from the assertion made by uttering some English sentence S_E.

Plainly, in order to establish such conformities, the radical translator is going to have to begin with what the Logical Positivists were fond of calling "observation sentences": sentences such as "It's raining," or "Ah! a rabbit!," whose function is simply, to employ a Quinean turn of phrase, that of commenting on presently salient features of the "passing show." But whereas the Positivists' account of observation sentences was linked to phenomenalism – and, thus, from Quine's point of view, to an outmoded, metaphysical epistemology rather than to the "naturalised" epistemology of Quine's preference – Quine's is, at least in ambition, rooted in behavioural science. For him, a sentence is "observational" just in case it evokes general agreement across a wide span of the Native speech-community under uniform environmental conditions.

> ... an observation sentence is one that is not sensitive to differences in past experience within the speech community.
> ... the observation sentences are those on which all members of the community will agree under uniform stimulation.[10]

Parity between S_N and S_E in the stimulus-conditions prompting assent to and dissent from each does not, of course, guarantee sameness of meaning. Stimulus-synonymy subsisting between Native "Gavagai!" and English "Ah, a rabbit" will also, in the nature of things subsist between "Gavagai!" and "Ah, an undetached rabbit-part!," "Ah, rabbithood!," "Ah, a quantity of rabbit-stuff," and a variety of optional translations. The impossibility of *observationally* warranting a choice between these options, and in general, of observationally warranting the English-derived structure of categorial distinctions and ontological commitments which a radical translator will perforce impose on Native in composing a Native-English translation manual, leads directly to Quine's celebrated principle of the Indeterminacy of Translation, to which we shall return in Chapter 13. Nevertheless, parity of stimulus-meaning is all we have to go on. The sensory evidence available to ground judgments of meaning come in the end to what we can discover of the observable circumstances under which native speakers will or will not assent to such sentences as can be classed, in virtue of the consistency of the circumstances prompting assent and dissent across the native speech-community, as "observational."

The evidence that, for Davidson, bridges the gap between utterance and interpretation comes to much the same thing. On the one hand, we have the disposition of speakers to treat certain sentences as expressing truths at the moment of utterance; on the other, what is observable about the surrounding circumstances.

> ... the evidence available is just that speakers of the language to be interpreted hold various sentences to be true at certain times and under specified circumstances ...
> On the one hand we have T-sentences, in the form:
> (T) "Es regnet" is true-in-German when spoken by x at time t if and only if it is raining near x at t.
> On the other hand, we have the evidence, in the form:
> (E) Kurt belongs to the German speech community and Kurt holds true "Es regnet" on Saturday at noon and it is raining near Kurt on Saturday at noon.[11]

The account of the observational grounding of judgments of meaning offered by both Quine and Davidson is, it is worth noticing, in general agreement with Referential Realism. So far as a sentence possesses cognitive content, that is, that content is directly derived from, and to be equated with, the observable, experiential, content of the circumstances under which it is "held true" by native speakers. Any feature of the sentence not determined in this way, whether grammatical, categorial or ontological, is a matter of convention, to be decided pragmatically, that is to say, in whatever way best serves the convenience of our best current theories concerning the nature of reality. The *bearing on Reality* of what we say is secured, just as in Locke, by a very sharp partitioning between these two types of meaning. According to the terms of that partitioning, the conventional in no way determines the cognitive content of what is said: that is determined solely by the nature of the natural conditions warranting assent and dissent. To follow Quine and Davidson on this issue would therefore be to abandon the defence of Wittgenstein's Slogan. Quine and Davidson hold that the one empirical constraint bearing on our attribution of assertoric content to a sentence is that exerted by the circumstances under which its affirmation elicits assent or dissent. For that constraint to be exerted, therefore, it must be possible to affirm the sentence before we have settled its assertoric content. And this is in flat contradiction with the contention of *Tractatus* 4.064, which rightly or wrongly we have taken to be one of the central expressions of Wittgenstein's Slogan, that one cannot affirm a proposition to which, as yet, no sense has been assigned, since "its sense is just what is affirmed." We shall pursue this point in the remainder of this chapter and the next.

iv. "True" as an undefined primitive

A good deal of discussion has addressed the question whether the "sensory evidence for meaning," if it were as thin and parsimonious as Quine and Davidson make it out to be, could serve to underpin empirically a concept of meaning as rich, as "thick" as the one we normally take to be appropriate in dealing with a natural language. That line of objection, however pursued, can hardly prove telling against either, because it is an essential part of both positions (1) that our ordinary use of the term "meaning" and its cognates is unclear as it stands, and in need of clarification, in part to be derived from the study of formal languages, and (2) that what such studies show is that much of what we regard intuitively as central to "meaning" is simply not empirically underpinned.

We shall take a different line, and enquire whether the "evidence for meaning," construed as thinly as Quine and Davidson construe it, is sufficient to afford empirical underpinning to the concepts of truth and falsity, together with such cognates as affirmation, negation, assertion, and denial. In this chapter, we shall sketch a case for such doubts in terms of

nothing more philosophically conclusive than some, admittedly rather persuasive, intuitions; in Chapter 10 we shall endeavour to give those intuitions
teeth.

Attempts to explicate the concept of truth, to answer the question "What
is truth?" have largely ceased within the mainstream of analytic philosophy. Those formerly hardy perennials, the Correspondence Theory and the
Coherence Theory, have continued to flourish on a reduced scale, but in
many quarters the concept of truth is simply taken for granted, on the
ground that it is analytically irreducible.

> . . . for Davidson, "literally true" just means "true." "True," for Davidson, is a concept
> that is not reducible to any other, and in particular has nothing non-trivial to do with
> correspondence or verification.[12]

The same might be said of Quine. Now, on the face of it, there is nothing
wrong in treating the concept of meaning as a dubious and imponderable
one, in need of analysis or explication, while at the same time taking the
notion of truth to be, on the one hand, fundamental to any such enterprise,
and, on the other, irreducible, in the sense that no explication of it is either
required or possible. To produce a satisfactory explanation of the concept of
meaning in terms of the concept of truth would be a considerable achievement, and it might seem reasonable to suppose that the achievement would
not be diminished if our understanding of the concept of truth were to
remain intuitive. And it is just that sort of achievement, it might seem, at
which Quine and Davidson are aiming. Explanations, as Wittgenstein observed, have to come to an end somewhere: some concepts must simply be
assumed, taken for granted, if we are to get anywhere explaining anything.

Simply helping oneself to a concept, though, is never an entirely safe
proceeding in philosophy. The assumption behind such a step is that, since
the concept in question is to be excluded from the process of analysis, in
which it is to function merely as part of the analysans, we shall not go far
wrong if we allow ourselves to deploy it in relevant philosophical discussion
much as we deploy it in everyday life. But once we move into the orbit of
philosophical discussion we abandon the world of everyday life for a realm
constituted by theoretical postulates introduced in the service of theoretical aims. In the world of the theory, ordinary concepts given sense by the
conditions of the everyday world may lapse into vacuity, in ways which the
theorist may fail to notice, because the needs of his theory allow, or compel,
him to suspend those conditions.

v. Assertion and registration

Let us return to the Quinean anthropologist embarking on the project of
radical translation, or to Kurt's English-speaking interpreter embarking on
that of radical interpretation. Both confront the gap identified by Davidson

between the linguistic goings-on of a subject and an observer's interpretation of those goings-on. Both consider themselves to dispose of evidence, in the shape of native dispositions to assent to or dissent from, or to hold true or false, sentences in consistent conditions of occurrent stimulation, sufficient to bridge that gap. It is clear, now, that both need to deploy the concept of truth and such cognate notions as assent, dissent, and so on, on both sides of the gap, for without doing so neither can formulate the nature of the evidence each takes himself to possess. And, although it seems clear that each can deploy those notions on his own side of the gap, the hitherward side as it were, it is quite unclear what justifies him in applying it on the other side of the gap, the side populated by Quine's natives, or by Kurt and those to whom he offers the remark "Es Regnet."

Both Quine and Davidson assume, that is to say, that the initially unintelligible utterances confronting the radical translator or interpreter are to be construed as *utterances of indicative sentences*; that is, as utterances making *assertions*, and as such, utterances to which *assent* and *dissent* are intelligible responses. But it is quite unclear what, observationally speaking, warrants that assumption. The Davidsonian gap, in other words, is wider than Davidson supposes. What has to be transported across the gap, and what therefore *also* needs some evidential basis for its passage, is not merely *some assertoric content* or other but also *the concept of the assertoric itself.*

The problem can be restated from another direction. The approach of the Quinean anthropologist to the task of constructing his Native/English "translation manual" can be compared to the approach of a zoological ethologist attempting to discover which stimuli prompt rabbits grazing in a group to thump with their hind feet. Like the Quinean translator, the ethologist observes the field of stimuli currently accessible in common to himself and the rabbits in order to determine which consistently prompt thumping. He finds, let us suppose, that thumping is consistently prompted, and prompted only, by the passage over the group of the shadows cast by cruising birds of prey, and he confirms this discovery by the use of bird-shaped kites to prompt thumping. Should he, therefore, begin the construction of a Rabbit/English translation manual with the entry "thump" = "There is a hawk-shadow passing over"?

Intuition suggests not. For there is at least a very strong intuitive inclination to say that the thumping response in rabbits is not part of a language. It does not *assert* that a given environmental circumstance obtains; it simply *registers* the obtaining of that condition, in the way that a barometer registers atmospheric pressure or a weighing-machine the weight of the person standing on it (for even a speak-your-weight machine doesn't *really speak* your weight!).

We do not, then, at least intuitively speaking, consider a rabbit's thump as constituting an assertion. We do consider Kurt's "Es regnet" as constituting an assertion. Intuitively, it would appear that the two cases must present to observation some disparity sufficient to ground this distinction. But, it appears, Quine's and Davidson's accounts of the sensory evidence available to ground judgments of meaning leave no room for any such disparity, because they place the two types of case, observationally speaking, exactly on all fours with one another.

It might be objected that this is unfair to Quine, as Quine's account does provide for behaviourally identifiable responses expressing, respectively, assent and dissent.

> . . . we have the linguist asking "Gavagai?" in each of various stimulatory situations, and noting each time whether the native assents, dissents, or neither. But how is he to recognise native assent or dissent when he sees or hears them? Gestures are not to be taken at face value; the Turks' are nearly the reverse of our own. What he must do is guess from observation and then see how well his guesses work. Thus suppose that in asking "Gavagai?" and the like, in the conspicuous presence of rabbits and the like, he has elicited the responses "Evet" and "Yok" often enough to surmise that they may correspond to "Yes" and "No," but has no notion which is which. Then he tries the experiment of echoing the native's own volunteered pronouncements. If thereby he pretty regularly elicits "Evet" rather than "Yok," he is encouraged to take "Evet" as "Yes." Also he tries responding with "Evet" and "Yok" to the native's remarks; the one that is the more serene in its effect is the better candidate for "Yes." However inconclusive these methods, they generate a working response. If extraordinary difficulties attend all his subsequent steps, the linguist may decide to discard that hypothesis and guess again.[13]

But this merely compounds the difficulty. If we have grounds for regarding the natives as making assertions, then we have grounds for regarding "Yok" and "Evet" as signalling assertion and denial, rather than just approval and disapproval. But, because nothing in Quine's description of the functioning of Native compels us to opt for the first assumption, the second, surely, offers the simplest way of accounting for Native verbal behaviour. It is perfectly possible, in other words to conceive of a human community whose "language" consists of a repertoire of distinct utterances, each of which registers some feature of occurrent stimulation. It is possible to imagine how such a language might find many uses in coordinating social activity, particularly in conjunction with a convention of pointing. When one member of the community was looking around for something with which to skin a deer, a repeated cry of "Knife! Knife!," "Knife" being a response prompted by the immediate presence of a sharp flint, might serve in conjunction with a pointing gesture to draw his attention to the requisite tool. We also may imagine that the items in the repertoire, unlike the rabbit's thump, are not instinctive, and have to be taught to children. The teaching process will employ an approval-noise (let's say "Evet!") signifying that the child has got it right, and a disapproval noise ("Yok!," maybe) signifying that the child has got it wrong and should try again. Nothing in Quine's account distinguishes the use of verbal response in this community (call them *R-speakers*, and their "language" *R* – for "registration") from their use among Quine's natives. But R-speakers, at least if what we are intuitively inclined to say is any guide, do not *have* a language, in the sense in which we do. R is not a *language*, but merely a system for *registering* occurrent environmental circumstances. If, therefore, we are to regard "Evet" and "Yok" as signs signifying assent and dissent, rather than approval and disapproval, we need some observational ground for introducing that distinction in the case of Native. And it is very difficult to see, either from Quine's or Davidson's discussion, what that ground could consist in.

vi. Quine on translation; Wittgenstein on ostensive definition

Suppose someone sympathetic to Quine and Davidson were to grasp this nettle and admit that Native speakers are *observationally* indistinguishable from R-speakers, and that, therefore, we have no *observational* grounds for regarding utterances such as "Gavagai!" as sentences, or as having assertoric content. Maybe we just have to assume that they are, and do. Couldn't it still be argued that, even allowing this to be an empirically ungrounded assumption, the terms of Quine's basic empiricism regarding the ascription of sentential meaning remain unassailable? Doesn't it remain unassailable, that is, that the only grounds we have for attributing assertoric content to an utterance are those provided by the project of isolating inductively the stimuli that prompt native speakers to give vent to or to withhold such utterances, or that prompt approval or disapproval of such utterances (if we are unhappy with the idea that Native speakers possess terms of assent and dissent) when produced by others?

Grounds for a pessimistic assessment of this suggestion can be derived from some remarks of Wittgenstein's at first sight very remote from Quine's discussion, namely, the ones, around §§28–29 of the *Philosophical Investigations*, which concern ostensive definition. The first outlines a general problem with attempts to define terms ostensively.

28. Now one can ostensively define a proper name, the name of a colour, the name of a material, a numeral, the name of a point of the compass and so on. The definition of the number two, "That is called 'two'" – pointing to two nuts – is perfectly exact. – But how can two be defined like that? The person one gives the definition to doesn't know what one wants to call "two"; he will suppose that "two" is the name given to *this* group of nuts! – He *may* suppose this; but perhaps he does not. He might make the opposite mistake; when I want to assign a name to this group of nuts, he might understand it as a numeral. And he might equally well take the name of a person, of which I give an ostensive definition, as that of a colour, of a race, or even of a point of the compass. That is to say: an ostensive definition can be variously understood in *every* case.[14]

The solution to the problem, according to Wittgenstein, is for the teacher to specify what type of predicate he is attempting to define:

29. Perhaps you say: two can only be ostensively be defined in *this* way: "This *number* is called 'two'". For the word "number" here shews what place in language, in grammar, we assign to the word. But this means that the word "number" must be explained before the ostensive definition can be understood. – The word "number" in the definition does indeed shew this place; does shew the post at which we station the word. And we can prevent misunderstandings by saying: "This *colour* is called so and so," "This *length* is called so-and-so," and so on.[15]

The discussion concludes,

30. So one might say: the ostensive definition explains the use – the meaning – of the word when the overall role of the word in language is clear. Thus if I know that someone means to explain a colour-word to me the ostensive definition "That is called 'sepia'" will help me to understand the word. – And you can say, this, so long as you do not forget that all sorts of problems attach to the words "to know" or "to be clear."

One has already to know (or be able to do) something in order to be capable of asking a thing's name. But what does one have to know?[16]

The first thing to be noticed, from the point of view of our present concerns, is that the situation of Wittgenstein's learner is effectively indistinguishable from that of Quine's anthropologist. He is confronted by a native speaker who proposes to convey to him the meaning of a word in Native, "two" by indicating the environmental circumstances to which "two" would constitute a linguistically appropriate comment. Since there is no evident disanalogy with "Gavagai!," there is no reason why we should not treat "two" analogously in this context, as what Quine would call a "one-word occasion-sentence": "Two!," or "It is twoing in the vicinity," or something of the sort. On that interpretation, Wittgenstein's teacher, like the anthropologist's native informants, is endeavouring to indicate which stimuli prompt assent to the affirmation made by uttering that sentence.

Early critics of Wittgenstein's argument found it difficult to see what the problem was supposed to be. If the teacher's object is to explain that "'two' means 'two *in number*'," can't he do that by supplementing the exhibition of two nuts with pairs of other things, and by correcting the learner who asserts "Two!" of exhibited groups displaying any other number of items? Like Quine, that is, such critics took it for granted that the assertoric content of a sentence can be ascertained, to whatever extent it can be ascertained, by inductively comparing and contrasting the stimulus conditions which variously prompt assent or dissent.

But the point Wittgenstein is making in §§28–30 is *already* one step ahead of this objection. What is often neglected in interpreting the passage is that the learner of §§28–30 is not a child or an alinguistic adult. He is not, that is, conceived as standing *outside language per se, but* as possessing a fully functioning language of his own. For how, except from within such a language, could he formulate the options, that "two" is a name for "*this* pair of nuts," that it is a name for "a colour, of a race, or even of a point of the compass," between which Wittgenstein represents him as hesitating?

The point he serves to dramatise is a very simple one, namely that from inside a language there will always be accessible alternative ways of characterising any dumbly presented scene, and that, therefore, the mere presentation of further scenes can never, in itself, offer empirical grounds for deciding between such alternative characterisations.

In other words, if we augment the two nuts with two gooseberries and three apples, in the last case replying in the negative to the learner's questioning "two?," we simply augment the range of possible alternative interpretations of "two!" available from within the learner's language. He knows that the gooseberries and the nuts share twohood and that the apples lack it. But there are plenty of ways, from within any reasonably developed natural language, of describing what two nuts and two gooseberries have in common that three apples lack. The original problem simply arises again with renewed force, in other words, and will continue to do so with each augmentation of the scene from which inductive reasoning alone is supposed to be capable of isolating the "sensory evidence" for the meaning of "Two!"

The credentials of Quine's way of construing the demands of a reasonable empiricism concerning ascriptions of meaning are thus directly impugned by Wittgenstein's argument. There seems only one recourse open to a Quinean at this point, namely to deny that there is, or could be, any observational ground for preferring one of Wittgenstein's learner's alternative options to another. This move would be consistent with Quine's general contention that much of what we ordinarily take to be empirically determinate in judgments of meaning is in fact observationally ungrounded and ungroundable. But in this case the consequences of such a move seem paradoxical to the point of absurdity.

Dummett is surely right to contend that differences of meaning, to exist at all, must in some way be *manifestable*. If Wittgenstein's learner can even *formulate* the distinction between a term's standing for a numeral and its standing for a type of plant structure (a nut), a colour, a point of the compass, and so on, then something *manifestable*, something observable, must have marked off these options from one another in such a way as to make it possible to formulate the distinctions between them in the first place.

The alternatives Wittgenstein's learner contemplates in effect propose alternative *assertoric contents* for "Two!" considered as a Quinean one-word occasion-sentence. The contention of the Referential Realist is that assertoric content is a reflection of the content of Given: is, in effect transcribed from Nature. Wittgenstein's suggestion is that what differentiates one assertoric content from another is "the overall role of the word in language," "the place in language, in grammar, we assign the word." That suggests that if we wish to understand the nature of assertoricity, with that the notions of assertion and denial, and with them the nature of truth itself, we should turn away, or at least half-away, from the extralinguistic world towards the interior of language. Early critics of Wittgenstein were under no illusion that this was the issue at stake in §§28–30, but found the suggestion paradoxical, not to say absurd, for reasons having to do for the most part with the threat of prison-house scepticism. If we locate differences of assertoric content as resulting from "the post at which *we* station the word" in language (our italics) doesn't that mean, absurdly, that *we*, and not Reality, decide the terms in which the latter is to be described? And doesn't that invoke precisely the fear that language might turn out to be an hermetic play, or game, of signs with which we have been concerned throughout this book. Quine's and Davidson's parsimonious assessment of the observational basis for judgments of meaning is designed, in part, precisely to allay those fears. It appears, though, that the observational basis they propose is not merely too slender to license our drawing the sorts of distinction between types of assertoric content that we actually draw; but too slender, even, to license our employment of the concepts of assertoric content, of assent and dissent, of assertion and denial, and for that matter even the concept of truth itself.

In Chapter 10, we shall enquire whether there is any way of plausibly augmenting the observational basis for ascriptions of meaning that might provide a satisfactory evidential basis for these rather indispensable notions.

10

Truth and Use

i. Negative description[1]

In Chapter 9, we presented some intuitive objections to a very widespread and popular account of the extent and nature of the observational basis available to ground judgments of meaning. Our business in this chapter is to explain the basis of the intuitions involved, in the process clarifying their relationships to one another and revealing the reasoning underlying what was in Chapter 9 no more than an intuitively founded scepticism.

A good place to start is the following – as usual extraordinarily condensed and so superficially gnomic – string of remarks from §82 of Wittgenstein's *Philosophical Remarks.*

"I haven't got stomach-ache" may be compared to the proposition "These apples cost nothing." The point is that they don't cost any money, not that they don't cost any snow or any trouble. The zero is the zero point of *one* scale. And since I can't be given any point on the yardstick without being given the yardstick, I can't be given its zero point either. "I haven't got a pain" doesn't refer to a condition in which there can be no talk of pain, on the contrary we're talking about pain. The proposition presupposes the capacity for feeling pain, and this can't be a "physiological capacity" – for otherwise how would we know what it was a capacity for – it's a logical possibility. – I describe my present state by alluding to something that isn't the case. If this allusion is needed for the description (and isn't merely an ornament), there must be something in my present state making it necessary to mention (allude to) this. I compare this state with another, it must therefore be comparable with it. It too must be located in pain-space, even if at a different point. – Otherwise my proposition would mean something like: my present state has *nothing to do* with a painful one; rather in the way I might say the colour of this rose has nothing to do with Caesar's conquest of Gaul. That is, there's no connection between them. But I mean precisely that there is a connection between my present state and a painful one.

I don't describe a state of affairs by mentioning something that has nothing to do with it and saying that it has nothing to do with it. That wouldn't be negative description.[2]

The central point at stake here is the very simple one that, in a natural language, *negative description* is possible. Saying that something, x, fails to possess a predicate *adds to the description of x*. At first sight this may seem paradoxical. How can we have *characterised* x, if all we have done is to *deny* x one or another characteristic?

ii. Affirmation-denial content connectors

What is needed to resolve the apparent paradox, however, seems evident enough. Take any simple subject-predicate sentence Fx, and its denial ~Fx. To say that one does not characterise x in asserting ~Fx is to say, in effect, that ~Fx lacks assertoric content. On that view only an affirmation possesses assertoric content. The corresponding denial simply cancels that content, voids, as it were, the affirmation. If that is right, there can be no such thing as negative description. But, because there is such a thing as negative description, it must be wrong. ~Fx must possess assertoric content. Moreover, that content must be related to the content of the predicate-expression F, as the expression ~Fx contains no other content-bearing sign. A statement Fx must, therefore, not only determine an assertoric content in contexts of affirmation, but also in contexts of denial.

There must, in other words, exist a linkage of some sort between the assertoric content of an affirmation Fx and that of the corresponding denial ~Fx. And that linkage must be of such a kind as to make it possible for someone who knows the meaning of the predicate-expression F to infer from that knowledge not only the assertoric content of Fx but also the assertoric content of ~Fx. Let us introduce a further technical term for whatever it is that constitutes that linkage. Let us call it, using a horribly clumsy locution whose sole merit is that it bears its meaning on its face, an *affirmation-denial content connector.*

iii. On not knowing the content of denial

The initial thread of argument along which we have advanced to the notion of an affirmation-denial content connector is so far a rather slender one. But other lines of argument, as we shall see, rapidly accrue to strengthen it. Consider a predicate, G, in Native, such that a nonnative speaker S_G is in a position to recognise some things of which Gx is correctly affirmed, and some of which it is not correctly affirmed; but not in a position to attach any content to ~Gx. S_G knows, for instance, that Gx is correctly affirmed of a large hut in the centre of the village, and of manioc plants. He knows, by experiment, that it is not correctly affirmed of jaguars, hoes, women, and the moon. But he does not know *what he is affirming of jaguars, hoes, women, and the moon in denying that they are G.* He does not know whether he is affirming, for instance that they are nonvegetable in composition, or that they are not under the protection of the ancestral spirit G, or that they are unconnected with the manufacture of G, or whether, to return to Wittgenstein's discussion in the passage from the *Remarks* quoted above, he is affirming that *they have nothing to do with being G*. But if he possesses no means of deciding between these alternative ways (and others) of construing the assertoric content of $\sim$Gx, have we any grounds for crediting him with a grasp of the assertoric content of Gx either?

So far, in other words we have talked as if the need to postulate affirmation-denial content connectors arose from the need to account for the possibility of negative description. Now we see that the problem is worse, or rather deeper, than that. Someone who has no access to an affirmation-denial content connector for a given predicate-expression F is not in a position to attach assertoric content to any assertion, either affirmative or negative, couched in terms of that expression.

iv. What determines affirmation-denial content connectors?

Someone who learns a language – his or her native language – *ab initio*, must in the process of learning it, if we have been arguing correctly, acquire a grasp of affirmation-denial content connectors. How could that come about, or to put it in another, and perhaps clearer way, what sort of thing would a learner be learning in acquiring such a grasp?

It seems clear that they cannot simply be read off from the natural world. It seems clear, in other words, that no amount of trial-and-error expansion, on the part of S_G, of, on the one hand, the list of natural objects of which the natives are prepared to admit the assertion of Gx, and, on the other, the list of natural objects of which they are prepared to admit the assertion of $\sim$Gx, will get S_G any closer to isolating an affirmation-denial content connector for G. It follows that the specification of affirmation-denial content connectors is something we, as users and constitutors of language, have to do for ourselves, since nature will not do it for us.

Granted, then, that *we* have to specify affirmation-denial content connectors, could the specification of the affirmation-denial content connector for a given predicate G be separated from the specification of G? Could we, that is, first stipulate what the assertoric content of Gx is to be, and then, as a separate act, stipulate what the assertoric content of $\sim$Gx is to be, and finally stipulate how the two contents are to be related? The problem with this is that, by the argument of §iii above, until we have access to affirmation-denial content connectors we have no access to assertoric contents either. Somehow or other, then, the linkage between the assertoric content of a predication and the assertoric content of its denial must be specified, not merely *in* determining the content of the predicate, but as a condition of determining its content.

If we are to grasp how this might be possible we need some example in which it is manifest both that it has been achieved and how it has been achieved. In *Philosophical Remarks* §82, and in the surrounding context, Wittgenstein provides just that. The example is that of learning to measure with a rule or yardstick. Consider how one might set about explaining what it is to measure in that way to someone who has no prior knowledge of, or prior experience with, such a practice, but who is already proficient in Goddard's "controlled counting" (Chapter 8 §xii). One might begin by explaining that there is a way of determining whether a large piece of furniture will go through a door without going to the trouble of moving it and making the attempt. That way is called "measuring," we might add, and it works like this. We take any object – this book will do – and we see how many times it can be laid end to end against the sides of the piece of furniture. In each case we count the number of iterations needed, arriving at a number. This number we call the *length* of the given side. If the number of one side is greater than the other, we say that that is the *longer* side, and the other the *shorter*. We now investigate the number of end-over-end applications of the book needed to span the doorway. If the piece of furniture, which we may suppose to be oblong in form, has a side which is shorter than the length – the number of book-iterations – required to span the door, the piece of furniture will pass through. Elaborating still further, we explain that it is not necessary to use a book; one can use anything, the only rule being that once one has started using one object to measure with, one must go on using it, as measurements made with objects that turn out to be of different lengths when measured with something shorter than either of them will not, evidently, be usefully numerically comparable. Choosing an object to measure with is, we explain, choosing to use it as a *modulus of measurement*. Different moduli can be numerically compared: thus the one we started with, a particular book, is equivalent (let's say) to 18.72 cm. And so on.

In teaching somebody to use this practice we have shown him how to set about answering the questions "How long is that?" "What is the length of that (side)?," and so on. He knows that the way to go about finding the answer is to lay the modulus, or better, a yardstick constructed by taking a long, thin piece of wood or metal and marking off iterations of the modulus one after another along it, against the object, and to check in that way how many iterations are required to span its length. He then replies by giving the number of iterations. His answers will include such sentences as "x is one book long," "x is two books long," "x is three books long," and so on. These are simple predicative sentences. But the predicates they employ are not *unrelated* to one another, in the way that " – is the colour of this rose" and " – is Caesar's conquest of Gaul" are unrelated to one another. On the contrary, they form a set whose members are intrinsically alternative to one another, and they do so precisely in the sense that what is asserted in denying any one of them of an object is the applicability to that object of one or other of the remaining ones. Given the nature of measuring as a practice, that is, and the role within that practice which we have assigned to numerical determinations of length, and thus to the concept of length, it follows automatically that if one denies that a given physical object is a certain length measured in books, eight books, say, what one is asserting is that its *length is some other number of books*. In the same way, if one asks "Are you giving that length in books?" and receives the answer "No," what is being asserted by the denial is that the length is being given in terms of *some other modulus*, centimetres, say, or inches.

In this context, in other words, ~Fx takes on an assertoric content because F is not an isolated predicate, but one of a family of predicates, {F, G, H, I, ... }, the denial of any one of which to a given object x asserts the applicability of one of the others without specifying which. It would be possible to think of what makes the members of the length predicate-family intrinsically alternative to one another, as concerning merely the physical constitution of the yardstick: the fact that the gradations on the yardstick are inscribed sequentially, so that only one of them can coincide with the edge of the object being measured. That makes it physically necessary, one might say, that whereas only one of the alternative predications represented by the successive gradations can be true of any one object, the others hang, as it were, in the wings, composing a field or "logical space" of alternative possibilities, ready to be reinvoked as possibilities by the denial (perhaps because of a mistake in measuring) of the predicate originally chosen. But that would be to ignore the fact that the physical yardstick has a significance *as such* (becomes a *yardstick*, rather than just a strip of wood or metal with some marks scratched on it) only in the context of the practice of measuring. It is thus the relationship of the expressions "one book long," "two books long" across the *practice*, rather than their relationship across the *yardstick*, which makes them intrinsically alternative determinations, and hence, by making clear the relationship of content between assertion and denial, gives them the status of signs expressing *predicates*.

v. Practice, predication, and the concept of truth

Before going any further it may be helpful to summarise, in this section and the next, two rather more general features of the account of the relationship between meaning and truth that is beginning to take shape on the basis of the foregoing, still rather slender, train of argument. One of them, which is beginning to come into focus, is a certain doubt relative to the view, characteristic of Davidson (Chapter 9 §iv), but in any case widespread in current discussion, that the concept of truth is basic and irreducible, admitting of no explication in terms of other concepts. Is this actually so? The notion of truth is, at the very least, difficult to make intelligible otherwise than against the background of the concepts of affirmation and denial. To speak truly

is, trivially, to make the right choice between affirmation and denial relative
to a given predication Fx, affirming Fx when circumstances are such as to
justify its affirmation, and denying it when circumstances are such as to justify its denial. But for this choice to present itself, the options of affirmation
and denial of Fx must be clearly specified relative to one another. It must be
clear, that is, what is denied in affirming Fx, and what is affirmed in denying
it. This, we have argued, developing Wittgenstein's suggestions at *Remarks*
§82 and *passim*, can only be made clear relative to a field, or logical space, of
predicates standing to one another as in some way intrinsically alternative.
And it begins to look as if there is only one way in which such a field could
be constituted: namely, if the way in which the predicates in question are
introduced *relative to some socially instituted and maintained practice* (such as
measuring) results automatically, given the nature of the practice, in their
organisation relative to one another as the components of just such a field
or space. It appears, then, that truth is a notion to which we gain access
as a by-product of the social constitution and maintenance of practices of
a certain sort: practices so constituted that (1) they define the conditions
under which the user is justified in selecting one or another out of a range
of verbally expressed verdicts or conclusions associated with the practice,
and (2) by so doing they structure the verdicts in question as intrinsically
alternative to one another, thus making precise the relationship between
the assertoric content of affirmation and that of denial, and in consequence
rendering accessible the concept of assertoric content *per se*. The concept
of truth, in short, far from being *sui generis* and irreducible, is erected on
the back of the notions of assent and dissent, and by way of those notions,
more fundamentally still, on the notion of a practice.

vi. Concepts and the natural world

A second general feature, worth noting at the outset, of the account of the
relationship between meaning and truth that we have begun to sketch in this
chapter, is its bearing on Peter Geach's version of the ancient, nominalist
or conceptualist doctrine that concepts are "made by the mind."

> Having a concept never means being able to recognize some feature we have found
> in direct experience; the mind *makes* concepts, and this concept-formation and sub-
> sequent use of the concepts formed never is a mere recognition or finding . . . [3]

Geach's way of putting it raises the worry we have been confronting
in different guises throughout this book. If *the mind* makes, if we *invent*,
the concepts in terms of which our thoughts are framed, and thus the assertoric contents that articulate those thoughts, how can anything we say
about the world ever have more pretence to capture a reality independent
of our minds than what we say about witchcraft or the Blood Libel? The
account of concepts swimming, still no doubt rather fuzzily, into focus here

is half-Geachean. Concepts are indeed "made," not "found in nature," but it is not "the mind" that makes them. If they were made by "the mind" they would be a species of "mental state": things constructed, or at least constructible, within the bounds of the individual mind, from materials available within those bounds. Such a view of course raises difficult questions concerning the relationships between Nature, or World, on the one hand, and Mind and its conceptual constructions on the other, and it does so because it is a view saturated with epistemic individualism (Chapter 7 §ix). That is, it views the individual mind in search of knowledge of concepts, and persuaded also that such knowledge is not knowledge of the world but knowledge of the constructive activity of human beings, as compelled to seek *within its own bounds* for understanding of the constructive activity in question. Each individual speaker, in other words, must look into his own mind to discover how *he* constructs *his* concepts. On the view recommended here, by contrast, concepts are not "made by the mind," but by the linguistic community. The creation of concepts is a function, not of the enacting of some species of inner stipulation by individuals, but of the devising of practices by social groups. It is difficult to see how an individual could have access to the concept of *length*, for instance, except through access to the practice of measuring. And although that practice might conceivably be invented by a single individual, what he or she would be inventing would be in its essence social. The purposes for which we measure are purposes which unite and engage different individuals; the methods by which we do so are standardised in such a way as to yield repeatable results precisely because the practice is one which engages the conflicting interests of different users. And it is just because individual decision, individual caprice, are excluded from the practice of measuring that philosophical worry concerning the relationship of concepts to "the world," conceived as the extraconceptual, vanishes with them. Absent the practice of measuring there are no lengths. But to say that is not to say that the concept *length* is in any way adrift from reality. On the contrary, its relationship to the practice of measuring – far from being something which alienates it from some deeper contact with reality that it might somehow or other possess, and that it might be the job of philosophy to make clear – is what stitches it to reality in the only way in which it could be stitched to reality. We have exposed, in other words, another aspect of the working of the two-level model introduced in Chapter 3 §ii. Linguistic expressions, including concepts, never take on meaning in virtue of relating directly, by mere association or stipulation, to parts or features of reality. They take on meaning in virtue of their relationships to practices. It is the practices that relate to reality: stand to it, indeed, in relationships whose complexity and diversity are persistently obfuscated and hidden from view by the one-level model characteristic of Referential Realism in all its forms. We shall turn in the next chapter to discuss the implications of this thought for the prevalent doctrine that there are such things as Natural Kinds.

vii. Semantic and contingent alternatives

We have argued that the siting of a sentence S_1 within a practice that relates it to other such sentences, $S_2 \ldots S_n$, in a way essential to the nature and point of the practice, serves to define what we have called an affirmation-denial content connector for that sentence. It does so by making clear what is affirmed in denying S_1; what is thus affirmed being that one or other of $S_2 \ldots S_n$ must be true. In virtue of their linkage to one another across the practice in relation to which we bestow a use$_E$ on them, $S_1, \ldots S_n$ are semantically alternative to one another. And we suggested that this feature of a natural language furnishes an explanation of the possibility of negative description.

To this it might be objected that the intention of a negative description, what alternative state of affairs is being asserted or suggested in affirming it, cannot always be extracted by reflection on the meanings of the words. The point is implicit, for instance, in J. L. Austin's comments on "real": "[something] may not be a real duck because it is a decoy, or a toy duck, or a species of goose closely resembling a duck, or because I am having an hallucination."[4] Similarly, the contrast intended by someone who cautions, "That's not a dagger you see before you" may be that between a dagger and a small pruning-saw, or between a dagger and a vaguely dagger-shaped stone or piece of wood, or between a dagger and a shadow, or between a dagger and a visual illusion created by the fold of a cloak and a silver buckle which creates the impression of a pommel. So are being a dagger and being a small pruning-saw, or a shadow, or a piece of wood, or a visual illusion, "semantic alternatives" to one another? If so, the proposed "explanation" of the possibility of negative description surely collapses into vacuity: in this sort of way, anything can given the right circumstances, turn out to be "alternative" to anything. But if not, what distinguishes sets of semantic alternatives from alternatives of this nonsemantic, contingent variety?

Two related things do. In the two examples we have just offered, negative descriptions figure as attempts to correct mistakes: "That's not a duck (dagger), it's a ——." The list of blank-fillers in such a schema is plainly (a) in principle indefinite in extent, and unpredictable, since membership of the list depends merely on the contingencies of error, which in human life are themselves indefinite in extent and unpredictable. And just because of that, there is in such cases (b) no principled way of granting or withholding membership of the list, in advance of experience, to any sentence, *whatever its content*. To learn what some fool or other may succeed in mistaking for a duck or a dagger, one just has to wait and see what turns up.

In the case of the sentences constituted as semantic alternatives in virtue of their relationship to a practice that confers meaning conjointly on them, neither condition (a) nor condition (b) obtains. There is a principled way, provided by the practice, of determining in advance of experience what sentences are, and what sentences are not, semantically alternative to a given sentence. And because of that, the list of alternatives is not indefinite in content, though it may be numerically indeterminate.

This is true, for instance, of the two other examples, besides measurement, offered by Wittgenstein in the passage cited at the start of this chapter. The statement "I haven't got a pain" finds its place in a practice of asking and giving estimates of the intensity of pain, with which doctors and physiotherapists are very familiar: "Is it a slight, niggling pain, or does it force you to pay attention to it?," "Where would you place your pain on a scale of one to ten?," "Is the pain getting worse?," "Does it still hurt when I press *there*?," and so on. This practice excludes a sentence such as "I am wearing a hat" as a semantic alternative to "I am in pain," because hat-wearing is, given the nature of the practice, an irrelevancy. Someone who said, in reply to the question, "What did you mean when you said you were not in pain?," "I meant, of course, that I had a hat on," would not be disobeying any rule of language: he would be saying something that cannot be made intelligible in the terms of the practice of estimating the level of pain – or in terms of anything else. It is simply this failure of intelligibility that excludes "I am wearing a hat" as a semantic alternative to "I am in pain." But that is enough, and it is a failure that relates directly to the status of "I am in pain" as one move in a practice in which other alternative moves are also possible, as the failure of intelligibility which excludes "I am wearing a hat" as a semantic alternative is its failure to qualify *as an intelligible move in that practice.*

That is why, if someone, one of Quine's natives, say, were to persist in insisting that when he said he was not in pain he meant (of course!) that he was wearing a hat, we would begin to doubt whether we had correctly assessed the meaning in Native of whatever Native sentence we have been translating as "I am in pain." Whereas the answer "A decoy-duck," or "A shadow in the grass," or "A barnacle-goose chick" in reply to the question "When you said it was not a duck, what did you mean it was?" would in no way incline us to reassess our estimate of the meaning of "duck."

The same is true of Wittgenstein's other example, "These apples cost nothing." Predicates of the form "costs βn," where "β" is a currency denomination and "n" a number, possible numbers to include zero, belong in, and take all the meaning they possess from their role in, systems of monetary exchange. The semantic alternative to some apples costing nothing is that they should cost a sum of money – not that they should cost some snow, or some trouble – because only that alternative is intelligible *relative to such a system.* Once again, someone who said "I meant that they cost no snow" would be saying something which, if he persisted in it, would make us either suspect some very bizarre, possibly ceremonial system of exchange (on a certain Autumn festival one "pays" for apples with snow brought in insulated boxes from mountain snowbanks remaining from the previous winter, for example), or, more simply, suggest that we should revise our previous estimate of the meaning of predicates of the form " – costs βn."

viii. Two further examples

The range of practices in terms of which sentences of various logical types can take on assertoric content relative to one another by taking on, relative to the nature and purposes of the practice, the status of semantic alternatives, is, of course, indefinitely extensive. Two further examples will illustrate its diversity.

The first is counting, as described by Goddard (Chapter 8 §xii). At the stage of what Goddard calls "the counting rhyme" there are no assertoric utterances, although there can be mistaken ones, as when the learner recites the numerals in the wrong order, or makes a mistake in applying the rules which ensure that there is always a specific numeral that *comes next.* Assertoric utterance makes its appearance at the next Goddardian stage, that of "controlled counting." Suppose the teacher points to a group of five objects, and asks *How many things are there?* Either the learner control-counts carefully, and gets the answer 5, or she counts carelessly and gets some other number. In the first case she says "There are five," in the second, let's say, "There are four." The second answer is wrong, or false, but *it is still a statement of number.* It has to be a statement of number, because statements of number are the only kind of response that can be generated by following the procedure of Goddardian controlled counting. If the learner responds to the question *How many things are there?* by saying "My teddy!" or "Teatime!" she is not playing the game of controlled counting, but making a joke, of a type that very small children, frequently do make, and find hilarious, the significance of which is precisely that she finds the game boring and refuses to play it any more. But, by the same token, if a little while later she wants to go on with it, as small children also often do, and if at this point the teacher says "No, five is wrong, what is it really?," the child will know that what is required is *some other numeral,* because all one can generate by putting one's finger on one object after another in a group and saying the numerals in succession until one gets to the last object in the group is – a numeral. The child has already learned, in learning to carry out operations of controlled counting, an affirmation-denial content connector for any statement of the form *There are n objects here.* The affirmation-denial content connector in question is simply the practice of controlled counting *itself.* For in the context of that practice the possibility one opens up by saying " 'Four' is the wrong answer" – or, more pedantically, "It is false that there are four objects here" is that, and only that, *some other number* is the right one. What is asserted in asserting "There are four objects here" is linked to the range of possibilities reanimated by asserting "∼(There are four objects here)" by the practice, controlled counting, in the context of which such statements "acquire meaning" in the sense of finding a use$_E$.

For a final example, at least for the time being, let us consider colour names. Wittgenstein sometimes talks as if the use$_E$, as we would put it, of colour names is to serve as labels for printed colour samples. Thus the grocer in *Investigations* I.1, responding to the request for five red apples, "looks up the word 'red' in a table and finds a colour sample opposite it." If we did use colour names in this way, that practice would, certainly, serve to equip a range of statements about colour including "That apple is red" with affirmation-denial content connectors. The possibility opened by the denial of "That apple is red" would be that of a match between the apple and some other colour sample. Plainly, though, this is not how we use colour words. Quine offers a more accurate account of their everyday use in the following passage.

One learns by *ostension* what presentations to call yellow; that is, one learns by hearing the word applied to samples. All he has to go on, of course, is the similarity of further cases to the samples. Similarity being a matter of degree, one has to learn by trial and error how reddish or brownish or greenish a thing can be and still be counted yellow. When he finds he has applied the word too far out, he can use the false cases as samples to the contrary; and then he can proceed to guess whether the further cases are yellow or not by considering whether they are more similar to the in-group or the out-group. What one thus uses, even at this primitive stage of learning, is a fully functioning sense of similarity, and relative similarity at that: a is more similar to b than to c.[5]

The sort of practice Quine is describing in this passage is precisely one in which members of a set of alternative descriptions are simultaneously defined relative to one another in such a way as to limit one another's conditions of applicability. Colour-predicates such as " – is red" and " – is green" are on this account by no means logically independent in the way that, say, " – is a hat," " – is red," and " – is in the Art Nouveau style" are logically independent of one another. Rather, colour-predicates represent points, or better, collections of points, on a continuum of hues, which, like the gradations on Wittgenstein's yardstick, are not independent of one another because they are not independent of the yardstick (the hue-continuum) and its role in measuring (in arriving at the correct, the linguistically authorised colour-designation). The relationship of colour-predicates to one another established by the process Quine describes, of subdividing the continuum of hues into linguistically marked zones for purposes of reference, automatically establishes affirmation-denial content connectors for colour predicates: establishes, that is, that the possibility reopened by the assertion of ∼(Red x) is the possibility that x is some other colour, and not, say, that x is a hat, or Art Nouveau in style.

ix. Feature-placing statements

But can it *really* be true, someone may argue, that *all* sentences acquire whatever assertoric content they possess from the relationships, mediated by practices, in which they stand to other sentences? Measuring, counting, arranging colours, assessing costs, reporting the intensity of pain surely represent, after all, rather specialised uses of language. Must we not at some point admit what is surely platitudinous, that many of the sentences we make daily use of, sentences like "It's raining" or "That ring is gold," function simply as comments on aspects of experience, and take their meaning not at all from their relationship to other sentences, but simply from the nature of the aspects of experienced reality on which they comment?

Strawson introduced the useful term "feature-placing statements" to describe such sentences. His examples are

> Now it is raining
> Snow is falling
> There is coal here
> There is gold here
> There is water here.[6]

What interests Strawson about such statements is their resistance to categorisation in terms of the familiar logic of the subject-predicate sentence. The universal terms, *snow, water, gold,* in such propositions function neither as characterising nor as sortal universals. They name kinds of stuff, not characteristics, and they introduce no "principle for distinguishing, enumerating and reidentifying particulars of a sort."[7]

That is also what makes them of interest to Quine, given the centrality to his position of the claim that such traditional categories are observationally underdetermined. What the Quinean anthropologist's methods are designed to achieve is, essentially, a rough matching (rough because those methods cannot filter out "shared collateral information") between natural features and Native feature-placing sentences. It is because the observational evidence available to the anthropologist supports no more than the feature-placing "Now it rabbiteth" as an English equivalent to "Gavagai" that alternatives such as "There is an individual rabbit," or "There is an instance of rabbithood for you," alternatives framed, that is, in terms of the traditional logical categories associated with the subject-predicate sentence, remain on Quine's view observationally underdetermined.

A further logical peculiarity of feature-placing statements deserves attention. It is one noted by Gareth Evans.[8] Evans suggests that there might be a language, "or quasi-language"[9] – an important caveat, to which we shall return – "which consisted of a finite number of utterance-types used to respond communicatively to the publicly observable presence of some general condition of the environment. There might be an utterance type appropriately used whenever it is raining in the vicinity of the speaker at the time of utterance, another whenever a rabbit or rabbits are in the vicinity at the time of utterance, and so on. Here there is no question of assigning any expression an extension, or of identifying any construction as that of predication, for there are no constructions to be explained."[10]

Such expressions, in Evans's imaginary language, can be employed on their own or compounded, to yield "expressions like 'Red Water,' 'Warm Fog,' 'White Rabbit,' and so on."[11] For this process Evans introduces the felicitous term *mereological compounding*:[12] we shall term a language of this sort a *mereological language* ("feature-placing language" would do as well). Evans's argument is, in essence, that in such a language there is no way of answering questions that are answerable in terms of the "apparatus of identity" associated with the predicative sentence. Thus there is no way, within the terms of a mereological language, of distinguishing between the disparate phenomena that might prompt an affirmative response to the mereological "Red Water." A drop of red ink falls into a swimming pool. Which "water" is being asserted to be red? The whole contents of the pool, the water immediately diluting the ink, "or one of the indefinitely many intermediate alternatives?"[13] Any modification of a mereological language to render it sensitive to such alternatives will involve stipulating truth-conditions in ways which move the language closer to the predicational model.

We take this argument of Evans's to be broadly sound, and we think it can be extended. But to do that we need to consider a different aspect of mereological language: not its relation to predication, which is what essentially interests both Strawson and Evans, but its relation to affirmation and denial.

To see mereological language under this aspect is to see it, in effect, in relationship to the passage from the *Philosophical Remarks* from which we set out (Chapter 10 §i). The sentences of a mereological language, interestingly enough, will mirror the leading characteristic of the "atomic propositions" of the *Tractatus*. That is to say, they will be logically independent of one another, in the sense that the truth or falsity of one such proposition will carry no consequences for the truth or falsity of any other.

This is precisely the feature of the *Tractatus* that Wittgenstein is in process of uprooting at *Remarks* §82. His argument is that the sentences of a natural language cannot be so related, because in such a language – effectively a mereological language – there could be no such thing as negative description. Negative description can be envisaged only in terms of a language, the truth or falsity of whose statements carries *intrinsic* consequences for the truth or falsity of other statements.

Let us look again at Wittgenstein's argument, then, viewing it now from the standpoint of Evans's thoughts concerning mereological language. In a mereological language the denial of one of the basic statements asserts merely the absence of the environmental condition or circumstance associated with the statement denied. Thus, "Water not-Red" signifies that there is water in the vicinity but no redness, or at least (if this is how the compounding is supposed to work) none in the vicinity of the water. "Not-fog Cold" signifies that while it is cold in the vicinity it is not foggy. The love-affair of analytic philosophy with such an understanding of the implications of assertion and denial go back far beyond Quine. The "atomic propositions" beloved of Russell and the Wittgenstein of the *Tractatus*, as we have just seen, function in exactly this way. An atomic proposition "p" in the *Tractatus* may be true or false, but its denial has no consequence for the truth or falsity of any other atomic proposition. Its denial asserts nothing; nothing, that is, beyond the mere absence, the blank failure to obtain, of the "state of affairs" expressed by "p." Moreover, the Fregean logic brought to philosophical prominence by Russell and the early Wittgenstein, that logic in whose power to illuminate the logico-semantic structure of natural language so many hopes have been vested, shares this feature. The expressions it employs to represent propositions are likewise logically discrete: "$\sim$p" or "$\sim$Fx" express merely the falsity of "p" and "Fx": what they assert is, respectively, the nonobtaining of whatever state of affairs "p" expresses, and the nonpossession of the predicate F by the individual x.

Both Strawson and Evans accept that there "might be" such a thing as a mereological, or feature-placing language. Their objections are merely to the suggestion that feature-placing statements are any more "basic" or "fundamental" than other kinds of statements, and in particular to Quine's suggestion that the kinds of observational evidence appropriate to feature-placing statements exhaust the kinds of evidence available for the assessment of meaning *tout court*. Now, at first sight, the presumption that mereological languages are, in principle at least, feasible, seems reasonable. Does not English, after all, permit the construction of feature-placing statements of all the kinds Strawson lists, and more?

But do the English sentences Strawson lists actually express *feature-placing statements*? Take, for instance, the familiar war-horse, "It's raining." What feature, what observable environmental condition prevailing in the vicinity is this sentence "cued" to? "Water falling in droplets" might seem to be the answer. But is that so obvious? Suppose there is a machine, used by filmmakers, say, which produces conditions indistinguishable from falling rain over a small, but reasonably extensive area. Has the inventor of this machine actually found a way of making "it rain"? Surely not, or not as the English sentence "It's raining" is actually used, although someone might say so as a joke. Yet the same "feature of experience" is present. In this situation a "Native" – that is to say, English-speaking – informant would have to tell the Quinean anthropologist, joking apart, "No, it is not raining," inexplicably contradicting the evidence of other occasions on which informants appear prepared to countenance an association of that sentence with just that feature. The linguistic fact of the matter is that, in English "It's raining" describes a *climatic condition*. That this is the case is evident from the fact that a competent English speaker will take "It's raining" uttered in the conditions created by the rain-making machine either to express a genuine error (i.e., the speaker does not know about rain-making machines,) or to be meant as a joke. The assumption in either case is that if the speaker did know about rain-making machines, he would not assert it to be raining, because "it" (the prevailing climatic condition, that is) is in fact fine.

The descriptions "rainy weather" and "fine weather" are, in short, semantically incompatible. They are so because they find their use$_E$ in the context of a system of classification: a classification of climatic, or weather, conditions. The natural background to the system is the cyclical changeability of weather on a planet such as ours. Rain falls, winds rise, storms break out and disperse, sunny days succeed ... the days grow colder, snow falls, frosts whiten the ground in the morning, fogs arise and dissipate, and so on. Sometimes the terms we use in classifying these changes are merely contingently alternative. It may be both foggy and warm, or crisp and sunny. But there cannot be a thaw and a hard frost, or rain and fine weather, or fog and a sparkling morning, because these descriptions are semantically alternative. They designate different points in one or other of the numerous climatic cycles that together make up what we call "weather." The relationship between semantically alternative statements in these cases is exactly parallel to that between "x is four inches long" and "x is five inches long": they represent, as Wittgenstein would say, different gradations on one and the same yardstick.

It is thus far less clear than Strawson or Evans, or for that matter Quine, imagine that the everyday English sentences as "It's raining" or "Snow is falling" fall outside what Evans calls the "apparatus of individuation." What gives plausibility to that proposition is the idea that such statements simply "respond communicatively to," as Evans puts it, or "are appropriately used" in the presence of "some general condition of the environment." But such phrases, so loose that one suspects them of having been, no doubt unconsciously, chosen to be loose, do not make clear what sort of communicative function utterances matching the description they offer are supposed to have. If the rule for using them really *is*, simply, that they may (should? must be?) uttered in the presence of the "general conditions of the environment" to which they are "cued," then they are not sentences, or statements, at all, but simply inarticulate cries. We have, to be sure, examples of such cries in actual human societies. The cry of "Heil Hitler" with which the functionaries of the Third Reich were enjoined to respond to the presence of their Führer is one such. And we can construct imaginary societies, like that of the R-speakers (Chapter 9 §v), in which such cries take on simple communicative functions. But such cries are not *statements*. They can no more be credited with assertoric force or truth-values than the warning thump of a rabbit startled by the shadow of a hawk.

Such is not the case with "It's raining," and "It's fine." They are semantically alternative characterisations belonging to a system of classification whose communicative function is not to warn or to salute but to convey information. The utterance "It's raining" conveys *information,* rather than just a warning or an assurance of solidarity, because the notion of *denial* finds a foothold in its case, as it does not find a foothold in the case of the rabbit's thump or the cry "Heil Hitler!" It finds a place because it is clear what is asserted by the denial of "It's raining," namely, that it is fine. That is clear because "It's raining" and "It's fine" are semantic alternatives. They are semantic alternatives because they are related as such across a practice: the practice of classifying the cyclic patterns of prevailing conditions presented by the weather by associating descriptive terms with different points in one or another such cycle.

But once we have got to this point – once we are dealing, in other words, with a pattern of utterance in connection with which the notions of assertion, denial, assertoric force, truth, and falsity find a foothold – the "apparatus of individuation" characteristic of the subject-predicate sentence has already entered the picture. Such predicates as " – is rainy" or " – is fine" are, logically speaking, perfectly straightforward characterising universals, the individuals they characterise being individual stretches of time: rainy days, fine weeks, and so on. To say "It's raining" is not to signal the immediate presence of a "feature," as the thump of a rabbit might signal the presence of a hawk's shadow; it is to assert that the present moment belongs in a span of time correctly characterisable, from the standpoint of the locality of the speaker, as a rainy one.

x. Ostensive definition again

Such ordinary English sentences as "It's raining," then, give no support to Evans' and Strawson's tacit presumption that the idea of a mereological language is an internally coherent one. The idea that they do arises from the idea that the component utterances of a mereological language are to be re-garded as sentences, rather than as mere cries. We have already questioned the intelligibility of that assimilation. We can perhaps obtain a clearer view of what makes it incoherent by returning, for one last time, to the discussion, begun in Chapter 9 §vi, of Wittgenstein's argument against ostensive defini-tion. We argued in the last chapter that what is at stake in that argument is not, as often assumed, the practical feasibility of ostensive definition as a way of teaching the meaning of general names to a learner with no prior grasp of language. Wittgenstein's learner, we suggested, has to be assumed to pos-sess a language, because the alternatives between which he has to decide – a colour, a race, a point of the compass, and so on – can only be specified from within a language. On this reading, the point of the argument is that *nothing in the teacher's procedure allows the learner to attach one assertoric content rather than another* to the sounds the teacher utters while pointing. The situ-ation is indeed the reverse of what it is generally taken to be. It is the *learner* who is the speaker of a language: the teacher, for all his performance can demonstrate to the contrary, merely an R-speaker; at best the possessor of a feature-placing or mereological "language." We noted earlier that the language of "atomic propositions" proposed by the *Tractatus* is mereological in this sense. Wittgenstein's target, in short, is – characteristically – primarily his own earlier views, and only secondarily or tangentially the long and immensely influential tradition of philosophical theorising about language in which those views were rooted, and in which the later developments represented by the thought of Quine or Davidson are still rooted. What the argument shows is that in a mereological language such as that of the *Tractatus* it is impossible to mark the distinction between one assertoric content and another. The conclusion is that natural languages are not mereological. "Who, except possibly a sense-datum theorist would have supposed that they were?" one might respond. But the adversary here is not, as we have tried to show, a straw man. "Sense-datum languages" of the sort proposed by the entire empiricist tradition from Locke to Russell, H. H. Price, or A. J. Ayer are indeed envisaged as mereological "languages." But, as we have seen, that writers of enormous current prestige, such as Quine or Davidson, also take feature-placing or mereological "language" as basic or fundamental to natural languages, can be seen to follow from the fact that they take the observational evidence for meaning in natural languages to be insufficient to support anything beyond the sort of "meaning" available in a feature-placing language.

According to Wittgenstein, what the learner needs to know, if he is to make sense of the teacher's attempts to elucidate meaning by ostensive definition, is "the overall role of the word in language"; a phrase amplified, in *Investigations* §§28–30 by two others: "what place in language, in grammar, we assign to the word," and "the post at which we station the word." That information is given by saying, for instance, " 'This *colour* is called so-and-so,' 'This *length* is called so-and-so,' and so on." This information will be unintelligible, of course, to someone who does not know how the words "colour" and "length" function in language. And it seems clear that nothing could be gained by attempting further *verbal* explications at this point: if the learner doesn't understand "length" he or she will understand "measure of linear distance" still less. But a recourse is available at this point that does not involve the foredoomed attempt to elucidate verbal formulae by appeal to other verbal formulae. It is to teach the learner *how to measure*, or *how to count*, or *how to group shades of colour under colour-names by reference to considerations of relative similarity*. In the process such terms as "length" or "red" will be positioned, "stationed at posts," both sententially and in the context of the practice, in ways that make clear the relative assertoric content of assent and dissent: make it clear, for instance that to deny that something is red is to assert that it is *some other colour*. To be clear about that is also to be clear about what the teacher is asserting when he says, pointing, "x is red"; for if what follows, semantically, from the denial of that assertion is that x is some other colour, then what is accepted, in assenting to it, is that x is a particular colour, namely, the one for which, in the teacher's language, "red" functions as a name. The passage from a system of reactive cries to a language, that is, to a system of signs with respect to which the notions of assertoric content, affirmation, denial, truth, and falsity find a foothold, runs by way of the involvement of utterances in practices. Although to demonstrate the point would require a sharper turn towards the exegetical mode than we have been allowing ourselves, these are the ultimate considerations in response to which Wittgenstein introduces such terms as "use" and "language game." In a celebrated review of the *Investigations,* Strawson once asked what philosophically interesting theoretical function was supposed to be served by the notion of a language game, pointing out that without a straight answer to this question anything at all might count as a language game, including, for instance, reading to an old man on a windy night to send him to sleep. The argument of this and the previous chapter has perhaps put us in a position to give Strawson, belatedly, the straight answer he rightly demanded: the function of the notion of a language game, and the associated notion of "the use of a word" is to explain how it comes about that the notions of truth and falsity are accessible to us.

xi. The sensory evidence for meaning

" . . . all inculcation of the meaning of words must rest ultimately on sensory evidence," says Quine. "Hence the continuing attractiveness of the idea of a *logischer Aufbau* in which the sensory content of discourse would stand forth explicitly."[14]

One central question, which has exercised linguists and philosophers at least since the work of Chomsky made it central to linguistics in the early 1960s, is: What is learned in learning to assign meaning, truth-conditions, to the sentences of a language? It is clear that whatever answer one gives must meet the criterion of adequacy here proposed by Quine. Whatever one learns in learning to assign meaning to sentences, she must have some observational ground, if not for thinking that she has got it right or wrong, at least for taking one hypothesis about the meaning of a sentence to be better grounded than another. Dummett's "manifestation argument" states the same condition.

The rather sharply restrictive answer given by Quine to this question is as we have seen, that what one "ultimately" or "basically" learns in learning to assign meanings is which natural features prompt assent to or dissent from comments on present features of the environment: comments classifiable as relatively "observational" by the criterion of consistency of response across the speech community. We have argued, in effect that such an account of what is learned in learning to assign meanings is too parsimonious to account for anything that could reasonably be described as learning the truth-conditions of sentences. So it would be disturbing if, as many readers of Quine have supposed, such an account of what is learned were to be strictly entailed by the need to satisfy the observationality condition.

It seems evident, however, that the observationality or manifestability condition for language-learning in itself places only weak restrictions on answers to the question "what is learnt?" Quine's answer follows strictly from the observationality condition only when the latter is supplemented by a general distinction, characteristic of Logical Positivism, between the form and the content of propositions. According to that distinction, one can differentiate sharply between linguistic conventions that govern the content, or "cognitive content" of what is said, and linguistic conventions which merely determine its form.[15] The latter would be exemplified, for instance, by grammatical-syntactic conventions such as those governing agreement of gender in French, or the conventions for expressing complex tenses by combinations of verbs in English. These conventions, so the view we are representing maintains, are variable from language to language and contribute nothing to the cognitive content of what is said. The cognitive content of a sentence, by contrast, is established solely in virtue of its conventional association with the natural features whose presence or absence confirms or disconfirms assertions made by means of it.

If one assumes the general adequacy of this distinction, then – and only then – it follows that the acquisition of the ability to assign meanings to sentences must begin with the assignment of meaning to sentences which are observational in something like Quine's sense of that term, for since it is only in the case of such sentences that any relationship between sentences and observable natural features will be readily discernible, it is only in such cases that the observationality requirement will be met.

One way of grasping the thrust of the argument in this and the preceding chapter is to see it as directed towards undermining the type of form-content distinction outlined in the penultimate paragraph. If we have argued correctly, learning the truth-conditions of the assertions made by means of a sentence cannot be a matter of learning to associate the sentence with naturally occurring features of experience. On the contrary, the notions of truth and truth-conditions can be introduced only via the involvement of the sentence, along with other semantically related sentences, in some practice or other. What has to be learned in learning to assign meanings is therefore the mastery of practices: a kind of knowledge-how, not a kind of knowing-that. Wittgenstein's Slogan is vindicated again, and on a deeper level. All questions of the meaning of an assertion must be settled before the issue of its truth or falsity can arise, because until we understand the role, the use$_E$, of the corresponding sentence in some practice, we have no means of relating the content of its assertion to that of its denial, thus no means of determining what is relevant to its truth or falsity, and thus no means of relating it to the notions of truth and falsity: no means, in short, of treating it as an *assertion*, involving the utterance of a *sentence*, rather than as a mere cry, like the cry of a seabird (which may, like Quine's "gavagai," be prompted by perfectly determinate, and determinable, natural circumstances).

The distinction between, on the one hand, linguistic conventions which determine the cognitive content of assertions because they relate sentences to natural features, and, on the other, conventions which, because this is not their function, merely determine the form of assertions, thus collapses. Conventions as little concerned with the first of these supposed functions as those defining such practices as chess, or counting, or measuring, now take their place as determinative of meaning. The acquisition of the capacity to recognise, as such, assertions in a first, or alien language, and to assign them meanings, thus becomes in large part a matter of coming to grasp the truth-relevant relationships in which sentences stand *to one another* across practices, rather than a matter of relating utterances, *taken one-by-one*, to natural features. A suggestion of this sort was advanced, in effect, by Gareth Evans. Evans's suggestion was that attention to the relationship, in point of truth-conditions, between "Rabbit" and "White Rabbit," would be sufficient to provide an observer with adequate observational warrant for the conclusions that, on the one hand, "White Rabbit" is predicational rather than mereological in its logical form, and, on the other, that "Rabbit" divides its reference over whole rabbits, not, for instance, rabbit-parts or rabbit-stages. Our argument in effect builds on this suggestion, although from a standpoint rather remote from Evans' later, deeply Russellian writing. The learner of a natural language can only, in fact, learn what native speakers are asserting *about the world* by determining how their assertions are related to one another across practices. This will be partly a matter of direct schooling in the practices, such as that involved in teaching Goddardian counting (in other words, "*training*," to use Wittgenstein's term for it), and partly a matter of inferring the practice from Native patterns of assent and dissent. Thus, that some natives who use "fish" freely of all kinds of fish deny the propriety of its application to whales may serve as one piece of evidence for the hypothesis that their vocabulary of animal-type names classifies animals in terms of evolutionary descent and not merely in terms of interbreeding groups of similar bodily form. In either case, no breach of the requirement of observationality or manifestability is involved. There can be as good observational evidence for the conventions of a practice such as chess as there can for the nature of the "feature" prompting a "native" to cry "Gavagai," with the important difference that evidence of the former type is in principle capable of underpinning conclusions regarding the truth-conditions of assertions.

xii. Two senses of "truth-conditions"

In conclusion, let us return to the familiar and plausible dictum, often attributed to Frege, that to know the sense of a sentence is to know its truth-conditions. Earlier (Chapter 9 §i), we suggested that this thought might most plausibly be formulated as the claim that to grasp what a sentence means, in the sense of grasping the propositional or assertoric content of assertions made by means of it, is to know, in some sense yet to be determined, under what conditions an assertion made by means of it would be true or false.

But what is it to know *that*? Does knowing it, for instance, involve knowing how to *recognise* whether some, or any, assertion made by means of a sentence S is true or false? And is the converse true? Does knowing how to recognise as true or false all (or maybe just some?) assertions made by means of S necessarily amount to knowing the *meaning*, in the sense of the assertoric content, of S?

Intuitively, it looks as though the converse must be false. Suppose it is the case, for instance, that each of a certain range of official measuring-vessels manufactured by a U.S. government agency between 1901 and 1934 is precisely 13.04 cm. in internal diameter, and that such vessels can be uniquely identified by the presence of an official stamp on the underside of their base. The presence of that stamp is thus, in one sense of "truth-condition," a truth-condition for the statement "The internal diameter of this vessel is 13.04 cm." Let us call a truth-condition in this sense an *observational warrant*.

It would surely seem absurd, now, to contend that this bizarre observational warrant has anything to do with establishing *the meaning of* "*a* is 13.04 cm in internal diameter." So it appears at least in principle possible for someone to possess an observational warrant for the truth of a statement S without knowing what S *means*: without, that is to say, being in a position to attach any assertoric content to S. And if this is in principle possible in the case of one true statement made by means of S, it surely equally possible for someone X to be in that kind of position with regard to *any* such statement. That is, X would *always* be able to answer correctly any question of the form "is *a* 13.04 cm long?," but would *always* do so by reference to some observational warrant as adventitious from the point of view of meaning as the one just considered.

Moreover, if argument by counterexample fails to persuade, there is a general argument which establishes the same conclusion; namely, that a grasp of the meaning of S cannot consist in the possession of even a wholly adequate set – a set adequate to all eventualities – of observational warrants for the truth or falsity of assertions made by means of S. Let us retain, for the moment, the measuring vessel example. Suppose we wished to enlighten X, as possessor of the observational warrant we have been considering, concerning the meaning of the words "The internal diameter of this vessel is

13.04 cm." Would we not have to explain, at least, *what it means, in general, to say that anything is n moduli in length?* How could we do that without teaching X *what linear measurement is?* And how could we do that without teaching him *how to measure?*

Once he knows how to measure, X knows what "The internal diameter of this vessel is 13.04 cm." means, in the sense of knowing its assertoric content, in the sense that we have been exploring throughout this chapter. He possesses an affirmation-denial content connector for the sentence: he is able to form the class of sentences semantically alternative to it, so he knows what alternative possibilities are invoked by its denial, and so on. But does "knowing the meaning of a sentence" in this sense, being in possession of an affirmation-denial content connector, that is, have anything to do with truth? It might seem at first sight not, as manifestly one can possess an affirmation-denial content connector for a sentence, grasp the nature of the "post at which it is stationed" in the context of a familiar practice, without being in a position to attach a truth-value to any assertion made by means of it. Like many readers of nineteenth-century Russian novels I am familiar with the Russian term *verst*. I would have no idea how to set about establishing the truth or falsity of any statement of distance framed in terms of *versts*. If someone were to tell me that the distance between Moscow and Kiev is seven hundred *versts* or fifteen hundred *versts,* I would have no means of assessing the plausibility of either claim, since I have no idea how long a *verst* is, or was, except for the rooted conviction, probably picked up long ago from the notes to some Penguin edition of Gogol or Lermontov, that it was a good deal longer than a mile.

Despite this, there are good grounds for crediting me with as full a knowledge as could be had of what *verst* means: both in the sense of what it contributes to the assertoric content of sentences in which it occurs, and in the sense of what it designates. The word designates an obsolete Russian modulus of linear distance, longer than a mile, used for establishing geographical distance. The connection of that with truth is not that knowing it puts me in a position to *assign truth-values* to any statement whatsoever, but that knowing it, by putting me in a position to relate the content of assertions employing it to the content of the corresponding denials, puts me in a position to discriminate *what is relevant to the truth and falsity of statements employing the term* from what is not relevant. Knowing it, I know how I would have to set about assessing the truth or falsity of "Kiev is fifteen hundred *versts* from Moscow": I should have, to begin with, to establish a conversion formula relating *versts* to some measure of linear distance familiar to me.

Notice, now, that this is not an ability that can be conferred by the possession of observational warrants: not even by the possession of a set of such warrants adequate to all the eventualities which will arise in any finite history of conversational interaction between a given set of speakers. The possession of an observational warrant for a statement S does not, that is in itself, place its possessor in a position to discriminate what is truth-relevant to S from what is not truth-relevant to S. One may, for instance, know that the presence of the little mark on the base of the Government vessel entitles her to assert, truly, "Here is something 13.04 cm. in internal diameter" without having the faintest idea what other considerations, if any, might be truth-relevant to that statement. And the same can in principle be said of any observational warrant.

We have here, then, two senses of knowing the truth-conditions of S: (1) knowing some set of observational warrants for S (being in a position to recognise the truth or falsity of S under certain conditions); and (2) possessing knowledge of an affirmation-denial content connector for S (being in a position to discriminate what is relevant to the issue of the truth and falsity of S from what is not relevant). It appears that it is only if we understand the phrase in the second of these senses that Frege's dictum stands any chance of coming out true. It is possibly this thought that Wittgenstein has in mind when, in his usual oblique and compressed way, he remarks at *Philosophical Grammar* §84:

The role of a sentence in the calculus is its sense.
A *method* of measurement – of length, for example – has exactly the same relation to the correctness of a statement of length as the sense of a sentence has to its truth or falsehood.[16]

xiii. Refutation of the Verifiability Theory of Meaning

The Verifiability Theory of Meaning is, or was, the thesis, or slogan, that "the meaning of a statement is its method of verification." One version of the theory holds that the meaning of a statement, in the sense of its cognitive content, is given by stating the observations that make it true or false; a second, known as Operationalism, that the meaning of a statement is given by explaining the procedures, or operations, required to assemble the observations relevant to its truth or falsity.

The central error of both theories can now be seen to be that, while both accept Frege's dictum that to give the meaning of a sentence is to specify the truth-conditions of statements made by means of it, both identify the "truth-conditions" of a statement, either directly with the set of observational warrants capable of establishing its truth or falsity, or with the "operations" that give access to those warrants. In so doing they collapse the relationship between language and reality from a two-level into a one-level relationship. For if the observational warrants relevant, respectively, to the truth or falsity of S just *are* "the meaning of S," then – as observational warrants are (no more than) natural phenomena – Nature, the Given, presents us, in effect, with ready-made concepts: dictates to us the terms in which we are to describe her.

What any such view ignores is the question why some natural phenomenon or other *should count as* an observational warrant for the truth or falsity of S in the first place. Someone who knows *the meaning of* S must be able to settle all such questions of truth-relevance in advance of settling any question of truth or falsity. The argument underlying this further application of Wittgenstein's Slogan is obvious enough. It is simply that if a speaker is not in a position to accomplish the former task for a given sentence S, there will be no possibility of his advancing to the latter, since the assertoric content of S will not yet have been made clear. Knowing the meaning of a sentence and possessing access to the means of observationally warranting the truth or falsity of statements made by means of it, are two quite different things. The former is a matter of knowing how words are sited, at what "posts they are stationed," within practices, and hence of being, in consequence of that knowledge, in a position to discriminate what is truth-relevant from what is not. It is prior to, and founds the possibility of, knowledge of what in fact may count as licensing us to affirm the truth or falsity of particular propositions. Concepts, *pace* a great many philosophers from Plato (on some readings) to Locke and beyond, cannot be read off from Nature. Nature offers us only phenomena. She offers us no concepts because there is no way in which she can be made to take over from us the task of defining the relationship between what we deny in affirming and what we affirm in denying. We ourselves must define that relationship if it is to be defined. And the only way in which we can define it is by way of the uses$_E$ which predicate expressions take on within human practices: such practices as counting, or measuring lengths, or arranging colours into qualitative series by appeal to relationships of relative similarity. In the next two chapters we shall examine in more detail the implications of this conclusion.

11

Unnatural Kinds

i. Universals

Does the universe contain, in addition to individuals, kinds and properties? This is the celebrated Problem of Universals. The traditional answers to it comprise Realism, which posits kinds and properties in addition to their individual exemplars and instances, and Nominalism, which allows the existence only of individuals. There is also a third answer, Conceptualism, which, recoiling both from the absurdities of an outright Nominalism and from the over-richly peopled universe of the Realist, assigns to kinds and properties the refuge of a shadowy existence as mental templates, or rules, for shuffling individuals into the sets, or as logicians say, *extensions*, associated with kind-names.

Realism was born with Plato. Nominalism, despite the efforts of Nelson Goodman or Hartry Field, is widely regarded as having died with Hobbes. The analytic tradition in philosophy has tended until very recently to alternate uneasily between the options of Conceptualism and some kind of platonic or quasi-platonic Realism. The Realism recommended both by Frege and by the early Russell was of this kind.

Thoughts, Frege agrees with Plato, are eternal, immutable essences which are neither created, nor sustained, nor in any way altered by any human activity; nor are they perceivable by any human sense. And so, Frege concludes, they exist neither in the external material world, nor in the subjective inner world: "a third realm must be recognized."[1]

"Third realms" and their contents sit ill, however, with the Positivism-derived naturalism and empiricism of so much analytic philosophy. John McDowell's defence of a "naturalised" platonism represents a recent attempt to bridge this gap. Like all other forms of platonism, it confronts an obvious problem: if the entities, Forms, Ideas, Thoughts, Concepts, postulated by the Realist are inhabitants neither of the mind nor of the external world, how does the mind acquire knowledge of them? In Plato the theory, or myth, of *anamnesis*, the soul's memory of a higher life before birth, is one answer to this question. Frege, in *Die Gedanke*, postulates a special faculty, "something nonsensible" which "could lead us out of the inner world and enable us to grasp thoughts."[2] McDowell proposes a process of *Bildung* that may be undergone, but that cannot be "viewed from the side": that cannot, that is, be described or spoken of save in terms of the very concepts that it renders accessible to us.

Conceptualism avoids this problem by representing concepts as creatures of the mind: things owing their existence to mental activity operating on a world containing only individuals. The doctrine is as old as Locke. In its more modern forms it has leant heavily on the notions of "intension" and "extension." The *extension* of a kind-name "F" is the set of items of which " – is F" or " – is an F" is true. The intension of "F" is the concept associated with the term. The relation between the two has been widely held to be that to grasp the intension of a term is to grasp a rule or criterion for selecting, assembling, the class of items that collectively constitute the extension of the term. Equally widely, the rule in question has been equated with a *description*, by appeal to which items can be *recognised* as belonging, or not belonging, to the extension.

For philosophers like Carnap, who accepted the verifiability theory of meaning, the concept corresponding to a term provided (in the ideal case, where the term had "complete meaning") a *criterion* for belonging to the extension (not just in the sense of "necessary and sufficient condition," but in the strong sense, of *way of recognising* if a given thing falls into the extension or not.)[3]

For the modern Conceptualist, in other words, grasping the *concept* picked out by a term is a matter of grasping the *intension* corresponding to that term, and grasping that is a matter of grasping a description adequate to confer upon the person who grasps it the capacity to "fix the extension" of the term: not just to say in principle, but to recognise in practice, of what items the term can, and of what items it cannot, be truly affirmed.

One great merit of Conceptualism of this type is that it offers a way of avoiding the implausible Nominalist contention that the mind is free to associate particulars under general names in any way it pleases. Like Locke, the modern Conceptualist can distinguish between descriptions "framed by the mind" and those that have a "foundation in the nature of things." On this account the content of the description that equips us to form the extension of a term such as "funfair" is indeed a matter of arbitrary human choice. The drift across time of particular decisions into settled custom alone accounts for the presence of the specific elements – mechanical rides, freak-shows, shooting-galleries, test-your-strength games, and so on – which jostle one another in it. The description that constitutes the intension of "gold" or "tiger," however, is for the modern Conceptualist, as for his intellectual ancestor Locke, read off from Nature. Some kinds, in other words, are Natural Kinds, the product of scientific investigation, rather than the creative ingenuity of the human mind. By allowing certain kinds to be in this sort of way Natural, Conceptualism takes itself, among other things, to have struck a balance between the Realist contention that Nature presents us with Kinds and Properties in addition to individuals, and the Nominalist contention that the work of framing concepts must reside in the human mind, unaided by *anamnesis* or by "special faculties" allowing a mysterious access to Fregean "third realms." By embracing Conceptualism, or so it has been claimed, we avoid both the otherworldly fantasies of the Platonist and the Nominalist's equally unappetising vision of a Nature infinitely plastic to the shaping powers of mind and language.

ii. Putnam's poser

Modern Conceptualism can be summarised, then, as the view,

(1) that the extension of a general name is fixed by its intension,
(2) that to grasp the intension of such a term is to be in possession of a recognitional capacity,
(3) that the ability to exercise the recognitional capacity in question results from the possession of a description, founded in the case of Natural Kinds on the observation of nature, knowledge of which is shared by all competent speakers.

A refinement of (3), widely known as the "cluster theory," says that what competent speakers associate with a general name is not a single description, but rather a cluster of descriptions, some but not all of which an item needs to satisfy in order to fall into the extension of the name.

The confidence of philosophers in this resolution of the Problem of Universals remained fairly general until, in 1975, it was disturbed by Hilary Putnam. Putnam, in effect, posed a question. An intension, whatever we take its exact nature to be, and however derived, is something capable of being grasped by a mind. A Natural Kind, let's say *water*, or *chlorine*, or *tiger*, is a part of Nature – a Nature that we must hold, short of embracing one or another form of Idealism, to be mind-independent. So how can an intension determine the limits of the extension of a Natural Kind? How can the question what is water and what isn't, say, turn on the contents of the description most competent English speakers happen to associate with the term "water"? It looks, on the face of it, at any rate, as if what is and is not water is a question to be settled by scientific investigation, and not by *our* adopting some *description* or other as criterial in the matter.

The obvious reply to Putnam's Poser open to the Conceptualist, a reply rooted ultimately in Locke's distinction between names of substances and names of "mixed modes," is that the descriptions we associate with names for the sort of thing Putnam considers a Natural Kind – things like *gold*, or *water*, or *lemon* – are descriptions derived from the observation of the natural world, descriptions, or as Locke would say, "ideas," which, as Locke puts it, "carry with them the supposition of some real being from which they are taken and to which they are conformable."[4]

But this altogether underestimates the extent and difficulty of the problems which Putnam's question raises. Putnam's reply is that, however the description was derived, it remains the content of a psychological state. Frege may indeed have argued that the sense, the *Sinn*, of a concept-expression cannot be a mental state because mental states are by their nature private, and sense must be accessible in common to all competent speakers. But even if the sense is not itself a mental state – as is the case, for instance if a sense is identified with the content of a description; with something, that is, which certainly can be publicly exchanged between speakers – *knowing*, or *grasping* the intension remains a psychological state. And the issue before us is whether any psychological state, including that of grasping the content of a description, can determine, or "fix," the extension of a Natural Kind.

Were intension sufficent to determine extension for kind terms, intension and extension would always coincide. The same term, used by two speakers with the same intension, that is, would always pick out the same extension. This, Putnam argues, is not the case.

> We claim that it is possible for two speakers to be in exactly the *same* psychological state (in the narrow sense), even though the extension of the term *A* in the ideolect of the one is different from the extension of the term *A* in the ideolect of the other. Extension is *not* determined by psychological state.[5]

iii. Twin Earth

Putnam's argument invokes a celebrated and subsequently much discussed counterexample.[6] Consider two possible worlds, Earth and Twin Earth. Twin Earth is *exactly* like Earth. Not only does it contain people like us who call themselves "Americans," "Englishmen," and so on, it even contains a *Doppelganger* for every individual person on Earth. The physical contents of the two worlds are identical also. On Twin Earth, in particular, there is a substance which Anglophone Twin Earthers call "water." To gross inspection it is indistinguishable from water on Earth. It tastes like water, quenches thirst like water, and so on and so forth. But Twin Earth water is not H_2O. It is a different liquid, whose "very long and complicated" chemical formula Putnam abbreviates as *XYZ*.

If a spaceship from Earth visits Twin Earth, the initial supposition will be that "water" on Twin Earth has exactly the same meaning as it has on Earth. But suppose the scientists aboard discover that Twin Earth "water" is actually *XYZ*. They will report this discovery, Putnam contends, as the discovery that "On Twin Earth the word 'water' means *XYZ*'," meaning by "means" here something like *has as its extension*. They would precisely *not* report it as the discovery that "On Twin Earth the meaning of the word 'water' is XYZ"– *unless it happened to be the case that every linguistically competent Anglophone adult on Twin Earth knew water to be XYZ*. For to report the discovery in that way would be to report not on the *extension* of the term, but on what competent speakers understand it to mean; that is, on its *intension*. Intension and extension are beginning to fall apart, in other words, with the latter beginning to appear as dependent not on what speakers may or may not suppose themselves to "mean" in the sense of *intend*, but on the results of scientific enquiry.

Putnam now develops the example into an argument for the conclusion sketched at the end of the last section. Suppose the year to be 1750. Chemistry has as yet not developed, either on Earth or Twin Earth, to a point at which H_2O could be distinguished from XYZ. Given the identity to gross inspection of H_2O and *XYZ*, Oscar$_1$ on Earth in 1750 and his *Doppelganger* Oscar$_2$ on Twin Earth at the same date may be supposed to have exactly the same beliefs about water, and given their *ex hypothesi* status as *Doppelgangers* to be in exactly the same psychological state in all other respects. Nevertheless the extension of "water" on Twin Earth in 1750 is different from its extension on Earth: in the one case H_2O, in the other *XYZ*. So, even in 1750, what Oscar$_1$ refers to when he refers to water is not what Oscar$_2$ refers to when *he* refers to water. For what each refers to in using the term is the extension of the term, and in one case that is "the set of all wholes consisting of H_2O molecules, or something like that," and in the other "the set of all wholes consisting of XYZ molecules, or something like that."[7] Thus, Putnam concludes, "the extension of the term "water" (and, in fact, its meaning, in the intuitive preanalytical usage of that term) is not a function of the psychological state of the speaker by itself."[8]

iv. Direct reference

Why does the "Twin Earth" example work? If we accept the force of the argument, we grant, among other things, that "water" must be regarded as having the same extension in 1750 as in 1950 on either Earth, or in other words, that the issue of what constitutes the extension of such a term is invariant with respect both to linguistic change and to the development of scientific theory. Granting that means granting, in effect, that the extension of a Natural Kind term turns, not on anything having to do with us, our language or our psychological or epistemic states, but simply on *how*, independently of all that, *things stand in the world*. The thrust of the argument, in short is towards Realism: towards the view that extension-fixing depends on how things really stand, not on how speakers envisage them as standing.

What is it, now, about the logic of Natural Kind terms, which makes the Twin Earth example sufficiently compelling to bear the weight of a version of Realism that radical? Putnam's rather traditional suggestion is that a Natural Kind term like "water" is initially introduced into the language by direct reference, or in other words by ostensive definition.

Suppose I point to a glass of water and say "this liquid is called water" (or "this is called water" if the marker "liquid" is clear from the context). My "ostensive definition" of water has the following empirical presupposition: that the body of liquid I am pointing to bears a certain sameness relation (say, *x is the same liquid as y*, or *x is the same$_L$ as y*) to most of the stuff I and other speakers in my linguistic community have on other occasions called "water."[9]

The sameness$_L$ relation, now, is a theoretical one, in the sense that whether one sample is the same liquid as another may take an indeterminate amount of scientific investigation to establish. It is therefore a matter about which speakers may be *mistaken*. It is not, in other words, for speakers to *say*, to *stipulate*, what is *to be regarded* as "the same liquid" as that, but for them, if they can, to *find out*. Putnam is offering, in other words, a sharply *externalist* account of the reference, or denotation, of natural kind names, in contrast to the *internalist* one offered by the modern Conceptualist.

v. Rigidity and indexicality

Another way of putting Putnam's point would be to say that the linkage between a Natural Kind term and its extension (collections of H_2O molecules in the case of "water," say) is a *rigid* one, in something like Kripke's sense of "rigid," because it is a linkage forged *indexically*, by ostensive indication of a sample. That in turn suggests a further argument against Conceptualism. The modern Conceptualist takes the extension of a term to be fixed by its intension, and the latter to be expressible by a description of some sort. But no description can forge a rigid linkage between a term and its extension. Whatever description a speaker may associate with a kind name like "tiger" may fail to discriminate some actual tiger as such. That remains true even if what the speaker associates with the term is a cluster of descriptions, only some unspecified subset of which have to be satisfied in order for what satisfies them to count as a tiger. For actual variation within the tiger population may at any time surpass the power even of a cluster of descriptions to predict its limits. If, by contrast, what links the term "tiger" to the world is ostensive indication of a sample, with the proviso that this, and any other animal which is of the same kind as this, is a tiger, then further applications of the term will depend, not upon any description available to speakers, but on what turns out as a matter of scientific fact to stand in the required sameness relation to the sample animal; an issue that, in the case of tigers, will presumably turn on genetic constitution. Treating extension-fixing as a function of the descriptions speakers associate with terms leaves open the possibility of referential drift across possible worlds. Treating kind terms as indexical preserves rigidity of reference precisely by putting it out of human power to determine the extension of such a term. What counts as water, or a tiger, will be whatever bears a given sameness relation to a sample, and since that question is one to be settled by scientific investigation in *the actual world*, it will have the same answer in every possible world. As Putnam puts it, "When I say '*this* (liquid) is water,' the 'this' is, so to speak, a *de re* 'this.'"[10]

vi. Stereotypes

The ability to fix the extension of a kind name is clearly, on Putnam's account, going to be a rather technical, and thus a rather sparsely distributed one. Only a competent analytical chemist with access to suitable equipment, after all, is actually in a position to determine whether a given sample is, say, potassium cyanide or not. To most of us the sample will be just another anonymous white powder in a bottle that might be anything at all. Similarly, it may take a competent botanist, in possession of a good flora and the knowledge required to use it, to determine with certainty whether a plant is of one species or another. Yet we commonly ascribe to ordinary speakers a grasp of the "meaning" of such terms as "potassium cyanide" or "cow parsley." What do we mean by "meaning" in such contexts, given that, if Putnam's argument so far is correct, "knowing the meaning" of such a term cannot imply the ability to form its extension?

Putnam's answer is, in effect, (1) that, for an "ordinary" speaker, knowing the meaning of a kind name is knowing roughly what things of that kind are like, and (2) that the extent of the required knowledge is socially determined. To justify the claim to know "what 'tiger' means," for instance, it will not be sufficient just to know that tigers are physical objects, or possess spatial extension, even though this knowledge might be sufficient to allow one to extract all the relevant implications-in-context of certain sentences concerning tigers.

Suppose a speaker knows that "tiger" has a set of physical objects as its extension, but no more. If he possesses normal linguistic competence in other respects, then he could use "tiger" in *some* sentences: for example, "tigers have mass," "tigers take up space," "give me a tiger," "is that a tiger?," etc. Moreover the *socially determined* extension of "tiger" in these sentences would be the standard one, i.e., the set of tigers. Yet we would not count such a speaker as "knowing the meaning" of the word *tiger*. Why not?[11]

It is worth noting that in commenting on this point, Putnam passes from the formula "he doesn't know the meaning of the word 'tiger'" to the formula "He doesn't know what a tiger *is*," as if the two formulae, however (strictly speaking) different in meaning, came to much the same thing in practice.

Before attempting to answer this question, let us reformulate it a bit. We shall speak of someone as having *acquired* the word "tiger" if he is able to use it in such a way that (1) his use passes muster (i.e. people don't say of him such things as "he doesn't know what a tiger is," "he doesn't know the meaning of the word 'tiger,'" etc.); and (2) his total way of being situated in the world and in his linguistic community is such that the socially determined extension of the word "tiger" in his idiolect is the set of tigers.[12]

This assimilation, as we shall see in a moment, is by no means philosophically harmless. Certainly it is what dictates Putnam's account of what a speaker must know if his knowledge of the meaning of a Natural Kind name is to "pass muster" among his fellow speakers. In Putnam's view, although a speaker need not be able to "fix the extension" of "gold" or "tiger," he must know, so to speak, *roughly what sort of things his fellow-speakers take gold or tigers to be.* He must share with them, therefore, knowledge of some collection of characteristics *generally attributed* to gold or tigers: that gold is a yellow, soft, precious metal, perhaps, or that tigers are large stripey cats. Such a collection of received ideas is in Putnam's terminology a *stereotype.* Such sets of characteristics can in no sense be regarded as sets of sufficient and necessary conditions for membership of the class *gold-sample* or *tiger.* Pure gold, as Putnam points out, is in fact almost white, the yellow colour seen in the sort of gold used in jewellery being the result of impurities, usually copper; albino tigers no doubt occur. Statements expressing the content of stereotypes, in short, enter no remotely plausible claim to the status of analytic truths. Nor can stereotypes offer a solution to Quine's problem, or paradox, of "radical translation" (see Chapter 13): "We cannot translate [an alien language] into English by matching stereotypes, just because finding out what the stereotype of [an alien expression] is involves translating [alien] utterances."[13] Stereotypes are no more than conventionally received bodies of belief which serve to "keep conversation on the rails." By contrast, when people point to samples which fit the stereotype of gold they will be, quite a lot of the time, pointing to samples of gold. Ostensive indications stereotypically guided will, that is, most often serve to set in train the complex nonlinguistic practices and processes which actually serve to give us a grip on the *extensions* of the terms we use, and where they do not, when we point in error to pyrites or to newly discovered marsupial carnivores strikingly similar in appearance to tigers, those processes themselves will serve to reveal the disparity.

vii. The thinness of linguistic knowledge

Subsequent discussion of Putnam's "The meaning of 'meaning'" has not focused very much attention on Putnam's doctrine of stereotypes, but has concentrated on what are much more evidently philosophically central issues raised by Putnam's argument: notably the internalism/externalism debate, Realism, and essentialism. We shall revisit Putnam on these issues later in the present chapter, and in Chapter 12 and the Epilogue. Nevertheless, and despite the evident importance of these other and much more discussed matters, it is with the doctrine of stereotypes that we propose to begin our discussion of Putnam's views.

One good reason for starting here is that the doctrine, even on its own terms, is scarcely plausible. Intuitively, we would say that we know what "potto" and capybara' *mean.* "Potto" and "capybara" are names for kinds of animal. But we have not the slightest idea what pottos and capybaras *are like.* Not only could we not recognise an individual of either species as such if it were put in front of us, we could not state a single feature either actually or generally presumed to be *characteristic* of either the potto or the capybara. So we appear to have nothing in the way of a Putnamian stereotype attached to either term. Of course there is the bare characterisation "kind of animal." But on the face of it that seems about as thin a piece of knowledge as (Putnam's example) the knowledge that a tiger is a physical object. Stereotypes in Putnam's sense ought, one feels, to be richer than that.

In part, that feeling is a consequence of the importance and centrality which Putnam's account of meaning bestows on the notion of ostensive definition. Putnam says at one point that the association of a stereotype with a kind name "is the sole element of truth in the 'concept' theory."[14] To a careless reader that pat on the back to the Conceptualist might convey the impression that the notion of a stereotype is marginal to Putnam's theory: a residual and harmless concession to an opponent, nothing more. That would be a mistake. Putnam is not merely casting a dry bone to the Description Theorist: he himself needs *that* much of the Description Theory. If sample-indication is, as it must be for Putnam, the link that connects language with the world, then knowledge of meaning must carry with it the ability to identify samples consistently from speaker to speaker. Hence, speakers who lay claim to knowledge of the meaning of a kind name must attach to it enough in the way of a descriptive content to enable them to indicate, independently of other competent speakers but in a way acceptable to them, one or more sample items to which the term applies. In taking meaning to involve a direct connection between a linguistic expression and some real-world correlate, Putnam is proposing, in other words, just as much as the modern Conceptualism he rejects, a version of Referential Realism. And, hence, like any Referential Realist, he needs some account of what guides the ability of a competent speaker to attach terms to their real-world correlates. For even if such abilities do not stretch as far as the "fixing" of extensions, they must at least run to the identification, in common with other speakers, of the samples on which the processes of scientific enquiry that accomplish the former task may be supposed to operate.

Thus it is a difficulty for Putnam that people are commonly said to "know the meaning" of a variety of terms – "potto," "capybara," "potassium cyanide," for instance – with which they associate no descriptive content which could possibly enable them to indicate, to *locate* in the world, any item to which the term in question applies. The difficulty is analogous to the one we encountered earlier (Chapter 5 §iii) in connection with proper names. And of course it is not just a difficulty for Putnam's account of meaning, but for the theory of meaning in general. Let us therefore address it.

viii. Salience and segmentation

Might the answer be that Nature just does come naturally, if only roughly, divided into kinds, and that what makes this division apparent, not just to language users but to prelinguistic children, and even to animals, is the evident *perceptual salience*, as psychologists say, of certain categories of phenomena? Quine develops a suggestion of this kind in an essay entitled "Natural Kinds,"[15] in which he discusses the processes by which the natural dimensions of salience exploited by folk terminology gradually become refined to fit the austere and more demanding requirements of science. And surely there is a great deal to be said for that answer. Colours, or animals, or plants, for instance, do on the face of it appear to offer perceptually salient domains awaiting further classification; domains whose status as coherent kinds appears quite independent of, and prior to, the sort of arbitrary choice of criteria of kind-formation envisaged, say, by the Nominalist. *Principles* of animal or plant classification clearly are open to the kinds of debate that, in the eighteenth century, produced the Linnaean system that provides the basis of present-day taxonomy. But the status of "the animal world" or "the plant world" as a *domain* of classification is surely assured by Nature. Equally, it might be said Nature supplies us with a range of one-item domains: kinds such as *Water*, or *Gold*, which, again, simply crop up in our experience as perceptually salient features of the natural environment. How could any choice, any "dividing-up of the world" by appeal to linguistic stipulation, enter into the introduction of a name for *water* into a natural language? How could *anything* be involved, over and above the bare association of a name with a sample which for Putnam, as for so many of his predecessors in the empiricist tradition, constitutes the point at which discourse ultimately makes contact with the reality which it concerns?

What could be more persuasive? The fact remains that outside the analytic tradition, and increasingly within it, there are to be found philosophers and linguists who reject such an answer. For such theorists, it is equally axiomatic that the stipulative dividing-up of the world by language goes all the way down; for whom, as Putnam himself has begun to put it in his Carus Lectures, written a decade after "The meaning of 'meaning'," *the trail of the human serpent is over all.*[16] As Samuel C. Wheeler III puts it,

The Platonist picture of language and truth requires . . . a natural segmentation of the world so naturally well-founded that any plausible language would have to have terms whose extensions matched that segmentation . . . .[17]

. . . For the languages in which we think and speak, as opposed to the mathematical constructions we might fantasize, the very items that are to be the elements of sets are not given by the nature of things. There is no truth-value or reference-bearing manifold prior to conceptualization, that is, prior to language or the languagelike. So there are no items of any kind waiting to be grouped into sets. Without a manifold of epistemologically given objects, no alternative "conceptual schemes" can be formulated as "constructions" or "artifacts."[18]

Chomsky has recently said similar things:

In general, a word, even of the simplest kind, does not pick out an entity of the world.[19]

On the face of it, such views may seem to raise the problem of how we are to avoid finding ourselves shut inside the Prison-House of Language, which has occupied us for so many pages. If there is not, at any level, any "natural segmentation" of the world into items "waiting to be grouped into sets," how can we claim for our kind names any grip on a world which, *ex hypothesi*, they themselves partition arbitrarily into kinds? Jerry Fodor, in a review, levels exactly this criticism at Chomsky.

The upshot is a familiar sort of postmodern Idealism according to which science speaks only of itself: "Il n'y a rien beyond the geology text," and all that. There are traces, in *New Horizons*, of incipient sympathy with this Wittgenstein-Goodman-Kuhn-Derrida sort of picture, but it is one that I think a respectable Realist should entirely abjure. Science is not just another language-game; and, no, Virginia, we didn't make the stars. Pray god that no miasmal mist from Harvard has seeped up the Charles to MIT.[20]

Wheeler is also, at least to all appearances, open to this kind of objection. The radical Nominalism apparently implicit in his view of things is hardly softened by the Davidsonian thought that in the absence of any possibility of contrasting the segmentation of reality imposed by the language we speak, with a segmentation proffered by Reality itself, the suggestion that the former is "artificial" or "constructed" lapses into vacuity.

However, appearances can mislead. We shall find reason to conclude that these remarks of Chomsky's and Wheeler's, save for the concluding, very Davidsonian, sentence of the latter, are entirely sound. The denial of "a natural segmentation of the world" need not, as we shall see, entail any form of Nominalism or Social Relativism or Linguistic Idealism. It is, as we shall see in the Epilogue, perfectly compatible with the attribution to the subject matter of geology of an existence independent of geology texts, and with scientific Realism in general.

To see how such things can be, we need to see two things. First, that segmentation, which is a linguistic phenomenon, is, as such, distinct from, and irreducible to, salience, which is a psychological one. Second, that although the segmentation a language imposes on the natural order may be determined by choice, or stipulation, that does not mean that the choices, the stipulations in question, are *arbitrary*, in the sense of lacking anything in the way of observational grounding or justification.

Let us start with the first point (we'll get on to the second in §ix). To say that colours, or animals, form salient domains of experience is to say, presumably, that they present us with collections of individual things united into a coherent set, or domain, by relationships of relative similarity holding between the items composing the set. Could one, then, as so many philosophers have supposed, introduce a kind-name, N_k, simply by correlating it with just such a naturally presented array of relative similarities? No, because while such systems of similarities may be sufficient to mark off *perceptual* boundaries, they are not sufficient, are not even the *kind* of thing required, to mark off *semantic* boundaries. (*Pace* the empiricist tradition in philosophy, not all our mental capacities are versions or aspects of our perceptual capacities, and in particular our linguistic capacities are not!) The reasons why semantic boundaries are not like perceptual ones are those developed in Chapters 9 and 10. Attaching assertoric content to a sentence, even a simple one such as "That's a dog" or "That's water" is a matter of relating what is asserted in affirming the sentence to what is asserted in denying it. Grasping such a relationship is a matter of grasping what *other sentences are* raised to the status of potential truths by the denial of a given sentence. Grasping it, in other words, is a matter of grasping *how sentences are related to one another* as alternatives relative to some practice or practices.

The kinds of similarity-systems that give *perceptual* salience to colours, say, or to animals, cannot, in other words, serve to delimit the assertoric force of a sentence, because the only thing that can serve to delimit the assertoric force of a sentence is the assertoric force of *another sentence*. This is the ultimate force, as we saw earlier, of Wittgenstein's objection to ostensive definition. Ostensive definition is the exhibition of a sample with the accompanying stipulation "this, *and anything which is the same* as this, is N_k (or "what we call 'N_k'"). The difficulty lies in giving a sense to *same:* "same" in what respect, in number, colour, shape, and so on? Solving that problem is a matter of limiting – circumscribing – the kinds of similarity capable of carrying the application of "N_k" into new contexts. And natural similarity, although it can provide grounds for extending the application of a term, can in the nature of things provide, of itself, no grounds for limiting or circumscribing a term's application. The patterns of similarity that the world offers to human perceptual capacities are so complex and so ramifying, that grounds can always be found for extending the application of a term. Individual books, for instance, are related to one another by an array of similarities of just the right kind to make the kind *book* a highly psychologically salient feature of our environment. Suppose, then, one defines "book" by ostensively indicating a copy of *Sesame and Lilies,* and saying "This is what we call a book," with the unspoken proviso "This ... *and anything similar*"? What *is* relevantly (i.e., from the point of view of deploying the word in other contexts) *similar*? Is the latest issue of *Vogue* a book? (It consists, after all, of a thickish wad of pages united at the spine, and if it has a soft cover, so do many books.) In some English idiolects it is, in others it is not.

Again, suppose someone defines "animal" for me by pointing to the most conveniently situated exemplar – a dog, say – and stipulating "this is an animal (or 'what we call an animal'), and anything similar to this is an animal too." Does a statue or a toy dog count as an animal in my informant's idiolect? Does a motile robot of dog-like form count as one?

One can get round this problem, as Wittgenstein notes, by adding some verbal specification of the type of similarity intended. This is, in effect, the path Putnam takes in incorporating into the stipulation accompanying the indexical indication of a sample of water the proviso "same liquid" (same$_L$). But this, by presuming access to a language with a fully functioning vocabulary of kind-names, begs the very question to which Putnam presents his theory of meaning as an answer, namely, how kind-names get established: how they are introduced into language in the first place.

ix. Cataloguing the world

The kind of differentiation of the world's contents effected by considerations of perceptual salience can never, we have suggested, be equivalent to, the kind effected by linguistic segmentation, because perceptual salience affords in itself no means of preventing the application of a term from extending itself indefinitely along endlessly ramifying perspectives of natural similarity. And we suggested, in line with the argument of Chapter 10, that the only thing capable of drawing the boundaries of the field of applicability of a given kind name is the field of applicability of another kind-name. The implication of that is, once again, that we must take seriously Wittgenstein's suggestion, in *Philosophical Remarks* §VIII, that what language lays against the world, as a yardstick is laid against what we measure with it, is not the proposition but the system of propositions. In effect, this means that we cannot think of the ultimate stipulations, or choices by means of which we give meaning to general terms, as associating individual terms with perceptually salient elements or aspects of the world. Rather, we have to think of the ultimate choices that institute one or another vocabulary of kind terms as twofold in character. On the one hand, there will be the choice of some set of principles for cataloguing the phenomena that go to make up some aspect or region of reality, chosen either because of its perceptual salience or because of its importance for various human purposes or interests. Those principles, once we have chosen them, will work to equip the resulting catalogue with a finite array of alternative heads. On the other hand, then there will be a second set of choices assigning phonemic strings as markers for the heads in question. In Chapter 10 §§vii–viii, we considered a short list of examples, including colours, counting, measurement, and price, which fit this description. Goddardian counting, for instance, in effect stipulates principles for cataloguing denumerable sets under the heads constituted by the natural numbers. On the one hand, there is the array of stipulations which constitute counting as a practice: these supply the principle of the catalogue. On the other, there is some set of arbitrary assignments of phonemic strings, "one, two, three . . . ," "ein, zwei, drei . . . " to fulfil the demands of the Counting Rhyme for the nonsense syllables that will, as the practice develops through the sequence of steps which Goddard sets out, become names for numbers. But there is, in all this, no assignment of names to stand for already discriminated, that is extralinguistically discriminated, aspects or items of reality.

Catalogues may be built on catalogues. Take, for instance, "book," in standard English. *Qua* artifact a book is a block composed of sheets of paper fastened together down one edge. On this level the term contrasts taxonomically with "sheaf of paper." And this simple taxonomy corresponds to a set of practices: we make paper, we cut it into square sheets, and for certain purposes we fasten it into books. We need terms for a block of loose sheets and a block of sheets fastened in this way. "Sheaf of paper" and "book" acquire the status of semantic alternatives in virtue of the manner in which we have chosen to insert, or integrate them, into the practice. Once we have the notion of a book, and with it the thing itself, other practices begin to weave themselves about the latter. Some books have a unique publication date, others are issued periodically, under the same title but with differing contents from issue to issue, as we say. We introduce "magazine" or "periodical" as kind-names for the second mode of publication, reserving "book" for the first. And now we have a second level of semantic contrast which, like the first arises in virtue of the way in which we have chosen to enmesh words in practices.

So far as the cluster of kinds "book," "periodical," "sheaf of paper" is concerned, then, it looks very much as if Chomsky is right. These terms don't pick out "entities of the world," at least of "the world" as a certain sort of Realism thinks of it: as a place, if one may put it this way, untouched by human hands. The entities they pick out are, like numbers, creatures of our practices: nomothetic entities (Chapter 5 §i). So does Fodor's criticism of Chomsky follow? Are we flirting with – or rather not just flirting with, but positively wallowing in – the absurd idea that nothing exists outside our practices and the functional roles for kind names with which they provide us: *il n'y a pas d'hors-pratique*, or something of the sort? Well, consider a further example, say that of organising a typology in archaeology. Suppose we are dealing with Classical Greek vases. There are many principles on which we could classify the potsherds that turn up in our excavations, from the general shape of the fragments themselves to the chemical composition or point of origin of the various clays used. But these have no immediate relevance to the primary interests of archaeologists in ancient techniques and their development, and the bearing of these on trade-routes, cultural influence, and so on. So classical archaeologists choose to classify Greek vases in the first instance, first by appeal to the various technical practices used in vase-painting: black-figure, red-figure, white-ground, and so on, and, second, by appeal to artists" identity and locality of origin so far as these can be determined on stylistic grounds. Suppose, now, some seventh-century black-figure vases showing a certain pattern of stylistic similarities have been turning up in excavations across the Eastern Mediterranean. There seems no reason to introduce a special name for the particular set of similarities concerned, any more than for any of the other indefinitely many other sets of similarities that can be discerned to hold between vases of this type. But now, on the island of Chios, the buried remains of an ancient ceramics workshop is discovered containing some hundreds of examples of pots all of which display just this pattern of similarities. Now there is a reason for baptising this set of similarities with a special kind name, "Chios black-figure," let's say; and archaeologists will at once set to work to refine the concept stylistically and to trace the occurrence at other sites of the type so defined.

The point of the example is this. The decision to attempt the construction of a classification of vases which will, *inter alia*, assign names to styles of vase-painting in ways which will reflect, as far as possible, the origin of these artifacts in geographically separated centres of production, is a decision of ours, or rather, of the Classical Archaeology community. But once that decision has been made, certain choices regarding *which* collection of stylistic resemblances to baptise with a name will rest not with the archaeological community but *with the results of excavation*. So to that extent Nominalism loses. We are not, as the Nominalist contends, free to fix the extension of "Chios black-figure" by appeal to just any collection of characteristics we choose arbitrarily to select. But the victory of the Realist is from his point of view a limited and ambiguous one, since our loss of freedom to do that is itself a consequence of a prior decision of ours; namely, our – or the Archaeological community's – decision to classify vases by stylistic criteria distinctive, as far as possible, of locality and workshop of origin. The Realist true to his platonic[21] roots thinks of kinds, or tends to think of them, as a class of *entities*, entities as much "out there in the world" as Mount Kilimanjaro or the Okapi. And just as it is a determinable question how many mountain summits over three thousand metres there are in Kenya, or how many species of large mammal, "large" being appropriately specified, are to be found on the African continent, and which these are; so to a certain kind of Realist – perhaps we should call him the Hardshell Realist – it is a determinable question how many kinds there are, and which they are. To the Hardshell Realist the contents of the List of Kinds is *in no way whatsoever plastic to human intention or decision.* It is in this sense that he believes in the existence of a "natural segmentation" of Reality into kinds. The view we have begun to develop here, however, is as unwelcome to Hardshell Realism as it is to Radical Nominalism. For on our view kinds do not exist independently of language, but only relative to our adoption of principles for the construction of catalogues. On the one hand, *pace* the Nominalist, it lies with Nature, relative to a determinate set of cataloguing principles, to determine both the contents of the list of kinds and the extensions of individual kinds. On the other hand, *pace* the Hardshell Realist, prior to the establishment of principles of cataloguing there are no kinds, only phenomena. There is no "natural" segmentation, in other words. There is a segmentation *determined by Nature,* but it is a segmentation determined by nature only in response to the application of principles of cataloguing chosen by us. It follows that not only the question *how many* kinds the world *naturally* divides into, but also the question *which* kinds the world *naturally* divide into, are vacuous ones. *Phenomena* are "natural" in the sense of prelinguistic, as are the relationships, phenomenal and otherwise in terms of which we characterise and recognise kinds, but kinds themselves are not natural. There are as many kinds, and as many varieties of kind, as there are viable and interesting principles on which to catalogue phenomena. And the invention of such principles is ultimately a function, not of "the way the world is," but of human interests and ingenuity.

x. Colours, species, kinds of stuff

The difficulty for Hardshell Realism is particularly clearly displayed in the case of colour kinds, if we take colour kinds to be the entities picked out by the basic colour names of a language. We discussed the example briefly in Chapter 10 §viii, but a fuller treatment will perhaps do no harm. The phenomena of colour, if we take into account surface as well as spectral colour, present us with a very large array of discriminable colours. Ordinary English speaks in this connection of "shades" of colour. It would be more exact, perhaps, to speak of "colour presentations," meaning by that a particular hue presented in specific degrees of saturation and tonality.[22] Understood in this way there are in excess of seven million discriminable colour presentations. What a name such as "red" picks out *in nature* is an indeterminately large collection of such presentations. Observably, all competent speakers of a language agree in the main, and agree independently of one another, which colour presentations lie within the extension of each basic colour name of their language, and which lie outside it. A natural question is, what is learned in acquiring the capacity to match, independently, other speakers' assignments of presentations to the extensions of colour names. And the answer cannot possibly be that for each speaker each colour name has been expressly associated with each of the presentations composing its extension; on the one hand, because the number of presentations is in each case far too large for such a procedure to be practicable, and, on the other, because the set of presentations composing the extension of a colour-name is at any given point in time indeterminate. No speaker will have observed all the shades of blue, say, that there are in the world, and there may be shades exhibited by compounds as yet unsynthesised by chemists (such was the case with aniline dyes in the first quarter of the nineteenth century) that no speakers have yet encountered, but that all will unhesitatingly agree to fall into the extension of "blue," or some other basic colour name, when they do encounter them.

It is not hard to envisage an account of colour-naming capable of answering this question. An adequate one, as we noted in Chapter 10 §viii, is furnished by the account of the learning of colour names first proposed by Quine in "Natural Kinds."[23] According to that account, we exploit the possibility of arranging colour presentations in series according to whether one presentation is more like another than it is like a third. Taking the capacity to form such series for granted, we associate specific colour names "A," "B," "C," . . . with specific sets of very closely related colour presentations, <a>, <b>, <c> . . . Then we introduce the rule that any presentation not included in any of these sets is to be called A if it is more like the presentations included in <a> than it is like the members of any other named set, B if it is more like the members of the <b> set, and so on. Cases of presentations intermediate between named sets are then dealt with *ad hoc* by the introduction of intermediate designations, "A-ish B," "B-ish C" (e.g., English "bluish-green," "reddish purple").[24]

It has long been known to linguistic anthropologists that the number of basic colour-names differs from language to language. Some languages have as few as three, some, like most modern European languages, have as many as sixteen. If one asks informants to indicate the best, the most typical samples of the colours named in their language, as it were the "foci" around which their colour concepts are organised, it turns out that there is a constant relationship between the identity of these foci and the number of basic colour terms present in the language. For a two-term colour vocabulary the foci of the two terms will be what we would recognise as (roughly) the foci of white and black. In languages with a third term the focus of the third term will be somewhere among what we would call the reds; in languages that add a fourth term its focus will be either in the greens or the yellows, and so on.[25] However, any language, whatever number of colour terms it honours, partitions the colour array exhaustively between the extensions of its basic colour terms. In two-term languages the colour "black" may be taken to include all the "darker" parts of the array, the blues, dark reds, purples, dark greens, while "white" will include all lighter colour presentations. In languages that add a third term, that term, call it "red," will cover all reds, oranges, most yellows, browns, pinks, and purples, the remainder of the colour array still continuing to be partitioned between "white" and "black."

This Quinean account of the transmission of colour names outlined above offers a plausible explanation of these phenomena. The partitioning of colour presentations into the extensions of however many colour names a language recognises will be a natural consequence of the rule that a colour presentation takes the name of the named set of samples it most resembles, taken in conjunction with the placing of names in association with specific foci. So changing the number of named foci, or moving the foci themselves, will produce a different partitioning of the colour array between the extensions of the same number or different numbers of basic colour names.

The difficulty for the Hardshell Realist is that these shifts in the procedures of what we may term the Colour-Naming Game will result in different partitionings of the *phenomena* of colour between the extensions of colour names, each of which will have an equal claim to be considered "Real." An Australian linguistic anthropologist once told one of the authors that although English and German both have a term, and the same term, for the colour orange, native German speakers and native English speakers consistently and independently form the extension of the term "Orange" differently, with the extension of German "Orange" shifted slightly towards the red. In terms of the notion of *kind* dear to philosophers, in other words, German and English "Orange" pick out different kinds. Which of the two is the *"Real"* orange? Or to put it another way, which of the two nations is *mistaken*, is *labouring under a misapprehension* about the segmentation of reality into kinds? Surely both these questions are absurd because vacuous: what could possibly count as relevant to an answer either way? The way to stop asking such questions is to see that what is "real" here are the phenomena of perceived colour, and that the partitioning of those phenomena into one or another array of named kinds is the result of, on the one hand, *how those phenomena are* (but not *how they are qua* array of kinds, rather, how they are *qua* phenomena), and, on the other, shifts in our manner of organising and conducting a certain linguistic practice.

To see this is to see that the supposed choice between Hardshell Realism and some form of relativism or Linguistic Idealism (the choice with which, in §viii, we found Fodor attempting to confront Chomsky, for example) is not an exhaustive one. What makes it look exhaustive is the unspoken and unexamined commitment to Referential Realism which has dominated, and dominates, so much philosophical discussion in this area. We think of the names of colour kinds, as of all kind names, as drawing their meaning from standing in a direct relationship of reference or designation to something "out there in the world." Because that something must be a kind, there must be a natural segmentation of Reality into such entities, for if there is not, then, since it will presumably be possible to segment Reality any way we please, the general names of our language will represent, will connect with, nothing save the caprices of the mind playing about a world infinitely plastic to its operations. These options cease to appear exhaustive, and the appearance of a forced choice between them vanishes, when we replace the one-level model of reference characteristic of Referential Realism with the two-level model advocated here. For now what gives meaning to a word is not a direct linkage between it and some "entity" in the world, but the relationship in which it stands, along with other terms, to some practice functioning to provide a set of rules or principles for the construction of a catalogue. In each case those rules will work to provide each term in the catalogue with an extension relative to a given domain itself individuated relative to the applicability of the rules in question. Each term will thus name, or designate a kind, but the kinds in question will be in effect, images cast by a Nature refracted through that practice, conducted according to that set of rules. Another practice, or a shift in the operation of the practice, will produce another set of kinds, equally ineluctably refracted from the un-changing face of Nature. The Linguistic Idealist is wrong, in short: we do not arbitrarily choose what kinds we shall honour, but only what sort of practice, what sort of system for determining the extensions of kind names, we shall adopt. Once we have made that choice, Nature determines what kinds we shall be required to honour in consequence of having made it. But, equally, the Hardshell Realist is wrong: the kinds we then find ourselves honouring are not parts or elements of Nature, nor do they uniquely characterise it. For were we to choose another method of determining the extensions of kinds, Nature would display itself to us under the aspect of a different set, with the same claim as the other to be considered Real.

The Hardshell Realist will surely wish to retort that such an appearance can only be the outcome of a careful choice of example. Colour may work like that; but then the status of phenomenal colour as an element of the real world has always been in doubt. Colour is, to put it bluntly, just one of the ways things look to us, not one of the ways things *are*. Maybe we do have that sort of control over how the colour array is to be partitioned into kinds, but is it plausible to maintain that such kinds as *tiger*, or *water*, or *gold* are artifacts of our schemes of classification; are not simply "out there in the world," waiting to be discovered, and when discovered, designated by direct reference?

The claim, of course, is not that colour kinds are *artifacts* of our schemes of classification, at least in the sort of way that canals on Mars were arte-facts of observation at the limit of resolution, but only that different sets of colour kinds are, as it were, *aspects* under which the phenomenal nature of colour (i.e. *the reality of things*, as far as our visual experience of colour is concerned) is displayed through the application of differing schemes of classification. The set of colour kinds into which the phenomena of colour arrange themselves relative to one or another way of conducting the Colour-Naming Game is, in other words, not in our hands, but in those of Nature to determine. But let us look more closely at the cases proposed.

Are *species* features of reality, or to put it another way, does the living world *segment naturally* into species? That the notion of a species is a fairly recent addition to the conceptual vocabulary of Biology is not in itself a reason for answering in the negative. Philosophers such as McDowell, or Kripke, or Putnam who argue that the conceptual segmentation of Nature has, like any other natural feature, to be discovered, have a point, even if they then complicate matters by their insistence, which we shall pursue in Chapter 12, that conceptual features characterise Reality necessarily or "essentially," with the consequence – one that sets off such features rather sharply from other sorts of empirically discovered feature – that it is impossible to contrast the world so conceptually segmented with a world segmented otherwise, or not at all.

A more instructive thought, from our point of view, is that the segmentation of the living world into species is not the only way of segmenting it. In ordinary English, or as the scientistically-inclined dismissively put it, in "folk"-English, an animal or plant kind is a community of individuals linked by a complicatedly interrelated collection of bodily resemblances displaying a high degree of consistency from individual to individual; a community, moreover, within which that pattern of resemblances is reliably passed on from parents to offspring. That is not, however, the same thing as a species. The notion of a species as that has come to be employed in biological taxonomy presumes the ordinary notion of an animal kind but adds to it the requirement that any individual in the community must be able to breed with any other to produce fertile offspring.

Of course this is an idealisation: putting the requirement as crudely as that will exclude some individuals whose incapacity to produce fertile offspring has nothing to do with speciation. But *ad hoc* adjustments will cope with that (in general, a lot more is *ad hoc* in scientific taxonomy and in science in general, than some philosophers are prepared to admit), and the intention is plain. The idea of classing individual animals into species is that of sorting them into groups separated from one another by the barrier of consistent infertility in the F_1 generation.

This has turned out to be, scientifically speaking, a most useful and informative project, because of the connections there have turned out to be between speciation and, successively, Mendelian genetics, the discovery of the chromosomal mechanisms entering into cell-division and their implications for sexual reproduction, and the rise of modern cellular biology. Has the success of these scientific endeavours, then, demonstrated that species are what the living world "really" segments into? No. To suppose any such thing is fatally to muddle science with metaphysics, with results that we shall pursue in the next chapter. The project of sorting animal and plant kinds into species is precisely that: a *project* – a highly useful and informative project, but a project nonetheless. It is as much a project, a principle of classification, as the project of sorting colour presentations according to the rules of the Colour-Naming Game relative to a certain selection of named foci, or the project of sorting books by subject, or by the identity of the bookbinder. There are other projects, other principles, other ways one might adopt of imposing an order, for purposes of reference, on the living world. The "ordinary," or "folk," taxonomy of animal kinds is just such a project. And while it yields, in practice, a perfectly clear and useful segmentation of the animal world into kinds having a very substantial overlap with the segmentation yielded by the species project, the overlap is by no means perfect. There are, that is, animal populations that consist of more than one species but whose members are sufficiently close in appearance for the species-differentiation to be detectable only to a biological taxonomist with experience in that area. Under the rubrics of the "folk" animal kind project, individuals of these species will be lumped together as constituting one kind of animal. Does this represent a *mistake* on the part of folk-taxonomists? Well, no: for how can it be a *mistake* to choose one principle of classification over another? To suppose anything of the sort is to commit oneself to the Correspondence Theory of Meaning (Chapter 1 §iii): to suppose that there can be "true" concepts as well as true assertions. Of course, access to some kinds of truth often requires one to order one's thoughts in accordance with one system of concepts rather than another. But that is a different matter. To say that is merely to say that one principle, or project, of cataloguing, may be more useful than another. That is undeniable, but is not, contrary to what is often assumed, equivalent to an assertion of the Correspondence Theory of Meaning.

What about substances, and more generally, kinds of stuff? A linguistic community that can count has all that is required to set up a linguistic contrast between count-nouns and mass terms. Count-nouns have plurals because the items composing their extensions are denumerable. The concept of a kind of stuff is the concept of a volume of something: a handful, a basketful. The principles on which a folk-language erects a taxonomy of kinds of stuff are various. Considerations of origin or manufacture predominate. Wood, in all its varieties, is what is obtained by dividing and shaping the trunks of trees. Stone, in its varieties, is what outcrops from the ground or, in more technologically advanced societies, is quarried from it. Agricultural commodities, wheat, lentils, rice, peas, wine, oil, are things obtained by various processes of cultivation and subsequent treatment of crops from various plants. Water, brackish or sweet, is what fills lakes, streams, and the sea. On these primitive taxonomies, naturally enough, a distinction between substances and mixtures imposes itself. A sample of wheat may be mixed with other grains or be "pure" wheat. Wine for drinking is, at least the ancient form of it, always a mixture of "pure" wine, the stuff made from fermented grape-juice, poured from a jar and mixed with water. Water and wine are distinct substances; what the guests at the *Symposium* actually drink is a mixture of two substances. In the same sort of way, bronze is a mixture of tin and copper, but tin and copper are not mixtures of anything: they are substances, each a separate, ultimate kind of thing in its own right. Struck by this, one might ask what kinds of stuff there *ultimately* are. It is not obvious at first sight, not only what answer one is to give to this question, but what considerations are, or may turn out to be, relevant to answering it. A very long history of scientific enquiry has led us to the conclusion that the most relevant considerations are those that began to emerge in the eighteenth and nineteenth centuries with the work of Dalton, Mendeleev, and others, and that led to the development of modern chemistry. But we could not have found reasons for thinking these developments relevant to the question "what kinds of stuff, ultimately, are there?," if the question had not *already* been intelligible to us.

The notion of an element, that is, is not theory-laden but, rather, practice-laden. One does not need to understand the modern chemical theory in which the term "element" finds for us its most natural use, to understand the concept of an elementary substance. An elementary substance is a kind of stuff that is not a mixture of other kinds of stuff, like bronze but, rather, is one of the kinds, like copper and tin, out of which mixtures are compounded. The project of making a catalogue of such kinds of stuff is again, in other words, a project, though again one that has proved over time both strikingly successful and extremely useful.

It is a project that has proved *explanatorily* more fundamental than the project of cataloguing kinds of wood, or kinds of agricultural produce. But that fact does not make it *metaphysically* more fundamental than they. The fact that olive oil, wine, or wheat are ultimately compounded out of the naturally occurring elements listed in the Periodic Table does not have as a consequence that only the kinds of stuff listed in the Periodic Table *exist*, or *really exist*, and that such kinds as *oil* or *wine or flour* are somehow illusions, capable of being explained away, like ghosts or the Loch Ness monster.

Philosophers, to whom reductive, or eliminative, analysis is an obsessively familiar technique, are often tempted to imagine that chemical analysis has, or could have, the same sort of function. But this is again to confuse science with metaphysics. The goal of reductive analysis is to show that sentences employing a given term "T" can be replaced without loss of meaning by sentences in which "T" does not occur. The immemorial project of "reducing" talk of physical objects to talk of sense-data, which for the moment appears to have died with Carnap, but will doubtless crop up again, is a case in point. Philosophers often appear tempted to think that giving an exact chemical analysis of olive oil would be an achievement of the same sort: that is, it would show both "what 'olive oil' really means," and that there is "ultimately no such thing as olive oil," but only carbon, hydrogen, nitrogen, and so on.

But giving an explanation of the properties of the items composing the extension of a term T_1 drawn from one type of catalogue in terms of the properties of the items composing the extensions of terms T_a, T_b, T_c, . . . drawn from another type of catalogue cannot amount to giving the meaning of T_1. For the meaning of T_1 is bound up with the nature of the principles defining the project of making the kind of catalogue to which it belongs. In the case of "olive oil" the name picks out, not a substance having a certain chemical composition, but the product of a certain agricultural process, namely that of pressing olives. Stuff having the appearance and chemical composition of olive oil but not produced in that way would not *be* ("what we mean by") olive oil. Moreover if we were to *dispense with* the name "olive oil" in favour of the names of the chemical elements entering into the composition of olive oil, all that we would achieve would be to make it impossible to refer to the kind of oil produced by pressing olives except by a very long and tedious circumlocution. It would, in other words, impede rather than assist us in cataloguing the kinds to be found in Reality. For that there is a certain distinctive kind of oil produced by pressing olives is as much a fact about Reality as it is a fact about Reality that there are ninety-six (or however many) naturally occurring elements, or that phenomenal orange is between phenomenal red and phenomenal yellow. Kinds are the faces that reality reveals in response to our taxonomic projects. And no one project, no one taxonomic practice, *pace* the philosophical reductionist, can prompt Nature to reveal all the kinds that she is capable of revealing.

xi. Linguistic and factual knowledge

Let us, one last time, recapitulate the argument of this and the preceding two chapters up to this point. Kind names do not acquire meaning through conventional association with anything in the extralinguistic world. Any such process would have to establish the assertoric force of an assertion "Fx": "This is (an) F." The bare act of associating one thing with another involves no conventional stipulation capable of conferring assertoric force on either. So if "Fx" is to acquire assertoric force through the association, that can only be because, once the association is set up, its assertoric force can be read off from the natural character of whatever it is associated with. But that can only come about if something extralinguistic, something in nature, already possesses assertoric force. And nothing in nature possesses assertoric force.

If assertoric force is not established by nature it must be established by convention. Part of grasping the assertoric force of a sentence "Fx" is grasping which other sentences are *semantically alternative* to "Fx," in the sense that their probability of turning out true is increased by the denial that x is F, and that are *semantically indifferent*, in the sense that their probabilities

of truth or falsity remain unaffected. So grasping assertoric force is a matter of grasping some conventionally mediated set of relationships between
sentences. Assertoric force – "meaning" at the sentential level – cannot, in
other words, be established by any conventional operation, including association with extralinguistic objects, samples or features, which operates on
sentences taken one by one. At the same time, the necessary relationships
between sentences cannot be established by blankly arbitrary stipulation.
For then assertoric force would in effect be established independently of
any consideration of the nature of reality. Linguistic Idealism, the triumph
of prison-house scepticism, would follow as an immediate consequence.

That consequence is avoided if we think of meaning, and assertoric force
as fundamentally established not at the level of sentences, but at the level of
practices. Initially, this move – familiar though it is to most philosophers as
a result of the prominence given to it by Wittgenstein's play with the notion
of a language-game in the *Philosophical Investigations* – looks unpromising.
Its striking absence from recent mainstream discussion in the philosophy of
language can be largely accounted for, indeed, by the apparent openness of
language-game talk to two obvious objections of contrary thrust. The first
is that games, at least in the ordinary sense, neither give foothold to nor
throw light on the two concepts most closely and essentially linked to that of
linguistic meaning, namely, the concepts of reference and truth. The second
is that a case for a conceptual connection between the concept of practice
and that of truth can be made out only within the context of some version of
verificationism or operationalism. Hence, as a majority of philosophers have
concluded, the stance of the *Philosophical Investigations* is either a version of
verificationism or is unintelligible.

We have suggested a way past this double impasse in the theory of meaning
and in the reception of Wittgenstein's work. It is to see that, for Wittgenstein,
what practices offer is not a criterion of truth but a criterion of relevance to
truth. That comes to the same thing as saying that they serve to make clear
the content of what is asserted in asserting Fx by making clear what propositionally formulable alternative possibilities are reopened by the denial of
Fx. A linguistic practice, such as counting, or colour-naming, offers in effect
a number of slots, or places, into which arbitrarily chosen sentential signs
may be inserted. These *simultaneously* take on specific assertoric contents relative to one another, as a result of assuming the status of *alternative outcomes
relative to the conduct of the practice*. It is crucial to see that what the conduct
of the practice establishes is merely *the status of a range of sentential signs,
relative to one another, as expressing alternative outcomes*. It does not determine
the success of one outcome relative to another: the truth of the assertion expressed
by the corresponding sentential sign (this is why the position is not a form
of verificationism).

This is difficult to see in the case of counting, because counting is one
way of establishing the truth of arithmetical propositions. But it is quite easy

to see in the case of a project of cataloguing, such as that of partitioning individual animals or plants into species. The conventional elements of the practice are (1) a specification of the conditions which must be met by a collection of individual animals if it is to be regarded as constituting a species; and (2) an indefinitely large array of places to be filled by signs which may be regarded either as names, "tiger" "panda," or as sentences "that is a tiger," "that is a panda." If the signs arbitrarily assigned to these places are construed as sentences, then they are related across the practice as semantic alternatives, since the practice determines what sententially formulated possibilities increase in probability as a consequence of the denial of one of the sentences it has brought into being. Denying that a given animal is of one species raises the likelihood of the possibility expressed by some sentence assigning it to *another species* turning out true, but not the probability of such possibilities as those expressed by the sentences "x is blind" or "x is brown," for example, turning out true. Finally, what is meant by difference of species is established by the conventionally stipulated criteria for settling that question incorporated in the practice. Hence the relationship of each sentence S to the practice specifies both the *assertoric content* of S, and what is *relevant to the truth* of S. What the practice does *not do*, however, is to *determine truth-values* for the sentences whose assertoric content it defines. To know what a species is, which is all that can be gleaned from knowledge of the practice, is not at all the same thing as *knowing what species there are*. To answer the latter question we need to know whether there are, in fact, communities of animals divided from one another by consistent infertility in the F1 generation, which communities those are, and how to recognise specific individual animals as belonging to one or other of them, and these latter questions are ones that can only be resolved by empirical investigation. To grasp the rules of what we may as well start calling the Species-Sorting Game is to know the meaning of "species" and, *ceteris paribus*, the assertoric content of sentences involving species-names: it is not, however, to know anything of substance *about biology*, or for that matter anything of substance about the natural world *tout court*.

We appear, then, to have arrived at a conception of what is involved in linguistic knowledge both richer and more parsimonious than Putnam's: richer in the content it assigns to grasp of linguistic convention, but poorer in the role it assigns to factual knowledge. On Putnam's account, the speaker who can be said to know the meaning of "tiger" has to share with other speakers knowledge of at least some commonplace or stereotypical truths about (some or most) tigers. He or she has to know that a tiger is a stripey cat about the length of a horse but considerably lower-slung, lacking the mane and tufted tail characteristic of lions, or something of the sort. This is why Putnam at times shifts easily, as we noted earlier, between the formulas "knows what 'tiger' means" and "knows what a tiger is." By contrast, on Putnam's view, the conventional mechanisms on the back of which animal kind terms are introduced into the language are of the simplest and barest kind, amounting simply to the establishment, by associative convention, of a direct link between a name and a sample.

We have argued throughout this book, following Wittgenstein in his debate with the early Russell, against the confusion of knowledge of language with knowledge of the natural world. This and the preceding two chapters represent the culmination of that argument. But there is, perhaps, something much more simply and intuitively implausible about the idea that to know what "tiger" means one has to know (even in the sketchiest, most amateurish way) "what a tiger is." For doesn't one, as we suggested earlier, know what "capybara" means even though he or she has not the ghost of an idea, even of the most sketchy and stereotypical kind, what a capybara *is*? One knows what "capybara" means if one knows that "capybara" is the name of a kind of animal, or more ambitiously, the folk-name, as distinct from the Linnaean name, of a species of animal. And one may know *that* without knowing anything at all *about capybaras.* For knowing it is a matter, merely, of knowing into which sort of language-game, into which sort of classificatory practice, the name fits, and how it fits into that practice. A matter, in other words, of knowing something, not about the world and its contents, but about us, about one part of the web of human contrivance, rule and stipulation. Here, of course, we come back to our old question: if knowledge of meanings comes down in the end not to knowledge of the world, but only to familiarity with, and competence in operating, a web of practices constituted by stipulation, how can knowing a language confer upon the knower the power to describe what lies outside that web of stipulations?

But now the answer seems obvious. The relationship between language and the world is a relation not between the world and linguistic *expressions,* but between the world and linguistic practices. Meaning, by contrast, is a matter of relationships between linguistic expressions and the practices in question. Grasping those relationships is a matter of competence, not information, of practical, not theoretical knowledge; and must necessarily be so, given the force of the Tractarian Wittgenstein's argument that, as there can be no propositional knowledge without a grasp of the meanings of the expressions in terms of which it is framed, knowledge of meaning has to be independent of, and prior to, knowledge of the truth of propositions.

xii. Indexicality, rigidity and kinds

If Putnam's suggestion of an indexical relationship between kind names and samples is mistaken, does that mean that the reference of kind names is nonrigid? And, more generally, how much is left of Putnam's celebrated account of the meaning of kind names if the contrary account sketched here goes through? The answer to the second question is, surely, quite a lot. We agree with Putnam that the extension of a kind name is not fixed by a description associated with the name in the minds of speakers, but is determined by empirical investigation. Russell, and to a certain extent Frege,[26] were wrong: there is no useful sense to be made of the idea that knowledge of the meaning of a kind name can be equated with a description. Knowledge of what in Chapter 10 we called "observational warrants," *pace* Dummett and the verificationist tradition, falls outside the ambit of linguistic knowledge: is no part of what is involved in knowing the meanings of general names. At the same time we go further. Not only are the *extensions* of kinds fixed by the investigation of nature; so are the *identities* of kinds. We cannot even decide in advance of the investigation of nature, that is, what is going to constitute a nonmisleading *sample* for the baptismal introduction (if that were possible) of a kind name taken singly. If we wish to inaugurate a classification of animals by species, for instance, we cannot do so just by differentially baptising some samples of individuals which happen to look a bit different, with the Putnam-style proviso "and the like likewise." For individuals resembling differently baptised samples might turn out on further investigation not only to be capable of coupling to produce an F1 generation but also to be capable of producing fertile F1 offspring. Animals of the same species from opposite ends of a wide geographical range often do tend to look a bit different. The accumulation of such differences through random mutation, combined with the restrictions imposed by distance on the transmission of the genes affected throughout the population, is one of the mechanisms through which differentiation into species occurs. But how could one possibly tell by bare inspection, prior to suitable genetic investigation, whether the formation of a new species had occurred in a particular case?

That in turn gives us a clue to the issue of rigidity. Putnam's argument for rigidity of reference of kind names runs parallel to Kripke's argument for rigidity of reference of proper names. Just as, according to Kripke, a description may pick out a different individual in another possible world, so according to Putnam a description may pick out a different kind in a different possible world. What is to all appearances a tiger might in another possible world be, genetically speaking, a member of an unrelated species; what is to all appearances water might in another possible world be *XYZ* rather than H_2O, and so on. In using a kind name such as "water" we do not mean to refer to *whatever may happen, whether it is water or not, to satisfy some description or other*, but to *water*. Hence, the reference of the kind name must be carried, not by its relationship to a description, which might or might not serve to pick out water, but by its relationship to whatever it is that *makes a substance water*: and what makes a substance water is its chemical formula.

Putnam's argument is that the indexicality of kind names links their reference tightly to essence; that is, in Locke's stately phrase, to "the being of any thing, whereby it is what it is."[27] In a scientific age, essence in that sense is widely taken to come down to microstructure. So Putnam's claim is that "water" refers to whatever has the same molecular formula as *this* sample of water, that "tiger" refers to whatever has the same genetic constitution as *this* tiger, and so on, *even when "water" and "tiger" are used referringly by speakers so situated in time as to lack any knowledge of modern chemistry or genetics.* When restated in terms of other examples, however, this linkage seems less plausible. Clearly not all that looks like bread, say, is bread (or is what we mean by "bread"). Possible worlds are imaginable in which a plausible imitation of bread is made from artificially synthesised carbohydrates formed into a bread-like mass by processes very remote from the milling of grain and baking of dough traditionally employed. If the meaning of "bread" were identifiable with a description of the appearance, texture, taste and physiological properties of bread, then the synthetic product would be bread. Plainly, given what we ordinarily mean by bread, such a product would not count as bread. But the reason for that could not be that it possessed a different *microstructure* from bread. For it might possess the same microstructure as bread: be composed of the same chemical substances organised in the same ways. The synthetic product would fail to count as bread not by reason of its microstructure but by reason of its method of production. Real bread is made by taking wheat or rye flour, making it into a dough, with or without yeast, and baking it. Nothing not obtained in this way could count as ("real") bread. But this is to say that the notion of "real" as applied to kind names ("is this *real* water?," "a *real* tiger?," "*real* bread?") is relative not to the current or future state of physics, or physical chemistry, but to the rules that constitute the particular taxonomy from which the word is drawn. "Bread," like "wine," or *"civet de lièvre,"* or "clam chowder" is a term drawn from a taxonomy of *culinary products.* For such terms, what makes the difference between reality and semblance is (not satisfaction of a description, but) *mode of production.* A *civet de lièvre,* according to French culinary authorities, is not a *civet* if it be not made with the blood of the hare, it is a mere *ragout.* Similarly, clam chowder is not clam chowder unless it is made from clams. If on Twin Earth dishes have been evolved, by rare if misapplied culinary skill, which look and taste sufficiently like *civet de lièvre* and clam chowder to fool not only the bucolic gastronomes of Twin Earth (who never go into the kitchen) but even discriminating visitors from Earth fresh from the *Tour d'Argent* (who never go into the kitchen either), but that contain neither hare's blood nor clams, those dishes are not ("really") *civet de lièvre* or clam chowder, *even if there is some sense in which they can be said to "possess the same microstructure" as those dishes.*

Other examples could easily be adduced to make the same point. Of course kind names refer rigidly, in the sense that their reference is not determined relative to a description. How could it be? The reference of a name is determined by its sense (Frege was right about this) and the sense of a kind name is determined by its place relative to some taxonomic practice. That practice will establish some conventionally chosen criterion for sorting the world into kinds: colour kinds, animal species, culinary products, chemical compounds, elements, literary genres, tennis strokes, varieties of tort, grammatical categories, and so on. For many kinds it will prove possible to evolve descriptive criteria – observational warrants, as we called them (Chapter 10 §xiii) – on the basis of which it will (mostly) be safe to count individual items into or out of the extension of the kind in question. Thus, something's being a big stripey cat may afford, most of the time, sound observational warrant for the conclusion that something is a tiger. A certain savour and appearance may, most of the time, afford sound observational warrant for the conclusion that the dish before one is *civet de lièvre*. As Putnam and Kripke point out, sound observational warrant in such cases never amounts to *de dicto* necessity. But the implication of that is not, as we shall see in the next chapter, that the reference of kind names must rest ultimately on *de re* necessities. On the contrary, the phenomena which Putnam adduces in support of his claim that kind names refer rigidly across possible worlds, can perfectly well be explained *de dicto*, that is, in terms of linguistic stipulations, provided we recognise that the stipulations in question serve not to fix the extensions of kinds (nothing stipulative can do that) but simply to establish what *kind* of kind a given name is supposed to pick out. It is the fact that "tiger" is a term drawn from a taxonomy of species that brings it about that nothing can be a tiger unless it is descended from tigers and capable of producing tigers as the offspring of couplings with other tigers; the fact that "bread" is a term drawn from a taxonomy of culinary products that brings it about that nothing can be bread unless it is baked from dough made with flour. But these facts are facts about (our use of) words, not about things: facts *de dicto*, not *de re*.

xiii. Qualified internalism

Finally, internalism versus externalism. The thesis of internalism is that the meanings of kind terms, and more specifically their extensions, are determined by the mental states of speakers, determined, that is, internally to the mind. The thesis of externalism is that the extensions of kind terms are fixed by appeal to considerations external to the minds of speakers, and that therefore the meaning of a term in use, what it refers to, what it "picks out" is determined externally to the minds of speakers. Speakers in 1750 who used the word "water" were referring to H_2O, even though they had no means of knowing that that was what they were referring to. The view suggested here strikes between these positions. On the one hand, it is in accord with the externalist insofar as extension-fixing is concerned. Determining the extension of a kind-name, of a species term, for instance, is always a matter of empirical investigation, never something which is, or could be, accomplished by linguistic stipulation. On the other hand, it denies the externalist's conclusion that the *reference* of a term in use is determined by considerations external to the mind. For on the present view the reference of a kind name, like that of a proper name, is a nomothetic object. What a kind name refers to, what it "picks out" in use, is not a natural object, nothing that could be regarded as a *constituent of nature* in the sense that electrons, or piezoelectric crystals are constituents of nature, nor, for that matter, a collection of natural objects, but a nomothetic object, a *kind*. If one says, for instance, "The tiger is found today only in India and in parts of North China and Siberia" what one refers to by means of the expression "the tiger" is a *species*. If one says "Is there any *civet de lièvre*?" what one refers to by means of the name "*civet de lièvre*" is a *dish*: what the French refer to as a *plat*. But species and dishes are nomothetic objects, objects which exist only relative to certain projects for classifying nature into kinds: which is not to say, as we have seen, that nature is not hospitable to such projects: sometimes very hospitable indeed, sometimes less so. One is in a position to refer to species just in case one grasps the principles governing the project of partitioning individual animals into that sort of collection; and one can grasp that, as we have seen, without having the slightest knowledge of what species exist, or what observations might turn out to be relevant to assigning an individual animal to one or another of them. Animal and plant taxonomy is neither a department of linguistics nor for that matter of metaphysics, but a department of empirical biology. Being in a position to *refer* to species, by contrast, is a matter, merely of grasping *what a species is,* and grasping *that* is a matter, merely, of grasping some linguistic conventions. And thus a matter internal to the mind. The externalist, in other words, is right about extension-fixing but wrong about meaning and reference. Meaning and reference *are* "internal to the mind" – and have to be, if Wittgenstein's Slogan is on the right track. For if Wittgenstein's Slogan is on the right track both have to be determined prior to, and as a condition of the possibility of, any ascription of truth or falsity to any proposition whatsoever concerning the world external to the mind. The Description Theory is as false for kind names as it is for proper names. But that is not enough to unseat internalism about meanings, since, as we have shown, the latter need not entail the former. According to the Description Theory, what the competent speaker grasps is a set of templates for forming the extensions of kinds; a procrustean bed of concepts to which, prior to any empirical investigation of Nature, we require Nature to accommodate herself. The present account requires no such *a priori* power to determine the division of nature into kinds. Nor, on the present account, need the competent speaker be able to assign items to the kinds to which he refers. All he need know are the principles upon which our variously successful attempts to catalogue nature proceed, and manner in which given kind names enmesh with given projects of this kind. Whatever other knowledge of kinds he may possess, that is all his knowledge of *meaning* in this area comes to. Slender as it is, however, and inherently practical as it is, it is surely "internal" in the sense given to that term in recent debate.

12

Necessity and "Grammar"

Essence is expressed by grammar.
— Wittgenstein, Philosophical Investivations, §371

i. Extensionality and the analytic

The central claim of metaphysics is that there are *de re* necessary truths other than those of mathematics and logic. Metaphysically necessary truths, if such exist, were long held to be characterised by the following combination of features:

(1) they capture the nature of Reality,
(2) they are discoverable by rational reflection alone,
(3) they are immune to disconfirmation at the hands of experience.

More recent and fashionable accounts of *de re* necessity dispense with (2): we shall come to them in a moment.

The tradition of belief in the accessibility to the mind of *de re* necessary truth is a very long one. It is commmon to Plato and Aristotle, most mediaeval philosophy, the major seventeenth century Rationalists, Kant and such major successors of Kant as Hegel, along with such twentieth century figures as Husserl and Sartre.

Vienna Circle Positivism, the philosophy of Schlick, Carnap, Reichenbach and Ayer, saw itself as committed to the defence of scientific rationality against all such claims. The positivists — although this is a gross oversimplification — held, by and large, that necessary truths are *de dicto*; a *de dicto* necessary truth being one that, although immune to empirical disconfirmation, and discoverable by rational reflection alone, cannot be said to capture the nature of Reality, as *de re* truths have been supposed to do, since the truth of the former is a consequence merely of the way in which we have chosen to give meaning to the signs of our language.

Very often, and particularly in connection with their accounts of philosophical analysis, the Logical Positivists interpreted the notion of *de dicto*
necessity in terms of something close to, though by no means identical with,
Kant's notion of the analytic. The positivists understood by an analytic truth
one true in virtue of the meaning of its terms. This forges a tight link between the notion of analyticity – and with it the notion of necessity – and that
of synonymy. Kant's stock example of an analytic truth, "All bachelors are
unmarried men" is necessarily-true, according to many Positivists, because
"bachelor" and "unmarried man" are synonyms: are identical in meaning.
In the same way a projected analysis of some everyday claim to knowledge,
aimed at making clear its experiential content, succeeds, if it succeeds,
just in case analysans and analysandum can be shown to be equivalent in
meaning.

Quine's more radical empiricism, his "hyperempiricism" as we called it
(Chapter 2 §iv), finds in this interweaving of meaning and necessity the
very combination of mentalism and mysticism characteristic of metaphysics:
the very characteristics, in short, which Vienna Circle positivism, like every
other decent version of empiricism, saw it as its function to expel from the
life of the rational and disabused mind. Like many subsequent writers, and a
short list of predecessors including the Wittgenstein of the *Tractatus*, Quine
sees the mischief that positivism opposes as going deep indeed: as involving
language itself, or rather "natural" language, as contrasted with the formal
languages of logic and mathematics. A formal language is *truth-functional*
in character. A truth-functional language consists of an array of simple sentences whose aggregation into complex sentences is governed by operators
defined in such a way that the truth-value of any complex sentence formulable in the language can be exhibited as a function of the truth-values of
the simple sentences entering into its composition. The notion of a truth-
functional language opens the way to a purely "grammatical" conception
of necessary truth. A necessarily true statement in a truth-functional language will be one which, simply in virtue of its logical syntax, comes out
true on every assignment of truth-values to its component sentences. Thus
Quine:

Now the further idea suggests itself of defining logical truth abstractly, by appealing not specifically to the negation, conjunction, and quantification that figure in
our particular object language, but to whatever grammatical constructions one's object language may contain. A logical truth is, on this approach, a sentence whose
grammatical structure is such that all sentences with that structure are true.[1]

By contrast, natural languages, enshrining as they do, in fundamental
ways, the notion of what is *meant* or *intended* by a given utterance, are *intensional* in character. Part of what is meant by that is that the truth-values of
compound sentences are not in any formally specifiable way a function of
their sentential components. This feature is most evident, and has been most

discussed, in connection with what are called "intentional," or in Quine's terminology "opaque" contexts: propositions, such as "John believes that p," which involve the concepts of meaning, belief and intention.

If we take as our standard the clarity of a truth-functional language, together with the purely "grammatical" accounts of necessary truth to which such languages appear to open the way, then any account of necessary truth involving intensionality in any form will appear suspect: something requiring explanation and reduction if we are to arrive at the empiricist-cum-positivist goal of expelling mysticism and metaphysics from our thinking. The intellectually opaque interweaving of the notions of synonymy and necessity implicit in the concept of an analytic truth, whether in the Kantian or the Vienna Circle version, is a case in point; which is why Quine's argument against the coherence of the notion of analyticity focuses on the way in which the effort to define analyticity revolves endlessly within the hermeneutic circle established by those notions, defying all attempts to break out of the circle in the direction either of an empirical or a "grammatical" account.

Quine's pragmatism, working by way of the arguments discussed in Chapter 9, in effect develops this rather specific argument against the coherence of the notion of analyticity into a campaign to extend truth-functionality to natural languages wholesale, as it were, by way of the denial of any observational content to the "folk" or "ordinary" notions of *meaning* and *intension* in general. The effect of Quine's arguments is to partition propositions into two groups. On the one hand, we have the truths of logic. These are necessary, but purely grammatical in character. On the other hand, stand all sentences whose truth-value is a function, not of their grammatical structure, but of their assertoric content, *including so-called analytic statements.* All the latter are, if true, contingently true, in the sense that any of them stands open to the possibility of revision in the light of recalcitrant experience. The "intuitive" boundary between the analytic and the synthetic, dear alike to Kantians, Ordinary Language philosophers, and empiricists outside the Quinean, neo-Pragmatist fold, turns out to be an illusory one:

... it becomes folly to seek a boundary between synthetic statements, which hold contingently on experience, and analytic statements, which hold come what may. Any statement can be held true come what may, if we make drastic enough adjustments elsewhere in the system.[2]

ii. Two senses of "logical grammar"

An account similar to Quine's, of necessary truth in terms of the logical grammar of formal languages is also to be found in the *Tractatus*. In many ways the main doctrines of that work are congenial to the aims of Vienna Circle positivism; so much so, that for a good many years Wittgenstein was generally regarded as belonging to that school. The *Tractatus* maintains that all sentences, so far as they have anything to say about the world, can be represented as truth-functional concatenations of simple, or "atomic," sentences; that atomic sentences are, if true, contingently true, and that necessary truth is merely a reflection of the "logical grammar" of extensionality; that is, of the rules that determine the ways in which truth-functional operators relate the truth-values of compound sentences to the truth-values of their simple sentential constituents. To the author of the *Tractatus* (cf. 3.322–3.325) it is as axiomatic as it was to the Positivists that the meaning of a sentence in "everyday language" is not necessarily perspicuous as it stands. The same sign is used with different significations, with the result that "words that have different modes of signification are employed in propositions in what is superficially the same way." The way to "avoid such errors" is to "make use of a sign-language that excludes them . . . that is to say, a sign-language that is governed by *logical* grammar – by logical syntax." In this respect Russell and Frege come in for a qualified pat on the back: "The conceptual notation of Frege and Russell is such a language, though, it is true, it fails to exclude all mistakes."[3]

In 1918, the date of the Author's Preface to the *Tractatus,* Wittgenstein believed himself, at least in all essentials, to have solved the problems of philosophy: "I therefore believe myself to have found, on all essential points, the final solution of the problems."[4] At some point in the second half of the 1920s this belief deserted him. The collapse of the *Tractatus,* according to Wittgenstein's own account, was brought about by a remarkably simple thought: the thought that the sentences "*a* is red" and "*a* is green," where *a* is the same object or surface, cannot both be true. The trouble with this example is that it breaches the requirement of extensionality built into the *Tractatus* account of how language ("everyday" or "natural" language, not just the formal languages of mathematics or logic) works. There is a case so strong as to be in practice unshakeable for regarding "*a* is red" and "*a* is green" as atomic sentences. A nonatomic sentence, for the purposes of the *Tractatus,* is by definition one that can be exhibited as a truth-functional concatenation of simple sentences, and it is utterly dark how one could even begin to set about exhibiting this in the case of "*a* is red" and "*a* is green." But central to the idea of an extensional language is the requirement that the basic sentences be truth-functionally independent of one another. The truth or falsity of any atomic sentence, that is, must be a contingent matter, one that for each such sentence could go either way, and thus not one dependent in any way on the actual truth or falsity of any other atomic sentence. This is the requirement breached by "*a* is red" and "*a* is green." The falsity of each seems to be required, necessitated in some non-truth-functionally-explicable way, by the truth of the other. To put it bluntly,

a is red & *a* is green

appears to be necessarily false, and necessarily false, moreover, in a sense of "necessarily" for which no persuasive explanation in terms of an extensional logic is available.

Down with the wreckage of the *Tractatus*, then, went the account of necessary truth, in terms of the logical grammar of formal languages, which has survived to the present day in the work of Quine and in that of the vast majority of other writers on the philosophy of logic. Between 1929 and 1934, Wittgenstein's thought takes an entirely new turn, and the "later" philosophy of the *Philosophical Investigations* and its voluminous battery of precursor-texts begins to emerge. In this new work the suspicion of "everyday language" that the Wittgenstein of the *Tractatus* shared with the positivists[5] has disappeared, and with it the project of reductively reinterpreting natural languages in terms of formal ones, regarded to this day by a great many philosophers as central to the work of philosophy. "Everyday" or "ordinary" language is, famously, said to be "in order as it stands." Curiously, however, talk of "grammar" remains in evidence; only it is now *natural*, "everyday" language that is said to possess a "grammar" and sometimes even a "logical grammar," which it is the task of philosophy to "elucidate."

In the course of this – not easily explicable – transfer of application from formal to natural language, the notion of "logical grammar" appears, when one encounters it again in the later work, to have undergone some curious mutations. The point of explaining necessary truth in terms of the syntax of formal languages – the philosophical gain achieved by that move – is that it frees one from the need to interpret necessary truths as truths *about the world*. This is the point of Wittgenstein's remark at *Tractatus* 5.43: "But in fact, all the propositions of logic say the same thing, namely nothing." There is in such views, though, no suggestion that logical truths are not *propositions*: it is just that their truth is a consequence of their logical syntax, not of their assertoric content. In Wittgenstein's later work, by contrast, the claim appears to be that propositions "about grammar" (about the "logical grammar" of natural languages, that is) are *not propositions*, although they appear to be. They are not contingently true, but they are not necessarily true either. The categories of truth and falsity cannot be applied to them, because such "pseudo-propositions" (another phrase popular with the positivists but given a new twist by Wittgenstein) *assert* nothing. They merely reveal, or "show" something about how we have chosen to use words. They reveal merely the nature of the stipulations that have gone into setting up a particular language-game, or something of the sort. According to the later Wittgenstein, an immense amount of error and self-delusion in philosophy arises from mistaking pseudo-propositions that merely express or indicate "the grammar of our language" for genuine propositions with assertoric content: remarks, in other words, in connection with which the notions of truth and falsity find a foothold. A very sharp distinction between the propositions of science and commonsense and those of "philosophy" is floated in the later work on this basis. Science and commonsense deal in genuine propositions, to which answers may in principle be elicited by empirical investigation. "Philosophy," by contrast, deals in apparent conflicts between pseudo-propositions, conflicts which no investigation could resolve, because no genuine assertoric content is at stake. The way out of these conflicts is not to seek to resolve them either way, but to recognise that the apparently competing propositions are not propositions at all, since they have no assertoric content, but are merely confused reflections of "grammar." The way to set about this is to strive to gain a clear view of "the grammar" (or "the logic," or "the conceptual geography") of our language. Where we succeed in this we shall find that we have laid philosophy to rest; but not through having found "the final solution to the problems" which the author of the *Tractatus* believed himself to have found; rather, because the problems will have evaporated: will have turned out to have been to have been illusory in the first place. "A cloud of philosophy," as he puts it, will have been shown to "condense into a drop of grammar." However, the "grammar" of which philosophical propositions are the misleading expression is the grammar of ordinary, everyday language, not the very different, and purely syntactic, "grammar" of formal languages. That is why the project of seeking solutions to philosophical problems through the construction of formal language has disappeared in the later Wittgenstein. Formal languages turn out not to be the essential tool of a fully Realistic, fully naturalistic philosophy, but a misleading diversion which distracts us from the real business of constructing such a philosophy.

If Wittgenstein is right, and there are no *propositions* in philosophy, then *a fortiori* there are no necessarily-true propositions. Statements apparently expressing the sort of nonlogical, nonmathematical necessities on which philosophers have immemorially based their systems – synthetic *a priori* propositions, essences, Husserlian *wesen* – indeed fail of contingent truth or falsity. But they fail of them not by reaching beyond them to necessity, but by falling short of it. They fail of contingent truth because they fail of assertoric content. They assert nothing that could be either true or false, but merely reflect the "grammar" of our language.

iii. Logical grammar and conventionalism

This programme, the programme of what was termed Ordinary Language Philosophy, or Conceptual Analysis, was briefly popular in the 1950s and early 1960s, when it yielded a rash of article and book titles in which the words "logic" and "grammar" were prominent: the "grammar" of this, the "logic" of that. The vogue passed, and Ordinary Language Philosophy became something of a byword for superficiality and triviality, mainly because it proved very difficult, not to say impossible, to give a clear sense to the crucial terms "grammar" and "logic" as used of "ordinary" (i.e., nonformal) language. Or, rather, it proved difficult to interpret them in any way that did not seem to entail, if not crude Verificationism, a still cruder Conventionalism. A rather simple argument suggests that the latter consequence must be ineradicable. If sentences that allegedly "express the logical grammar of our language" *say nothing about the world*, what is it that they "express"? Presumably the content of some set of conventions governing the use of words. But how can linguistic convention be the key to the resolution of any substantial problem, in philosophy or elsewhere? Take the apparent necessity of "Nothing can be red and green all over," which led Wittgenstein to abandon the extensionalism of the *Tractatus*. How could the appearance of necessity here be an artifact of linguistic convention? Only, it seems, if by changing our linguistic conventions we could render the claim false. But how could that come about? All that changing our linguistic conventions could achieve, it would seem, is that red and green might come to be called by different names; and how could *that* affect the truth of the statement that the two colours exclude one another necessarily, or "by their nature"? For the fact that red and green exclude one another is a fact about *those colours*, not a fact about what they *are called*.

Despite the apparent force of this argument, it is not impossible that there is more to the late Wittgensteinian conception of the "logical grammar" of a natural language than this rather swift way with it allows. Certainly, if the notion is to do the work that Wittgenstein seems to have thought it could do, there will be certain senses of the term "convention" in terms of which it cannot be explicated. In a penetrating essay, Cora Diamond discusses the grounds for regarding certain types of claim recurrent in hagiography less as pretenders to literal truth than as conventions of genre. In noting the airiness, the detachment from ordinary considerations of corroboration and truth licensed by such conventions, she contrasts the latter with "conventions of the sort Wittgenstein occasionally speaks of in connection with necessity," observing drily, "There has been a certain amount of confusion of these very different sorts of convention in some philosophical writings influenced by Wittgenstein."[6]

But what sort of conventions could Wittgenstein have had in mind as constitutive of the "logical grammar" of a natural language? One could attack this question in two ways. The first would be by way of Wittgenstein exegesis, but that is a route which, at least for the present occasion, we have (largely, at any rate) forsworn. The second way of approaching the question would be to ask in general terms, without particular reference to Wittgenstein, what other sorts of linguistic convention there *are*, if not "pure" conventions, like the conventions that saints "always" try to conceal stigmata, or that red is called (in English) "red"? Not only is this second way forward open to us; we have already travelled a considerable distance along it. Let us look again, in more detail, at the argument which convicts Wittgenstein of conventionalism. Its form is that of an *ad hominem*. Wittgenstein wishes to claim that the seeming propositions of philosophy say nothing about the world. This is, indeed, a major point of contact between the early and the late Wittgenstein. For the Wittgenstein of the *Tractatus* "the correct method in philosophy would be the following: to say nothing except what can be said, i.e. propositions of natural science – i.e. something that has nothing to do with philosophy – and then, whenever someone else wanted to say something metaphysical, to demonstrate to him that he had failed to give a meaning to some of the signs in his propositions." This translates in the later work into the claim that good philosophy produces no *theories* of its own, but only *elucidations* which work by showing any attempt at such a theory to be based on a misunderstanding of "grammar," or "the way our language works." But, runs the argument we are considering, if philosophical propositions have no bearing on the world because they are about "grammar," it follows that propositions about "grammar" can have no bearing on the world; and that can only be the case if they concern some class of purely *syntactic* conventions: of conventions, that is, governing merely the relationships of sign to sign, and not those of signs to the world.

There are at least two things wrong with this argument. The first is the assumption that there is a clear distinction to be drawn between conventions that relate signs to one another and conventions that relate signs to the world. That assumption is central to the one-level account of meaning characteristic of Referential Realism, against which we have been arguing throughout this book. On a one-level account, "semantic" relationships introduce "content" into language by linking signs, one by one, directly to extralinguistic, real-world correlates. Once linked in this way to its "meaning" (its referent) a sign carries that meaning with it into all subsequent contexts of use, including philosophical ones. It follows that if "grammar" is not infected in this way with content, that can only be because "grammar" concerns only the relationships of signs to one another, not to the world. The dominance of Referential Realism in Anglo-American philosophy makes such a distinction appear essentially inviolable to the Anglophone mind. By contrast, quite a number of quite celebrated, mainly French, philosophers and linguists of the past century outside the Anglo-American sphere of intellectual influence have held it to be unworkable. F. de Saussure, Maurice Merleau-Ponty, and Jacques Derrida are cases in point. When such writers fall into the hands of readers innocent of the perception that the distinction in question is under threat in their work, much confusion ensues. To the Anglophone reader they seem, like the later Wittgenstein so interpreted, to be men almost ludicrously blind to the absurdities of the conventionalism seemingly entailed by their views. Equally, from the opposite, Francophone, standpoint, the English-speaking critic seems a man incapable of reading what is on the page before him without cramming it into some gratuitous straitjacket of Anglophone philosophical assumptions. The dismaying bulk of the resulting polemics either way constitutes a sufficient answer to those who think that the clarity sought by good philosophy is of no value ("is just a matter of words" is the usual way of putting it); if only by demonstrating the alarming consequences, in terms of wasted effort, obfuscation and misplaced contempt, of embracing its opposite.

As will by now be evident, we stand with the trio of French writers just mentioned in denying the adequacy of the distinction, though we come at the matter from a standpoint quite different from any of theirs. If one rephrases the distinction as a dilemma, the two-level account of the relationship between language and the world passes neatly between its horns. On a two-level model, the conventions establishing what expressions in a natural language mean are neither conventions stipulating relationships between sign and sign, nor conventions stipulating relationships between signs and elements, "constituents," of the world. They are conventions establishing practices. The practices thus established stand between language and the world. On the side of language they define places to which linguistic expressions can be assigned, "posts," as Wittgenstein puts it, at which "we station the word." Its station, its post, relative to a practice, establishes the "logical grammar" of a word. It determines, among other things, in which positions in sentential contexts the word can sensibly occur, as speakers' grasp of the assertoric content of a sentence is achieved, on a two-level view, by manipulating, relative to one another, the conventions of the different practices invoked by the component expressions of the sentence. A word supplied with "meaning" in this way does not carry that "meaning" with it into all subsequent contexts of use. Whether some seemingly profound, or even seemingly necessarily-true, remark in which it is employed possesses assertoric force, or on the contrary is senseless or vacuous, will depend on how practices, or parts of practices, can be made to mesh with one another. And that, in turn, will depend, not on some set of "purely linguistic" stipulations of the chimerical kind imagined by philosophers, but on the nature of our linguistic practices considered from the standpoint of their opposite pole: the pole of their engagement, not with words, but with nature, with how things stand in the world presented to us by experience. Explaining philosophical puzzles – apparent necessities, the persistent appeal of questions which seem to lead nowhere in direct proportion to the amount of ingenuity expended in pursuing them – by appeal to "linguistic convention" does not necessarily lead to philosophical "conventionalism," in short, because the actual "conventions" of language, the conventions that establish actual linguistic practices, with their bipolar systems of engagement, on the one hand, with language and, on the other, with the world, are not the sort of "conventions" the philosophical conventionalist has in mind: not the sort that *can* yield his conclusions. Only "pure conventions" could do that, and the linguistic conventions which establish meaning are not, in the required sense, "pure conventions."

We said a few paragraphs ago that the argument which apparently convicts Wittgenstein of conventionalism has two things wrong with it. The first is the one we have just discussed. The second is that the argument fails to distingish between a remark which *mentions* the world and one which *concerns* the world, *asserts something* concerning it. In describing the manner in which a linguistic practice meshes with the world, it will no doubt be necessary to mention any number of aspects or features of the world: colours, physical objects, measuring devices, denumerable sets, or whatever else the practice happens to engage with. The description of the practice, though, *says* or *asserts*, in itself, nothing about the world. It *mentions* the world, but *concerns*, *says* something about, the constitutive conventions of the practice in question. It is thus possible (following at this point well-known parallel claims of Wittgenstein's) for philosophy to be *descriptive*, for there to be philosophical *descriptions* (of linguistic practices), without its following from that that there are, or could be, *theories* in philosophy in anything like the sense that there are theories in natural science: that is, theoretical explanations of natural phenomena.

We shall not waste time here considering whether a reconstruction of the later Wittgenstein's use of the term "logical grammar" along these lines receives support from the texts. Instead we shall enquire whether such a conception of "logical grammar" can take us any distance towards an understanding of the nature of necessary truth, insofar as the latter defies, or appears to defy, explanation in terms of the logical grammar of extensional languages. We shall consider first analyticity, and then incompatibilities of colour. Finally we shall turn to *de re* necessities of essence of the sort associated with the work by Putnam and Kripke discussed in Chapter 11. There are, of course, many other kinds of putative necessary truth that present difficulties to the extensionalist. But success is these, rather central, cases may at least indicate routes likely to lead to success elsewhere.

iv. Analyticity

Quine's account of analyticity, as is well known, dissolves the supposed difference between analytic and synthetic statements by showing the difficulty of arriving at any principled way of distinguishing analyticity from mere coextensionality. Any two predicates which are *coextensional*, in the sense of happening to be true, and false, of exactly the same objects, will be interchangeable *salva veritate*. Such is the case with "creature with a heart" and "creature with kidneys." The same is true of "bachelor" and "unmarried man." As it appears to us "intuitively," it is a merely contingent matter, a trick of evolution, that "creature with a heart" and "creature with kidneys," share the same extension, but necessary that "bachelor" and "unmarried man" do so. An explanation of the difference is supposedly offered by the thought that "bachelor" and "unmarried man" are *equivalent in meaning*, are *synonyms.* But how far does this thought take us? What does it *mean* to say that two expressions are synonymous? If we could define *meaning* we could no doubt define *sameness of meaning;* but the notion of meaning for natural languages is notoriously cloudy. A natural recourse would be to define synonymous expressions as expressions *necessarily* interchangeable *salva veritate;* but this embroils the notion of synonymy with the very necessity we thought we could introduce it to explain. The notions of analyticity, synonymy and necessity appear, in other words, to compose an hermeneutic circle.

A possible way out of the circle, Quine suggests, might be to retire from natural to formal languages, and to define analyticity for a given formal language L in terms of the Carnapian notion of a *semantical rule.* Having thus got rid of the fuzzily intentional notions of meaning and synonymy, we might then be in a position to content ourselves with saying that an analytical statement such as "All bachelors are unmarried men," as distinct from the statement of the coextensionality of two predicates, is one that is – indeed – not merely contingently true, but true by virtue of a semantical rule. But what is a semantical rule? Unless we have some prior account of analyticity, says Quine, a semantical rule is "distinguishable apparently only by the fact of appearing on a page under the heading "Semantical Rules"; and this heading is itself then meaningless."[7]

In short, Quine concludes, there is no empirical sense to be made of a distinction between coextensionality and synonymy. At first sight this seems paradoxical. As Strawson and Grice argued very early on,[8] if it is meaningless, cognitively vacuous, that is, to talk of synonymy, it must equally be cognitively vacuous to talk about the meaning of a sentence. Quine's reply to this would be that the notion of the meaning of an individual sentence is indeed empty of cognitive content; as empty of cognitive content as that of synonymy. It poses no threat to Quine's outlook at this point to protest that such a conclusion is counterintuitive. For what is the force of the appeal to "linguistic intuition" here, if it can be grounded neither in "rules" nor in any conception of necessity not itself dependent on the very conception of "intuitive" evidence it was introduced to explain?

The debate at this point divides, it is worth noticing, along familiar lines. On one side are ranged those who follow Frege in holding that although meanings, or "senses" cannot be identified with mental states, since they must be accessible in principle to all competent speakers, yet, nevertheless, grasp of sense is a mental capacity, so that judgments about meaning can be taken as issuing from the exercise of "linguistic intuition" by competent speakers reflecting upon their own mental capacities. On the other side stand those who, like Quine, take meaning to be a relationship between sentences and their truth-conditions: one ascertainable, if at all, by appeal to sensory evidence concerning the empirical circumstances of native assent to and dissent from assertions framed in terms of simple sentences. We have before us, in short, yet another version of the dispute between "externalists" and "internalists" about meaning. That dispute, in all its forms, is internal to Referential Realism. For the purposes of the past century of discussion, the original form of the doctrine is Frege's. In Frege's version, Referential Realism maintains that there are two root senses of "meaning." In one (*Bedeutung*) meaning is a relationship between a linguistic expression and an aspect or element of reality. In the other (*Sinn*), meaning is something grasped by all competent speakers, which serves in some way to connect the linguistic expression with the aspect or element of reality it picks out. Internalists argue that a theory of meaning lacking the second of these elements is in some way explanatorily incomplete; externalists argue the contrary. Thus in the present version of the dispute, Quine's position is in effect that talk of "meaning," "synonymy, "analyticity," and so on, adds nothing, contributes no additional cognitive content, to what can be empirically ascertained by tabulating the circumstances of native assent and dissent.

On this ground, Quine wins. His victory can even, as many writers have noted, be given a Wittgensteinian twist.[9] On this view Quine's argument has two wings, both reminiscent of Wittgenstein. The first is that neither "lintuition" nor Frege-style "senses," at least to the extent that the latter have to be construed as "mental states," can be relevant to the determination of meaning, because the latter are irredeemably "private," in the discredited Cartesian sense, whereas language and meaning are essentially public and intersubjective. The second is that we do not in practice determine meaning by consulting our own mental states, but by consulting usage. So reconstructed, Quine's argument works, very much in the manner of Wittgenstein, by demonstrating reference to "mental states" to be, here as elsewhere, explanatorily redundant: a fifth wheel.

The account we have developed here, however, since it rejects Referential Realism, rejects both sides of the debate over analyticity. It rejects the idea that what is grasped in grasping meaning is the content of a mental state: a "sense" or a description. But equally it rejects the idea of meaning as a special sort of linkage between a linguistic expression and some aspect or element of Reality. For an expression to possess a meaning is for it to be assigned to some place or "post" relative to the conduct of a practice: a practice itself occupied in some way with the manipulation of real things. With such a view in place nothing seems simpler than to define synonymy of expressions, and with it analyticity. Two expressions are synonyms when they are assigned to exactly the same place, stationed at the same "post," in exactly the same practice or practices. One such practice is marriage. The existence of the institution of marriage divides people into two classes, the married and the unmarried. Because we admit only two sexes (another practice, and one which exhibits the combination of general utility with fuzzy edges characteristic of most of the practices human beings devise) we need convenient terms under which to refer to the four classes thus generated. "Wives," "husbands," "spinsters," "bachelors," are the terms provided by English. But in English one can equally well say "married woman," "unmarried woman," "married man," "unmarried man." The items in this terminology slot into places in the practice identical with those into which the items in the other terminology are slotted. We are thus dealing with a set of synonyms.

Notice, now, that no reference to *meanings*, or to any other class of *intensional entity* occurs in this explanation. The intensional has been routed as thoroughly as Quine could wish, in favour of an account that is, in that respect, as naturalised as his. Second, the issue of *how we come to know that* "bachelor" and "unmarried man" are synonyms simply vanishes. There is no need, in other words, to explain cognitive access to intensional relationships by postulating a special mental faculty of "linguistic intuition," on pain of having otherwise to grant that knowledge of meanings rests, in company with other forms of empirical knowledge, on "sensory evidence." On the present account it is wholly unmysterious how we know that "unmarried man" and "bachelor" are synonyms. We know it because people just do know how to operate the conventional practices which constitute the glue of the particular society to which they belong. The moment they do not, the practices lapse into oblivion, and if enough of the characteristic practices of a particular society lapse into oblivion, at least if they do really lapse into utter forgetfulness, as distinct from simply undergoing change and development, and lapse all at once, that society lapses into oblivion also. Knowing that two terms are synonyms, that is to say, is merely a further case of the kind of commonplace knowledge-how elsewhere exemplified in the ability to play chess, or trace a client through the telephone directory, or undertake property conveyancing.

Now for the Big Question: Does "All bachelors are unmarried men" express a necessary or a contingent truth? The answer suggested by the account of synonymy which we have just offered is: neither, because it expresses nothing which could sensibly be said to be either true or false in the first place. What guarantees the substitutability *salva veritate* of "bachelor" and "unmarried man" is not a piece of knowledge-that, but a piece of knowledge-how. What identifies them to the competent speaker as synonyms is not access to some piece of *information*, either about "meanings" or about the environmental circumstances surrounding their occurrence in discourse, but rather her mastery of a web of practices which, among other things, define a certain sort of slot to which both words are related as alternative fillers. In effect, Wittgenstein's Slogan is vindicated: here as elsewhere, all questions of meaning must be settled prior to the raising of questions concerning truth; and that goes for questions of equivalence of meaning also.

There is, evidently, nothing necessary about the substitutability of the expressions "bachelor" and "unmarried man" as alternative fillers of the same slot relative to the web of legal, verbal, and customary practices associated with the institution of marriage. One might express the relationship in the form of a rule *licensing* the substitution in English of "bachelor" for "unmarried man." As a license asserts nothing, there is, given this form of words, no temptation to suppose that the relationship affords any foothold to the notions of truth and falsity, let alone those of necessary truth or falsehood. The sentence "All bachelors are unmarried men" expresses, now, nothing more than the content of the rule in question: nothing more than that the substitution of the one expression for the other is licensed in English. It is the form of the sentence alone, not what it expresses, that creates the impression that truth and falsity are at stake. But the impression it creates is quite a strong one, especially when viewed from the standpoint of a general philosophical commitment to the system of assumptions associated with Referential Realism. And, because the magisterial universality of the sentence appears to rule out contingent truth, we feel tempted to treat it as expressing a necessary one; not, perhaps, about the persons designated by the terms "bachelor" and "unmarried man," but about some class of intensional entities associated with those expressions: "meanings" or "senses." Quine's impulse is to grasp the nettle, at whatever cost to intuition, and treat the sentence as an assertion of contingent coextensionality of the same type, logically speaking, as "all creatures with hearts are creatures with kidneys." If we are right there is no need for us to rush in this fashion into the arms of paradox. "All bachelors are unmarried men" embodies neither a contingently true nor a necessarily-true assertion, because it embodies no assertion whatsoever. It merely expresses, in a logically misleading fashion, a feature of the logical grammar of English, namely, the status of "bachelor" and "unmarried man" as alternative occupants of the same meaning-bestowing "post," or place, or slot in the web of legal, social, and linguistic practices surrounding the institution of marriage.

v. Incompatibilities of colour

How are we to explain the necessary falsehood of "*a* is red and *a* is green"? A suggestion of Wittgenstein's in the *Philosophical Remarks* is that such a sentence is analogous to, say, "*a* is four inches long and *a* is five inches long." How does this help? Wittgenstein's thought seems to be that "*a* is four inches long" and "*a* is five inches long" are not *independent propositions*, in the kind of way that, for instance "a is a mole" and "a is black" are. What it means to say "*a* is a mole" can be explained independently of what it means to say "*a* is black," and vice versa. That is not true of "a is four inches long" and "a is five inches long." No explanation can be given of either which is not an explanation of *what it is to measure*. That practice determines what conditions are relevant to the truth and falsity of such statements as "*a* is four inches long" and "*a* is five inches long," along with indefinitely many other statements of the same kind. But it does not determine any conditions as relevant to the truth of "*a* is four inches long and *a* is five inches long." The practice of measuring, in other words, fails to make clear what would be relevant to the attachment of a truth-value to that form of words: and what else could make that clear? The form of words "*a* is four inches long and *a* is five inches long" is thus not the vehicle of a necessary falsehood because it is not the vehicle of an assertion. Hence, the fact that it cannot be true does not show that it is necessarily false. It merely shows something about the "logical grammar" of such sentences; namely, something about the way in which such statements as "*a* is four inches long," "*a* is five inches long," take on their meanings from the post at which they are stationed relative to the practice of measuring, given the rationale of that practice.

Can we extend that solution by analogy to the case of "*a* is red and *a* is green"? "Red" and "green" are names of colours. The first thing to note is that *colours,* if one means by that the entities picked out by colour names, are not natural but rather nomothetic entities (Chapter 5 §i). What is given in experience are *colour-presentations:* hues presented in specific degrees of saturation and tonality. The extension of a colour name is some subset of colour presentations. In order for the colour names of a language to be understood in the same way by different speakers, each speaker must have access to some practice, call it Practice C, the operation of which results in the sorting of colour presentations, including colour-presentations encountered for the first time, into the extensions of colour-names in a uniform way from speaker to speaker. Individual colour names will then take on meaning, not from their relationship to anything already on offer, independently of Practice C, "out there in the world" ("out there," remember, there is only the linguistically unstructured drift of colour presentations), but from the place to which we assign them relative to the operation of Practice C.

Practice C, we have argued, following earlier work of our own and a still earlier suggestion of Quine's, sorts colour presentations into the extensions of colour names by exploiting the fact that it is possible to arrange colour presentations into smoothly graded series in which each member lies "between" the two most adjacent members of the series. The nature of the "betweenness" relation to which we wish the learner to pay attention in forming such series cannot, of course, be verbally explicated. It can be explained to a learner only by showing him examples of how such series are constructed, and inviting him to continue them. Here as elsewhere in language, in other words, the level of propositional discourse, the kind of discourse to which the notions of truth, falsity and assertoric content are relevant, floats on, and is sustained by, an underlying level of pure practice, of "just acting": "it is our acting," as Wittgenstein says in *On Certainty* §204, "which lies at the bottom of the language-game."

The sorting-game proceeds by reference to an arbitrarily selected number of sets $<p_R>$, $<p_G>$, . . . , of closely similar presentations, each associated with a colour name "Red," "Green," . . . , and so on. The object of the game is to assign every colour presentation to the extension of some colour-name. The principle on which the sorting proceeds is that a given presentation p_n

is to be added to the set whose founding members it most resembles, with the proviso that for presentations falling between named sets, sets bearing compound colour-names ("blue-green," "yellow-green," for example) may be created.

Suppose, now, that the operation of Practice C has resulted in the assignment of a given colour presentation to the extension of the colour name "red." *A fortiori* that presentation will not have been assigned to the extension of the colour name "green." The same will be true of every other colour presentation assigned, as a result of the operation of Practice C, to the extension of "red," and vice versa for presentations assigned to the extension of "green." It follows that nothing homogeneously coloured – no colour presentation, in our terminology – which the operation of Practice C makes it correct to call "red" can also correctly be called "green," and vice versa. It follows that there is nothing of which the characterisation "a is red and a is green" could be true. But the emptiness of the extension of "a is red and a is green" arises in precisely the same way as that of the extension of "a is four inches long and a is five inches long." The emptiness of the extension of the latter characterisation is a consequence of the fact that we have assigned the expressions "four inches" and "five inches" to mark different gradations on measuring rods *employing one and the same modulus*. The emptiness of the extension of the former arises as a consequence of the fact that we have used the words "red" and "green" to label two of the small collections of colour presentations which are used as *alternative* foci in the process of partitioning the total set of colour presentations into named subsets according to the procedures of Practice C. "Nothing can be red and green all over" is thus not a necessary truth about "colours," in the sense of the entities colour names name. It is not a necessary true assertion about anything "in the world," because it is not an assertion about anything in "the world." Rather, it is a misleadingly expressed remark about the "logical grammar" of the words "red" and "green": about the relationship in which they stand to the operation of one of the practices by means of which we divide up the contents of the world into named kinds.

Notice, now, that it is not being claimed that "Nothing can be red and green all over" is "true by convention." What is being claimed is that neither truth nor falsity can be ascribed to "Nothing can be red and green all over," because "red and green all over" fails to designate a predicate: misfires as an attempt at formulating a predicate-expression. That it fails, or misfires in that way, is a consequence of *our* having chosen to partition colour presentations between the extensions of colour names by appeal to the operation of a certain practice, given a certain initial choice of sets of colour presentations to function as the named foci in terms of which the practice is to operate. And the choice of that practice and those foci for its operation was indeed a *choice*, a decision that could have been taken otherwise. To that extent we are indeed dealing with a *conventional* device for dividing up the array of colour presentations between the extensions of colour names. But once we have made the initial choice of practice and foci, which, and how many, discriminable colour presentations sort into the extensions of which colour names is a function of the perceived relative similarities holding between colour presentations; in other words, a function of how things stand in the world. There is a substantial overlap between the extensions of "green" and "yellow": a body of colour-presentations for which considerations of perceived relative similarity leave it a toss-up whether we assign them to the extension of "green" or "yellow." Their existence gives a kind of sense to the expression "green and yellow all over," although it would be better English to say "greenish-yellow (or yellowish-green) all over." That no such body of presentations exists for green and red is a function, not of any decision, or convention, of ours, but of the way we (or at least the normally sighted: matters are different for the red-green colour blind, who will often claim to find expressions like "reddish-green" intelligible) *see colours.*

Doesn't that mean that "Nothing can be red and green all over" is, after all, a truth about the nature of the world: specifically a truth about colours? No, because colours, in the sense of the referents of "red" and "green," are not to be found in "the world" in the sense intended: the prelinguistic or extralinguistic world, that is. Colours are nomothetic entities, creatures of linguistic convention. What is "in the world" extralinguistically is the array of colour presentations. And there is nothing either necessary or contingent about *them.* We perceive them as we perceive them. They exhibit the relative similarities we perceive them as exhibiting. They are what they are. Necessity and contingency, like named colours, are creatures of language. A *statement* may be necessarily or contingently true. But a colour-presentation cannot intelligibly be said to be either "necessarily" or "contingently" what it is. As Wittgenstein puts it at one point in the *Philosophical Remarks,* "Immediate experience cannot contain any contradiction . . . it is beyond all speaking and contradicting."[10]

vi. Intrinsic relations

"But you admit," someone might object, "that there are relations of relative similarity between colour presentations. These relations, surely, are internal, or intrinsic, in the sense that they could not help but hold between the presentations which they characterise, given the qualitative nature of the presentations in question. What is to stop us, in the spirit of the early Russell, introducing names, a, b, c, . . . , to stand for individual colour presentations, together with a relational predicate Rxyz informally explained as "x is more similar to y than to z," or something of the sort. Now, by some appropriate replacement of the variables in this formula with names for colour presentations, we obtain "Rabc." Why isn't this, or some English sentence of the same logical form, a necessary truth?"

It isn't, because "Rxyz" is not a genuine predicate expression. The logical form of the expression creates the impression that, on the one hand, there stand a, b, and c, and, on the other, a relation of some sort, in which they stand to one another. But this apparent distinction corresponds to no difference. The "relationship" in which a, b, and c stand to one another, as the Russellian would like to say, *in virtue of* their qualitative characters, *is nothing over and above*, those qualitative characters themselves. We are not dealing with an "internal," or "intrinsic," or necessary relation here because we are not dealing with a relation. That colour presentations, given how we perceive colour, can be arranged in qualitative series by different speakers acting independently of one another, is what lies at the root of colour language, colour talk. Nothing is clarified – indeed, the nature of the situation is obscured – by our choosing to say that what such performances depend upon is not our sharing the ability to perceive colour presentations, but our sharing the ability to perceive internal relations holding between colour presentations. Such a shift in the way things are put offers a characteristic example of philosophical obfuscation. It preserves, or appears to preserve, the credit of a theory, while not merely failing to offer any gain in understanding, but actually alienating us from an adequate grasp of what is really ultimate, prelinguistic, in our relationship to our own capacities and to the world they reveal to us. It offers a palmary example of the sort of thing Wittgenstein has in mind when he speaks of the perennial endeavour of philosophy to attempt to "use language to get between language and the world": to cover up as swiftly as possible the naked presence of the prelinguistic, the arbitrary quiddity of the world, with a concealing layer of verbal obfuscation. The anguish that fuels such attempts is born of the fear that the human mind lacks the power ever *finally* to grasp and dominate the world into which we find ourselves, as Heidegger would say, "thrown" (*geworfen*). We hope to allay such fears by showing that there is a point at which meaningful utterance and necessity cohabit, and cohabit there, if not elsewhere, because it is the point at which language and reality mysteriously coalesce and become one. But this introduces a topic that can only be properly dealt with in the Epilogue.

vii. Essences

Thirty years ago, belief in essences (in somewhat different senses of "essence") was confined to Aristotelians and those phenomenologists still faithful to Husserl's ideas. Their recent popularity among Analytic philosophers is due entirely to the work of Saul Kripke and (independently) Hilary Putnam on the logic of direct reference. The Kripke-Putnam argument for essences is, at least in its most general form, easy to state. Names, whether proper names or kind names, are *rigid designators* (Chapter 6 §i). Such expressions as "Richard Nixon," or "water," that is, refer to the same individual, the same substance, in all possible worlds. Our capacity to refer by means of names cannot, therefore, be tied to any description of the entity a name picks out, because for any description it is possible to envisage a possible world in which different individuals satisfy that description. Hence names refer directly to their bearers, whether individuals or kinds. There is a baptismally established association between name and bearer, and that is the end of the matter. Suppose, now we discover that water is H_2O, or that Nixon is the child of certain parents, or originated from a certain zygote. Could anything, in any possible world, be water that was not H_2O? Could any individual, in any possible world, not derived from that zygote, be Nixon? Intuitively, it would seem not. But to say that is to say that "Water is H_2O" and the proposition that Nixon developed from a certain zygote are propositions true in all possible worlds which contain water or Nixon. And a proposition true in all possible worlds is what we mean by (or at any rate one of the central things philosophers have meant by) a necessary truth.

Moreover, "Water is H_2O" and "Nixon developed from zygote N" are clearly not true *de dicto.* They cannot plausibly be regarded as propositions "made true by definition," or anything like that. We are dealing here, then, with *metaphysical,* or *de re* necessary truths. "Water is H_2O" and "Nixon developed from zygote N" are remarks about *essence.* They say what a thing has to be, *de re* necessarily, in order to be water, and how a thing, *de re* necessarily, has to have originated in order to be Nixon.

At the same time that water is H_2O, that Nixon developed from zygote N, are facts about the world that have to be discovered. Such truths are not discoverable by rational reflection alone: empirical enquiry is needed. But that just shows, as Kripke argues,[11] that philosophers have been wrong to suppose that epistemological notions like *a priori* and *a posteriori* align themselves neatly with modal ones such as "necessary" and "contingent." That scientific enquiry was needed to establish that water is H_2O simply shows that some (modally) necessary truths are (epistemically) *a posteriori.*

The account of meaning implicit in these views is a *strongly externalist* one. On the direct reference view of meaning, that is, extension-fixing passes altogether out of human hands. We can make clear what we *take ourselves to be referring to* in referring to gold by indicating a certain sample. But what we are *actually referring* to by means of the expression "gold" can only be determined by the successful prosecution of scientific enquiry; and is then determined retrospectively; as in the "Twin Earth" example, in which it transpires that speakers in 1750, in speaking of water, were "really" referring to H_2O, even though they had no idea that that was what they were doing.

Those who cling to the belief that science deals in contingent truths have on the whole tended to attack the new essentialism by attacking the externalism of the theory of meaning that provides its main support. Both essentialism and strong externalism require the identity conditions of individuals and kinds to be determined by nature. The conditions that ultimately justify an affirmative answer to the questions, "Is this Individual NN?," "Is this a sample of kind K?," must, that is, be (1) discoverable through the investigation of nature, (2) unambiguously applicable in all circumstances, that is to say, across all possible worlds. There must never come a point, in other words, at which nature places the terminological ball back in our court, leaving it to us to decide what considerations are to be decisive in determining whether something is to count as Nixon, or water.

One awkward case for strong externalism, as Hugh Mellor[12] pointed out early in the discussion, is presented by the existence of isotopes. Isotopes of the same element differ in microstructure. According to Putnam's "Twin Earth" argument, difference of microstructure is what compels us to conclude that XYZ is not, appearances to the contrary, water. Are we then to conclude from the discovery of the two common isotopes of chlorine, that chlorine has been found not to be a natural kind after all, but a mixture? As Zemach[13] has argued, taking that line will very likely lead to the conclusion that we have no natural kind terms. In any case, it isn't the line we take.

In the case of individuals, origins provide the best candidate for naturally constituted identity conditions. On this view, what makes an individual thing or organism NN is its originating in a certain collection of material precursors, or as Graeme Forbes engagingly puts it, "propagules."[14] So just as, what makes an individual Nixon is his having originated in a given zygote, what makes an axehead *this* axehead is its having originated in a given mass of forged steel. What makes a ship the *Galveston* is its consisting of just these steel plates, and so on; the supposed intuition operating here being that just as any human being who developed from a different zygote couldn't be *Nixon*, so an axehead made from a different lump of steel couldn't be *this* axehead, a ship made from different plates *this* ship, and so on. Unfortunately, an opposing intuition of equal plausibility inclines one to think that slight variations in the constitution of propagules might be compatible with the continued assertion of identity. How slight? The attempt to formulate a version of origin-essentialism accommodating this second intuition has been pursued in the journals with considerable ingenuity but uncertain success. Teresa Robertson and other recent writers[15] have argued persuasively, indeed, that no such concession is compatible with the aim of constructing a version of origin-essentialism that would be both interesting and internally coherent.

All these discussions proceed on the assumption that the available options in the theory of meaning are restricted to two: on the one hand, Direct Reference, on the other, "Fregeanism," which in this context means some version of the theory that the reference of a term is determined in use by appeal to reference to an associated description. On this view, any blow struck against essentialism is a blow in favour of the Description Theory, and vice versa. The weakness of the Description Theory, its inability to "give an account of reference stability through theory and belief change," as Kim

Sterelny[16] puts it, thus constitutes something of an albatross around the neck of the anti-essentialist.

Can what appears increasingly an unappetising choice between essentialism and the Description Theory somehow be evaded? Let us begin by restating the case for the former. A substance, water for instance, reveals itself to us as a clump of qualities. And there is, presumably, something, some underlying nature, which accounts, causally speaking, for the stuff in question exhibiting just those qualities. But something other than water might exhibit just those properties. So what are we referring to when we speak of "water"? Just *any* kind of stuff, provided it exhibits a certain clump of properties? Surely not! – we mean to refer to *this* stuff, the stuff a sample of which is – let's say – in this glass. But in that case, what we must take ourselves to be referring to when we speak of water is the stuff which possesses the underlying nature whose presence accounts for the manifestation of the clump of properties in question by the sample in this glass. The universality of the laws of nature now ensures that wherever that underlying nature recurs, in any possible world, water will recur. There can never, in short, be a case in which it will be uncertain whether a possible world contains water or not, and certainly never a case in which such an uncertainty might have to be resolved by taking a *decision* about the application of the word "water." And that is just as well, because down that road lie nominalism and radical relativism, and with them the threat of finding ourselves immured in the Prison-House of Language. A language, the conditions of application of whose terms is fixed by human decision, is a language which has lost its grip on Reality. Speaking such a language we move among conceptual phantoms of our own devising.

Against this background, consider the account of kind names advanced in Chapter 11. Consistently with the argument of this book we argued that what makes a name not merely a kind name, but a name for a *kind* of kind – a substance, a species, a type of artifact, a type of outlook, a type of offence – is a matter, on the one hand, of the relationship of the name to some practice, or system of practices, and, on the other, of the ways in which that practice or system of practices engages with the world. In the case of names for substances, we suggested (Chapter 11 §x) that the concept of a substance arises in the context of sorting volumes of material according to whether they consist of a single kind of thing or a mixture of different kinds of thing. We offered bronze as an example. Bronze is a mixture, because it is smelted of two distinguishable kinds of metal, copper and tin. Copper and tin are substances because we have no way of showing samples of either to be composed of further distinguishable kinds of material. We suggested that to know the meaning of the terms "bronze," "tin" and "copper," it is enough to know (1) the rule according to which this kind of catalogue is constructed, namely, that one enquires whether there is any way of constituting a given material out of materials of other kinds; (2) what logically different types of "post" or "place," at which to "station" words, the practice gives rise to: in this case, names for mixtures and names for substances; and (3) which sort of post a given name has been stationed at. All a competent speaker needs to know, to know the "meaning" of the three terms, in other words, is that "bronze" is the name of a mixture, specifically an alloy, while "copper" and "tin" are names of substances "in their own right."

Note, now, that on this view it is not a condition of semantic competence that the speaker attach *any description whatsoever* to any of the terms "bronze," "copper" and "tin." So no description *attaches analytically* to any of the three terms. What tin, bronze, and copper *are like*, what *properties* these substances exhibit, is entirely a matter for metallurgical investigation to determine, and thus *an entirely contingent matter*. And, in general, once we have evolved the concept of a substance along the lines just set out, the question of *what clumps of properties characterise substances* is just as much a matter of empirical investigation as the question of what underlying natures account causally for the occurrence of properties in just these clumps. Hence, although the concept *substance* is defined relative to a practice, a system of stipulative requirements, that is, the issue of what substances there are in the world and what characteristics they exhibit is not determined by stipulation, but by empirical investigation.

Such an account of the grammar of the term "substance," and of names for substances, cuts between the Direct Reference and the Description theories. On the new account the reference of such terms is determined neither by a term-description linkage nor by a term-sample linkage, but by the assignment of the term to a certain role in a practice. Someone who is familiar with this practice, and knows that "water" is the name of a substance, knows the meaning of "water" even if he has never encountered liquid water and has no idea what its properties might be. He just knows that it is the name of one of those kinds of stuff which we have no means of demonstrating to be composed of other kinds of stuff. Not only may he have no idea that water is H_2O, he may be unable either to state or recognise *any* property of water. Let's suppose he is a member of a desert tribe that has adapted, like some antelopes, to obtaining their entire water-supply from solid food, and like all reptiles and birds, to excreting urea in solid form. In his desert there is no standing water because it never rains there: the plants he uses for food get their water via long taproots from a deep water table. So he has never seen liquid water, and has absolutely no idea what properties the stuff is supposed to have: he just knows that "water" is the name of a substance. No doubt if he travels, his views on the matter will rapidly expand. Encountering rivers and faucets he will learn that water is wet, encountering chemistry he will learn that it is H_2O. But just as in learning that water is wet he will be learning a contingent fact about water, so in learning that water is H_2O he will be learning a contingent fact about it. The reason for that is that he has learned the meaning of "water" in a way that dissociates *the meaning of "water"* from the issue of what water *is*. To know the meaning of "water" he just needs to know something about the linguistic practices of his tribe (we"ll suppose his language community extends into more pluvial areas, and that's how the word "water" reached him in the first place). To know what water *is like*, and what it *is*, he needs on the one hand to have acquired a wider knowledge of the world, and on the other to have done some science.

How does this divorce of meaning from identity-conditions address the issue of what Sterelny calls "reference stability through theory and belief change"? In the ordinary way of things we expect property-clumps and underlying properties to turn out on investigation to correlate one-to-one. The present state of scientific theory shows how remarkably this expectation has been rewarded by enquiry. As long as nature fits in with this assumption, keeping the reference of "water" stable through theory and belief change presents few problems. We have a practice, of sorting materials into mixtures and substances, according to whether or not they can be shown to consist of different types of material. We introduce two sorts of name in connection with this practice, names for mixtures and names for substances. To know the meaning of "water" is, we said, to know that it is the name of a substance. Which substance? Whatever substance it has become customary, among the substances recognised by those operators of the practice best equipped to operate it – smiths, merchants, herbalists, artisans of various kinds, later on alchemists, and still later scientists – to bestow that name on. Until serious science comes along, the answer to the question "What is water?" is "Water is a stuff which has a certain set of properties that we take to correspond to a certain underlying nature." If our theories and beliefs about the underlying nature change over time, they remain theories and beliefs *about water* because they are theories and beliefs about *the stuff having a certain collection of properties*. If our theories and beliefs about the properties of water change over time, they remain theories and beliefs *about water* because (leaving aside the fact that such investigations are hardly likely to call into question all the properties of a substance at once) they remain theories and beliefs about what has the underlying nature of water (i.e., about H_2O).

But now, suppose we find ourselves on Twin Earth? Now we are in trouble. And we are in trouble, notice, at just the point at which Putnam, the originator of the example, thinks we are *not* in trouble. The whole point of Twin Earth is that it is a place in which the ordinary one-to-one linkage between collections of properties and underlying natures falls apart. On Twin Earth we have a substance with all the *properties* of water, but a different underlying nature, *XYZ*. Putnam takes it to be intuitively evident that *XYZ* isn't water. But is that so evident? Couldn't one equally say that what we have on Twin Earth presents such an awkward case for our ordinary notion of *substance* that the decision could go either way? The game of sorting materials into mixtures and substances works out so smoothly in the ordinary way of things because in the ordinary way a given collection of properties corresponds to a single underlying nature. Now we have a collection of properties that corresponds to two underlying natures. Luckily all the XYZ in the universe is (let's say) on Twin Earth. But the spaceship that took us to Twin Earth in the first place can easily be employed to bring some XYZ back to Earth. And suppose, by some regrettable inadvertence on the part of a technician, some of it gets into the water-supply. Now when we draw a glass of water from the tap, what does it contain? A substance, a mixture of substances, what? *Pace* Putnam, what one is tempted to say is that *there isn't any answer to this question,* or at least, none decided in advance, none that could be elicited by appeal to "the meaning of" any term in our language. It isn't true, in other words, as Wittgenstein says,[17] that the meaning of a word is like a set of tramlines leading to infinity – that once we have established "the meaning" of a word it carries that meaning with it into all subsequent contexts of use.

What tempts us to think that that is so is the idea that meaning is, or could be, established by direct reference. For then, since the eternity and stability of the world would guarantee that whatever element or aspect of the world had been thus baptised would always, as it were, be *on hand,* just so the meaning of the word would always be on hand. If, by contrast, words are given a meaning by their use in connection with practices, then they continue to enjoy a clear reference just as far as, or to the extent that, the questions that a given practice teaches us to ask of nature continue to encounter a nature willing to yield a clear and unambiguous answer to those questions. When an awkward case arises, when the attempt to apply the practice no longer yields a clear and unambiguous result, the only thing capable of restoring clarity and univocity is a decision. In the present case, as in any case, including that of Mellor's isotopes, in which the properties of a substance fail to correspond to a single underlying nature, we simply have to decide whether we prefer to have substance-identity turn on properties or on underlying nature. No doubt we shall take this decision differently in different cases, and no doubt there will be, in each case, good reason for deciding to do whatever we decide to do in that case. In the Twin Earth case, so far as Putnam establishes its ground-rules, it looks as though the chemistry of Twin Earth has to be supposed to be so different from that of Earth that the parity of properties with such Earthly compounds as water, including parity of properties revealed on interaction with the Earthly physiologies of the visiting astronauts, as to require major revisions, if not a complete upheaval, in chemistry. In that case, what ended up counting as water would depend upon what had become of chemistry when the dust had settled. But certainly there seems no reason why we should not end up, exactly as in Mellor's case of isotopes, where the issues in chemistry are less momentous, deciding that one and the same substance could, on occasion, correspond to more than one underlying nature. Such decisions are never arbitrary, but equally they are never wholly constrained by the nature of things.

Kind-names refer, in short, not *rigidly*, as Kripke and Putnam suggest, but, as one might put it, *semi-rigidly*. On the present account, when we speak of a kind – "water," for instance – we refer to a thing, identifiable in other possible worlds, because the reference of such a term is not tied to a description of a clump of properties. Given the grammar of substance terms we can identify a substance by its underlying nature even when its properties are not what one would normally expect (when one is examining materials under extreme conditions of temperature or pressure, for instance). But in some possible worlds it will be indeterminate whether a given kind exists in that world or not. The reason for this is that the identity-conditions of a kind are set, not by the underlying nature of a sample, but by the logical grammar of the type of kind-name in question: the mode of engagement of names of that type in the practice or system of practices through which they acquire meaning, and the mode of engagement with the world of the practice or practices in question. As Wittgenstein observes, "Grammar tells us what kind of object anything is. (Theology as grammar.)"[18] The ideal to which Kripke and Putnam subscribe is that of a language in which no doubt about whether a possible world contains or does not contain a named kind can arise – or at any rate no doubts settleable only by a stipulative modification of our linguistic practices – because the issue of whether or not something is a sample of a kind has been taken out of our hands by nature. "We all," says Merleau-Ponty, "secretly venerate the ideal of a language which would deliver us from language in delivering us to things." But no such deliverance is possible. Kinds are nomothetic entities. Essence expresses itself as (logical) grammar. Grammar tells us what kind of object anything is. Grammar settles the question of what is and what is not relevant to membership in the extensions of the kinds it defines.

Of course grammar, conceived as we have conceived it here frees us from the ancient conception of meaning enshrined in the Description Theory, according to which a concept is a list of features culled from experience. The mind does not passively receive its concepts from nature: it makes them – out of practices, and the way in which practices, through their modes of relationship to the world, order it for purposes of discourse. So of course the possession of a concept confers a certain degree of rigidity on the acts of reference we are able to accomplish by means of it. But the inherent power of phenomena to outstrip the provisions so far enshrined in our practices means that the degree of rigidity of reference our concepts allow us is never absolute. "Nixon" refers to an individual, and not to a collection of properties, for the trivial reason that the criteria of identity on the basis of which the Name-Tracking Network operates to a considerable extent transcend questions of who a person *might appear to be*. But suppose, in another possible world, the Nixon-zygote has produced an adult with the character, opinions and personal mannerisms of Hubert Humphrey? Is *this* Nixon? *Pace* the Origin Essentialist it just isn't clear what one would say in such a case.

It would depend on the circumstances; and those might be structured in such a way as to make nonsense of the supposed "intuition" of a *de re* necessary link between zygote-identity and personal identity. They might, for example, include the probability that the newly-instituted Physics of Unitary Consciousnesses (PUC) rapidly developing at MIT and Stanford looked like injecting some hard physics into that old mystical talk about reincarnation, with difficult consequences for the law of property. The trouble with natural-kind and origin essentialism is not, or not primarily, that they hand over to science provinces long governed by humanists, but that they foreclose the progress of science. Of course, the essentialist confronted by the above example could retort that the discoveries of specialists in PUC merely insert a new level of "underlying nature" below the biological one. But if the claim of essentialism is merely that the criteria of identity of a name, whether of a kind or an individual, tend to fall back on appeals to "underlying nature" in the most fundamental sense of that phrase currently available, the reply must surely be that that claim, while rather obviously correct, is also rather obviously a claim about "the logical grammar" of such names.

Artifact kinds offer a still less promising prospect for essentialism. It is simply not clear either that the identity of an individual artifact is tied to its origin in a particular mass of material, any more than that the identity of an artifactual kind is defined by reference to samples. What would "This is a chair, and anything which is the same$_C$ is a chair also" come to in practice? Sameness$_C$ here can't possibly mean either "sameness in appearance" or "sameness in method of construction" (there are indefinitely many kinds of chair, and indefinitely many ways of constructing them).[19] It can only mean "same in function." But what function defines a chair? And how are chairs "functionally" distinct from stools, or thrones, or seats (in buses or on tractors) or saddles, all things after all, made to be sat on? There are criteria according to which we draw these distinctions, and even criteria formulable as principles of fairly wide application. But such principles as govern our usage here are, as elsewhere, of only "fairly" wide application. At the edges, where their applicability peters out, they are riddled with *ad hoc* exceptions; and even in more central areas can make no pretence to be governed by anything beyond contingencies of linguistic practice and usage, pursuing now one perceived analogy, now another.

Again, suppose Harrison's daughter, who happens to be a furniture designer and maker, makes him a small maple table, of a given design, for his birthday. She makes it of maple planks delivered the week before. In a different possible world the maple planks delivered come from a different shipment. Does this make any difference to the identity of the table? Intuitively, none. Similarly a ship might have been made of different plates, by a different shipyard, to a given design for a given fleet, or made by the same shipyard, of the same plates, to the same design, for a different fleet (after the shipping line which originally ordered her went bankrupt), . . . , and so on. Where numbers of practices yielding different criteria of identity cohabit as promiscuously as they do here, identity becomes a very moveable feast indeed. Nothing is *de re* necessary here, and nothing is "analytic," either. Our ways of speaking are underpinned neither analytically, by associated descriptions or sets of sufficient and necessary conditions, nor metaphysically, by the nature of things. But that does not mean that they are underpinned by nothing: that we are adrift among conceptual phantoms of our own devising. They are underpinned by the logical grammar of the practices in which they find their uses. And those practices in turn are underpinned by the humdrum, utterly contingent nature of the everyday world in which it has seemed useful to us to devise them.

It might seem that this just misses the essentialist's point. For suppose the essentialist replies, laying his hand on the table in Possible World 1, the table made from one set of maple boards, and gesturing in thought towards the table which in World 2 has been made, *ex hypothesi*, from different boards, "THAT table isn't "the same" as this one, because it isn't THIS VERY TABLE." Doesn't that, intuitively, clinch the matter in his favour? No, because the phrase "this very X" is as grammar-relative as the term "essence," and "intuition" is either itself grammar-guided or impotent to decide the issue. Call the table in World 1 Table A. Suppose, now, in World 2, Harrison's daughter makes the Birthday Table out of a different set of maple boards from the set she used in World 1. Call that table Table B. In World 2, again, another craftsman makes a table to an identical design from the planks used in World 1 to make Table A. Call this Table C. Which of Tables B and C is *the very same table as* Table A? Both, perhaps – or neither. That is to say, we can argue it any way we please. Table B is *the very same table as* Table A, since it is the table made by Harrison's daughter, for his birthday, at the same point in a given day, and so on. By contrast, Table C is *the very same table as* Table A because it is made from the same planks as Table A. But then, what would "intuition" say if it turned out that the craftsman who made Table C, though he used the same planks as Harrison's daughter used to make Table A, cut different members from different planks? Do the very members of Table C have to consist, molecule for molecule, of the same timber as the members of Table A, for A and C to be *the very same table?* Again suppose Harrison's daughter in World 3, though she makes the table from the same planks, and cuts the members of the table from the same portions of those planks, as in World 1, decides at the last minute to cut a cunning little chamfer unobtrusively around the plinth on which the table top rests? Is the table with that addition *the same table as* Table A? The issue is, surely, not how we are to answer such questions but whether they are answerable otherwise than by our *deciding* what answer we are prepared to deem appropriate: what we are going to *mean by* "the same" in a given context? Whether they have an answer, that is, determined by the nature of things, rather than by the manner in which, and the purposes for which, we have chosen to give a sense to "the same" in one or another specific context.

The desperation-move for the essentialist at this point is to go for absolute identity: Leibnizian – or quasi-Leibnizian – identity. On that view, no table can be THIS VERY table if it differs in (at least) origin, design or physical constitution from THIS table in any respect whatsoever. No cunning little chamfers, no differences of material constitution even at the molecular level, no question of some of the members having been finished by Harrison's daughter's husband, and so on, and so on. The decision to use the phrase "this very X" for pieces of furniture in this way will indeed compel us to recognise certain features of tables, say, as necessities of essence. But doesn't that in itself constitute a sufficient reason for not deciding to use the phrase in that way (with that "grammar") in this context? For why should we adopt a self-denying ordinance denying sense to Harrison's daughter's observation that the Birthday Table would have been even prettier if she had thought to put a little chamfer on it just there, or that it would have been finished sooner if her husband had been available to make some of the members, or that an almost invisible blemish could have been avoided if she had used a different board from the back of the stack. The reply, "Ah, but then it would have been a different table, dear," foolishly consoling as it is, seems an unpromising candidate for metaphysical profundity.

PART IV

PARADOXES OF INTERPRETATION

The criteria which we accept for "fitting," "being able to," "understanding," are much more complicated than might appear at first sight. That is, the game with these words, their employment in the linguistic intercourse that is carried on by their means, is more involved – the role of these words in our language other – than we are tempted to think.

(This role is what we need to understand in order to resolve philospohical paradoxes. And hence definitions usually fail to resolve them; and so *a fortiori* does the assertion that a word is "indefinable.")

Wittgenstein, *Philosophical Investigation*, §182.

13

Indeterminacy of Translation[1]

i. Introduction

Philosophy exists to trouble the peace of minds secure in their assumptions. Its shadow has always lain athwart the paths of commonsense thinking. To be fertile in paradox is part of its nature. At the same time the mind can never for long rest content with conclusions which smack of it. Paradox is not a resting-place, rather a spur to further thought. And for that reason, philosophical paradox is a serious matter, to which, when it is the product of a considerable mind, real intellectual importance can attach. It is something to be resolved, transcended if possible; it is not, by contrast, at least at its best and most serious, something to be laughed off.

In this Part, we have to deal with two such flights of paradox. The first, which will occupy us in this chapter, is Quine's celebrated argument for the indeterminacy of translation. The second is an argument of Kripke's which seems to show that our ordinary criteria for ascribing belief on the basis of sincere assent to propositions lead in certain cases to irresoluble contradiction. We shall argue that both are plausible only when their supporting arguments are advanced against the background of a certain, widely pervasive intellectual outlook, namely, the one we have been attacking throughout this book. Dispensing with Referential Realism, along the lines argued in Parts I–III, allows one, as we shall see, to deal rather swiftly with them. And the very swiftness of the countermeasures we shall find ourselves deploying, given the considerable mass of the discussion to which each has given rise, may suggest that we regard them as mere errors, the product of bad reasoning, or inattention, or something of the sort. That would be a mistake. The business of philosophy is with argument: with what follows, or fails to follow, from what. To demonstrate that certain conclusions no longer follow from certain premises, when those premises are deprived of the support of a range of hitherto unchallenged supplementary assumptions, even if the demonstration withstands criticism, in no way impugns the achievement of having, in the first place, shown those conclusions to follow from those premises so supplemented. As we hope will have been evident from the general tenor of the proceedings so far, this book, to whatever extent its arguments are successful, stands as much on the shoulders of those philosophers with whom we disagree as on those of its presiding spirits.

With that *caveat* in mind, let us begin with Quine's principle of the Indeterminacy of Translation. In Chapter 1 §iii, we introduced the term "hyperempiricism" to mark the fact that Quine's philosophy in one way represents a continuation, rather than a rejection, of Vienna Circle positivism. Like Carnap and the rest, he holds that a concept is explicable, if at all, only in terms of the empirical grounds we have for treating statements employing it as true. Unlike his positivist predecessors, he is prepared to apply this criterion to the founding notions of the positivist account of philosophical analysis: meaning, synonymy, analyticity. This move, we argued, commits Quine to Referential Realism. To establish that an utterance is meaningful, that is, is for Quine to show that it can be correlated with some set of experiential conditions taken by speakers to warrant assent or dissent. Meaning, cognitive content, consists, for Quine in other words, not in the relation of the members of a collection of utterances to some body of conventional procedures, some "practice," some collection of "rules," but in their relation, singly or collectively, to some collection of "stimuli." Supplementary arguments show, as we have seen, that the relationship must be a collective one. If to know the meaning of a sentence is to know which collections of stimuli count in favour of, or against, its truth, we face the immediate difficulty, when it comes to isolating these collections for a specific sentence, posed by the fact that the truth of one sentence of a theory can be saved by sacrificing the truth of other sentences. The implication of that is the "holistic" one that theories "face the bar of experience" as wholes, not as collections of specific sentences. Is it not a further implication, now, that, when we set out to establish a "translation manual" for an alien language, we shall find ourselves faced with empirically undecidable alternatives when it comes to selecting English equivalents for Native sentences? And may not such choices, depending how we take them, lead to the bifurcation of the translation manual into alternative manuals? Quine's answer is that they may; that in fact it is perfectly conceivable that two translation manuals, assigning to certain sentences meanings sufficiently at odds to yield contradictory truth-values, might be compatible with the totality of the evidence for meaning in a given language. This is the so-called thesis of the Indeterminacy of Translation. Quine illustrates it, in Chapter 2 of *Word and Object*, and elsewhere, with the much-discussed example of an anthropological linguist attempting to translate the Native one-word occasion-sentence "Gavagai!" The sensory stimuli prompting Native assent to and dissent from "Gavagai!" are such that "Gavagai!" correlates well with English "Rabbit!"

Unfortunately they are such as to offer equal warrant for adopting other possible English translations: "Rabbithood!", "A mass of rabbit-stuff!", "It rabbiteth here!", "Undetached rabbit-parts!", and so on. Which is the linguist to choose? The Indeterminacy Thesis says that this choice is empirically underdetermined. Worse, the indeterminacy does not result merely from a contingent lack of evidence, which might be remedied. The lack is an in-principle one. It is not that these is no evidence to be had concerning the actual fact of the matter. It is that, in the case of such choices, *there is no fact of the matter.*

Quine's thesis has been widely regarded as in some deep sense paradoxical, without its ever becoming quite clear what that sense is. Quine and Quineans maintain that Quine's conclusions are merely *surprising* consequences which, however surprising they are, we must accept because they are inescapable. We shall argue for the former view, taking the term "paradox" in the strict sense; the sense in which it is commonly used, say, in connection with Russell's Paradox, and other paradoxes of self-reference. According to that usage, in order to demonstrate that a view is paradoxical one must show that it entails pairs of propositions one of which must be true, but neither of which can be true.

To begin with, we shall argue, there is a level on which Quine's views could be seen as, in an odd way, *methodologically* paradoxical. Quine starts out, after all, with a version of the familiar empiricist project of placing meaning on a sound empirical footing: a project as old as Locke, and foundational to Vienna Circle positivism. Central to that project is the thought that unless a sign can be provided with empirical content, or as the positivists sometimes put it, with "cognitive content," it is an empty vocable, a mere *flatus vocis.* Quine, however, by pursuing the project with greater pertinacity and logical rigour than any earlier writer in the tradition, ends up with the conclusion that there is no empirical basis for the greater part of what we regard as meaning. It is thus not easy to say whether, in Quine, one is dealing with an exceptionally rigorous form of empiricism or with a *reductio ad absurdum*, if not of empiricism *tout court*, at least of its pretensions to be capable of delivering a coherent theory of meaning. On a more detailed level we shall argue that the Indeterminacy Thesis as Quine develops it does in two respects yield paradox in the strict sense of that term. One concerns his account of *observation sentences*, the other his assumption that, on his view, it remains an option for the anthropologist investigating Native, or for one English speaker attempting to understand another, to "*regress*," as Quine puts it, "*into a background language.*" Finally we shall argue that these, formally paradoxical, consequences of Indeterminacy are neither tolerable (though "surprising") nor unavoidable. They can be avoided, along with the Indeterminacy Thesis itself, by abandoning, along the lines we have opened up in the foregoing chapters, Quine's commitment to Referential Realism.

ii. Empiricism at odds with itself

Quine gives various, and varying, statements of the Indeterminacy Thesis throughout the corpus of his work;[2] the examples that follow are from *Word and Object*.[3]

The thesis then is this: manuals for translating one language into another can be set up in divergent ways, all compatible with the totality of speech dispositions, yet incompatible with one another. In countless places they will diverge in giving, as their respective translations of a sentence of the one language, sentences of the other language which stand to each other in no plausible sort of equivalence however loose. The firmer the direct links of a sentence with non-verbal stimulation, of course, the less drastically its translations can diverge from one another from manual to manual. It is in this last form, as a principle of indeterminacy of translation, that I shall try to make the point plausible.... [4]

Sense can be made of the point by recasting it as follows: the infinite totality of sentences of any given speaker's language can be so permuted or mapped onto itself, that (a) the totality of the speaker's dispositions to verbal behavior remains invariant, and yet (b) the mapping is no mere correlation of sentences with *equivalent* sentences, in any plausible sense of equivalence, however loose.[5]

This thesis is connected to another of his claims given in a well-known passage from "Ontological Relativity,"[6] where he writes,

... the inscrutability of reference is not the inscrutability of a fact: there is no fact of the matter.[7]

This might seem an odd and disturbing conclusion if it merely concerned our ability to understand "Natives": speakers of some very remote and unrelated language. But the difficulties Quine takes himself to have uncovered do not disappear when we leave the native's land. Even "closer to home" we are plagued by precisely the same difficulties.

But our troubles do not end here; for the fact is that I see no hope of making reasonable sense of sameness of meaning even for English.[8]

There is nothing, Quine argues, that forces us fellow language speakers to mean the same thing when we make the sound "S"; indeed there is nothing that forces (or, indeed, even allows) *me* to attach an unambiguous interpretation to *my own* remarks from occasion of utterance to occasion of utterance. And this is so because there is, on Quine's account, nothing in the world capable of grounding interpretation that could narrow interpretation to a unique outcome.

Quine arrives at this conclusion as the result of an attempt to find an empirical basis for judgments of meaning; it thus stands as a contradiction of his initial aim. This is the methodological paradox of which we spoke earlier. It justifies us, perhaps, in labelling the conclusion Quine's Paradox (**QP**) for short.

Quine's Paradox (**QP**): There is no fact of the matter.

iii. Quine's linguist and his Native subjects

Quine's empiricism about meaning, his Referential Realism in our terms, commits him to the view that judgments concerning the meaning of a statement S can be grounded only in knowledge of the experiential conditions prompting Native assent to and dissent from S. Not surprisingly, therefore, Quine's anthropological linguist, or translator, differs from actual members of the profession in paying remarkably little attention to the Native-speakers' relationships to, and conduct towards, *one another*. Meaning must emerge, according to Quine's founding assumptions, solely from whatever takes place between the triad consisting of the translator, some individual Native informant considered as source of canonical assents and dissents, and the surrounding environment. Because the Quinean translator does, in effect, obey the following two self-denying ordinances, it is to all intents and purposes as if he were required to obey them by the methodology of Quinean translation.

(1) The translator must treat every native utterance in total isolation from the rest of the native utterances;

(2) the translator must discount, or at any rate ignore as irrelevant, any parallels in nonlinguistic behaviour, and in interactions between linguistic and nonlinguistic behaviour between the natives and the members of the linguistic community to which the anthropologist belongs.

An actual anthropological linguist confronting an alien community will embark on a programme of *translation* only if he can take it that he is *prima facie* confronted with a *language*. But under restrictions (1)–(2) it is not clear, to say the least, what could motivate such an assumption. A real anthropological translator would, presumably, avail himself of the total context in which the natives engage in their verbal activity. As one of Wittgenstein's remarks correctly suggests, a would-be translator *must* employ the total context of utterance.

The common behaviour of mankind is the system of reference by means of which we interpret an unknown language.[9]

This, however, violates restriction (1). Quine's, linguist/translator, therefore, *cannot* adopt this approach.

An obvious question, now, would be: why should Quine, for all that appears to the contrary in his development of the "Gavagai" example, place his imaginary linguist under restrictions (1)–(2)? The answer has, surely, much to do with Quine's notion of an observation sentence, and the place which that notion plays in the structure of his thought.

iv. Observation sentences

To salvage whatever empirical warrant can be assigned to talk of meaning is, for Quine, conformably to his attachment to empiricism, and with it to Referential Realism, to find some way of anchoring meaning in the world via some empirical connection between linguistic entities (for Quine, sentences) and things outside language (empirically accessible features of reality). This anchor must connect language to a world which entirely excludes human convention and practice. For the latter cannot be, in the required sense, external to language unless it is entirely mind-independent.

Taken by itself, language can only provide us with linguistic entities, along with the relationships that hold between them. Within the boundaries of language we can define and redefine terms by drawing and redrawing the relationships between them. But satisfying as this might be for passing an idle Saturday afternoon, at the end of the day, no matter how many connections we have redrawn, we will be no closer to understanding what is "out there" than we were when we began. This seemingly unbounded ability to draw and redraw the connections between linguistic items as the needs of theory dictate is a large part of Quine's holism, and it works to keep us imprisoned in language envisaged as an hermetically sealed system.

If we are to reach out to a world independent of language, then, we need linkages capable of connecting language directly to the world that makes up the surroundings in which our utterances occur. For Quine, all that language taken by itself can give us is *more language*. If language is to take us any way towards the world, it must be because the meaning of at least some linguistic entities derives from what surrounds their utterance in the world, *not* from what surrounds them in the human practices in which they occur.

Because Quine locates meaning at the level of sentences,[10] he dubs the required entities *observation sentences*. Observation sentences are sentences whose meaning derives maximally from its links to extralinguistic reality (to "stimulation") and minimally from its links to other sentences in the language from which it is drawn. That is precisely what allows such sentences to serve as a constraint upon translation, whether between languages or between sentences in the same language.

The firmer the direct links of a sentence with non-verbal stimulation, of course, the less that sentence can diverge from its correlate under any such mapping.[11]

The firmer the direct links of a sentence with non-verbal stimulation, of course, the less drastically its translations can diverge from one another from manual to manual.[12]

This is why, to return to the question we raised at the end of the last section, the Quinean linguist, to all appearances, operates under restrictions (1)–(2). He is uninterested in the relationships of Native sentences *to other Native sentences,* or to Native conduct, because these matters are, to him, matters *internal to language* (to Native), and what he is interested in are the relations obtaining between language, taken as a whole, and its *experiential,* not its *social,* surround.

v. Are "observation sentences" *sentences?*

We are still facing, however, the question we raised at the end of §iii. Why should a linguist operating under restrictions (1)–(2) take himself to be confronted by beings endowed with language? *Ex hypothesi,* the hypothesis being Quine's, the "language" spoken by Native speakers (or at least that part of it accessible to an anthropological linguist guided by Quinean principles) consists of the following elements:

(i) a repertoire of utterances, each cued to some experientially accessible environmental condition;
(ii) a pair of utterances construable as expressing, respectively, assent and dissent.

In Chapter 10, we discussed the case of what we there called feature-placing or mereological language. Such a "language," we argued, is at best a quasi-language because it cannot be used to make assertions; at most, it can *register* features of the "passing show," but such registrations cannot be construed as constituting *assertions,* any more than a bored committee member's idly lining paper clips up along the side of her notebook can be construed as *measuring* the length of the notebook in paper clips. *Registration,* we argued, falls short of *assertion* because the notions of affirmation and denial find no footing in connection with it. To speak of an utterance as asserting something it must be possible to attach propositional content to its denial: to say what is affirmed in denying it. And that something – we called it an affirmation-denial content connector – must link the two propositional contents to one another: must make clear, for instance that what is affirmed in denying that x is three inches long is that x *is some other length,* and not that x is a hat or some snow. But to establish which affirmation-denial content connector governs a given Native sentence S_n a linguist would have to examine S_n's relationship to other Native sentences and to Native conduct and social convention: that is to say, he would have to acquire precisely those interests that are proscribed to the Quinean anthropologist by restrictions (1)–(2).

It follows that the anthropological linguist operating under restrictions (1)–(2) has access to no empirical grounds for concluding that Native is a language, rather than a system of registrations, hence that he has access to no grounds for supposing the notions of affirmation, denial, truth or falsehood to find a foothold in connection with it, and hence no motivation for the project of "translating" Native "sentences" into English ones. It now begins to look also as though the Indeterminacy Thesis must begin to totter. Can it really come as any surprise, that is to say, that the Quinean linguist finds himself with inadequate empirical grounds for arriving at unique English translations for Native sentences, if there are no Native sentences to begin with, because Native is not a language, but only a mereological repertoire, a system of registrations? To put it another way, if Quine's conclusion is to be of any philosophical interest, his example of radical translation must be a case of genuine translation, that is, the mapping of one language on to another language. But the considerations adduced above show that the very restrictions that Quine introduces to secure this provision function to defeat it, as to the extent that he conforms to those restrictions the Quinean linguist will have no means of establishing that Native is a language. Hence, whatever other arguments there may be for the Indeterminacy Thesis, those contributed by the "Gavagai" case must fall.

vi. Are observation sentences a part of language?

One can perhaps make the point sharper by looking a little more closely at the role played by observation sentence in Quine's philosophy of language.

An observation sentence, to whatever degree it is observational (and one must remember that observationality is for Quine a relative notion), is defined as unlike the rest of language in a crucial respect: it cannot shift its meaning or truth-value by having the lines between it and other sentences in the language redrawn at the behest of theory. Their "post" is fixed externally by a world over which we have no linguistic control. It is only the experiences in which they are grounded that give them meaning. Observation sentences with their stimulus meaning lie at the boundaries of language. They face reality (the world) directly (at the periphery) and alone (not in the context of the rest of language, subject to redrawing and redefinition). In short, they are exempted from the consequences of holism.

This view of observation sentences cannot, evidently, sit entirely comfortably with Quine's holism. On the face of it, the view of observation sentences just propounded seems, and is, contrary to the spirit of holism. It would be possible to reply that observation sentences are at best an ideal, a fiction forced on us by empiricism. One could retort though that the problem for Quine is precisely that his meaning-empiricism, his Referential Realism, forces him to a series of untenable conclusions, one of which is the formulation of a concept of observation sentence at odds with his holism. If we begin from Quine's initial position and take seriously the idea of a Referential Realism in the context of a commitment to holism, we find, and this is a further paradox, in the strict sense, to which Quine's project ends by committing him, that in pursuit of the attempt to define the observational content of statements about meaning, Quine is forced, on the one hand, to attribute observation sentences a special status as entirely unaffected by holism, and, on the other, to deny them that status.

Quine's Referential Realism and holism taken together entail that in the context of theories, sentences confront reality in groups: there is play, room for shifts in their relationships and meanings, realignments amongst them are possible. Analogously, any account of meaning that would explain the meaning of one expression, e_1, in terms of another expression, e_2, e_2 in terms of e_3, and so on, is always open to having the intralinguistic links redrawn in such a way that the overall system remains the same while the internal links shift dramatically.

To break out of the circle of language requires a unit of meaning that derives from a direct connection with whatever in the world confirms (or disconfirms) it, with no reliance on anything linguistic. Observation sentences must, therefore, be conceived as facing reality alone. "[O]bservation expressions are expressions that can be learned ostensively"[13] and thus must be held apart (or separate) from the holistic fabric of language; they are sentences that we can grasp without regressing into any background language. For, if they were enmeshed in the language, they, too, would become subject to the possibilities just discussed of redrawing linguistic links.

Because so much depends on observation sentences, what are we to make of their status as elements of language? Looking again at what they are expected to do to allow us to escape the Prison-House of Language, we can ask where in fact they are positioned. Quine tells us that they are at the periphery of language; that they are firmly linked to nonverbal stimulation; that they have direct links to the stimuli that prompt assent to them; that their meaning is nothing more or less than pure stimulus-meaning. But where exactly are they? Are they *inside* or *outside* language? They must be one or the other, but neither option is acceptable.

If Quine says they are inside language, as he mostly seems to do, then he is immediately forced by his holism to admit that they are as much subject to holistic shuffling as any other sentence. This isn't, however, the end of the matter. If observation sentences are to be counted as genuine parts of language, they must have assertoric content. But this, if we have argued rightly in the preceding four sections, is precisely what they must lack if they are to escape the consequences of holism. If they are to be immune from holism, observation sentences at most can serve to register natural conditions – stimuli or the "passing show." But to restrict them to that role will be to render them incapable of "founding meaning," if "meaning" is what attaches to the sentences of a natural language; to expressions, that is, capable of expressing assertoric content. Positioning observation sentences inside language or outside it are, therefore, equally untenable moves. Put another way, Quine must either treat observation sentences as inside language or outside it. To whatever extent he treats them as inside it (as standing in meaning-determining relationships, that is, to other sentences of the language) he must treat them as subject to holism. To whatever extent he treats them as outside language, as insulated, that is, from relationship with other sentences, he weakens the case for treating them as potential bearers of assertoric content.

Quine's treatment of observationality as a relative notion to some extent obscures this problem. Yet the problem remains, and partakes of the character of paradox as we defined that earlier. The paradox is that for Quine some sentences in language must both be insulated from the ploys of holism, and yet be potential bearers of assertoric content. On the face of it, such a specification appears internally incoherent.

vii. Ontology and the background language

To understand how deeply Quine's commitment to empiricism runs, one might start by reading Quine's *oeuvre* as a search for the fixed meanings that would allow us to gain sure and reliable access to the world in which we live. On such a reading, Quine begins by looking for what might be called "*absolute* meaning," in the sense of meaning not tied to a background language. Using the framework of a background language allows us to fix meanings in such a way that we can sensibly ask whether our neighbour is talking about a rabbit or a group of undetached rabbit parts. However, it is only a relative sense; once we leave the assumptions of that language, we lose the sense and the ability to ask or answer the question.

... we need the background of language to regress into. The background language gives the query sense, if only relative sense; sense relative in turn to it, this background language.[14]

It is only after he fails to find such an account of meaning that Quine concludes that *empirically* there can be no reason to prefer one interpretation over another.

If Quine's conclusion is accepted, however, it ceases to be clear *what*, if any, distinctions we are marking in the background language. Specifically, when the critic examines the linguist's translation manual and asks, "But are you really sure that 'Gavagai' is 'Lo, rabbit' and *not*, perhaps, 'Lo, undetached rabbit parts?'," has she asked a significant question? If the question is to be significant and not a mere play of words or a "wheel that can be turned though nothing else moves with it,"[15] it must be possible for the critic and the linguist to mark an ontological distinction between rabbits and undetached rabbit parts within the background language, the language into which the native's utterances are being translated. Given this, we can now go on to ask whether these ontological distinctions have manifestable truth-conditions (*à la* Dummett) that distinguish them from one another. There are only two possible answers to this question: either they do or they do not.

If we suppose that they do, then there is no reason to suppose that these same manifestations are unavailable to the natives or to the linguist while in the field. And if they are thus accessible, then the linguist has an answer to the critic roughly along the lines that the reason for pairing "Gavagai" with "Lo, rabbit" rather than "Lo, undetached rabbit parts" is to be found in the manifested truth-conditions that correspond to the former rather than the latter.[16]

Quine's discussion of the "Gavagai" case has philosophical significance for language, meaning, and so on, only on the assumption that we (as speakers of English) can mark the distinction between (e.g.) rabbits and undetached rabbit parts; but on this assumption, his argument loses its distinctive (and destructive) conclusion. If we can mark the distinction, then so, too, can the natives. Even if they presently do not code this distinction in their language, all the manifestable truth-conditions in terms of which it can be marked are there for them and there is no reason to suppose that they cannot be brought to introduce the distinction into their language. Once the distinction is coded in Native, the linguist can discover whether "Gavagai" corresponds to "Lo, rabbit" or to "Lo, undetached rabbit parts." Even prior to the natives' coming to see things from the two separate perspectives (rabbit versus undetached rabbit parts), the linguist can mark *this* fact in the manual by noting that "Gavagai" may be translated by either "Lo, rabbit" or "Lo, undetached rabbit parts," leaving the final choice to the translator.

If, by contrast, we suppose that there are no manifestable truth-conditions, then we find that we are forced to treat the purported distinction between "Lo, rabbit" and "Lo, undetached rabbit parts" marked in the background language as mere verbiage – a distinction without a difference. There could be, on this account, no rabbits or undetached rabbit parts *out there in the world*. All we would be left with as the basis of the distinction would be the *stimuli* connected with the respective utterances.

But this is to commit ourselves to combine a *radical* form of Realism about the stimuli with an equally radical Linguistic Relativism about all other ontological categories. Yes, there are what we might call "rabbit-stimuli" existing independently of the human mind and all human conventions, but there are not "rabbits." "Regressing into the background language" cannot dispel this. In the background language we marked a distinction between rabbits and undetached rabbit parts; but there is no such distinction – the only distinction is between sets of stimuli.

viii. Psychological and linguistic salience

On Quine's account, in effect, then, all one can say is that there are stimuli that speakers treat as detached from other stimuli; but no account can be offered of the ground on which the detachment is based. In "Perceiving and Learning,"[17] Quine uses the notion of *salience* in connection with the role similarity plays in language learning.

A subject's perceptual similarities are reflected in his behavior: in the reinforcement and extinction of his responses: in a word, in his learning. Perceptual similarity relates his present episode to a past episode.[18]

Noticing is a matter of degree, and perceptual similarity is sensitive to this variation. Thus suppose a cat is visible at times *a*, *b* and *c*; suppose that the broad visual setting of the cat is much the same at times *a* and *c* but quite different at *b*; but suppose the cat is salient at times *a* and *b*, because of motion or spotlighting or focal position, and not at *c*. Then the subject may find *a* perceptually more similar to *b* than to *c*, despite the sameness of landscape at *a* and *c*. . . salience has the power to swing perceptual similarity the other way.[19]

Psychologists ordinarily speak simply of the stimulus, where I am speaking of what is salient in the episode . . . there can be multiple salience, and in varying degrees, within an episode . . . *the salience version suggests a field of gradations rather than just one or several clean-cut stimuli*, and this I find good (emphasis added).[20]

What Quine misses in this discussion is that a psychological account of salience does not yield a linguistically relevant salience. His treatment of salience is a version of psychological salience; it cannot provide any means for establishing meaning. Having established that the cat stimuli are salient in *a* and *b* (but not *c*) goes no way toward establishing anything relevant to meaning.

We need to return here, for one last time, to the obvious but real parallels we noted earlier between Quine's treatment of observation sentences and Wittgenstein's treatment of ostensive definition. Wittgenstein in effect addresses the issue of the relationship – or more correctly absence of a relationship – between psychological and linguistic salience in the following passage.

Now one can ostensively define a proper name, the name of a colour, the name of a material, a numeral, the name of a point of the compass and so on. The definition of the number two, "That is called 'two'" – pointing to two nuts – is perfectly exact. – But how can two be defined like that? The person one gives the definition to doesn't know what one wants to call "two"; he will suppose that "two" is the name given to *this* group of nuts! – He *may* suppose this; but perhaps he does not. He might make the opposite mistake; when I want to assign a name to this group of nuts, he might understand it as a numeral. And he might equally well take the name of a person, of which I give an ostensive definition, as that of a colour, of a race, or even of a point of the compass. That is to say: an ostensive definition can be variously interpreted in *every* case.[21]

No amount of talk about salience will guarantee that the learner get it right – no matter how many times one varies the scenario, as *per* Quine's discussion in "Perceiving and Learning," the fact remains that salience of the sort available to the learner is psychological salience. In order to move to linguistic salience, we need access to language; that we are able to say "This *number* is called 'two'," to continue Wittgenstein's case. We must be able to explain the function of the word "two" within language.

> For the word "number" here shews what place in language, in grammar, we assign to the word. But this means that the word "number" must be explained before the ostensive definition can be understood.[22]

But this is precisely to say that without a clear concept of linguistic salience, no amount of psychological salience will serve to establish meaning. No matter how salient the pair of nuts may be in the environment, no matter how many times we vary the presentation to force the learner to focus on just these two nuts, the simple fact is that until the learner can grasp that it is the *number* of nuts that is at issue – until that is she can count, until she grasps the use$_E$ of number words in relation to the practice of counting – she will not get it.[23] The world is a mass of psychological saliences: the problem for the theory of meaning is to determine which of these are significant for the application of terms – and why.

   If he is correct, then what Quine has shown is that the categories honoured by the "background language" are *one and all illusory* and possess no objective correlate in the world. The effect of this is to rule out the motivating question of the Indeterminacy Thesis (Is it rabbit or undetached rabbit parts that the native is talking about?) and to rule it out in a deeply problematical way for Quine's philosophy. It can stand in no way as a criticism of a translation manual (or anything else for that matter) that it fails to mark distinctions that have no force or basis in the first place. Quine's quest for meaning turns on his quest for an "absolute" meaning, one which is not relative to any background language; but if there are no manifestable truth-conditions for utterances in a language, the quest cannot even begin.

   Quine's demand for absolute meaning comes out in such passages as these, where he explores what would be required to break out of the Prison-House of Language. The first passage below is especially interesting since it might be taken as turning the metaphor inside out, with the world breaking into the Prison-House.

> For observation sentences are precisely the ones that we can correlate with observable circumstances of the occasion of utterance or assent, independently of variations in the past histories of individual informants. *They afford the only entry to a language* (emphasis added).[24]
>
>   What makes ontological questions meaningless when taken absolutely is not universality but circularity. A question of the form "What is an F?" can be answered only by recourse to a further term: "An F is a G." The answer makes only relative sense: sense relative to the uncritical acceptance of "G."[25]

This turns out to require that meaning and ontology be grounded and determined by the world, that is, the very *facts* that (**QP**) rules out.

Could anything else serve in this role? Could stimulus-meaning, for instance? Quine does not take this path, and for good reason. For Quine it is only a *fact*, in the sense of something possessing assertoric content, which could eliminate the possibility of linguistic relativism. Since experience gives us access to no such entities, Quine concludes that there can be no fixed (or absolute) meaning. There is no world that can fix meaning absolutely; therefore, there is no world to be referred to or talked about independently of our so referring or talking. For him, language is relative right down to the ground; whether talking of meaning or reference, one cannot speak of things that exist independently of their being referred to in some particular language.

In other words, for Quine, rabbits (as commonly understood) gain purchase in the world *only* through some community's having a language in which a word picks out rabbits. Put another way, the purchasing power of rabbits in the world depends on a rabbit-discourse. If a particular language fails to have a term which picks out rabbits, then any and all talk of rabbits is out of the question. It is not that the speakers of this language get it wrong when they remain mute in the face of a rabbit-strewn field before them; they have the stimuli of the rabbit-strewn field, but they simply have nothing to say about it *in their language*. Nor could they be said to have made a mistake about "what is there before them," for there is no fact of the matter about which they could be mistaken.

For Quine ontology is an unanalysed category. Once we are operating within a language, we can draw distinctions and propose rules of individuation that fit, or don't fit, the linguistically parsed "facts." However, by itself, all of this takes us no closer to the world or to meaning in any absolute (non-relativistic) sense; all we have are the furnishings within the Prison-House of Language. As we have already argued in Chapter 3 and §§iii–iv above, the only hope for escape that Quine offers lies in *sensory evidence*. But there is no interpretation of "sensory evidence" that will do the job Quine requires that notion to do in his theory.

The sensory evidence or stimuli (Quine's "shared experience") that could play this role has to be of a very special sort indeed: it must be able to bear the entire burden of bridging the gap between the private – our sensations – and the public – the language we use to communicate with one another. Absent such evidence, we are confined to the Prison-House of Language. Regardless of how comfortable, commodious or convenient we may find being there, it is an illusion that we are in any contact with an independently existing reality.

If we accept Quine's starting point of empiricism and the attendant assumptions about observation sentences (viz., that the only evidence for science is sensory and that meaning rests on sensory evidence), the conclusions he draws are inevitable. In other words, if we agree that the only reliable meaning is stimulus-meaning and that observation sentences alone could form the basic element of meaning in virtue of their facing the world alone and directly (i.e., unmediated by other linguistic meanings), then we must accept (**QP**) (There is no fact of the matter) and the Indeterminacy Thesis.

ix. Nature and human decision

It will help us to focus on a third level of paradox in Quine's account if we revert to an example from Chapter 3 §i, the "Islets of Langerhans." Let's explore this in a bit more detail to show more clearly the play between Nature and human decision involved. On our account, the way in which the term "Islets of Langerhans" comes to acquire its use$_E$ is through a process of practical interaction between us and the order of Nature. For Nature is not the only thing that plays a part in the term's acquiring its use$_E$: our interests and decisions also play a part. We might have chosen to divide the body into zones by reference to the procedures of acupuncture. Assuming that acupuncture has a solid basis, as contrasted with an hallucinatory one, this might have led to a vocabulary of bodily areas or zones, rather than of cells. By the same assumption, the terms in this vocabulary also would have a "foundation in Nature."

One could not, by contrast, explain either system of dividing up the body in terms of anything like Quine's "observation sentences": until one understands what kind of catalogue one is trying to draw up, one does not know which observations will or will not be relevant to the drawing up of that catalogue. And understanding what kind of catalogue one is trying to draw up is a matter of understanding the practice in play – be it histology or acupuncture.

Quine's views on such matters as this are quite different. For him the question is whether one could have a way of distinguishing between vocabularies that is *entirely internal to language.* There is no play between human decision and Nature: for Quine either it's all a matter of decision or it's all a matter of Nature. He insists that either one be able to determine entirely within language whether a term (e.g., "rabbit") is to be used as a name for a whole animal or for a collection of undetached animal parts or something else entirely, or else that the world "imposes" the correct meaning on us via the breaking in of *salient* features of the "passing show" upon our passive sensibility. Quine confronts us with two options – all Nature or all human decision – neither of which yields an intelligible account of publicity, communication, or *linguistic* salience.

Quine goes on to say that in practice, of course, things seem much less relativistic than this. In practice we engage such devices as pointing and going on as it seems everyone else is going on, to stop the relativistic downward spiral. But at the end of the day, even these devices are relativistic.

In practice, of course, we end the regress of coordinate systems by something like pointing. And in practice we end the regress of background languages, in discussions of reference, by acquiescing in our mother tongue and taking its words at face value.[26]

... in the case of position and velocity, in practice, pointing breaks the regress. But what of position and velocity apart from practice? what of the regress then? The answer, of course, is the relational doctrine of space; there is no absolute position or velocity; there are just the relations of coordinate systems to one another, and ultimately of things to one another. And I think that the parallel question regarding denotation calls for a parallel answer, a relational theory of what the objects of theories are. What makes sense is to say not what the objects of a theory are, absolutely speaking, but how one theory of objects is interpretable or reinterpretable in another.[27]

The point is not that bare matter is inscrutable ... for it is that things can be inscrutably switched even while carrying their properties with them. Rabbits differ from rabbit parts and rabbit stages not just as bare matter, after all, but in respect of properties. ... [28]

But this only means that we are comfortable with our own assumptions about meaning, it does not mean that meaning is not relative. The parallel Quine draws between the status of position and velocity in the relational doctrine of space, and meaning is instructive. Just as there is no absolute position or velocity, but only position and velocity relative to the other, so, too, there is no absolute meaning, only meaning relative to some other locus of meaning. Quine here can be read as expressing his deep disappointment at meaning theory, indeed even the world, for failing to provide the fixed point from which he could construct an unassailable theory of language, science and everything. Having striven for what, to distinguish it from the version of realism we argue for in this book, we might call Absolute Realism, Quine settles for total relativism. In short, he embraces (**QP**).

x. Referential Realism as the root of Quine's difficulties

How does Quine end up in this position? We argue that it traces back to his Referential Realism. His initial suggestion that it is only a (fictitious) observation sentence that could defeat relativism is doomed from the start. The possibility of pure observation sentences commits Quine to a view that holds that, whereas generally sentences face reality *en masse*, not all of them are quite as enmeshed in the *masse* as others. And this contradicts his own view that all meaning is embedded in a theory (holism). As we argue, Quine fails to take into account the implications of, on the one hand, the embedding of sentences within practices, and, on the other, the embedding of those practices within the world. Language itself – speaking, writing – is embedded in an even larger pattern, viz., human life. Once we grasp this, relativism, with its attendant scepticism, fades. But what remains is not the false hope of Absolute Realism; rather it is the Relative Realism for which we argue in the Epilogue.

His commitment to Referential Realism is what drives Quine to posit pure observation sentences as the only anchor for meaning and ontological realism. However, once he commits himself to this move, he is faced with the following choice. Either abandon holism, indeterminacy and (**QP**), or abandon the very Realism that was his initial goal. In view of his pragmatism, Quine opts for the latter, thereby, seeming to further entrench holism and indeterminacy. (**QP**) then emerges almost as an explanation of why absolute meaning and determinate ontology are forever logically elusive. But, this is to turn things inside out. Meaning-Realism does not require Referential Realism as its ground. Once the requirements of Referential Realism are abandoned, we are free to construct a realistic theory of meaning.

Earlier, we argued against Quine on the grounds that observation sentences, if they are to avoid becoming enmeshed in the holism Quine attributes to language, must be construed as mereological utterances, that is, as utterances lacking in assertoric content. From this standpoint, Quine's contention (**QP**) that there is "no fact of the matter" in which the choice between attributing one or another assertoric content to such an utterance is concerned could be taken as roughly equivalent to

(**QPA**): There is nothing assertoric in Nature.

We have no quarrel with (**QPA**) so construed. It does not, however, support Quine's thesis of the indeterminacy of translation. By contrast, if he indeed intends (**QP**), then our arguments show that it is incoherent, and indeterminacy fails.

But none of this provides the basis for adopting Meaning-Relativism. Quine is led to this conclusion only because he conflates the two treatments of observation sentences: either they are genuine parts of language or they are, somehow or another, not subject to the demands of holism. Drawing on the first, he treats "Gavagai" as a full-fledged sentence, with assertoric content; drawing on the second, he treats it as lacking what we call affirmation-denial content connectors. According to his own views, the first renders them inappropriate for grounding meaning in the sense required to escape the Prison-House of Language because they can be assigned meaning only relative to the language in which they are located; the second, however, fares no better as now they are utterly incapable of bearing, let along grounding, linguistic meaning. We have argued that this is the result of misunderstanding the nature of language; this misunderstanding stems from Quine's conviction that Referential Realism provides the only viable account of meaning sufficiently strong to avoid meaning-relativism. When he demonstrates that Referential Realism is untenable, Quine draws the only conclusion open to him, viz., meaning relativism. None of this need follow once the misunderstanding about the nature of language is uncovered.

14

Linguistic Competence[1]

i. Paradox and understanding

In "A Puzzle About Belief,"[2] Saul Kripke argues that linguistic moves to all appearances normal in reporting the beliefs of others can be shown to generate paradoxical results. The paradox lies in the impossibility of giving a straight answer to this question: Does Pierre, or does he not, believe that London is pretty? We can neither say that Pierre believes London to be pretty nor that he believes it not to be pretty; worse still, we cannot say that he believes neither that it is nor that it is not pretty; and certainly we cannot say that he believes both that it is and that it is not pretty. As straightforward as this outline of the options appears, it is mistaken. There is indeed a straight answer to the question: viz., that Pierre believes that London is not pretty and that *Londres est jolie*.

In this chapter, we show that the supposed paradox is one in appearance only, and that the appearance rests on a Kripke's covert vacillation between two conceptions of linguistic understanding, a weak, or "minimal" one, and a "strong" one. The weak conception allows Kripke to set up the example that allegedly generates his paradox; but only the strong allows the generation of a philosophically significant paradox. However, a conception of linguistic understanding strong enough to generate the paradox turns out to be strong enough to block it. The fundamental problem for Kripke's position turns on his commitment to Referential Realism (as we have already argued in Chapters 5 and 6).

ii. Kripke's principles

To construct the puzzle, Kripke uses the following two principles.

- Disquotation (**DQ**): If a normal English speaker, on reflection, sincerely assents to "p" then he believes that p (where "p" is replaced by a standard English sentence in both instances).[3]

- Translation (**T**): If a sentence of one language expresses a truth in that language, then any translation of it into any other language also expresses a truth (in that other language).[4]

The qualifiers "sincere" and "reflective" rule out cases in which the "speaker . . . , through careless inattention to the meaning of his words or other momentary conceptual or linguistic confusion, assert[s] something he does not really mean, or assent[s] to a sentence in linguistic error" and cases of "mendacity, acting, irony, and the like."[5] He also excludes "indexical or pronominal devices or ambiguities, that would ruin the intuitive sense of the principle."[6] Furthermore, he assumes that "we are dealing with a normal speaker of English," by which he means that the speaker "uses all words in the sentence in a standard way, combines them according to the appropriate syntax, etc.: in short he uses the sentence to mean what a normal speaker should mean by it."[7]

iii. The paradox

Suppose Pierre is a normal French speaker who lives in France and speaks not a word of English or of any other language except French. Of course he has heard of that famous distant city, London (which he of course calls *"Londres"*) though he himself has never left France. On the basis of what he has heard of London, he is inclined to think that it is pretty. So he says, in French, *"Londres est jolie."*[8]

From Pierre's "sincere French utterance" we can infer that (4) Pierre believes that London is pretty.

Pierre satisfies all the conditions for the application of (**DQ**) and (**T**). He is a normal French speaker who satisfies all the criteria "we usually use to judge that a Frenchman (correctly) uses *"est jolie"* to attribute pulchritude and uses *"Londres"* – standardly – as a name of London."[9]

But, unlike most of his French neighbours, Pierre moves to London, where,

. . . like most of his [London] neighbors, [he] rarely if ever leaves [his] part of the city. None of his neighbors know any French, so he must learn English by "direct method," without using any translation of English into French: by talking and mixing with the people he eventually begins to pick up English. In particular, everyone speaks of the city, "London," where they all live . . . Pierre learns from them everything they know about London, but there is little overlap with what he heard before. He learns, of course – speaking English – to call the city he lives in "London." Pierre's surroundings are, as I said, unattractive, and he is unimpressed with most of the rest of what he happens to see. So he is inclined to assent to the English sentence:

(5) London is not pretty.

He has *no* inclination to assent to

(6) London is pretty.

Of course he does not for a moment withdraw his assent from the French sentence, *"Londres est jolie"*; he merely takes it for granted that the ugly city in which he is now stuck is distinct from the enchanting city he heard about in France. But he has no inclination to change his mind for a moment about the city he still calls *"Londres"*.[10]

The paradox arises from two competing inclinations. First, that on the basis of Pierre's behaviour while in France, we are entitled to draw the conclusion that he believes that London is pretty (4). Second, that on the basis of his behaviour in England, we are entitled to draw the conclusion that he believes that London is not pretty. That is to say, from Pierre's assent to (5), using (**DQ**), it follows that

(7) Pierre believes that London is not pretty.[11]

Kripke argues that there are no reasonable grounds for denying the truth of either (4) or (7). We cannot conclude that Pierre once believed that London was pretty, but no longer holds that belief, because by hypothesis, he continues to assent to *"Londres est jolie."* Nor can we deny that, while in London, he believes that London is not pretty.

... His French past aside, he is just like his friends in London. Anyone else, growing up in London with the same knowledge and beliefs that he expresses in England, we would undoubtedly judge to believe that London is not pretty. Can Pierre's French past nullify such a judgement? ... [12]

To attempt to deny Pierre both beliefs encounters the difficulties just stated for each considered individually; "[t]he option does not seem very satisfactory."[13]

However, if we credit Pierre with believing both, we seem to be committed to saying that Pierre has contradictory beliefs: an alternative with seemingly "insuperable difficulties."[14] And thus we arrive at the position outlined in §i above.

We have examined four possibilities for characterizing Pierre while he is in London: (a) that at that time we no longer respect his French utterance (*"Londres est jolie"*), that is that we no longer ascribe to him the corresponding belief; (b) that we do not respect his English utterance (or lack of utterance); (c) that we respect neither; (d) that we respect both. Each possibility seems to lead us to say something either plainly false or even downright contradictory. Yet the possibilities appear to be logically exhaustive. This, then, is the paradox.[15]

Two paragraphs later, Kripke restates the paradox in its question form.

To reiterate, this is the puzzle: Does Pierre, or does he not, believe that London is pretty? It is clear that our normal criteria for the attribution of belief lead, when applied to *this* question, to paradoxes and contradictions.[16]

iv. Kripke's challenge

According to Kripke his "... main thesis is a simple one: that the puzzle *is* a puzzle. And, as a corollary, that any account of belief must ultimately come to grips with it ...,"[17] although coming to grips with it cannot involve denying its validity.

> I have no firm belief as to how to solve [the puzzle]. But beware of one source of confusion. It is no solution in itself to observe that some *other* terminology, which evades the question whether Pierre believes that London is pretty, may be sufficient to state all the relevant facts. I am fully aware that complete and straightforward descriptions of the situation are possible and in this sense there is no paradox. Pierre is disposed to sincere assent to *"Londres est jolie"* but not to "London is pretty." He uses French normally, English normally. Both with *"Londres"* and "London" he associates properties sufficient to determine that famous city, but he does not realize that they determine a single city. (And his uses of *"Londres"* and "London" are historically (causally) connected with the same single city, though he is unaware of that.) We may even give a rough statement of his beliefs. He believes that the city he calls *"Londres"* is pretty, that the city he calls "London" is not. No doubt other straightforward descriptions are possible. No doubt some of these are, in a certain sense *complete* descriptions of the situation.
>
> But none of this answers the original question. Does Pierre, or does he not, believe that London is pretty?[18]

This passage contains the essence of Kripke's challenge. The paradox cannot be solved by being dissolved: it will not count as a response to this puzzle to show that there is really no paradox. Instead, Kripke insists, any would-be critic must accept the reality of the paradoxical nature of the case, and do so presumably, in Kripke's own terms. Resolution is possible only if, having agreed to Kripke's terms, the critic can then provide an answer, which has no paradoxical, contradictory or false consequences, to the question: "Does Pierre, or does he not, believe that London is pretty?"

In one sense Kripke's challenge is legitimate; but in another it isn't. What makes the challenge illegitimate as Kripke presents it is that his way of formulating it implicitly assumes that the content of beliefs can *always* be specified without mentioning the language in which the speaker himself formulates his beliefs: that, *even when dealing with someone whose situation is characterised as Pierre's is characterised*, we can state *the content of* what he believes, or formulate the *proposition* he believes, or something of the sort, in a way entirely neutral with respect to the distinction between one natural language and another.

This assumption arises from Kripke's misunderstanding of what a language is, and what counts as linguistic understanding. Using the arguments of the present book, we show how Kripke fails to see the problems with the assumption. Once it is dismissed, the response to Kripke's challenge is clear: what Pierre believes is that *Londres est jolie* and that London is not pretty.

v. The Principle of Insulation

Kripke maintains that the paradox is the result not of this or that theory of meaning or reference but, rather, that it is a result of being able to use language to refer to the world, regardless of what theory of meaning one accepts. Kripke argues that the paradox arises simply in virtue of language's being used to make claims about the world.

At first blush, a critic might suppose that the puzzle arises for Kripke only because of, and directly as a result of, his semantic externalism.[19] After all, one might argue, it is only because of Kripke's commitment to an account of names according to which the meaning of a name is fixed by its referent, that Pierre can get into trouble with "London" and *"Londres."* An internalist account of names, such as the Description Theory, might block generation of the same puzzle. However, Kripke rejects this line of reasoning, insisting instead that the puzzle presents itself regardless of whether one is a semantic externalist or an internalist.

It is noteworthy that the puzzle can still arise even if Pierre associates to *"Londres"* and to "London" *exactly* the same *uniquely identifying* properties. How can this be? Well, suppose that Pierre believes that London is the largest city in (and capital of) England, that it contains Buckingham Palace, the residence of the Queen of England, and he believes (correctly) that these properties, conjointly, uniquely identify the city. (In this case it is best to suppose that he has never seen London, or even England, so that he uses *only* these properties to identify the city. Nevertheless, he learned English by "direct method.") These uniquely identifying properties he comes to associate with "London" after he learned English, and he expresses the appropriate beliefs about "London" in English. Earlier, when he spoke nothing but French, however, he associated *exactly* the same uniquely identifying properties with *"Londres."* He believed that *"Londres,"* as he called it, could be uniquely identified as the capital of England, that it contained Buckingham Palace, that the Queen of England lived there, etc. Of course he expressed these beliefs, like most monolingual Frenchmen, in French. In particular, he used *"Angleterre"* for England, *"le Palais de Buckingham"* (pronounced *"Bookeengam"*!) for Buckingham Palace, and *"la Reine d'Angleterre"* for the Queen of England. But if any Frenchman who speaks no English can be said to associate *exactly* the same properties of being the capital of England, etc., with the name *"Londres,"* Pierre in his monolingual period did so.[20]

Contrary to the critic's contention that this entails that there is a nonparadoxical answer to the question whether or not Pierre believes that London is pretty, Kripke argues that it doesn't.

Suppose Pierre had affirmed *"Londres est jolie."* If Pierre had any reason ... to maintain "London is not pretty," he need not contradict himself. He need only conclude that "England" and *"Angleterre"* name two different countries, that "Buckingham Palace" and *"le Palais de Buckingham"* (recall the pronunciation!), name two different palaces, and so on. Then he can maintain *both* views without contradiction, and regard *both* properties as uniquely identifying.[21]

On first reading, these passages are somewhat disconcerting. It looks as though Kripke intends us to spend philosophical energy on what, while no doubt true, seems philosophically unremarkable, viz., the fact that people can (and often do) believe the most implausible things, including things which are incompatible with the rest of their seemingly sincerely held beliefs. This reading would, however, miss the point at issue; Kripke intends his example to differ from, say, someone's holding that all the time we say he was having dinner with us, he was really abducted by aliens and we didn't notice because the aliens put a robot in his place.

These passages show the role language plays in Kripke's account. The denials required to keep London and *Londres* apart are internal to language, while the denials required to place the "abductee" on the UFO require actual changes in the world. Pierre's misunderstandings are of the first sort. Simply in virtue of his being able to understand and use the names in these circumstances, Pierre is open to the paradox.

Indeed, Kripke's remarks show us more than this. Even if Pierre were to impose extraordinary standards of understanding on himself; for example, if he were to accept Russell's Principle, he might still end up assenting to both "London is not pretty" and *"Londres est jolie."* London is not, after all, something seen at a glance. Pierre might take his friends to St. James Park when showing them *Londres,* and take them to some wretched area when showing them London.[22] Even direct acquaintance with the objects named is not enough to prevent paradox.

Such a blanket susceptibility to the puzzle requires that all nonlinguistic aspects of Pierre's understanding of French and English must be removed from consideration. If the paradox is to have any philosophical implications, the following two things must hold.

(a) Pierre must be competent in both French and English, and
(b) he must understand the sentences he assents to and affirms.

Removing all nonlinguistic aspects from Pierre's understanding of his languages means that Kripke must be able to characterise *in purely linguistic terms* the content of the capacities covered by (a) and (b). If Kripke were to allow philosophical issues concerning belief or reference to enter into the satisfaction of (a) or (b), any argument for the puzzle would constitute a *petitio.* This requirement of linguistic insulation, which we call the Principle of Insulation, entails that (a) and (b) conjointly be taken as defining linguistic competences, and that linguistic competences can (and in this case *must*) be kept entirely independent from philosophical and all other competences, including epistemic and empirical competences. In short, one's ability to use and understand language cannot depend on any ability to understand anything about the world; all that is needed is grasping the use$_E$ of the language, not the use$_P$ of the practice. We call this "minimal linguistic understanding." Because Pierre can only be credited with minimal linguistic understanding of English and French, we say that he is minimally bilingual. All that is needed for minimal bilingualism is understanding use$_E$, and this alone allows Pierre to correlate the Name-Tracking Networks across the two languages.

vi. How not to generate Kripke's Paradox

According to Kripke, linguistically, Pierre is just like his fellow language users; consequently we draw the same inferences *vis-à-vis* Pierre as we would for any speaker of the language. In England, Pierre is

... just like his friends in London. Anyone else, growing up in London with the same knowledge and beliefs that he expresses in England, we would undoubtedly judge to believe that London is not pretty.[23]

The same is true of Pierre and his French friends with regard to *"Londres est jolie."* And this is the puzzle. If anyone in Pierre's English condition believes that London is not pretty and anyone in Pierre's French condition believes that London is pretty, and as Pierre is in both conditions, then it seems that Pierre believes both.

In order to force us to hold both (4), "Pierre believes that London is pretty," and (7), "Pierre believes that London is not pretty," as true descriptions of Pierre, Kripke must maintain that Pierre understands both *"Londres est jolie"* and "London is not pretty" in some sense strong enough to count him as a "normal speaker" of both French and English. Furthermore, he must maintain that, even given this status, the fact that Pierre does not see that *"Londres"* and "London" name one and the same city simply as a result of his competence as a speaker of both French and English puts him in an intolerable position. That Kripke does maintain that Pierre counts as a normal speaker of both French and English and that Pierre doesn't make the connection between London and *Londres* is evident from the passages already cited.

The argument that linguistic competence alone leads to the paradox provides further grounds for taking Kripke to be committed to the Principle of Insulation. In order to generate the puzzle, there must be some way of describing Pierre's abilities, as respectively a speaker of French and a speaker of English, that introduces into the relevant description of French-Pierre and English-Pierre no difference, no unshared characteristic that in any way affects or is relevant to the generation of the paradox. This can be done only by limiting the understanding necessary for a normal speaker to minimal linguistic understanding. Thus, Kripke counts Pierre as minimally linguistically competent in both of his languages, and, therefore, as minimally bilingual.

vii. The content of minimal linguistic competence

Is minimal linguistic understanding sufficient to generate the puzzle? Before we can answer this question, we must first look more closely at what "understand," in (b) above, means. What, in other words, counts as minimal linguistic understanding?

In the case of Pierre's understanding *"Londres est jolie,"*[24] at least the following must be true.

(i) He understands the syntax of the sentence, though he certainly need not be able to express this understanding by talking about subjects, predicates, verbs, adverbs, adjectives, and so on;

(ii) he knows the function/meanings of *"est"* and *"jolie"; and*

(iii) he knows that *"Londres"* names a city and that a city is something that is capable of being pretty or not pretty.[25]

Could anything else be required for Pierre to understand this sentence, or by extrapolation, his language? In the case of names, there are three candidates: (1) the ability to locate the named object; (2) the belief (not necessarily true) that one could locate the named object; and (3) the association of an (allegedly) identifying description with the name. None of these, however, is a viable addition to (i)–(iii).

We cannot require that Pierre actually be able to locate the named object. Apart from violating the Principle of Insulation, if this were the standard for normal use, most of us would fail to qualify as normal speakers of at least vast portions of our language.

Nor can we require that Pierre believe that he is able to locate the city. While weaker than the first suggestion and not a violation of the Principle of Insulation, this, too, would rule out too many normal speakers. For example, someone (including at least one of the authors) might know that Caracas is the capital of Venezuela, but at the same time, know that given a map of Venezuela that had dots for all the cities but no names next to them, she could not locate Caracas. However, there is no reason to suppose that she doesn't understand "Caracas" and cannot use it in a fully normal sense.

Finally, we cannot add any requirement to the effect that Pierre possess an (either actual or allegedly) identifying description. Even if one were inclined to want to do this, it's clear that Kripke doesn't include this in minimal linguistic understanding. Therefore, (i)–(iii) exhaust minimal linguistic understanding.

But something interesting emerges from this. Minimal linguistic understanding is compatible with what we call Wittgenstein's Slogan. On this account, Pierre's linguistic understanding is entirely linguistically contained, or, to borrow from the Slogan, it "looks after itself." As we shall show, if this is all the understanding attributed to Pierre, no paradox arises. It is only by violating the Principle of Insulation that Kripke can generate the paradox;

but violation of the Principle of Insulation entails violation of Wittgenstein's Slogan, and thus shows that Kripke's violation of the Principle of Insulation is a result of his commitment both to Referential Realism (see Chapters 3 and 5) and to a version of Russell's Principle (see Chapter 4).

viii. The puzzle disappears

The question now is whether granting only minimal linguistic understanding we are justified in concluding that Pierre believes anything at all about the *city* (whatever it's called).

The short answer is that we aren't. It would be more accurate to say that Pierre believes something about the-city-that-French-speakers-call- *"Londres."* But, put in this way, it is not possible to drop reference to the French language as (T) authorises. In order to specify Pierre's belief, given only minimal linguistic understanding, we must retain reference to the language in which it is initially expressed; in other words, how Pierre himself puts a belief is crucial to any (re)statement of that belief. The very same is true for Pierre's statement "London is not pretty." Given only minimal linguistic understanding, it's the-city-that-English-speakers-call-"London." This puts us in the position of concluding that Pierre holds the following non-contradictory beliefs: the-city-that-French-speakers-call- *"Londres"* is pretty, and the-city-that-English-speakers-call-"London" is not.

To restate this in terms of our earlier argument (Chapters 4 and 5), all that minimal linguistic understanding authorises is access to *nomothetic objects*. Minimal linguistic understanding gives Pierre license to use$_E$ of "London" and *"Londres"* within their respective languages; this establishes a relationship of name-bearership between the words and the nomothetic objects that the use$_E$ picks out. This, however, does not put Pierre into contact with any actual object; for this, Pierre must acquire some extralinguistic knowledge about the world. On the basis of minimal linguistic understanding, Pierre is ready to learn about the actual cities (including whether they exist, are one or two, etc.), but he does not yet have this nonlinguistic knowledge.

Earlier in §iii, we quoted Kripke's argument that the paradox arises whether one holds semantic internalism or externalism with respect to the meaning of names. There Kripke says that the puzzle arises "even if Pierre associates to *"Londres"* and to "London" *exactly* the same *uniquely identifying* properties."[26] Something about that passage strikes a false note given the earlier arguments of this book, namely, the appeal to the association of *properties* with names. In light of Kripke's antecedent commitment to Referential Realism, this isn't a surprising turn of phrase. However, in view of the theory argued for in this book, we can now see that in fact, it is not actual properties (i.e., things in the world) that speakers are in touch with;

rather it is nominal properties that we are in touch with when we acquire the meaning of a name. Thus, even to say that Pierre associates "exactly the same" properties with "London" and *"Londres"* is to violate the Principle of Insulation.

ix. Dissolution versus redescription

A Kripkean might contend that our solution of the puzzle doesn't meet Kripke's challenge that it is no solution to provide an alternative description of Pierre's situation which does not have paradoxical consequences.[27] Are we guilty of having simply redescribed Pierre's situation in terms which, though in a sense straightforward and in a sense complete, evade Kripke's straight question: "Does Pierre, or does he not, believe that London is pretty?"

The short answer is that we are not. Our response to Kripke's straight question is that Pierre believes that London is not pretty but that *Londres* is pretty.[28] Kripke's description of Pierre's situation (the paradox-generating description) is itself illegitimate, because it rests on using (T) to detach something supposedly identifiable as the *content* of the belief Pierre expresses in French from the language (French) in which it is expressed. Pierre's beliefs about *Londres* have, for the reasons already set out, no content expressible wholly in English. Names acquire their meaning only via the Name-Tracking Networks that give them use$_E$ within a language (a practice with a use$_P$), as we have shown; but this ties (or indexes) names to the language within which they acquire their meaning (as use$_E$).

From Kripke's point of view, the problem is that Pierre's minimal linguistic understanding of the sentences "London is not pretty" and *"Londres est jolie"* not only need not, but if Kripke's argument is to get off the ground *cannot*, include the knowledge that *"Londres"* and "London" designate one and the same city. And Kripke is right on this point. But what he misses is that minimal linguistic understanding does not, indeed cannot, require that Pierre (or any language user) have access to this nugget of information. That London is *Londres* remains elusive even if we suppose Pierre to have learned the names "London" and *"Londres"* in association with what *we* regard as "the same" city. In other words, for Pierre to understand "London" and *"Londres"* is not for him to be in touch with the city, but to be in touch with the Name-Tracking Network that gives the name its use$_E$, regardless of how one comes to be in touch with the Name-Tracking Network.

In Chapter 5, we argued that knowing a language is knowing-how to operate within a practice. Understanding "London" consists in knowing-how to use the word within a practice; in this case, the practice is English (more precisely, British English). His minimal linguistic understanding, puts Pierre "in touch" with the nomothetic object associated with the name. Since nomothetic objects are determined by the practice within which they acquire name-bearerships, there is nothing to connect them across languages, that is, nothing to connect the nomothetic objects London and *Londres*). To show that Pierre is only in touch with a nomothetic object, consider the following fanciful case, in which Pierre gains access to both the Name-Tracking Network associated with "London" and the Name-Tracking Network associated with *"Londres"* while in "direct contact" with the same city.

Imagine that rather than growing up in France, Pierre in fact grew up in London. His parents were very protective and wanted to ensure that their little Pierre learned only French and had a idyllic "French" childhood, filled with beauty. So they spoke only French to him and took him only to beautiful spots in *Londres* where they happened to live. So thorough were they in their efforts to keep Pierre "French" that they had special earphones made for him so that when outside he heard only French; indeed, they were so concerned that Pierre experience his childhood as a "French" boy that they arranged for a special pair of spectacles that removed all traces of English in advertisements, menus, signs, and so on. Now, his parents were not so obsessed as to try to make Pierre think that he lived in France. No, they were very honest about the fact that they lived in London, except, of course, they called it *"Londres."* And so little Pierre learned all about his hometown, *Londres*, and indeed it was a pretty place; full of places like the Tate, Westminister Abbey, St. James Park, Kew Gardens, Hampstead Heath, and so on (all these, of course in French). Later in his life, he loses the spectacles and earphones; ends up in some wretched neighbourhood where he learns English on the streets and comes, alas, to think that London is not pretty.

At this point, Pierre connects *"Londres"* as directly with the city in which he lives as he will later come to connect "London" with London. Earlier we used this to justify our removing the reference to English in order to allow us to say that Pierre believes that London is not pretty. Are we now justified in saying that Pierre believes that London is pretty? Or should we instead say that Pierre believes that *Londres* is pretty?

Minimal linguistic understanding does not warrant our claiming or assuming that *"Londres"*/*Londres* and "London"/London, either in their entirety or piece by piece, are interchangeable. Understanding that *Londres* is a city and that a city is something capable of being pretty/not pretty doesn't even hint at, let alone entail, that *Londres* is identical with London. But, if we can only say that Pierre believes that *Londres* is pretty, then once again we fail to generate the puzzle; there is no contradiction between "London is not pretty" and *"Londres* is pretty."

Thus, even in a case where Pierre directly connects the names with a city, and these cities are in fact one and the same city, we still have no paradox. Since Kripke doesn't require Pierre to make such a connection between the names and the city, he certainly cannot have his paradox.

x. DQ and T

It is perhaps worth going over again one last time the reason why Kripke is entitled to (**DQ**) but not to (**T**).

The degree of understanding specified by (i)–(iii), is sufficient to warrant appeal to (**DQ**). When Pierre says "London is not pretty" and minimally linguistically understands it, he has met all the conditions for application of (**DQ**) as specified by Kripke; likewise, in France when he says *"Londres est jolie, "* use of (**DQ**) is warranted. If Pierre lacked any of (i)–(iii), he would be like a parrot. When our colleague's parrot, Greenbird, says "New York, New York; it's a helluva town," there's no temptation to conclude that Greenbird believes that New York's a helluva town. Likewise, if Pierre had simply learned the sounds "London is not pretty" and repeated them at various times, no matter how appropriate the times, we would not conclude that he believed that London is not pretty.

But as described by Kripke, Pierre is not a parrot, therefore, we can use (**DQ**) to infer "Pierre believes that London is not pretty" and *"Pierre croit que Londres est jolie. "* The next step in generating the puzzle is the application of (**T**) to get (4) "Pierre believes that London is pretty." As plausible as this step seems, we argue that it is not warranted under the conditions of minimal linguistic understanding and minimal bilingualism.

There is an intuitive sense that a "normal speaker" need not understand the sentences she asserts or assents to upon reflection in any especially exalted way. One can, for example, understand "The pot is aluminium" without having the slightest idea of the molecular structure of aluminium or being able to sort the aluminium pots from the molybdenum pots. Minimal linguistic understanding was defined to capture this sense. But it is crucial to distinguish this sense of understanding from a more extended sense of understanding, which includes a wider range of background (and foreground) knowledge. This latter sense, which we may call "integrated language understanding," is what a person must possess in order to be considered a sophisticated or adult member of the *community* of speakers. We use the term "integrated" here to indicate that someone with this level of understanding does indeed integrate language use with all other aspects of her life; she, in short, happily violates the Principle of Insulation. (**DQ**) does not require membership in the community of speakers, but (**T**), as used by Kripke in "A Puzzle About Belief," does.

Integrated language understanding sets a much higher standard than minimal linguistic understanding; indeed, it is a standard that breaks down the barrier between the linguistic and the philosophical encapsulated in the Principle of Insulation. However, it is only when this standard is met that (**T**) can be used in conjunction with (**DQ**) to generate statements about someone's beliefs, and it is these statements that are essential to Kripke's puzzle. But if Pierre has integrated language understanding of both French and English, Kripke's puzzle cannot arise, because Pierre's understanding of his languages now violates the Principle of Insulation.

In order to make this clear, let's look at the example used above, where someone, call her Esther, talks about aluminium pots, but doesn't know much about the chemistry of aluminium or even how to distinguish aluminium from molybdenum. Esther, in addition to talking about aluminium pots, even goes so far as to pick them out in cook shops and distinguish them from copper pots and stainless steel pots. Indeed others may rely on Esther to help them select their new cookware. Why and how is this possible? It is possible only on the condition that Esther's understanding of "This is an aluminium pot" goes beyond minimum linguistic understanding.

It is only in virtue of Esther's being situated in a community of speakers that the statement "This is an aluminium pot" gains any authority in the world. While she cannot tell an aluminium from a molybdenum pot, she knows how to find out which is which; while she doesn't have the criteria for drawing the distinction, she knows that others do and that such criteria exist. Esther is confident that she doesn't have a molybdenum pot in her hand when in the cook store she says, "This is an aluminium pot, but this one's stainless steel," because she knows that cook stores in America and Great Britain don't stock molybdenum pots.

It is this knowledge, along with other things like it, that constitutes the background and foreground knowledge that identifies Esther as a member of the community of speakers of English. In considering Esther's assertions in English we can drop reference to the language because she is a member of the community of English speakers.

But it is crucial to note that someone may have integrated language understanding of one language and only minimal linguistic understanding of another. In such a case, the person would be counted as minimally bilingual. To be bilingual in any stronger sense requires integrated language understanding of both languages. In order to generate the paradox, Kripke also ignores this point.

If (**T**) is to authorise treating a statement in one language, L_1, as entirely equal to a statement in another language, L_2, it must presuppose that the speaker has membership in the community of speakers in both L_1 and L_2. In other words, (**T**) breaks down any distinction between language communities and membership conditions for belonging to them. Put as bluntly as possible, (**T**) allows us to treat statements in all languages on an exact par with each other. It makes no difference if I speak French and only French, statements of my beliefs in French are exactly like statements of my beliefs in English; and whatever holds for the English statements of these beliefs, I believe *that*.

Kripke must treat (**T**) in this way to generate the puzzle. And here's the rub. The stock of background and foreground knowledge that entitles one to membership in a linguistic community is always strong enough to give the speaker a readily available access to the means of correcting mistaken or ill-considered agreement or assertion. Thus, if Pierre is to be credited with believing both that London is pretty and that London is not pretty, it is necessary that Pierre himself be in a position as a speaker of French to know that there is some way of going about associating *"Londres"* with a city in the world, and as a speaker of English to do the same with "London" (although in neither case need he be able to do so himself). And part of what this entails is knowing that cities often have several names (i.e., to be a member of the English community, I must know that there are English names of cities and there are also other names in other languages of these same cities); thus for any one city name, I always hold open the possibility that I may come to learn that what I think about another city name might be true of the first city. But this is a fact about the world and not about language or grammar, and as such violates the Principle of Insulation.

Looked at in another way, we might say that for Kripke there is simply one community of language users, and speaking any language makes one automatically a member of that larger community; from this larger community we can be shuffled off into smaller subsets and be held to the very same standards that the speakers of these specific tongues are held to.

xi. Externalism and Russell's Principle

How does Kripke miss this point? The answer lies in his semantic externalism, but the precise way in which this comes about may be surprising.

In Chapter 4, we discuss Russell's Principle as stated by Gareth Evans in *The Varieties of Reference.*

RP: it is not possible for a person to have a thought about something unless he knows which particular individual in the world he is thinking about.[29]

To use a referring expression, the speaker must be in contact with the referent. Semantic internalist accounts of names have the contact occur internally through the mind of the speaker via the description associated with the name. In "Naming and Necessity," Kripke argues that the referent of a name is fixed externally. However, rather than entailing a rejection of Russell's Principle, this merely moves the contact between the speaker and the named object *outside* the speaker's mind, placing it entirely in the world. For Kripke, then, if English-Pierre and French-Pierre both understand sentences using "London" and *"Londres"* (respectively), it is because they are in some sense in contact with the named city (i.e., London). This entails that English-Pierre and French-Pierre are making remarks about *the same* subject matter. Thus, it is only on the assumption of Russell's Principle that we can suppose Pierre to have contradictory beliefs.[30]

The arguments of this book show that adherence to Russell's Principle is not a condition of linguistic understanding, one can understand sentences involving referring expressions without being in contact with the referents. All that is required is to have linguistic understanding of the use$_E$ of the expression in a language. Such minimal linguistic understanding allows access to the referents of the expressions, but this access is entirely nominal. This does indeed reject Russell's Principle. The only contact between the speaker and the object is indirect, running through the use$_E$ of a referring expression.

15

Paradox and Substitutivity[1]

But is *language* the *only* language? Why should there not be a mode of expression through which I can talk *about* language in such a way that it can appear to me in co-ordination with something else?

Ludwig Wittgenstein[2]

i. Kripke's cautionary lessons

In Chapter 14 we showed that, in "A Puzzle About Belief,"[3] Saul Kripke relies on antecedent commitments to Russell's Principle and Referential Realism, which lead him to embrace a notion of linguistic competence that is both incompatible with the alleged paradox and with ordinary practice. In this chapter we show that the roots of these commitments run deep, so deep that Kripke's Referential Realism would, if successful, allow him to sustain his Millian view of meaning and reference, along with the version of *de re* essentialism in *Naming and Necessity*. We argue here that these conclusions are unwarranted: neither Millianism nor *de re* essentialism are defensible. However, as our earlier arguments show, and as will be more fully spelled out in the Epilogue, this does not result in an abandonment of Realism.

Kripke's paper ends with a cautionary conclusion.

When we enter into the area exemplified by Jones and Pierre, we enter into an area where our normal practices of interpretation and attribution of belief are subjected to the greatest possible strain, perhaps to the point of breakdown. So is the notion of the *content* of someone's assertion, the *proposition* it expresses. In the present state of our knowledge, I think it would be foolish to draw any conclusions, positive or negative, about substitutivity.[4]

And, in our *present* state of clarity about the problem, we are in no position to apply a disquotation principle to these cases, nor to judge when two such sentences do, or do not, express the same "proposition."[5]

There is even less warrant at the present time, in the absence of a better understanding of the paradoxes of this paper, for the use of alleged failures of substitutivity in belief contexts to draw any significant theoretical conclusion about proper names. Hard cases make bad law.[6]

This cautionary stance leaves open the possibility that the solution to the pertinent problems in the philosophy of language – including the meaning and reference of names, general terms and sentences/assertions, as well as the notions of propositions and propositional content – might in the end produce results that diverge sharply from Kripke's own Millian views.

Among these alternatives is the view advanced in this book. It might seem that to the extent Kripke's arguments go against Frege-Russell and Millian theories of meaning, we should be sympathetic to them. However, as we have argued in Chapter 14, the paradox Kripke uses to support his claims is unfounded and does not present a challenge to any view of meaning or reference. The account of the present book provides an answer to the question "Does Pierre, or does he not, believe that London is pretty?," which shows that there is no paradox. Our criticisms of Frege-Russell and Millian views lie elsewhere; Kripke's puzzle only confuses matters in ways that betray the underlying mistakes in Referential Realism as they affect philosophical understanding of belief and other propositional attitudes. For this reason it is worth exploring them in greater depth.

ii. Substitutivity of identicals

One of Kripke's aims is to show that certain well-known problems attending the substitution of codesignative terms within belief contexts do not favour internalist theories of names over externalist theories. Kripke argues that the paradox cuts as deeply against the internalist as the externalist. The source of these problems is rooted in something beyond the particular theory of names one happens to advocate.

The criticism has traditionally taken the following form. According to a Millian view of names, substitutivity *salva veritate* – indeed, *salva significatione* – must hold in all contexts. Because "Cicero" and "Tully" are names of one man, from "Jones believes that Cicero is bald" it follows that "Jones believes that Tully is bald." This leads to problems if, for example, Jones is unaware that "Cicero" and "Tully" name the same man. In this case, she might even go so far as to hold that "Tully is *not* bald" is true. Further, in a case where Jones maintains that Cicero is *not* Tully, we seem committed to claiming that Jones denies the obvious truth that Cicero is self-identical.

The Millian has, it is argued, no way out of this conundrum. An adherent of a Frege-Russellian view, by contrast, does: the apparent anomalies simply reflect the distinction between the descriptions associated with the two names, or the mode of presentation of the referents.

Kripke proposes undermining this attack on Millian theorists by constructing a version of the puzzle that does not appeal to any principle of substitutivity of codesignative terms. On his account, the paradoxical results have a source independent of the principle of substitutivity of codesignative terms. In the end, he advises us to refrain from making any judgment about the appropriateness of appeals to substitutivity in belief contexts, the actual content of anyone's beliefs in Jones/Pierre cases, principles of disquotation, and indeed the very notion of the content of someone's belief or the proposition believed.

This advice may be justified, but we argue that Kripke's puzzle does not provide any evidence for it. We argue that the very construction of the example commits Kripke to a view of propositions strong enough to block the construction of the puzzle. Furthermore, that view of propositions is connected to Kripke's view of names as presented in *Naming and Necessity*, and to the strong version of *de re* essentialism that this view entails. Once again, we show that it is Referential Realism which creates the difficulties here.

In Kripke's version, Realism can be salvaged only at a high cost: not only does meaning depend on the world, but the world itself turns out to be made of objects having *de re* essences that fix the meanings of words in language. This does have a certain appeal, and if true it might provide all the connection between language and world anyone could ever want as a means of ensuring the accessibility to language users of an independent reality. A world consisting of objects with such *de re* essences and in which meanings were completely determined by the world, would be one in which Relativism could gain no foothold. But, not only is this vision unreal, it is, in fact, not necessary to preserve Realism from the attacks of Relativism.

iii. Kripke's constraints on the construction of the puzzle

To maintain that the paradox is not simply a variant of the puzzles arising from attempts to substitute codesignative terms within belief contexts, Kripke must impose certain constraints on its construction. The significance of Kripke's paradox lies in its alleged support for the claim that proper names are subject to paradoxical behaviour within belief contexts quite independently of any attempt to employ a principle of substitutivity.

. . . I shall present – and this will form the core of the present paper – an argument for a paradox about names in belief contexts that invokes *no* principle of substitutivity. Instead it will be based on the principles – apparently so obvious that their use in these arguments is ordinarily tacit – of disquotation and translation.[7]

If correct, this shows that seemingly unremarkable and unquestioned practices – disquotation and translation – are somehow suspect, and that even without substitution of codesignative terms, names behave in unexpected ways within contexts of belief and, presumably, other propositional attitudes. It calls into question our conception of what language can and cannot be used to do.

Since so much turns on this strategy, Kripke describes it at some length.

The usual use of Jones's case [where Jones believes both that Cicero is bald and that Tully is not bald, and where he uses both names in their normal senses] as a counterexample to the substitutivity principle is thus, I think, somewhat analogous to the following sort of procedure. Someone wishes to give a *reductio ad absurdum* argument against a hypothesis in topology. He does succeed in refuting this hypothesis, but his derivation of an absurdity from the hypothesis makes essential use of the unrestricted comprehension schema in set theory, which he regards as self-evident . . . Once we know that the unrestricted comprehension schema and the Russell class lead to contradiction by themselves, it is clear that it was an error to blame the earlier contradiction on the topological hypothesis.

The situation would have been the same if, after deducing a contradiction from the topological hypothesis plus the "obvious" unrestricted comprehension schema, it was found that a similar contradiction followed if we replaced the topological hypothesis by an apparently "obvious" premise. In both cases it would be clear that, even though we may still not be confident of any specific flaw in the argument against the topological hypothesis, blaming the contradiction on that hypothesis is illegitimate: rather we are in a "paradoxical" area where it is unclear *what* has gone wrong.

It is my suggestion, then, that the situation with respect to the interchangeability of codesignative names is similar. True, such a principle, when combined with our normal disquotational judgments of belief, leads to straightforward absurdities. But we will see that the "same" absurdities can be derived by replacing the interchangeability principle by our normal practices of translation and disquotation, or even by disquotation alone.[8]

This passage provides a clear statement of Kripke's first constraint.

(C1) There can be no appeal, either explicit or implicit, to a principle of substitutivity of codesignative terms.

The second is introduced on pages 260–2, in which Kripke maintains that the puzzle is not dependent on any particular theory of the meaning of names; it is a puzzle about "the behavior of names in belief contexts" that cuts across all theories of names. Thus, the puzzle must be consistent with Kripke's own externalism, but not simply be a feature or consequence of that externalism.

(C2) The puzzle must be consistent with an externalist theory of meaning of the sort Kripke defends in *Naming and Necessity*,[9] but not be a feature of this externalism itself.[10]

Finally, the puzzle must be *paradoxical* in a philosophically significant way. Many things in life that are puzzling (e.g., why otherwise intelligent people continue to enter sweepstakes despite an extensive understanding of probability); however, none of these rises to the level of philosophical interest because they contain no paradox.

A philosophical paradox is, at the very least, one that calls into question certain widely accepted assumptions; in order to resolve such a paradox, one must reconceive these assumptions. Genuine philosophical paradoxes show something adrift at the level of our theories and fundamental understanding of how things are.[11] Perhaps Kripke comes closest to describing a philosophical paradox in the final section of his paper, where he says that his paradoxes preclude our drawing "any significant theoretical conclusion about proper names."[12]

(C3) The puzzle must constitute a philosophical paradox.

We argue that it is not possible for Kripke to satisfy (C1)–(C3) conjointly. We first show that to meet (C1) Kripke must constrain our "normal practices" of translation and disquotation to ensure that they do not implicitly rely on or include a principle of substitutivity. While it is possible to do this, once the necessary constraints are in place, the case no longer yields a paradox.

Finally, we argue that contrary to what he claims, the "paradox" is in fact entailed by Kripke's externalism, a violation of (C2). Rather than providing a paradox about the behaviour of names in belief contexts, the puzzle at most presents a difficulty for a certain type of externalist theory of names, and is not equally destructive of Frege-Russellian theories.

iv. "Normal practices of translation and disquotation"

Before confronting Kripke's arguments directly, it is perhaps worth restating the two principles that Kripke describes as our "normal practices of translation and disquotation."

> Translation (**T**): If a sentence of one language expresses a truth in that language, then any translation of it into any other language also expresses a truth (in that other language).
>
> Disquotation (**DQ**): If a normal English speaker, on reflection, sincerely assents to "p" then he believes that p (where "p" is replaced by a standard English sentence in both instances).[13]

v. How to avoid substitutivity: **DQ**

To satisfy (C1), (**T**) and (**DQ**) must explicitly outlaw all appeals to substitutivity. To this end, we define paradigmatic senses of these principles, that is, senses which are entirely free of any appeal to substitutivity.

In an older terminology, what Kripke is trying to accomplish with (**DQ**) is analogous to the move from direct quotation to *oratio obliqua*.

> *Oratio Obliqua* (**OO**): It is permissible to move from a sentence, Sq, of the form "A says 's'," to a sentence, Si, of the form "A says that s."

Let's introduce a variant of (**DQ**) in this spirit.

(**DQO**): It is permissible to move from a sentence, Sq, of the form "A asserts/assents to 's'," to a sentence, Sb, of the form "A believes that s."

An unstated, but significant, *proviso* of both (**OO**) and (**DQO**) is that all the sentences be in the same language.

Using the French analogue of (**DQO**), Kripke's reasoning can be reconstructed as follows.

(a) *Pierre donne son assentiment à "Londres est joli."* (by hypothesis)
(b) *Pierre croit que Londres est jolie.* (from (a) by (**DQO**))
(c) Pierre believes that London is pretty. (from (b) by (**T**))

This again takes us from what Pierre assents to in French to a statement that conveys Pierre's beliefs to an English-speaking audience. The rest of the puzzle proceeds as before, with (**DQO**) in place of (**DQ**).

vi. How to avoid substitutivity: **T**

Appeal to (**T**) outside belief contexts, such as the move from

(1) *Londres est jolie*

to

(4) London is pretty,

works well to set the standard for the paradigmatic sense of (**T**). If (1) is true, so is (4), and vice versa; no one is likely to contest (4)'s status as an English translation of (1). This, and this alone, is what (**T**) authorizes.

In a reasonably straightforward sense,

(3) Pierre believes that London is pretty

is a translation of

(2) *Pierre croit que Londres est jolie.*

It is, however, essential to understand that (**T**) is simply a principle that ensures the transitivity of truth value across translations taken as a whole. This means that (**T**) can be applied only to *complete sentences as translated.* Nothing Kripke writes goes counter to this. Thus, from the truth of (2), we can infer the truth of (3), but not the truth of (4), even though (4) is contained within (3), and even though (4) is a translation of (1), which occupies in (2) exactly the same place (4) has in (3).

vii. Paradigmatic roots of **DQO**

To find a paradigmatic use of (**DQO**) (and thus (**DQ**)) it is easiest to look for a sense in which the fact that it derives statements of belief attribution is entirely free of any illicit appeal to substitutivity. The access to the principle of *oratio obliqua* (**OO**) afforded by (**DQO**) makes this reasonably straightforward.

Simply put, (**OO**) is a principle that allows us to move from direct quotation to indirect quotation by removing the quotation marks from a sentence sincerely assented to. This is uncontroversial provided one has the sentence right in the first place. It becomes problematic if one tries to paraphrase, but as this is a thinly disguised appeal to substitutivity, it is ruled out by (**C1**).

Thus, from

(i)   Jones said "London is pretty,"

to

(ii)   Jones said that London is pretty

is a valid inference by (**OO**). However, from (i) to

(iii)   Jones said that the financial capital of Europe is pretty

is not. Whereas Jones may say that London is pretty, and whereas he may even believe that London is the financial capital of Europe, as the leader of a German political party that has as the central plank in its platform the contention that Frankfurt is the financial capital of Europe, he cannot be supposed to assent to (iii), nor, by (**OO**) does he. In such cases, the *specific words* do count.

The problem in the inference to (iii) arises from an implicit attempt to use substitutivity. By hypothesis, London is the financial capital of Europe; therefore, it would seem that "London" and "the financial capital of Europe" can be exchanged *salva veritate*. Regardless of the virtues of such reasoning, it has the unfortunate effect of rendering the inference from (i) to (iii) a *nonparadigmatic* use of (**OO**), and thus unsuitable for Kripke's purposes.

There is an analogous sense of (**DQO**). If (**DQO**) is restricted to a simple "stripping-away" of quotation marks, the fact that the statement being inferred is a belief attribution poses no problem for (**C1**). Thus, from

(iv)   Jones assents to "London is pretty,"

we can infer

(v)   Jones believes that London is pretty,

but not

(vi)   Jones believes that the financial capital of Europe is pretty.

The moral of all this is that a principle of disquotation can only avoid appeal or commitment to substitutivity by remaining true to (**OO**)'s initial function of the simple "stripping-away" of quotation marks, which means that the sentences embedded in the belief context must remain unaltered.

viii. The puzzle restated and **DQO** recast

With these appropriately qualified principles of translation and disquotation, we turn again to the statement of the puzzle itself.

(A) *Pierre donne son assentiment à "Londres est jolie"* (by hypothesis)
(B) *Pierre croit que Londres est jolie.* ((A) by (**DQO**))
(C) Pierre believes that London is pretty. ((B) by (**T**))

The puzzle then follows as presented by Kripke.

(D) Pierre assents to "London is not pretty." (by hypothesis)
(E) Pierre believes that London is not pretty. ((D) by **DQO**)

Thus, we are once again confronted with the question that Kripke takes to embody the paradox, "Does Pierre, or does he not, believe that London is pretty?"

Taken singly, none of the steps in the generation of the puzzle seems problematic. However, while substitutivity is never explicitly used, in the step from (B) to (C), the reasoning itself seems to embody some violation of the principle that (**DQO**) not alter the embedded sentence. If an alteration were to have occurred, this would violate (C1), and the example could not be used to generate Kripke's paradox. As interesting as it might be on its own, it would be just another illustration of the failure of substitutivity in belief contexts.

The immediate response to this challenge is to say that the "alteration" of *"Londres est jolie"* in the step from (B) to (C) is not introduced by (**DQO**), but by (**T**). (**T**), as a principle of *translation*, cannot be required to avoid alteration: by its very nature, translation alters sentences. The question that should be asked is whether (**T**) can justify the inference from (A) to (C) via (B), without any appeal to substitutivity of the sort Kripke eschews.

The answer seems clearly to be that it can. There is no problem of substitutivity with (**T**) as used here. Kripke's appeal to (**T**) can hardly be faulted as extravagant or in any danger of leading anyone to suppose that Pierre believes anything as esoteric as that London has a high degree of pulchritude or, worse yet, that the city where one of the authors spent Thanksgiving in 1994 is pretty.

However, when (**T**) is used conjointly with (**DQO**), genuine problems involving substitutivity might arise. If left unaddressed, these could lead to illegitimate appeals to substitutivity that would undermine Kripke's line of argument. We propose, therefore, to address this by modifying (**DQO**) to allow sentence alteration of the sort that occurs in straightforward, and generally unimaginative, translations between languages that are reasonably close linguistically and that have well-established translation manuals.[14]

(**DQO**$_E$): It is permissible to move from a sentence, Sq, of the form "A asserts/assents to 's'," to a sentence, Sb, of the form "A believes that s."

In case one wishes to apply a principle of translation such as (**T**) to Sb, one may do so provided that the two languages are reasonably close linguistically and have well-established translation manuals between them, and that the translation of "s" is as literal as possible.

On this understanding, the mere fact that (A) and (B) are in French, and (C) is in English, does not disqualify the use of disquotation. Replacing the appeals to (**DQO**) with (**DQO**$_E$) in (A)–(E) above, we can restate the puzzle without even the appearance of any illegitimate appeal to substitutivity.

ix. The puzzle as a paradox

We now have a statement of the puzzle that does not rest upon any appeal to the principle of substitutivity of codesignative terms. But, even in this form, the puzzle appears to have philosophical bite only because Kripke is committed to the view that understanding, belief, and other propositional attitudes are not exercised about *words* but, rather, about what the words pick out, with no attention to the language used by the subject. That is to say, Kripke presupposes a Millian interpretation of names and sentences. This makes it seem possible to consider the sentences embedded in (C) and (E) separate from the larger context of their occurrence, and, thus, to compare them directly with one another.[15]

This puzzle is about Pierre's beliefs and our ability to make statements about these beliefs. For Kripke the puzzle is expressed by the question "Does Pierre, or does he not, believe that London is pretty?" It does not involve any claim about whether Pierre's individual beliefs are true or false; instead it concerns itself only with the logical connections between these beliefs. For this, we must have access to and be able to make claims – statements that are either true or false – about what it is that Pierre does, or doesn't, believe.

This point cannot be overemphasised. While Kripke maintains that he will restrict his discussion to a *de dicto* reading of belief contexts, in the construction of his puzzle, it is not clear that he succeeds. Indeed he seems to violate the condition stated on pages 241–2.

Of course there is a *de re* or "large scope" reading under which the second sentence ["It is necessary that Jones's favorite number is even"] is true. Such a reading would be expressed more accurately by "Jones's favorite number is such that it is necessarily even" . . . Such a *de re* reading, if it makes sense at all, by definition must be subject to a principle of substitutivity *salva veritate*, since necessary evenness is a property of the *number*, independently of how it is designated; in this respect there can be no contrast between names and descriptions. The contrast, according to the Millian view, must come in the *de dicto* or "small scope" reading, which is the *only* reading, for belief contexts as well as modal contexts, that will concern us in this paper.

But, Kripke's very way of posing the puzzle in the form of a question about what Pierre believes about a city, and his claim that in expressing Pierre's beliefs we are talking about what Pierre believes about London (the city), not about its name, be it "London" or *"Londres,"* indicate that he remains interested in the *de re* reading. Indeed, this reading seems to be deeply implicated by our "ordinary" practices in understanding each other when we express our beliefs.

Kripke has hit on one quite ordinary sense in which we speak of ourselves as understanding what our beliefs are about. When asked whether Pierre believes that London is pretty, there is a sense in which we take ourselves to be asking how Pierre stands in relationship to a city, London. It is, however, a mistake to imagine this as a direct relationship between Pierre and London. As we have argued, any such relationship is mediated through the Name-Tracking Network associated with the name. To be in a position to access this Network doesn't depend on knowing or believing anything about London. Thus, any alleged "paradox" arising from asking what Pierre believes about London provides no basis for drawing conclusions about meaning.

What Kripke would have us consider in the construction of the paradox is our apparent ability to strip sentences out of belief contexts in order to examine them to ascertain the content of the speaker's belief, independently of how she might express her belief. On this interpretation, belief functions as a two-place nontruth functional operator that takes a person, P, and a sentence, S, as its arguments, B(P,S). Although we cannot infer the truth of S from the truth of "B(P,S)," we can examine S on its own to see *what exactly it is that* P *believes*. Thus, we take *"Londres est jolie"* and "London is pretty" to represent what Pierre's believes.

When Kripke invokes (**T**) to justify the move from (2) to (3), it is important to realise that this entails our viewing the embedded sentences (*"Londres est jolie"* and "London is pretty") as coequal descriptions of Pierre's belief. This makes (**T**) a very important principle indeed. But it is only (3) *taken as a whole* whose truth is guaranteed by (2). "Stripping-away" the belief operator to reveal Pierre's *belief* means that we need a principle of translation that guarantees preservation of the *content* of the belief, that is, the content of the embedded sentence, S. For the paradox, we must be able to make claims about S as expressing Pierre's beliefs, regardless of the language in which S is expressed.

x. Meaning

There is a straightforward sense in which (1) *"Londres est jolie"* means (4) "London is pretty;" it is just that (4) translates (1). This sense of "meaning" is, however, essentially indexed to a particular language. In the case at hand, (1) gives the *French-meaning* of (4), and (4) gives the *English-meaning* of (1). It is precisely *and only* this that can be at issue in (**T**).

When dealing with (2) *"Pierre croit que Londres est jolie"* and (3) "Pierre believes that London is pretty," this entails that (3) is the *English translation* of (2), nothing more. Kripke's puzzle, however, depends on its being more. For the paradox, Kripke needs to maintain that (3) gives an English-speaking audience access to the content of French-speaking Pierre's belief.

This requires him to assume a connection between (2) and (3), which is closer than anything authorised by the ordinary sort of translation that preserves truth value. Kripke must assume that (3) captures the meaning of (2), and vice versa; but, more importantly, that both equally capture the content of Pierre's beliefs. This in turn entails that (1) and (4), the sentences embedded in (2) and (3), each equally captures the *content* of Pierre's belief. And it is precisely here that being able to consider the embedded sentences on their own enters into the generation of the puzzle.

There are four different possibilities.

(P1) (1) and (4) represent Pierre's beliefs.
(P2) (1) and (4) translate each other.
(P3) (1) gives the French-meaning of (4), and (4) the English-meaning of (1).
(P4) If (1) is true, then (4) is true (and the reverse).

Generation of the paradox requires (P1). However, all (**T**) can give us access to are (P2)–(P4). For (P1), we need another principle.

TB: If s_1 is a translation of s_2, and if s_1 conveys the content of a belief held by speaker P of L_1, then s_2 conveys the content of P's belief in L_2.

This is a much stronger principle than (**T**), and it requires further justification. An answer to the following question would provide this.

(Q1) What does (1)/(4) mean *simpliciter?*

Telling someone what (1) means in another language is not an answer.[16]

The notion of meaning in the paradox at the point where (**T**) is invoked can be used to answer

(Q2) What does (2) mean in English (or Urdu or Mandarin or Italian)?;

but it cannot be used to answer

(Q3) What exactly, and independently of any particular language, does Pierre believe?

Another way of putting (Q3) is to ask: Why is it that (1) and (4) can stand in the relationship that they do *vis-à-vis* one another in their respective languages? In other words, why is (1) a French-translation of (4)?

To construct his paradox, Kripke requires that we be able to answer (Q3), that we can connect (2) and (3) in such a way that a monolingual English speaker, for example, gains direct access to what Pierre believes. And for this, that is, the answer to (Q3), we need to answer (Q1) *not* (Q2). (Q3) requires more than the sense of meaning implicated in (**T**), it requires the further claim that the sentences that stand as translations between languages are linked by something they share. In other words, if (1) and (4) equally represent Pierre's belief, they must have something in common.

But all this may seem too quick. In a spirit more sympathetic to Kripke's argument, one might say that (1) and (4) do have something in common: they just mean the same thing. Hence, (**T**) has already settled the issue; all the talk about (Q1)–(Q3) is beside the point. Unfortunately, this won't do. (**T**) only authorises appeal to a sense of meaning which is essentially indexed to a particular language. The claim that (1) gives the meaning of (4) must be read as

(M1) (1) is (gives) the (a) *French-meaning* of (4),

and this doesn't provide the shared element required for the puzzle. Instead, the puzzle requires something like the following.

(M2) *m* is the *meaning* of (4).

However, even to state (M2) requires a vehicle to serve as a language-neutral expression of meaning. Armed with this, we could go on to state that since *m* is the meaning of both (1) and (4), (1) and (4) equally express the content of Pierre's belief. None of this, however, is authorised by (**T**). It would be authorised by (**TB**), but absent the language-independent *m* we cannot justify any appeal to (**TB**), and, hence, cannot generate the paradox.

xi. Translation as based on propositional content

There are two considerations to be dealt with here. First, Kripke requires access to Pierre's beliefs in order to generate his paradox. Second, he needs this access to be free of all necessity of indexing Pierre's beliefs to the particular language in which Pierre happens to express them. In other words, we need to gain access to the content of Pierre's beliefs in some completely language-neutral fashion.

One way of doing this is to appeal to propositions, senses, thoughts in the role of *m*. If Pierre assents to a sentence, S, we infer that he believes that S. S, by hypothesis, means *m*; therefore, Pierre believes that *m*. It does not matter whether Pierre expresses *m* in French or Urdu or English or Italian, the belief is *m*, period. What Pierre believes is the same regardless of whether he or we express it in English or in French. On this understanding, as statements of the content of Pierre's belief, (1) and (4) are on all fours.

Kripke assumes that two features of our ordinary way of talking are true: first, that it makes sense to talk of different sentences (including sentences in different languages) as having exactly the same content in the sense that the content of the different sentences is literally the same; and second, that it is possible to identify and access this content independently of any particular language – in fact that this is not only possible, but that it is done routinely. We might say that this is what, on Kripke's account, serves to get us out of the Prison-House of Language: language, by giving us direct access to the nonlinguistic, is the key to defeating the scepticism and Relativism that are the primary targets of Referential Realism. The term "proposition" designates whatever it is that enables us to talk about an independent world and, in the case at hand, to access the content of our beliefs about that world.

A proposition, it is true, cannot be accessed without using a specific language, but once accessed, we are no longer dealing with a piece of language. While it makes sense to ask for the "English meaning of '*Fa fresco oggi*'," it makes no sense to ask for the "English proposition expressed by '*Fa fresco oggi*.'" Traditionally, the introduction of propositions has been viewed as a means of avoiding having to manoeuvre between languages; they are supposed to get us outside specific languages. On such a view, what secures the translation relationship between (1) and (4) is the fact that they are both associated with the same proposition.

One might try to avoid this move by returning to (**T**). (**T**) does not concern translation *per se*, it only says that if two sentences, s_1 and s_2, stand as translations of each other, and if s_1 is true in its language, L_1, then s_2 is true in its language, L_2. By itself, however, this is not enough. It is, after all, patently unconvincing to say that all sentences with the value true in L_2 are translations of all sentences with the value true in L_1, and nowhere does Kripke suggest this.

It is only when we are able to restrict the range of true sentences when applying (**T**) that it can generate the puzzle. Thus, if in our application of (**T**), we are actually appealing to the propositions associated with (2) and (3), then the test of truth value is more convincing. (2) is true because the proposition, p_1, with which it is associated is true; (3)'s truth derives from the truth of its proposition, p_2. As it turns out, however, p_1 and p_2 are one and the same proposition; therefore, both (2) and (3) *derive* their truth values from that same proposition. This is the identity that connects (2) and (3), and justifies our claim that they are translations of each other. It is this apparent connection between (2) and (3) that gives the puzzle its *prima facie* plausibility or, to be more accurate, that gives the puzzle its *prima facie* paradoxicality. It does this as follows.

If Belief is an operator applied to two arguments, then the sentences "*Pierre croit que* (1)" and "Pierre believes that (4)," can be represented as "B(P,(1))" and "B(P,(4))." Now we know that these express the same proposition; therefore, the content of the sentences "believed," (1) and (4), must be identical as they express the same proposition. This, in turn, justifies (**T$_B$**).

So it looks as though the paradox remains. With an understanding that in the contexts at issue here translation rests on an identity of propositional content, ($\mathbf{T_B}$) and ($\mathbf{DQO_E}$) seem to yield an appropriately paradoxical puzzle.

There is one further qualification on this line of reasoning. It may, on the one hand, seem to run the risk of introducing substitutivity, and perhaps if analysed more carefully, it does. On the other hand, it seems reasonable to hold that all talk of substitution is irrelevant once we have access to propositions. Since they are not themselves pieces of language, when dealing with propositions, we do not, properly speaking, have codesignative items, as we do with, say, "Cicero" and "Tully." In the latter case, after we discover the identity of Cicero with Tully, the separate words still remain; in the case of propositions, on the other hand, once the identity is uncovered, there is only *one* proposition. Any talk of what initially seemed to be two propositions is now, at the very least, misleading.[17]

For the purposes of our argument, we assume that an appeal to propositions does not violate (C1). We now show that while propositions give ($\mathbf{T_B}$) the force it needs to yield the puzzle, in the end, they subvert the resulting paradox by violating (C3), as they render the paradox philosophically uninteresting. Furthermore, this appeal to propositions uncovers Kripke's commitment to externalism in his construction of the puzzle, a violation of (C2).

xii. Externalism unmasked

Assuming access to propositions, the puzzle arises as follows. When in France, Pierre assents to

(1) *Londres est jolie.*

This entails that Pierre has a belief that is associated with a particular proposition, P. Later, in London, he assents to

(5) London is not pretty.

This belief is associated with a particular proposition, Q. As it happens, Q is related to P in virtue of its being equivalent to ~P. Thus, without taking a position on whether Pierre's beliefs are true or false, we are able to see that the set of beliefs contains two individual members which, when taken together, are contradictory. We cannot, therefore, answer the question "Does Pierre, or does he not, believe the London is pretty?" This construction of the puzzle involves no appeal to substitutivity, that is, it satisfies (C1).

The promise of this construction of the puzzle is short-lived: it is not paradoxical, it's merely one of life's little puzzles. But, we are now in a position to see why this is so, and to uncover the source of the problems with conjointly satisfying (C1)–(C3).

If there were such things as propositions accessible independently of any linguistic expression of them, we could use them to gain accurate access to Pierre's belief when he assents to (1) or (5). But, if we can access the propositions connected with these sentences and see the relationship between them, so, too, can Pierre. The plausibility of Kripke's puzzle rests on an assumption that Pierre assents to (1) because of the proposition that it is associated with; it is this proposition that allows Kripke to link (2) and (3) via translation. In turn, it is the relationship between the propositions associated with (4) and (5) that allows him to link (3) and

(6) Pierre believes that London is not pretty

with paradoxical results for Pierre's belief set. The same holds for assent: Pierre would not assent to (1) except that it is associated with a particular proposition; so, too, for (5). It is only at the level of propositions that the paradox concerning Pierre's beliefs emerges.

But at this level, the paradox evaporates. All that remains of it is the fact that, for whatever reason, Pierre hasn't yet come to see that the propositions associated with (1) and (5) are related in the same way that the proposition connected to

(3) London is pretty

is related to (5), viz. that they are contradictory.

Most people who speak both French and English would feel some sense of discomfort in connection with holding both (1) and (5); however, there is nothing paradoxical about failing to do so. Kripke's puzzle shows us how someone might end up in such a situation. If one just fails, for whatever reason, to see that London is *Londres*, or that the capital of England is *la capitale d'Angleterre* or that St. James Park is *le jardin de St. Jacques* or any of a number of other similar "facts," one might easily be in Pierre's situation. That Pierre fails to feel this any discomfort with respect to this particular combination of beliefs points to a contingent, and eliminable, gap in his awareness of the relationships between his beliefs. It is a failure of Pierre's knowledge of the world, not of his understanding of language.

There are all sorts of reasons he may fail to feel any disconnection between his utterances. Perhaps Pierre actually doesn't understand one or the other of his utterances (e.g., he is merely parroting sounds he has heard) or that he just hasn't discovered Q's equivalence to $\sim$P. Much as one might wish that we all saw all the connections between everything to which we assent, the fact of the matter is that often we do not. Whatever the reasons – self-deception, inattention, failure of will, or ideological biases – such lapses are too common to be remarkable.

This "failure" on Pierre's part may well point to issues relevant to belief maintenance and Pierre's personal history, but, by itself, it tells us nothing about the nature of belief or belief reporting. More to the point, it is not a philosophically significant puzzle; in fact, it tells us nothing about language or meaning, or the behaviour of names in belief contexts apart from Kripke's externalist theory of meaning. It is only when, captured by a picture, we impose a theory's constraints on what actually goes on in language (and, for that matter, the world) that we are tempted to find mystery and paradox. The correct conclusion is to examine the theory, not to insist on the mystery and paradox.

What Kripke may have shown us is that as *observers*, rather than as believers, we have difficulty in ascertaining what someone believes. Pierre, after all, is not bothered by the alleged contradiction; he would respond to the question "Do you, or do you not, believe that London is pretty?" that he does not believe it is pretty, with no difficulty at all; similarly he would answer the question "*Croyez-vous, ou non, que Londres est jolie?*" affirmatively with no difficulty. If this is so, it seems that the puzzle is a version of the thesis of underdetermination of theory by data or of some form of other-minds scepticism. We, the observers, are not able to answer the question because of some problem with our data, though oddly enough in this case, it's because we have too much data; it is not, on this reading, an argument for meaning-scepticism.

In *Fact and Meaning*,[18] Jane Heal gives a fascinating analysis of meaning which takes as its starting point Wittgenstein's remarks at *Philosophical Investigations*, Part II, page 224.

I can be as *certain* of someone else's sensations as of any fact. But this does not make the propositions "He is much depressed", "$25 \times 25 = 625$" and "I am sixty years old" into similar instruments. The explanation suggests itself that the certainty is of a different *kind*. – This seems to point to a psychological difference. But the difference is logical.

"But if you are *certain*, isn't it that you are shutting your eyes in face of doubt?" – They are shut.

Heal uses this remark is to argue that to vindicate "realism about meaning" it is not necessary to answer the sceptic by showing that meaning ascriptions can "fit together in only one way."[19] Instead, to avoid scepticism, "all we have to do is keep our eyes shut, to ignore the possibility of alternative interpretation which the sceptic thrusts at us. And we are not to be criticized for so doing."[20]

Although she is not taking on Kripke's arguments, Heal's insight can be extended to them. In constructing his paradox, Kripke allows Pierre to do something analogous to "shutting his eyes," while preventing our doing so. Pierre can ignore his French-condition while in his English-condition, and thus avoid the contradiction Kripke alleges to hold between *"Londres est jolie"* and "London is not pretty"; we, however, cannot. But why can Pierre ignore his French past, while we cannot? Kripke gives us no answer, and thus fails to produce a puzzle that satisfies (C3); it is not, therefore, a philosophically significant paradox. We now turn to (C2) and show that the appearance of paradox derives from Kripke's particular version of externalism and his commitment to Referential Realism.

xiii. The root of the problem

Kripke assumes that what Pierre believes or thinks about is not just a sentence; Pierre's beliefs are about something other than the words in which he expresses them. In the case of proper names, especially names of people, this works tolerably well, and it is effective when used to argue against the Description Theory of names. Pierre is not talking or thinking about "the teacher of Alexander" when he uses the name "Aristotle," he's talking or thinking about *Aristotle*, the philosopher, the man.

In *Naming and Necessity*, Kripke argues that when I talk about Richard Feynman, I'm not giving you information about my mental state, or whatever description I associate with the name "Richard Feynman," I'm talking about the man, *Richard Feynman*. Even if I do not know who he is and I cannot pick him out or distinguish him from Murray Gell-Mann, I am still talking about and giving you information about *Richard Feynman*, not *Murray Gell-Mann*.

Although this sort of argument was effective in the context of *Naming and Necessity* it isn't here; in fact it contributes to a *petitio* and violates Kripke's avowed restriction of interest to *de dicto* readings of belief attribution. Here Kripke isn't concerned with what the audience takes a use of a name to mean or designate or how it comes to designate this rather than that particular individual, as he did in *Naming and Necessity* instead he is concerned with the *beliefs held by the subject*, beliefs expressed by means of such sentences as

(1) *Londres est jolie,*
(4) London is pretty, and
(5) London is not pretty.

In Chapter 12, we discuss Kripke's version of *de re* essentialism and argue that it is implicated in externalism, as his arguments in *Naming and Necessity* show. More surprisingly perhaps, it also affects the arguments now under consideration. Its influence is seen in Kripke's interpretation of statements of belief (whether made by the subject or her audience) as statements about real, rather than about nomothetic entities. Without denying that some statements are about things external to the speaker, as we have shown in this book, from the analysis of meaning alone, one is only entitled to infer attributions concerning nomothetic entities In effect, the substitution of the real for the nomothetic violates Kripke's claim that in constructing the paradox he does not give a *de re* reading to statements of attributing belief.

By contrast, our arguments in Part II entail that Pierre's beliefs are mediated by a specific language. In the case at hand, it would be more accurate to say that what he believes is that *Londres* is the city that French speakers call *"Londres."* However, even this is somewhat misleading. The full account of what's going on is that Pierre has beliefs *about whatever is picked out in response to the name "Londres" by the French Name-Tracking Network*, in short, Pierre only needs to understand the use$_E$. This, as we have already seen entails that any belief about, *Londres* is to be analysed along these lines: "that place that French speakers call *'Londres'* is xyz." Thus, contrary to Kripke's claims and his externalist assumptions, reference to the French language is not dispensable.

It is entirely possible that Pierre is so ignorant that he has no idea that the English Name-Tracking Network for "London" and the French Name-Tracking Network for *"Londres"* pick out the same city; indeed this is precisely the situation that Kripke's case describes. In fact, it is likely that more people are in similar situations more often than one might suppose. Looking at a Flemish map, many English-speaking tourists are no doubt unaware that "Leeuwen" picks out the same city as "Louvain." Kripke doesn't see this as a simple fact about how we express our beliefs; for him it betrays contradiction and deep-seated paradox within language itself. Why does he think this? Again, we find the source of Kripke's conclusions to lie in his version of externalism.

An antecedent commitment to *de re* essentialism helps ease the transition from Pierre's affirming *"Londres est jolie"* to Pierre's believing *of* London that it is pretty. This is not, of course, to say that pulchritude is an essential property of anything. However, if one agrees that objects do possess certain properties (origin, material, etc.) essentially, and, furthermore, that speaking about these objects entails a commitment on the part of the speaker to statements about their essences, regardless of whether the speaker actually knows what the essence is or can even identify the object, one is already committed to the claim that simply in virtue of using the name of an object, one is directly in touch with object. And the same holds for the meaning or sense of the sentences used to make the claims about the objects.

Unless Kripke supposes that sentences pick out something to which we enjoy a type of access quite distinct from that afforded us by any given language, it will be impossible to resurrect the paradox. It is only on the assumption that Kripke's version of externalism about names extends not only to certain natural kind terms but also to sentences that a puzzle can reemerge; this would be to extend Kripke's version of Referential Realism to the level of sentences. Under such an assumption, there is no longer a need for disquotation or translation. On the present view, we could move directly to the proposition (as an extralinguistic entity) expressed (or picked out) by the affirmed sentence. But that violates (C2).

xiv. The solution

If we reject the underlying assumption of Kripke's externalism, viz., that belief, understanding, and other propositional attitudes work on what our words pick out rather than on the words, it becomes clear that there isn't even the hint of a puzzle.

On such a view, (1) expresses Pierre's belief at a specific time, in a specific set of circumstances (e.g., he's dreaming of other places while living in France and speaking only French); (5) now expresses his belief at another time, in another set of circumstances (viz., when he's living in London and speaks English). In order to understand (1) and (5) *as asserted by Pierre* (or as representing Pierre's beliefs), we must look to the times and circumstances, *including the language*, complete with its Name-tracking Networks, in which Pierre expresses them. This is not intended to suggest that when Pierre says (5), he *really* means something else; rather, it's intended to indicate that belief ascriptions cannot ignore the context in which the belief is held. Nor does it entail that now, while living in the London he says to be "not pretty," Pierre no longer affirms *"Londres est jolie."* He does, and indeed he still believes that *Londres est jolie*.

And such cases aren't nearly as rare or peculiar as one might suppose. In *Philosophy and Mystification*,[21] Guy Robinson discusses the case of a "bicultural" Trobrian Islander who attends university in Port Moresby. "When he was in Port Moresby engaged in his studies and the university world, he said, he *knew* that ghosts didn't exist. When he was back home in the Trobrian Islands, he *knew* that they did."[22]

Robinson's subtle argument supports the understated claim of his next sentence: "They [the ghosts] were part of the world-view and the practices of the society that he had reentered. To ask which of these seemingly incompatibles he *really* believed is perhaps not helpful here."[23] Robinson's points about the relationships between the various vocabularies we employ in different contexts and the bridges that can and cannot be built across them all bear on the argument of this chapter in useful and instructive ways. It goes a good way towards removing the sting from Kripke's "paradox" to note simply that "on the whole these different practices and ways of viewing the world are not in competition with one another."[24] Likewise, what Pierre says in French and what he says in English are not necessarily in competition with one another.

The precise language in which something is expressed is an integral part of its meaning. However, we must take care in saying this; it might be taken to imply that there is another – perhaps extralinguistic – part of meaning. That is a mistake. It's only within a language that meaning, use$_E$ has any place; and it's only with a language that one can express beliefs. Apart from being sentences that Pierre has assented to at one time or another in his life, there is nothing simply as bits of language that (1) and (4) share. When

Pierre assents to (4), it is only on pain of contradiction that he can also assent to (5), and when he assents to (1) it is only on pain of contradiction that he can also assent to

(7) *Londres n'est pas jolie.*

Nothing, however, connects these two pairs in a way that warrants claiming that (1) contradicts (5).

This blocks the generation of Kripke's paradox, and undermines the very possibility of the puzzle as paradox. There is nothing in the puzzle that suggests that Pierre would hold (1) and (7), or (4) and (5) simultaneously. It is only when we try to infer from the fact that Pierre assents to (1) and (5) simultaneously that he is somehow committed (however weakly) to including their translations as members of the set of his beliefs, that the paradox gets a grip on our thinking. This solution meets Kripke's challenge by not simply being a redescription.

The fact of the matter is that we think inside a context of practices. Human thinking is linguistic, and any theory of language, like Kripke's, which ignores this cannot succeed. Because Kripke's views as expressed in "A Puzzle About Belief" and *Naming and Necessity* not only ignore it, but actually entail that it is not so, that, for example, we think in translingual propositions, they are bound to get the matter wrong. When we think of the Tower of London or the Houses of Parliament, we think of them as "the Tower of London" and "the Houses of Parliament"; our French friend Pierre, by contrast, thinks of them as *"la Tour de Londres"* and *"les chambres du Parlement."* Neither of us thinks of the buildings *simpliciter.*

At the end of the day, what Pierre believes is that *Londres est jolie* and that London is not pretty. What he comes to do with these beliefs is an open question, to be decided by Pierre's particular propensities. It is not a question that can be decided by logic or by language. It does not generate the paradox. Nor does it give rise to sceptical doubts about our ability to understand one another or to attribute beliefs to others; most significantly, it does not entail the meaning-scepticism that attends Referential Realism.

EPILOGUE

Not empiricism and yet realism in philosophy, that is the hardest thing.
– Wittgenstein[1]

Epilogue: Relative Realism

i. Realism Restored

"To say that self-sufficient thought always refers to a thought enmeshed in language," says Merleau-Ponty, "is not to say that thought is alienated or that language cuts thought off from truth and certainty."[2] If we have done nothing else in the foregoing pages, we have offered a rich series of amplifications of that teasing remark. Analytic philosophers, though, are apt to take a dim view of talk of thought being enmeshed in language. The atmosphere of many departmental coffee-rooms when that sort of thing comes up is nicely caught by J. A. Fodor in a passage which we have found occasion to quote already (Chapter 11 §vii n. 20).

The upshot is a familiar sort of postmodern Idealism according to which science speaks only of itself: "Il n'y a rien beyond the geology text", and all that. There are traces, in [Chomsky's] *New Horizons*, of incipient sympathy with this Wittgenstein-Goodman-Kuhn-Derrida sort of picture, but it is one that I think a respectable Realist should entirely abjure. Science is not just another language-game; and, no, Virginia, we didn't make the stars. Pray god that no miasmal mist from Harvard has seeped up the Charles to MIT.[3]

Philosophers since Russell have, broadly speaking, taken a commitment to Referential Realism, in one or other of its many forms, to be essential to the preservation of the sort of "respectable Realism" Fodor here invokes. One might reply that Referential Realism, far from proving a reliable bulwark against Idealism and relativism, has itself proved a fertile source of such doctrines, from Dummett's anti-realism, or the semantic nihilism of Kripke on rule-following, to the varieties of paradox we examined in Part IV. But Fodor's question is fair enough, and a *tu quoque* is not a sufficient answer. How far are we committed to the sort of "postmodern Idealism" which respectable Realists should abjure?

Jane Heal gives two criteria for what she calls "mimimal realism."[4] The first is that for a statement S to be construed as making a realistically intended

claim about some subject matter, S must obey the principle of noncontra-
diction. It cannot, that is, be a matter of taste, or convention or personal
preference whether we choose to assent to S or to ∼S. There must be some
reason for regarding one or the other judgment as not merely regrettable,
or "bad form," but erroneous. The second criterion is that to be minimally
Realistic about some subject-matter is to presume the mind-independence
of that subject-matter. As Heal puts it, "If I am a realist, for example, about
the existence of marigolds in my flower bed, then I take it that the existence
of those marigolds is not constituted by my thinking or sincerely saying that
they are there."[5]

How do we stand with respect to these criteria? At first sight we might
appear to fail on both. Haven't we insisted all along that individuals (at least
in the sense of name-bearers), concepts, assertoric contents, natural kinds
and kinds in general – all those entities, in fact, which might be supposed to
provide respectably Realistic *Bedeutungen* for one class of linguistic expressions or another – are linguistic constructs, having no existence in Reality
prior to, or independently of, the institution of language? Well, yes. But as
we have also argued all along, the link between a linguistic expression and
its reference, in the sense of its meaning, what it "stands for;" is not what supplies the connection between language and the extralinguistic. The relation
between a term and its referent – a kind, a colour, a name-bearer, for example – like that between a sentence and its assertoric content, is a relation
internal to language. It would follow that language is an hermetic system
governed by laws internal to it, affording no access to anything beyond itself, only if it were the case that those relations provided the only means of
mediating such access. And we have argued, contrary to a long tradition in
philosophy, that that is not the case. Such a view appears compelling only if
one assumes that the connection between language and the world, the extralinguistic, must take the form of a relationship of some kind between the
members of some class of "constituents" of reality, and *linguistic expressions*.
To assume that is to assume that all there is to a language *is* its spoken or
written expressions: that English, say, *just is* the class of well-formed English
sentences, or the collection of terms recorded in *Websters* or the *OED*.

Such a view is crucially incomplete, as we have argued throughout this
book, because it leaves out of account practices. It neglects, therefore, precisely what must be taken into account if we are to understand not only what
it is for a term to have a meaning, a *Bedeutung*, but what must be taken into
account if we are to grasp how it is that we achieve access to the concepts of
assertoric force, assertion, denial, truth, and falsehood.

Language gives its expressions meaning by sowing them across the face of
a vast web of socially created, possessed and maintained practices. The meaning of an expression just is the mode of insertion of that expression into the
practice or practices in connection with which it finds a use$_E$. The vast majority of the practices in question – measurement, for instance, or counting,

or differentially comparing colours, or sorting animal or plant populations into species – have nothing particularly "linguistic" about them. They are not, at least on the face of it, games played with words; rather, they are techniques of mensuration, or mathematics, or colour-theory, or biological science. Nevertheless, they remain procedures in whose conduct *words play a role*, are *given* a role, and it is only because such roles exist for words, are bestowed on words, that we become beings who speak, beings with something to say about the world, rather than silent manipulators of the world like Köhler's apes, who can grasp the use of simple tools to achieve results, but cannot comment on their own performance because the manipulative procedures of which they are capable are too simple to include a place, a mode of insertion, for words. It is for these reasons that Wittgenstein's choice of the expression "language-game" (*Sprachspiel*) is an unfortunate one, one which sits ill with the entire tenor of the arguments in which it is deployed, and tends to distort the reception of those arguments. For the apparent implication of the term is the one presumed by Fodor in the passage cited above: that a language-game is *a game played with words*.

Such, then, is the account whose Realism in some respects, and lack of it in others, we have now to assess. Such an account is certainly anti-Realist about many of the entities that have traditionally populated the theory of meaning. It affords, for instance, no place to Realistically intended talk of senses, or "meanings," where these are supposed to be mental contents. Plenty of philosophers, of course, from Russell onwards, have smelt a rat where Fregean *Sinn* is concerned. But most have responded by looking for ways of making do, in the theory of meaning, with Fregean *Bedeutung*. The present account, by contrast, is as anti-Realist about reference as it is about sense. According to it, the references of expressions are one and all linguistic constructs. There are, for instance, no such things as "individuals," if "individuals" are supposed to be both the bearers of proper names and "constituents of Reality" in something at least analogous to the sense in which physicists hold electrons to be among the constituents of reality. Nor are there "facts" or "states of affairs" considered as entities invested with a similar ambiguity: half creatures of "logic," half creatures of physical nature. None of these notions, on the present view, correspond to anything real. They are creatures of theory only. Although there is a sense in which they meet the first of Heal's criteria for minimal Realism (the sense provided by the fact that one can be correct or mistaken in one's exposition of a theory, of Frege's theory of *Sinn*, for instance) they fail to meet the second. They fail, one and all, of mind-independence.

Finally, the present account is anti-Realist, or at least anti-platonist, about concepts. Concepts exist only relative to practices. To put it bluntly, talk of concepts is talk of the roles which we bestow on words relative to practices. Reality is not conceptually partitioned prior to, or independently of, the constitution of some language. The Forms are figments of discourse.

So much for the respects in which the present account flirts with Idealism. Now for the respects in which it remains rather staunchly Realist.

The first and most obvious of these respects is a direct consequence of the anti-platonism to which we have just nailed our flag. In making practice prior to conceptual thought, the present view outlines a picture of the relation of Mind to World that allows us to credit ourselves with *preconceptual*, or *extraconceptual*, access to reality. Philosophy since Descartes has viewed the individual mind as a theatre on whose intangible boards are staged, through the medium of a shifting cast of mental entities, *representations* of a reality putatively external to the mind. Since Kant, philosophers have been constrained, with varying degrees of willingness, to accustom themselves to the further possibility that mental representations constitute, wholly or partly, the world they affect to represent.

The nature of the representing states of mind has been variously conceived. Candidates favoured at one time or another include ideas, sense-data, concepts, propositions, theories. But it is essentially in connection with, and against the background of, the picture of thought as *representative* that the options of Idealism and Realism have defined themselves. To Putnam, for example, *metaphysical realism* is the thesis that the world is "independent of any particular representation we have of it."[6] Idealism, by contrast, is, precisely, the thesis that we enjoy epistemic access only to our representations of Reality, not to Reality as it exists independently of human mental activity. Prison-house scepticism, as defined in Part I, puts a Kantian spin on the basic theme of Idealism. Kant introduced the thought that the world epistemically accessible to us is in part the produce of the spontaneity, the conceptual fertility, of the mind. "Concepts" originating in the mind organise experience into an intelligible field of representations. The suggestion of the prison-house sceptic is that the spontaneity, the conceptual fertility, of the mind is inherently at odds with the claim of thought to be representative. Semantic foundationalism has been thought, and by some philosophers[7] is still thought, to provide the Realist with a natural and and effective response to that kind of scepticism, just because it envisages conceptual content as issuing from the experienced content of the Given, rather than from the conceptual fertility of the mind. We have rejected (Chapter 1 §iii) what McDowell calls the Myth of the Given, for reasons related to, although not quite the same as, his.

Metaphysical realism can be attacked, though, and has been, over the past two decades, by Putnam, Dummett, and others, for reasons having nothing to do with the inadequacies of foundationalism, and everything to do with the concept of truth. Putnam's doubts about metaphysical realism are (or perhaps one should say *were*, since Putnam is, admirably, the sort of philosopher whose thinking never comes to a halt) partly motivated by Dummett's arguments in favour of the Manifestation Principle. The Manifestation Principle says that if attaching a meaning to a sentence is a matter of knowing under what conditions statements made by means of it come out true or false, then those conditions must be publicly manifestable: must be capable of being shown, or demonstrated, by one speaker to another. Dummett has argued that satisfaction of the Manifestation Principle is incompatible with a Realistic conception of truth, according to which truth-conditions may be in principle inaccessible to observers. Dummett has therefore proposed replacing the belief in the accessibility of truth Realistically conceived with a more epistemically modest conception of truth as warranted assertability.

Putnam has pointed out in turn that Dummett's arguments bear on the more general issue of the truth of metaphysical realism, as the latter pre-supposes a *"radically non-epistemic"*[8] conception of truth. For metaphysical realism to be true, that is, it has to be conceivable that our best representations of reality, in terms of the best available scientific accounts of things, might wholly misrepresent its nature. And the intelligibility of that supposition seems to require access to a sense of truth in which "is true" is not defined relative to any means we have, or might have, of actually warranting the truth of any statement. Putnam has therefore proposed an "internal Realism," according to which truth and conceptual content are always internal to some theory.

As usefully summarised by Evan Fales,

The internal realist, as depicted by Putnam, can make use of all the semantic devices associated with realism . . . only those devices have to be understood only in relation to some background theory we have about the world, and not *de novo.* Putnam's version of realism – a realism "internal" to some theory or other – is antifoundationalist, and represents a rejection of the correspondence theory of truth and of the causal theory of reference, if these are construed as giving access to a reality independent of our conceptual apparatus.[9]

One advantage of internal realism over metaphysical realism, as Putnam sees it, is that it gives us a reply to a certain kind of sceptic; the sort who asks whether the total reality presented to us in experience, and worked up by us into scientific theory, might not be a total illusion: whether we might not really be, as Putnam puts it, "brains in vats." The metaphysical realist, it would seem, must be constrained by the nature of his realism to credit the sceptic's hypothesis with at any rate minimal intelligibility, to grant that it might be so, even if we can never know either that things so stand or that they do not so stand. The internal realist, by contrast, can counter the sceptic with the charge that his hypothesis is self-stultifying. If we were brains in vats it would be impossible for us to attach a conceptual content capable of truth or falsehood to the suggestion that we were, as such a suggestion can be given no sense, that is to say, assigned no truth-conditions, from within the perspective of our total theory.

Back, now, to the question of the Realist credentials of the account presented here of the nature of the relationship between language and reality.

The first, and most important thing to be noted about the present account is that, according to it, neither a language nor the system of concepts – the "conceptual scheme" enshrined in it – can be said to *represent* anything, or to be *representative* in function. That is the implication of our rejection of the Correspondence Theory of Meaning. There is nothing in the world to which a concept *corresponds*: concepts are creatures of the fertility of the mind in devising practices. By the same token we do not, as linguistic creatures, confront the world, as it were, from behind, or amidst, a system of *mental representations* which might turn out to represent falsely. As linguistic creatures we confront a world that offers itself, mutely and preconceptually, as the foundation on which we erect our practices. The foundation offered by the world to our collective activity as constitutors of practices, is plainly not an *epistemic* foundation. Epistemic foundationalism, for that matter epistemology *tout court*, addresses the issue of the ultimate justification of knowledge-claims; that is to say, the nature of our ultimate grounds for supposing certain *propositions* to be *true*. At the level of the constitution of linguistic practices we are below the level of truth, of conceptual or propositional thought, because what we do and devise at the level of linguistic practices is foundational to the notions of assertion, denial, proposition, truth, concept. If metaphysical realism is, as Putnam puts it, the claim that the world is independent of any particular representation of it, then at the level of the constitution of linguistic practices we confront a world of which metaphysical realism is simply true.

But that claim perhaps needs a little more spelling-out. In which of their aspects, and how, exactly, can linguistic practices be said to be "below the level of," or "logically prior to," or "foundational to" the notions of truth, conceptual thought, linguistic meaning, and so on? Two objections suggest themselves here. One, which we owe to Samuel C. Wheeler III, is that (in his own words, in correspondence) "if practices are really separable from the world, then there ought to be a way to directly describe the world." The second, which we owe to Guy Stock, is that we seem to want to say that Nature, or Reality, supplies us with the truth-values of propositions. And we seem to want to say also that linguistic practices show the bearing of natural circumstances on the truth of propositions. But if that is what practices are supposed to do, how could a prelinguistic child, with no prior grasp of the notions *concept* or *proposition,* grasp that that is the function which the practices into which he is being intitiated are supposed to serve. The answer to the second objection turns on the answer to the first. The answer to that is that there is indeed, acording to us, no way to describing the world other than by means of propositions, but that the sense in which, according to us, practices are "sepaparable from" the extralinguistic world is not such as to carry with it any such absurd implication. We hold, rather, that the world external to language can be, and is, known to us, but – reasonably enough – that the knowledge in question is not linguistically formulable knowledge. There are, after all, ways of encountering the world other than, as Russell would say "by description," and the remaining options extend far beyond Russell's single alternative of "acquaintance." We encounter the world primordially, as Merleau-Ponty strove to remind us, not as wielders of conceptual thought and its linguistic expressions, but as perceivers of a world of physical objects and forces, in which, by reason of our physical embodiment we are immersed, and as actors upon and manipulators of that world. And our actions and manipulations evoke from the physical world responses, in the shape of repeatable outcomes precipitated by conduct of one or another kind. The world we inhabit at that level is not, in other words, a realm of concepts, or truth-values, or truth-conditions, but rather a *realm of outcomes*. Such a realm is replete with perceptual and causal structure: what it lacks is conceptual structure. Hence the introduction of linguistically marked practices cannot, on our view, be taken as establishing a relationship beteen the realm of outcomes and the *conceptual realm* (or the *realm of truth-values*, or however else one might wish to characterise it), *as if the latter already existed*. A practice, on our account, is simply that: a practice: a way of manipulating the world which is socially maintained because it serves certain purposes. What distinguishes linguistic practices from animal practices of other sorts, such as the ritualised grooming of one individual chimpanzee by another, or the digging of termites out of anthills with a stick, is simply that they include, meaning by that that they are not merely accompanied by, but *functionally involve*, the utterance of repeatable phonemic strings. Through their functional involvement in one or another such practice, phonemic strings gradually aquire the roles of such proto-propositional entities as questions and answers, for example, "(is it to the) left or right?," "(to the) left," "How many (there)?," "three," in which the bracketed portions represent contextually presented circumstances. At this point we have a beginning grasp of such concepts as position and number. But, and this is the important point, in acquiring, or beginning to acquire, such notions we have not begun to depart from the Realm of Outcomes, the bodily-cum-perceptual realm, into another realm whose component entities and powers, concepts, truth-telling, description, might intrinsically function to impede access to the natural world we encounter perceptually. For *the answers to the questions whose conceptual possibility our practices shape and bring into being for us are still dictated by what occurs in the realm of outcomes*. In ascending to the conceptual realm we never leave the realm of outcomes, or the direct, prelinguistic access to the physical world that we enjoy in consequence of our own embodiment. We simply acquire vastly augmented means of directing and analysing it. We also acquire access to that augmented realm of outcomes which includes the human, a world of political, moral, legal and cultural entities as "Real" in the sense of "contitutive of what there is" as the entities, the medium, sized, middle-distance physical objects, as Quine would say, which make up the realm of outcomes from which we started.

But – to move on to another species of anti-Realism – doesn't the power of these thoughts to reassure us against the inroads of Prison House scepticism lapse the moment we enter, via the constitution of practices, into the possession of concepts, the power to assert and deny? Doesn't the demon of Cartesian scepticism recover all its wonted powers, that is, the moment we are in a position actually to *say something* about the world and determine its truth or falsity? Even if meaning is a nonepistemic concept, that does not in itself show the concept of truth to be nonepistemic in character. And if it is not, might not the totality of what we say about the world be warranted, but false? No, because the manner in which we have acquired the power to assert carries with it the means of equipping ourselves with the "radically nonepistemic" account of truth which Putnam rightly takes metaphysical realism to presuppose. Earlier, we distinguished two senses of "truth-condition." On the one hand, there is the sense commonly understood, in which a truth-condition for a statement S is an observational warrant: some natural condition whose occurrence warrants the *assertion* of S. On the other hand, there is the sense we have distinguished here, in which the truth-conditions of S are those circumstances, whatever they may be, which make clear how what is asserted in affirming S is related to what is asserted in denying S. We argued earlier that truth-conditions in the second sense, since they cannot be extracted from inductive reflection on the circumstances of native assent and dissent, must be stipulated, by relating statements to one another across some practice. Frege's dictum that to know the meaning of a statement is to grasp under what conditions it would come out true and false, is what lies behind the commonly asserted claim that to know the meaning of a statement is its truth-conditions. But fidelity to the spirit of Frege's thought is better served by understanding "truth-conditions" in the second of the two senses we have just distinguished. For to grasp the nature of the relationship between what is asserted in affirming S and what is asserted in denying it is to grasp what is *relevant to the truth of S*. And grasping that gives one an *open-ended* grip on the question of what natural conditions are to be regarded as assertion-warranting for S. If I know, that is, because I have been trained to count and to measure, that "three" is a number word and "foot" the name of a modulus of measurement, then I shall be in a position to characterise indefinitely many natural conditions as assertion-warranting for "x is three feet long," because I know what, given the meaning of the words, makes each such condition *relevant*, causally or otherwise, to the truth or falsity of S. By contrast, if I know, because I have been told, that certain objects are three feet long, but know nothing of measurement or counting, I can neither be said to know the meaning of "x is three feet long" or to have made any significant progress towards knowing it, despite knowing that the objects in question possess the status of observational warrants for its assertion.

Let us therefore conclude that the meaning of a statement S is its "truth-conditions" in the second of the above two senses. We know the meaning of S, that is, when we know how the issue of what is relevant to its truth or falsity is determined via the modes of insertion of its component expressions into some practice or practices. Dummett's Manifestation Principle, although remaining unimpeachable in itself, now also takes on a new sense. What has to be manifestable, in order for the meaning of S to be in common accessible to speakers, is not the set, or nececessarily any subset even, of S's observational warrants but, rather, the detailed workings, rationale and modes of interaction of the practices from which the component expressions of S derive their meanings. But to restate Dummett's principle in this way is to break the connection it is commonly held to forge between truth and the epistemic. If access to manifestable practices is sufficient to make clear what would be relevant to the truth of a statement S asserted under envisaged circumstances, then the impossibility, even the in-principle impossibility, of determining, under those circumstances, whether any truth-relevant condition actually obtains or not, weakens speakers' grip neither on the meaning of S nor on the notion of truth to which they have access. The projection of truth-conditions of the first kind from practices, in other words, projects truth-conditions in the ordinary, Realistic sense: truth-conditions defined in terms of how things stand in the world, not in terms of how things stand with respect to our epistemic capacities. There is thus a sense, even, in which the rejection of the Correspondence Theory of Meaning opens the way to a harmlessly naturalistic version of the Correspondence Theory of Truth. The Correspondence Theory was long ago buried by Strawson,[10] and has shown few signs of life since. Strawson's reasons for dispensing with it possess force, however, only against versions of the theory made out in terms of alleged mapping relations between sentences and such putative real-world correlates as "facts" or "states of affairs." On the present view a sense of correspondence can be made out that makes appeal to no such entities. It involves, one might say, an inverse notion of correspondence. As usually conceived, that is, the notion of correspondence has been taken to involve some sort of mapping by sentences or statements of pre-existing structures in the world. The required correspondence has therefore been conceived as correspondence *by* the sentence or statement *to* the world. The present account suggests the converse relation: correspondence *of* the world *to* the statement. Let us try to spell this out. We define, decide, by relating statements to one another across practices, what is to count as relevant to the truth or falsity of any given statement. In terms of that decision we put a question to the world: the question whether there obtains in reality any relevant circumstance capable of settling the question one way or the other. The answer belongs wholly to the world. It will be, whatever it is, as indifferent as a reality conceived as external to the mind must be, to our decisions, hopes, wishes or linguistic manipulations. The answer, when it comes, will thus be in no sense "the work of the mind." The trail of the human serpent, in Putnam's graphic image, is not, after all, "over all." The questions we put to the world glitter with it: the world's answers, blankly and indifferently inhuman as they are, are innocent of it: as innocent of Mind and its machinations as the boot-button eyes of a bear seen at close quarters. We do not, in short, confront the world from within a web of theories, or representations, from which there is no exit save the intrinsically epistemic one which runs by way of the evidence for their truth. We confront the world from within a web of practices which operate directly on the inhuman material confronting them, because their roots remain firmly embedded in the Realm of Outcomes. That makes the difference – all the difference – between, on the one hand, both Idealism and Putnam's internal Realism, and, on the other, the version of metaphysical realism we have espoused here.

ii. Brains in vats

Where does that leave Putnam's brains in vats? Does the espousal of something as close to metaphysical realism as we have just outlined leave us with no means of countering the sceptic who raises that possibility? The example raises the central puzzle informing the debate between Realists and Idealists: if anything regarding the real nature of the world can be in principle epistemically inaccessible to us, why should not the "real" nature of things be *in its entirety* epistemically out of reach?

One might ask where the vats that putatively contain our brains are supposed, according to the sceptic, to be situated. Are they somewhere in the world we encounter when, waking in the morning, we reach out and touch with our hands the familiar objects that furnish our lives, the alarm clock, a teacup: the world, in short, which also contains the machinery in the laboratory? If the sceptic answers that they are indeed in that world, he is, one would have supposed, foiled, for the investigation of *that* world is well within our reach. So his answer must be that the world that contains alarm clock, teacup, and laboratory machinery is a phantom world: that *real* reality inhabits a world elsewhere, a Beyond. But "Beyond" in what sense, exactly? If that Beyond is causally disconnected from the phantom world we supposedly inhabit, then indeed it is a Beyond to which, even in principle, we must lack epistemic access. But in that case it becomes difficult to see in what sense the latter world is supposed to be a "phantom" one, as, in that case, we are just dealing with two universes, both equally real, to one of which we lack epistemic access indeed, but only because we lack causal access to it. In any case the world that possesses Ultimate Reality cannot on the sceptic's hypothesis be envisaged as causally disconnected from the phantom world to which alone, supposedly, we enjoy epistemic access, as what happens in the phantom world is supposed (by the sceptic) to be completely causally determined by what goes on in the Ultimately Real world. It follows that the vats, their operators and the surrounding machinery enjoy causal commerce with the vatted brains. So why can't the vatted brains investigate those causal connections? The sceptic's answer can only be: *because the vatted brains enjoy epistemic access only to their own mental representations,* and these systematically distort reality.

Let us approach this last point once more, from a slightly different angle. One might ask why, if the vatted brains enjoy causal contact with the Ultimately Real world, they do not enjoy epistemic access to it? After all, there is a sense in which we *are* all brains in vats, namely, the sense in which we are brains in skulls. But being brains in skulls does not stop us investigating the nature of the causal links which connect world and brain. Something other than the idea of the brain as "only" *causally* connected with the world, some further thought, has to be operating here, therefore, in order to generate the sceptic's puzzle. And it is easy to see what that further thought must be. It cannot be, as the stage setting of the example suggests, the thought that the nature of the causal mechanisms disposed of by the Mad Scientists who control the vats, given their mastery of neurology and cognitive science, is such as to rule out *in principle* the possibility of any investigation of those mechanisms on the part of the brains. Such suppositions are free, of course, but are for that reason weightless. How can the Mad Scientists rule out *any* passing anomaly which might alert the vatted brains to their situation? *In principle* is a big word, in short, and invites the response: what principle, exactly? In fine, the only thought that will do the work the sceptic needs done here is a very old and familiar one that owes nothing whatsoever either to contemporary or to speculative cognitive science; namely, the *ur*-thought of Cartesian scepticism: the thought that neither in contemplating our mental representations of reality, nor in amassing the sensory evidence for those representations, do we ever encounter anything extramental: anything but our own mental states.

There are many reasons for regarding *that* thought as simply false. Metaphysical realism, reached by the route we have followed here, adds another. If we have argued correctly, our possession of "mental representations," if by that is meant concepts, theories, ideologies, in general, systems of propositions, is dependent on our enjoyment of practical access, physical, manipulative access, to a world *whose properties and modes of response under manipulation are independent of any representation we may construct of it.* What metaphysical realism asserts is the epistemic transcendence of that world: its permanent power to escape and to frustrate any representation we may make of it. It is just that characteristic of the world – its power to surprise us, to defeat our expectations – which we intend in calling it "real." If the sceptic wants to raise the possibility that we might be vatted brains, therefore, he has to build that feature into his description of what it is like to be a vatted brain. But in that case what is the difference between being a vatted brain and being a real human being living in a real world? Presumably that, if we are vatted brains, the physical world we encounter in our practical lives is just *not the real one*. But that move makes the sceptic's suggestion simply imponderable, for now he must face the question, *in what way not real?* And it is not clear what answer he can give. When an investigator in the supposed shadow-world of the vatted brains takes a pair of calipers and, laying them first across a group of tree-rings visible in the cut surface of the trunk of a bristlecone pine, and then across a scale, writes down in a notebook a cypher, "3.25 mm," in what sense could his practical activity here be said to be occupied about *mental representations?* Well, he uses some signs, which have meanings. Aren't meanings *mental* entities, then? No. Meaning goes to ground in practice. It is socially instituted and maintained practice, and not "thought," or thought only in a sense that owes everything, including assertoric content, to practice, which guides his actions here. And for that reason, the investigator is operating beyond the sphere supposedly occupied by the Cartesian category of Mind. Hence, he is, like ourselves, in touch with a real world: a world that displays its reality precisely in its possession of a power to subvert the representations we form of it having no limit that our minds can encompass. Contrary to the sceptic's belief, we lack a way of rendering intelligible the "possibility" that that world could be, "really" an unreal world, just because it is a metaphysically real world in the sense of one which exhibits a permanent power to transcend, through our practical interactions with it, any representation we may make of it. Metaphysical realism, *pace* Putnam, is no friend to the sceptic.

iii. Meaning-Realism

Meaning-scepticism is the thesis that there is no "fact of the matter" about meaning, the consequence of which is widely taken to be some form of relativism or semantic nihilism. We might be thought to be in a poor position to dissent either from the meaning-sceptic's premise or from his conclusions. Central to the position outlined here are two theses that might seem to play straight into the meaning-sceptic's hands. The first is that "meanings," "concepts," "propositions" are neither mental entities, nor constituents of extramental reality, but nomothetic entities, in the sense in which the King in chess, or the ampersand are nomothetic entities. The second is that the knowledge of meanings grounds out, not epistemically, in the truth of some propositions but, rather, in practices. Each might seem to rule out, in different ways, the possibility of there being any "facts of the matter" about meanings.

That would be a mistake. For a grasp of meanings to ground out in practice is still for it to ground out. And that subverts a crucial step in the meaning-sceptic's argument. To get from the claim that there is no fact of the matter about meaning to any form of relativism or nihilism about meaning, it has to follow that, in the absence of any "fact of the matter" where meanings are concerned, judgments of meaning are in certain crucial respects *ungrounded*. Different kinds of meaning-scepticism handle the necessary passage of argument in different ways. For Quine what is empirically ungrounded is the choice between different translation manuals. For the Kripke of *Wittgenstein on Rules and Private Language*, what is empirically ungrounded is the choice between different 'rules' for the guidance of linguistic performances. Either way the lack of empirical grounding for these choices, according to the sceptic, leaves speakers with no option but to repose their claim to linguistic competence on the approval of the linguistic community to which they belong. For Quine, this involves acquiescence, for purposes of translation, in the ontological categories of a "background language." For Kripke, it involves allowing the supposition that one is continuing to act in accordance with a given rule to rest solely on continuing acceptence by his linguistic peers of the performances he takes to represent successive applications of that rule.

We agree with the meaning-sceptic that there is no *fact*, knowledge of which would be logically equivalent to knowledge of the meaning of a linguistic expression S. For no S, that is to say, is there, according to us, any proposition p such that "A knows the meaning of S" is logically equivalent to "A knows p to be true." But that is merely to say that the knowledge of meaning possessed by a semantically competent speaker does not reduce to knowledge of the truth of some propositions, not that the notion of a semantically competent speaker is vacuous. To be semantically competent in a language L is on our account to be in a position to participate intelligently in the socially devised and maintained practices in the context of which the linguistic expressions of L find their uses$_E$. Semantic competence of this kind, rather than a matter of knowing some propositions to be true, is a matter of having received sufficient training in the conduct of the practices in question to allow one, first, to grasp their rationale, their point, the practical and communicative advantages they bestow; and, second, to deploy them in communicative contexts with the sure-footedness and fluency required if misunderstanding is to be avoided.

How does this move defeat the meaning-sceptic? In two ways. First, and most important, it allows us to represent language as an essentially public, because *essentially social*, phenomenon, without being compelled by that thought, as so much recent philosophy has imagined itself to be, to embrace a *socially relativist* account of the justification of linguistic performances. The semantically competent speaker, on our account, is justified in asserting the semantic propriety of what he says and does in execution of linguistic practices in whose conduct he has been adequately trained, by the mere fact that what he says and does is an adequate expression of that training. Someone who has been trained to count, or to measure, say, and who counts or measures with due care, is justified in accepting the results of his counting or measuring as correct, simply because *they are the results which have issued from a carefully conducted episode of counting or measuring*. Moreover, no prior epistemic question, no question of whether he is right to conduct the practices of measuring or counting as he is in the habit of conducting them arises. He does not need to refer to the approval of the linguistic community to satisfy himself that he is justified in counting *this* way, rather than some other way. He counts as one counts, as he has been trained to count, and gets the result one gets. If there is any doubt about the result, the remedy lies in counting again, more carefully, not in a foredoomed attempt to find some "justification" (what justification could there possibly be?) for counting as he has been trained to count.

The training he has received, in other words, although it is training in the conduct of socially devised and maintained practices, places the learner in a position to monitor the correctness of his own responses, without further guidance from the community. Nor could it be otherwise. A linguistic device, if it is to be an effective vehicle of communication between independent speakers, and more particularly if it is to assist in making clear the assertoric content of assertions, must contain within itself whatever may be needed to distinguish correct from incorrect employments of the linguistic expressions it governs. That would be one way, indeed, of expressing the purport of Wittgenstein's Slogan. For suppose that a speaker S of language L really did have to defer to the opinion of fellow speakers of L on the propriety of "67" as a reply to "What is the sum of 28 and 39?" That would merely show either that no viable system of counting had yet been added to L, or else that A had not yet been sufficiently trained in its use; for no viable system of counting could leave the result of an addition sum to be determined by considerations arising outside the system.

In terms of Jane Heal's criteria for minimal realism, then, the semantically competent speaker is in a position to be minimally realistic about the correctness and incorrectness of linguistic performances. He is justified in intending realistically the claim that there are such things as correct and incorrect linguistic performances, because, on the one hand, there will necessarily be some objective ground, in the structure and use$_P$ of the practice which governs it, for regarding a given linguistic performance as correct or incorrect; and because, on the other, that ground will necessarily be mind-independent: will be constituted, that is, by considerations transcending the mere *ad hoc* say-so, either of the individual speaker or of the linguistic community.

The second sense in which the meaning-sceptic stands confuted by the present account is that on that account there turn out to be, after all, "facts about meaning": namely, social-anthropological facts. We do not, because we could not, "gain entry to" an alien language by attempting to establish correlations between the truth-values assigned by native speakers to native observation-sentences, and the environmental circumstances in which those speakers are prepared to assign those truth-values to those sentences. Such an account fails, as we have argued at length in Chapters 9, 10, and 13, because it disregards the question of what empirical grounds we have for taking the natives to possess a language, rather than a repertoire of responses for registering natural conditions, and thus the question what grounds we have for regarding their utterances as *assertions*, that is, as expressions capable of taking truth-values, in the first place.

How, then, *do* we gain entry to an alien language? The suggestion arising naturally from the account of the nature of meaning pursued here is that we do so by framing testable hypotheses concerning the nature of the native practices in the context of which native expressions acquire their uses$_E$, and across which native sentences come to be related as semantic alternatives in such a way as to make clear the semantic implications of denial *vis-à-vis* assertion, and vice versa, for any given native sentence. Like Quine's anthropologist, the anthropologist pursuing *this* enterprise will make mistakes: will find himself required on empirical grounds to revise, from time to time, his initial hypotheses. But what this empirically guided process of trial and error bears on is not the construction of an English/Native *translation manual*. It has two goals: first, to connect native utterance with the web of practices that constitute native social and practical life; to arrive at a *detailed* integration of native utterance into native practice; and, second, to equip the anthropologist with a mastery of the relevant practices equivalent, ideally, to that of a native speaker. The goal of the anthropologist, in short, is not to dominate the native language from the standpoint of a "background" language, English, say. His business is not to force the uncouth utterances of "Native" down on the Procrustean bed of English, and to dismiss as empirically irrecoverable anything that fails to fit the imperial mould of the latter's canonical constructions. Rather, his goal is to submit himself to the mercy of the alien culture and its language, to let it instruct him in its ways so that it can, in the end, speak to him, and be spoken by him, in, and on, its own terms.

What he will learn in this way, what his competence in the new language will consist in, is the ability to deploy, freely and effectively, in communicative situations, the practices with which its linguistic expressions engage. How far will he be able to couch that knowledge in English sentences? What kind of account, in English, of the content of his competence, can we reasonably demand of him? Philosophers and linguists over the past forty years, partly under the influence of Noam Chomsky, have set themselves the theoretical aim of giving a complete account, in propositional terms, of what a competent speaker knows in knowing his native language. Various philosophical enterprises stand committed to this aim, including Davidson's project of constructing a truth-theory for a language, and Dummett's of constructing a theory of meaning.

If, as we have argued, linguistic competence reduces to competence in the conduct of practices, the question of what modes of description of linguistic competence are available to us reduces to the question what modes of describing practical competence are available to us. And there are reasons to suppose that the "content" of practical competence may not be exhaustively propositionally expressible. The most obvious reason for this is that practices do not possess "content" in the sense that sentences, or propositions, or assertions do. Practices are not assertoric, but preassertoric. The second is that, while verbal descriptions, explanations and elucidations of the structure and point of practices, and of the roles linguistic expressions play in them, are abundantly available, there is no reason to regard any of them as "exhaustive." Someone might grasp any such explanation, in other words, and still stumble when it comes to actually playing chess, or actually extracting the implications of a set of directions framed in terms of the words "left" and "right," because of some bizarre misunderstanding unique to him. Of course, such misunderstandings can be cleared up by further verbal specification, but the possibility of misunderstanding remains. Normally one relies on a certain level of nonverbal, practical, intelligence in those with whom one discusses, and to whom one has to communicate, such matters. Suppose one encounters someone in whom such intelligence appears to be lacking. To some extent one can address his misunderstandings by means of further, more elaborate, verbal explications. And those will no doubt in many cases suffice to dispel some misunderstandings. But suppose they work only to reveal still more profound misunderstandings? And others lurking beneath those? Isn't it always possible that a point will be reached at which one has no option but to fall back on an observation of Wittgenstein's: that although it is generally possible to tailor a verbal explication to address a particular misunderstanding, there is no way of tailoring a verbal explication that will address *all possible* misunderstandings? At some point we must simply rely on the capacity of the learner to "catch on," to "pick it up"; and if that point never arrives, the only recourse left to us will be to shrug our shoulders and mutter, resignedly, some such Wittgensteinian tag as "He is very unlike us!" Explanations must, as Wittgenstein observes, end somewhere. The idea that *everything* we know must be capable of propositional expression perhaps has its roots in what Merleau-Ponty called the "intellectualism" of most modern philosophy; that philosophy that is to say, which began with Descartes and has remained broadly in the Cartesian tradition. Descartes taught us to think of the body, of our bodily situation in the world, as inessential to mind. That thought carries with it two further ones: that thought, including cognition in all its forms, is essentially a matter of apprehending "mental states," and that language is a device for neutrally representing the "content" either of such "states" or of their presumed extramental correlates. Those preconceptions die hard, even now. A considerable part of what we have said here has been directed towards helping them on their way towards the dustbin of defunct ideas. We have argued, in effect, that the content of a thought cannot be viewed in isolation from the language in which it is expressed, and that language *per se* cannot be viewed in isolation from the substratum of practices through which its expressions gain whatever meaning they possess; and that in consequence we have no means of representing ourselves, as beings capable of knowledge, in abstraction from practical life: the life we enjoy as physical, embodied beings, manipulators of an equally physical world, and devisers of the practices through which alone we are enabled to question that world and assess the implications of its answers.

That suggests a further limitation on the verbal explication of linguistic competence. It is that teaching most practices involves a mixture of verbal instruction and demonstration. We show the learner mechanic how a crankshaft operates to return the pistons to their cylinders in order, giving a crude verbal explanantion eked out with passes of the hands. "And that," we conclude, "is what we call the camshaft." For the beginning engineer the verbal explanations will be longer and involve different matter, but they will still be eked out with demonstrative aids, with blueprints, for instance. An engineering training, or any other form of practical training, which confined itself wholly to verbal explications is, simply, inconceivable.

These arguments might make it appear impossible to give any effective account of semantic competence. But that again would be a misunderstanding. As we argued earlier, semantic competence consists on one level simply in a grasp of how linguistic expressions fit into practices, not necessarily in the ability to use those practices, to enter into communication involving them, with the ease of a native speaker. And the role linguistic expressions play in practices is something that can be expressed in reasonably brief descriptions grounded in empirical observation. So we can say that "camshaft" in English belongs to a certain nomenclature, the nomenclature of the functional elements of an internal combustion engine. Its use as one item in that nomenclature, that is, is what gives it all the meaning it possesses. The demand to "know the meaning" of "camshaft," therefore, ends there. There, as Wittgenstein would say, "The spade turns": there is nothing more to know. And, for most purposes, such an account of the meaning of "camshaft" will be good enough. Let us call it an *effective account*. An exhaustive account of the meanings of expressions in a language in terms of effective accounts is perfectly possible. Such accounts are clearly going to be capable, *pace* Quine, of being rendered entirely determinate on empirical grounds. To take a readily translatable expression, it will take a monoglot English mechanic half an hour helping to strip an engine in a French workshop to determine with certainty that the French for "camshaft" is *l'arbre à cames*. To take two terms for which no equivalent exists in English, it will take only a little experience of French bars and restaurants to determine with equal certainty what contrast is marked by the expressions *bon viveur* and *bon vivant*.

The Chomskean revolution transferred the study of linguistic competence from the social to the biological sphere, breaking the link between linguistics and anthropology. Parallel developments in philosophy have referred studies of semantic competence to formal semantics, including possible-worlds semantics. The present view, in effect, transfers the study of semantic competence back to the anthropologist: not the Quinean anthropologist, but the empirically based linguistic anthropologist of former days. Language becomes once more a socially, rather than a genetically, based phenomenon, and the study of alien meaning fuses with that of the social customs and practices of alien cultures.

iv. The idea of a logically perfect language

What is the relationship between metaphysical realism (MR), defended on the sort of grounds presented here, and scientific realism (SR)? Bas van Frassen has characterised the latter in the following way:

Science aims to give us, in its theories, a literally true story of what the world is like; and acceptance of a scientific theory involves the belief that it is true.[11]

Putnam has argued that metaphysical realism is actually incompatible with scientific realism. That, though, has much to do with Putnam's deeply Russellian assessment of what one has to hold concerning the relation between language and the world to be a metaphysical realist, an assessment deeply imbued with Referential Realism. Putnam has characterised metaphysical realism as involving the following three claims:[12]

(1) The world consists of a fixed totality of mind-independent objects and properties.
(2) Truth involves some sort of correspondence relation between words or thought-signs and external things or sets of things.
(3) There is exactly one true and complete description of "the way the world is" [though we may never have a language capable of expressing it or may never know it].

The trouble with identifying MR and SR, according to Putnam, is that the former "is supposed to apply to *all* correct theories at once . . . and THE WORLD is supposed to be *independent* of any representation of it."[13] Lepore and Loewer have argued that "the heart of [this] argument is that the reference and correspondence relations invoked by MR cannot be placed with[in] a scientific account of the world."[14]

In this Putnam is clearly correct. But the version of MR defended here escapes Putnam's argument, since it is not Referentially Realistic, and so involves no dependence upon referential relationships between "words or thought-signs and external [i.e., presumably, extramental, or extralinguistic, or both] things or sets of things." We can claim, therefore, to have a grip on a type of metaphysical realism giving van Frassen's type of scientific realist a good deal of what he wants.

It still might be objected, however, that it doesn't give him by any means all that he wants – or thinks he should want. Closer attention to van Frassen's characterisation of SR will show us why not. It falls into two parts, each of which formulates a quite different demand. The demand that science give us a "literally true story of what the world is like" might be equated merely with the demand that science *yield true statements*. By contrast, the addendum "and acceptance of a scientific theory involves the belief that it is true" might be taken to express a further demand: the demand that "theories," in addition to being assessable in terms of utility, simplicity, plausibility, and so on, should be capable of truth or falsity. This demand is reminiscent of the third of the claims ascribed by Putnam to the metaphysical realist, the claim that there is (even though we might never succeed in formulating it) one true and complete description of the way the world is. That demand can be seen as roughly equivalent to the belief in the possibility of a *characteristica universalis*, or as Russell called it, a logically perfect language. For when we demand, not merely that a theory prove fertile in truths, but that *the theory itself* be true, what are we demanding? A theory is, among other things, a general way of representing the nature of the world. Thus it will have a language, a vocabulary of concepts, peculiar to it. The claim that a theory is true thus equates with the belief that the terms in which it represents the world represent it correctly. The intelligibility of such a belief carries with it the intelligibility of the belief in the possibility of an ultimate, finally adequate, description of reality, and that in turn seems to carry with it the intelligibility of the notion of a finally adequate language. For the Ultimate Theory must, it would seem, be couched in a language appropriate to it. Thus if the theory correctly represents the nature of things, that language will also correctly represent the nature of things. Its terms and relations will exactly mirror the structure of entities and relationships that ultimately go to make up the world.

Our grounds for advancing a version of MR, as they require assent to none of the three clauses that Putnam considers essential to metaphysical realism, allow us to reject the third. But they do more than that. They throw doubt on the intelligibility of the idea of a unified, ultimately true description of the totality of things from a direction and in a manner which in no way impugns the credentials of metaphysical realism about truth. On the present view, the considerations that determine what is and what is not relevant to the truth of a statement S, and thus the assertoric content of S, are constituted internally to some language or other. To raise the question whether or not S is true, however, is to raise a question which is not, and cannot be, settled internally to language: the question whether nature exhibits features that would, *according to the criteria we have established,* resolve the matter one way or the other. On the present account, it is possible that such features may exist in nature without our being in a position to say whether they exist; because, on our account, fixing the assertoric content of S does not involve saying anything about how either the assertion or the denial of S is, in practice, to be *warranted.* The link between meaning and observational warrant, forged in different ways by verificationism and by Dummett's version of anti-Realism, on our account falls apart.

By the same token, however, it becomes difficult to make sense of the idea that language *represents* anything, let alone "the world." The idea of language, or of a scheme of concepts, as representative, as capable of "corresponding" or failing to "correspond" to reality, has a very long history. In the shape of the so-called Picture Theory of Meaning it played a central role in the *Tractatus.* It could, we think, be easily shown to be one of the chief among the features of that work against which Wittgenstein set his face in his later writings. We have chosen to follow him in that. If, as we have argued, the considerations which establish the assertoric content of a sentence are constituted internally to a language, then they are devised, not found in nature. It follows that none of the vocabularies of concepts in which we frame our explanantions of natural phenomena, no matter how successful those explanations may have proved in illuminating particular tracts of phenomena, can be regarded as final. There will always remain the possibility that further flights of conceptual inventiveness, of the sort associated with what T. S. Kuhn famously called "paradigm shifts," may lead to our coming to view things under the aspect of some new, and even more explanatorily successful vocabulary of concepts. The objection to such accounts as Kuhn's has always been that they usher in an unbridled relativism according to which nothing we say about the world can ever be regarded as simply true, but only as true in some suitably diminished and relative sense: "true relative to theory *T*," "true-in-language L," "true relative to the beliefs and values of linguistic community C," or something of the sort. An entirely honorable dislike of that sort of thing is what largely motivates many of those, such as Russell, or Evans, for instance, whom we have labelled "Referential Realists." We have argued at length against Referential Realism, but without any animus against the essentially scientifically realist values motivating many, at least, of its defenders. What we hope to have rescued from the wreck of Referential Realism is, among other things, an acceptably realistic account of the notion of truth.

By the light of that account we can perhaps begin to see how Kuhn's account of the nature of scientific progress might be rescued from the charge of relativism. It is nature, as we have argued, that certifies as true the true statements of any theory concerning it. The obverse of that thought, as we have defended it, is that nature remains outside theory, outside language, outside thought: accessible to thought only by way of assertoric discourse,

and to the latter only by way of the devising of practices capable of establishing the relative content of assertion and denial. We dream, vainly, of
establishing a thoroughgoing conformity between the structure of Nature
and that of our accounts of it; and we feel, confusedly, that one of the
things that impedes us in that endeavour is the fertility of thought itself, the
protean character of human conceptual inventiveness, the "spontaneity." as
Kant termed it, of the mind. Because language is the locus and fount of conceptual fertility, we dream, as philosophers since Locke and Berkeley have
done, of circumventing language, of passing somehow beyond language to
Nature herself, of somehow founding thought, not on the shifting sands
of our own spontaneity, but on whatever structure of descriptive categories
founds Nature herself. As Merleau-Ponty put it, "we all secretly venerate the
ideal of a language which in the last analysis would deliver us from language
by delivering us to things."[15] Such an ideal is essentially metaphysical: is indeed the essence, the heart, of metaphysics as that developed from Descartes
to, say, Husserl. It is implicit, for instance, in Proposition VII of Part II of
Spinoza's *Ethics*: "The order and connection of ideas is the same as the order
and connection of things."[16]

We have shown why, in the last analysis, no such deliverance is possible. A
"conceptual scheme," a "system of concepts," or, by contrast, the assertoric
contents of the set of sentences which compose a theory, cannot "represent"
Reality more or less adequately, cannot correspond or fail to correspond to
how things stand in the world, because there is nothing in the world for
concepts or assertoric contents to correspond to. There is nothing conceptual, or assertoric, about the world: no Forms, no "properties," no "facts," no
"states of affairs": just phenomena. The conceptual and the assertoric are
creatures of language. We also have shown why that thought has no sceptical implications: does not carry with it the conclusion that language is a
veil of illusion, cutting us off from contact with the world. Contact between
thought and world is established, not at the level of the conceptual or the
assertoric, but lower down, at the level of the practices through which the
concepts of the conceptual and the assertoric become accessible to us. At
that level we confront phenomena directly, through the medium of practice,
not through that of propositional thought. It follows that it is at the level of
practice that the springs of the conceptual fertility of the mind are ultimately
located. And from that it follows that the conceptual fertility of the mind
in the constitution of new conceptual content is not, as philosophers have
imagined, something that threatens continually to bar us from an adequate
knowledge of the nature of things, but rather what makes such knowledge
possible. That thought, as we have shown, has as one of its consequences
the accessibility of a realistic account of truth. What remains inaccessible
on the present account is the philosophers' dream of a Finally Adequate
Theory equipped with a Finally Adequate Language; a language that, as all
truths would necessarily find expression in it, could serve as a touchstone

for the detection of nonsense and error. The natural world is not an image of thought. It exceeds thought in the absolute sense that it is simply other than, external to, thought, honouring in itself none of the categories internal to thought. Our cognitive relationship to it hinges on the permanent possibility of devising questions to which, when put to it, the world will deliver a clear answer. But we have to recognise that that possibility, endlessly explanatorily fruitful though it has proved in modern times, really is a *permanent* possibility. At any point in our investigation of the natural world, no matter how far that investigation may have proceeded, there will always remain open the possibility that some new experiment, some new model, will open a new conceptual vista from which things will look different, new types of explanation become available, problems that appeared solved turn out to display new aspects. Hence, there will never come a time when we "know everything" about the natural world, not because we suffer from some bizarre, philosophically locatable cognitive defect, but because, as Wittgenstein puts it in the penultimate paragraph of the *Tractatus*, "we have failed to give a sense to certain signs in our propositions": because, that is, the notion of "everything" in its employment here is simply imponderable.

v. The human and the subjective

One reason for believing in the availability in principle of a single language, a single conceptual scheme for the description of the natural world is, of course, the presumption of the causal unity of that world. That presumption, even if correct, does not entail the accessibility, even the ultimate accessibility, of a single language of description. But it does turn the idea of such a language into something like a Kantian regulative principle. One object of theory in natural science is to unify the conceptual basis of explanation wherever and to whatever extent possible, and many of its more striking advances have achieved just that.

By contrast, a great deal of discourse, that part of it which comprises what used to be called "humane letters," appears to proceed in the opposite direction, wantonly multiplying conceptual vocabularies without limit. Serious fiction and poetry, literary studies, ethics, theology, even law and politics, all display this characteristic. That fact raises a natural doubt concerning the claim of such works to investigate anything real. If students of ethics, let us say, or theology, or literary studies, had as their subject matter something real, would they not be led, like the natural scientist, since the principle of the Unity of Nature would apply to their subject matter as much as to hers, to seek, as she does, to arrive at a common conceptual vocabulary in terms of which to pursue their enquiries? And, since they do not, must it not follow that they are occupied with nothing real, but rather with figments of discourse, fancies of the mind?

The Logical Positivists made themselves a name in the 1930s for offering that sort of critique of ethics, aesthetics, theology. But the critique is of much older provenance, and its influence lurks everywhere in our intellectual and cultural life. It is implicit, for instance in Frege's treatment of the sentence "Odysseus was set ashore asleep at Ithaca," with its governing assumption that, since there is no real individual for "Odysseus" to be the name of, one's interest in the sentence, and with it the rest of the *Odyssey*, can only be an extrarational one; an interest, as Frege puts it, in "the euphony of the language" or "the images and feelings thereby aroused." Such interests, as Frege sees it, would be frustrated if questions of truth and reason were to raise their ugly heads: "the question of truth would cause us to abandon aesthetic delight for an attitude of scientific investigation."[17] Such attitudes, indeed, go back to Plato. But they are no less widely felt today. In this respect we seem a schizophrenic culture. We pay lip-service to "the Arts," we fund innumerable university departments devoted to the study of literature, institute Chairs of Theology, or Talmudic or Islamic Studies. And yet in our hearts very many of us believe that all these admirable institutions are concerned only with the study, or the propagation, of subjective fancies, and that the only person who has a seriously defensible claim to be busied about anything real is the natural scientist.

In this mood, the mood in which (some of the time, at least) we feel ourselves drawn to Positivism, things look like this. When we turn towards nature, towards the life-cycle of the sea-turtle, say, or the inner workings of volcanoes, we seem to get a grip on something real, something outside the mind. But when we turn back towards ourselves, towards Romantic poetry, towards the theology of Greek Orthodoxy, towards the philosophies of Hegel or Bentham and their political consequences, we seem to be entering a world of words, a world made of words, constituted by fold on fold of involuted, self-referential discourse: a vast palimpsest formed by the endless recursions and superimpositions of the mind's conversations with itself.

That mood has specific roots in two thoughts which recur constantly in our thinking. The first is the thought that to pursue reality is to be permanently at war with the tendency of the self, the ego, to deceive itself, to betray itself into fantasy, wishful thinking, refusal to look facts in the face. The second is the thought that we have pursued throughout this book, the thought that language itself may work to advance the forces of self-deception, unless in some way we can take the formation of its descriptive concepts out of the control of the mind, and place them instead under the control of the objective realities we wish them to describe.

The first of these thoughts is central to what Cora Diamond has called the nonphilosophical uses of the term "realism."[18] It is, for instance, what Iris Murdoch has centrally in mind when she argues, in *The Sovereignty of Good*, that the novel, and great art in general, since they work to discipline our tendency to self-deceiving fantasy, work not against but in favour of

Realism, at least, of Realism understood in Diamond's nonphilosophical way.[19] That "nonphilosophical" thought, that the impulse to Realism struggles constantly against the urge to remain deceived, is one gateway, though, to more "philosophical" uses of the term. The development of the methodology of the natural sciences, since the middle of the seventeenth century, after all, has very largly consisted in the formalisation and implementation of that thought. Through the development of practices, from increasingly precise standards of measurement to the institution of standards for making and reporting observations and experiments aimed at making both repeatable by any competent observer, natural science has aimed at freeing observation and experiment as far as possible from the private wishes and idiosyncracies of individual observers.

The project of natural science has thus become that of giving an account of the world independent of everything about human beings which makes for subjectivity: an account of the world, in effect, as it would appear if human beings were not part of it. Of course, human beings *are* part of the world. But that thought has seemed to many to require very little adjustment to the project of natural science. That project simply widens, as many have thought, to include within it the project of giving an account of human beings as one component of an objective world. Such an account, many have supposed, as it would be couched in the "objective" language or languages of the more general accounts of nature of which it would form a special department, would necessarily dispense, on grounds of "subjectivity," with the greater part of our commonplace self-descriptions: with the greater part, indeed, of what we fondly consider to constitute humane culture. Out would go "folk psychology," out would go the subjective discourses of of poetry, the novel, criticism, theology, and so on. It would describe human beings as they are, not as they imagine themselves to be. The language of such a description would indeed, as Merleau-Ponty put it, "deliver us to things": would finally expel us from all the saving obscurities, all the hiding places offered to subjectivity by the conceptual constructions of "ordinary language," which is to say, of language.

To formulate the project of natural science in this second way is to see science as aiming at an account of the world which, like the account aimed at by seventeenth-century metaphysics, would be final because radically comprehensive. Since the account given by its theories of the nature of things would be, *ex hypothesi*, finally adequate, the language in which those theories were couched would be, necessarily, perfectly fitted to the description of reality: a logically perfect language, in short. Such a vision of the end of enquiry is necessarily a vision of what we ultimately aim at in endeavouring to "be Realistic," and thus of what "Realism" means, what it involves. It brings us face to face with just that version of Realism that Cora Diamond takes to be "philosophical" in a bad sense of "philosophical." Philosophical Realism in this sense is the project of divorcing meaning from the practices, the experiences, through which, as human beings, we interact with the world, vesting it instead in something altogether beyond the human, something from the standpoint of which, neverthess, we may attain final epistemic dominance of the human. At that point, which is also the standpoint of the logically perfect language, language ceases to be capable of conceptual change and revision, because, in effect, frozen before the gaze of the ultimate reality by which, in absolutely mastering it, it has been absolutely mastered.

Diamond holds that there is a better sort of philosophical Realism; the one invoked by the remark of Wittgenstein's which forms the epigraph of her paper and of this chapter: "Not empiricism and yet realism in philosophy, that is the hardest thing."

Realism in philosophy, the hardest thing, is open-eyedly giving up the quest for such an elucidation, the demand that a philosophical account of what I mean make clear how it is fixed, out of all the possible continuations, out of some real semantic space, *which* I mean.[20]

The operative phrase here is "fixed . . . out of some real semantic space." We are to recognise, if we are to be Realists in Wittgenstein's and Diamond's sense; that what I mean – how I am to "go on," that is – is fixed by the conditions through which the words achieve a use in human life, not by something "real" in the sense of something altogether beyond the human, something which prescinds absolutely from the human.

The question whether we can speak, or mean, beyond the human, has been the topic of this book. Let us pursue it a little further yet. Let us begin with morals. The late Bernard Williams, in *Ethics and the Limits of Philosophy*, offered a clear-eyed, if depressing, account, not only of the prospects of moral philosophy, but of the prospects for the coherence of a society around an agreed set of moral principles. At one point in his argument, he asks the reader to envisage a "hypertraditionalist" society, whose members, although little given to moral reflection, believe in the "truth" of a range of moral judgments on which they agree. A more "reflective" society, viewing the hypertraditionalists from the outside, may deny truth to the latter's moral beliefs, on the grounds that those beliefs are in certain respects unreflective, have implications their holders have never considered, but which if considered might shake the hypertraditionalists' faith in what they have held to be moral truths. May we hope that moral knowledge, in the sense of access to moral truth, will prove available at the level of the reflective society? No, Williams argues, because the concept of moral knowledge is a philosophical chimaera. What enables us to speak of "knowledge" in connection with natural science is, on the one hand, the tendency of different investigations to converge on an answer, and, on the other hand, the possibility of accounting for this convergence in terms of "the way the world is," where "world" is to be explicated in terms of what Williams calls an "absolute conception," formed by selecting "among our beliefs...some that we can reasonably claim to represent the world in a way to the maximum degree independent of our perspective and its peculiarities."[21]

This appeals, in effect, to the first of the two conceptions of the goal of science distinguished above. Williams's question now is: could ethical reflection lead to a process of world-guided convergence upon answers such as we observe in natural science? Several reasons, he thinks, motivate an answer in the negative. First, not all ethical concepts are even partly world-guided. Some are, at least in part: they are what he calls "thick" ethical concepts; such concepts as *coward, lie, brutality, gratitude.* "A concept of this sort may be rightly or wrongly applied, and people who have acquired it can agree that it applies or fails to apply to some new situation."[22] But the more searching kinds of ethical reflection employ more general moral notions, *right, ought, good,* for example; and these are not in the same sort of way world-guided.

The very general kind of judgment that is in question here – a judgment using a very general concept – is essentially a product of reflection, and it comes into question when someone stands back from the practices of the society and its use of these concepts and asks whether this is the right way to go on, whether these are good ways in which to assess actions, whether the kind of choices that are admired are rightly admired.[23]

At this level one necessarily falls back on the voluntarism which has been such a *leitmotiv* of analytic moral philosophy since the 1930s. That is, one evolves a set of preferences which collectively adumbrate a life different from that prized by the hypertraditionalists, and one presents the picture of such a life to them in terms persuasive enough to secure the assent of many of them, and as a result, to lead them to change their opinion concerning the moral validity of their present opinions and practices. Simply on the evident grounds that belief in the truth of moral claims *can* be shaken in this way, Williams thinks, one must reject an "objectivist" for a "nonobjectivist" model of what is going on in the hypertraditional society. We shall not see the members of that society, in other words, "as trying, in their local way, to find out the truth about values." Rather, "we shall see their judgments as part of their way of living, a cultural artifact they have come to inhabit (though they have not consciously built it)."[24] The same, however, is true of the reflective society. Moral reflection is not a way of seeking truth. Rather, and especially when viewing events from the standpoint of the hypertraditional society, "we reach the notably un-Socratic conclusion that, in ethics, *reflection can destroy knowledge.*"[25]

It is not, as we shall see, far-fetched to see such a critique of the moral life as embodying a commitment to philosophical Realism in the first of the two senses distinguished by Cora Diamond. Let us look more closely at this. For Williams, the content of morality is expressed, essentially, by a collection of sentences in the imperative mood, such sentences, perhaps, as, "One does not behave brutally," "Lying is wrong," "A good wife should obey her husband," and so on. To take morality seriously is to believe that the members of some collection of such statements are "true." If that belief can be sustained, well and good; but if not, one emerges into the realisation that what one had considered moral truths represent merely expressions of the nature of a "cultural artefact," which one had no hand in instituting in the first place, and whose terms one can at any time transcend through processes of "moral reflection" which proceed to a great extent free from any restraint on the part of "the world." That Williams has here identified, and given admirably clear and concise expression to, a vision of the nature of our engagement with morality very widespread today, mostly in less clearly formulated versions, is beyond question. But is it correct? Is that in fact how we engage with morality?

Take, for instance, the conviction, widely shared by nonutilitarians, and indeed by many utilitarians, that it is wrong to punish the innocent. Do we respect this maxim because we believe it to be "true"? It would be odd if we did, given that the only sort of truth it can seriously be supposed to express is a conceptual one. It follows from what we *mean by* "justice," "innocent," "guilty," that it would be unjust to punish an innocent person. But what does "mean by" mean here? The preceding chapters suggest an answer. The society in which we live disposes of a vast range of devices, developed over long periods of time, first, for devising laws which no citizen may have reason to feel bear more heavily on him or her than on others; and, second for identifying those who have broken the law, to the disadvantage of others, and imposing suitable penalties on them. The first include among others, representative democracy, including such things as the institution of a second, revising, chamber, and the device of precedent central to the common law. The second include all those rules, of evidence and the conduct of court proceedings, whose purpose is to ensure that the innocent are not wrongly subjected to penalties that they have not justly, that is, through acting in a manner proscribed by the law, incurred.

If someone asks, now, "*Why* is it wrong to punish an innocent person," the only sensible response available to us, other than "because he is innocent, silly!," must surely take the form of redirecting the enquirer's attention to the role, the use$_E$, assigned to the words "innocent" and "just" in the fabric of practices to which we have just adverted. We are not, that is, confronted, as Williams supposes, with a choice between either taking a moral notion seriously because we take it to relate to an "absolute" reality, a reality wholly independent of human constitution; or, if we find that it relates merely to a "cultural artefact," waking as from a curiously moralistic dream to the realisation that it has no serious weight. We have, as a third option, what one might call Wittgensteinian Anamnesis. Wittgensteinian Anamnesis consists in the attempt to recollect in detail – "assembling reminders" is the phrase

Wittgenstein actually uses – how a concept functions, what place it occupies, in our lives.

I think one can see what Williams would make of such a move. He would see it as simply caving in to hypertraditionalism. And moreover as an ineffectual cave-in: as offering the hypertraditionalist not a lifebelt, but a mere straw. On Williams's view, the only thing that can save hypertraditionalism in morals is an ascent beyond the merely human, beyond the mere conceptual geography of a "cultural artifact," to something "real" in the sense that it might conceivably figure in an account of how things stand in the world framed in accordance with the "absolute conception" of enquiry. And there is nothing of that sort which could serve.

It is in this sense that Williams's views – like, incidentally, Kripke's on rule-following – can be read as philosophically Realist in the sense Cora Diamond thinks is wrongheaded. Diamond sees us as asking ourselves, in that mood,

> ... ordinary questions, to which we reject, as inadequate, ordinary answers, in the belief that we are asking something that passes those answers by. An adeqate elucidation of what I meant by "he is always to go on in that way" must pick out something in the realm of things-that-might-possibly-be-meant: not possibly-in-human-practice but in some other sense, *not dependent on what goes on in our lives*.[26] [our italics]

Let us not, then, be too shaken by the demolishing reply we have just offered ourselves on Williams's behalf. Given that there is indeed nothing *not dependent on what goes on in our lives* that can save the hypertraditionalist's bacon, and given also that we are all, in some respects, hypertraditionalist in our attitude to morals; let us consider a little further to what extent Wittgensteinian Anamnesis, the giving of answers which *are* "dependent on what goes on in our lives," may help the hypertraditionalist to keep his flag flying and his ugly head obstinately raised. Suppose we do see why, given the role that the institutions charged with maintaining justice, and with determining what is just, play in our lives; and why it is, given the meanings that terms such as "just," "innocent," "guilty," play in our lives, that to say that one ought not to punish an innocent man is to make a remark about the meaning, the conceptual content of the terms "just" and "innocent." And suppose that the only answer we have to offer an enquirer, or ourselves, in answer to the question, "*Why* is it wrong to punish an innocent man?," is merely to embark once again on a tour of recollection around and about those familiar facts concerning the roles the relevant notions play in our lives? How far is the belief that it *is* wrong to punish an innocent man, so sustained, vulnerable to "moral reflection"?

The answer that springs to mind is: not very; indeed, really not much at all. How could one set about showing that, after all, it may on occasion be right to punish an innocent man? The usual route taken is a Utilitarian one, the argument being that, since increase of welfare, either distributively or globally, provides our only measure of rightness, it may on occasion be right to practice injustice if that is necessary to produce a greater balance of welfare. Such arguments are usually buttressed by the suggestion that to maintain the contrary is mere "rule-worship." Such arguments do indeed display the features that Williams sees as characteristic of moral reflection: the deployment of cut-and-dried arguments of an extreme degree of abstraction, employing moral notions whose generality frees them from being "world guided" because it deprives them of any contact with the detailed realities of human life. Such reasonings have in the past persuaded many astute minds. But is there not a price to be paid for accepting them? Can one not see, rather clearly, at the close of the twentieth century where they lead: namely, to put it bluntly, to the institution of regimes in which increasingly empty claims to maximise welfare in fact mask the most abject *raison d'état*; regimes whose ruling élites display endemic kinds of tyranny and kleptocracy that can no longer be brought before the bar of a common justice because the institutions of justice have been effectively dismantled? Is not the reflection that these observations suggest that to abandon the moral respect commonly given to the principle that the innocent are not to be punished is to abandon the moral respect due to the notion of justice *per se*, and by so doing to embrace a world in which justice no longer exists? Might one not prefer not to take that step? And would not the reasons for not taking that step – the ones we have just rehearsed – constitute merely a further round of Wittgensteinian Anamnesis: a further stage in the process of remembering why we have, and need to have, such notions as "just" and "innocent" in our language; notions that we treat with moral respect because treating them with moral respect is integral to the leading of a certain kind of life: a life governed by justice rather than by unbridled tyranny founding itself on moral cant?

Williams has a reply open to him: namely, that not all moral notions can, as plausibly as these, be represented as indispensable. This is fair enough. At one time higher education was considered by many to be *morally* inappropriate for young women, as damaging the purity and innocence essential to femininity, and unfitting them to become the mothers of the race. "Moral reflection" has indeed played a part in relegating these notions to the history of morals. But one needs to remember that "moral reflection" involved in this case more than the deployment of a few smart arguments. It involved the painful invention, over more than a century, of new modes of accommodation between the sexes; a process that is still, in many respects, proceeding. What happened was not that certain *propositions*, which earlier were supposed to express "truths," were found on reflection not to be *propositions* at all, but to be merely expressions of sentiment, or of the internal logic of a "cultural artifact." It was rather that, as relations between the sexes gradually altered, in response to a vast variety of causal and cultural influences, the terms "purity," "innocence," "motherhood" ceased to play the role in *what goes on in our lives* that they formerly played. They were left stranded, on some Arnoldian beach, by the melancholy, long, withdrawing roar of the vast changes in the practices and assumptions governing social and personal accommodation between the sexes in Western societies that have taken place over the past century and a half.

At any given time some of our "moral beliefs," if one wants to put it that way, will be vulnerable to revision at the hands of such changes. Others – the vast majority – will not. The effect of the kind of "Realism" Diamond deplores, in the hands of such able reasoners as Williams, is first to misrepresent the nature of the processes through which such revisions occur, and second, and in consequence, to make it appear that because some moral convictions are vulnerable to revision, *all* are.

The heart of the illusion worked by such arguments is the move Diamond identifies: the move of first suggesting that something beyond the role it plays in our lives is necessary to confer "objectivity" on a moral observation, and then pointing out that no further, "external" consideration of the type allegedly required is available. What happens if we resist this move? Don't we find ourselves envisaging a different conception of objectivity: one different, that is, from the one we commonly envisage in terms of what Williams calls the absolute conception of enquiry? It is a conception foreshadowed by much of what we have been arguing in this book. Earlier, in Part II, we suggested that the conception of *who someone "really,"* that is to say objectively *is*, is made available to us only through the existence of the vast web of socially devised and maintained practices – the "cultural artefact," if you like – constituted by the Name-Tracking Network. The thought that suggests is that objectivity and the culturally artifactual are not the polar opposites they are commonly supposed to be, but rather part and parcel of one another. Let us pursue that point by looking once again at the notion of justice. Justice is, as we say, "a reality" in a society in which it is a reality, because in those societies the institutions for establishment and application of justice are (to a great extent) scrupulously maintained and conducted, and are respected by the vast majority of the citizens. Justice exists in such a society, no doubt, only because it is, in this sort of way, continuously willed into existence by the citizens, acting both individually and collectively. If they ceased to will in that way it would cease to exist. But as long as it is, in this way, borne up on a continuously flowing tide of settled wills, it exists, as a perfectly real, perfectly "objective" feature of the society it characterises.

Such realities, such objectivities, moreover, enter into the constitution of types of human being. The Just Man can come into existence only in a society that possesses a conception of justice. But once he exists he is real, he is objectively present in the world as what he is. The same is true of indefinitely many human types, the Romantic, the Marxist, the Catholic, the Sceptical Chymist, the Hobbist. And that thought may yield, in conclusion, the solution to a puzzle we raised earlier: why we allow so much cultural weight to attach to the study of literature, literary criticism, theology, when the subject matters of these studies appear – or can appear to us, in certain moods – to be no more than tissues of words, bearing on nothing objective. The answer is that they *do*, all of them, bear on objectivities, namely, the kind of objectivities we collectively constitute, make out of ourselves, out of our own perishing flesh and blood, through our activity as constitutors of practices: that founding activity to which we owe both our humanity and our status as language-users, as articulate beings.

Such a thought lies at the heart of Wallace Stevens's poem "Men Made out of Words":

> What should we be without the sexual myth,
> The human reverie or poem of death?
> Castratos of moon-mash – Life consists
> Of propositions about life. The human
> Reverie is a solitude in which
> We compose these propositions, torn by dreams,
> By the terrible incantations of defeats
> And by the fear that defeats and dreams are one.
> The whole race is a poet that writes down
> The eccentric propositions of its fate.[27]

Paul De Man taught us that a poem can be read in contradictory ways. Something of the sort happens here, though without the sceptical implications De Man tends to attach to the thought. At first sight the poem grants the sceptic's point: there is nothing to words, and so nothing to men, beyond their own dreams, for words are all that either are made of. But at the same time the poem turns that thought upside-down. By means of words we make ourselves, change and elaborate our nature; and since we, and our changing natures, are real, the words by means of which we accomplish that are, after all, occupied with realities.

By means of words we make ourselves. Words seem, as we have argued, empty vocables only if we consider them in abstraction from the modes of insertion into our lives which confer upon them all the meaning they possess. A language, a vocabulary of concepts, is the expression of a way of life, of a mode of being. Consider the issue of how we are to describe what it is to be an individual human person. Anyone of common sense and experience in encountering and dealing with the oddities of others will be inclined to doubt whether the range of conceptual distinctions adequate to express the way in which life and the world in which it is lived present themselves to one person, will prove entirely adequate to express the way in which they present themselves to another. Always there comes the moment at which someone will say, "No, that's not quite how it seems to me"; and as he or she attempts to say how it *does* seem to them, it is familiar enough to find one's interlocutor groping towards the articulation of what are, in

effect, grounds for accepting a shift in the content of some common word
or phrase, "love," for example, or "Englishness," or "what is owed to one's
children." Understanding another person is, in part, understanding why he
or she wishes, or feels compelled to, give words a slightly different meaning
from the meaning another might give to them. And as one enquires further
into what might motivate that shift of meaning, and what its implications
might be, the lineaments of another life, another consciousness, come into
view.

Merleau-Ponty takes that experience to be central to the reading of literature.

With the aid of signs agreed upon by the author and myself because we speak the
same language, the book makes me believe that we had already shared a common
stock of well-worn and readily available significations. The author has come to dwell
in my world. Then, imperceptibly, he varies the ordinary meaning of the signs, and
like a whirlwind they sweep me along toward that other meaning with which I am
going to connect.[28]

It is easy enough to think of examples of this process. "Sensibility" in the
period when Jane Austen was writing, had been established by that comparatively recent growth, the Novel of Sensibility, as a term of positive connotations, denoting sensitivity both on the moral and the aesthetic plane, and
contrasting with brutality, dullness and insensitivity. Part of Jane Austen's
achievement in *Sense and Sensibility* is to take the shine off the term by sup-
plying rather compelling grounds for connecting the state of mind it designates with kinds of aestheticising egotism not normally dwelt upon by its
admirers. The grounds she supplies are, of course, only imagined, but they
are imagined with a degree of coherence and verisimilitude that, by making
it easy to connect them to instances in the life of the reader, make them
difficult to dismiss as mere polemic. When we open the book we are able to
grasp what Jane Austen is talking about because, just as Merleau-Ponty says,
we can rely on a common fund of commonplace meanings linking us to the
author. But as we read on, contrary impressions accumulate one by one, and
by the end of the book, if we have grasped what is going on, "sensibility"
will be for us a term of slighly different content, and rather less favourable
connotations, than it was for us at the outset.

Someone of a resolutely Referential Realist turn of mind will tend to find
these choppings and shufflings of words irritating and pointless; typical of
literary studies; but then, typical of what makes literature of so little relevance, as he sees it, to the formation of an objective picture of the world
and our place in it. Either, he will want to say, the word "sensibility" has a
meaning, in the sense of picking out some definite, identifiable constituent
of reality, or else it has no meaning, or can mean anything you please; is in
short a mere bit of literary verbiage, part of one of those "folk" languages
that will one day, it is to be hoped, be discarded in favour of a properly

"scientific" language for the description of human affairs, based, perhaps, on an "objective" psychology or on one of the languages of neurophysiology or Artificial Intelligence.

That irritation is reasonable, at least in its own terms, and deserves an answer. Would it make sense to accuse Jane Austen, or the writers of the Novel of Sensibility school, of being "just wrong" in the content they assign to the notion of sensibility? Clearly not. To ask such a question, in fact, would show a complete misunderstanding of what literature is about. If two chemists hold incompatible views about the properties of a certain substance, say the element cadmium, it will make sense to ask which of them is mistaken in the content they assign to "cadmium." But that is because "cadmium" is a label for a naturally occurring substance whose properties are open to investigation. The case of Jane Austen and the Novel of Sensibility is not analogous. There is no object, no "constituent of reality," whose properties remain to be investigated, and for which the term "sensibility" serves as a label. Neither Jane nor the author of *The Man of Feeling*, therefore, can be "just wrong" about the content attaching to the term "sensibility."

In that case, why isn't the term a mere arbitrary counter, whose meaning, or lack of it, can safely be left to the literary-minded to determine as they please? The question sets out to force a choice beween two replies which, it is presumed, conjointly exhaust the options. One reply would be that the term in this context is just an arbitrary counter; the other would be that it refers to, or "picks out," some entity, posited as enjoying an existence independent of any linguistic, conceptual or otherwise "constitutive" activity of the human mind, which Jane Austen and the Novel of Sensibility are setting out to "investigate" and "describe," in something analogous to the way in which our inorganic chemist might set out to investigate and describe the properties of cadmium. That is the pair of options allowed us by Referential Realism. The chief ground for thinking it an exhaustive option is identical, moreover, with the chief ground for accepting Referential Realism itself: deny either, and you will find the doors of the Prison-House of Language closing on you.

When anything in philosophy looks as watertight as this, however, the chances are that mirrors and trapdoors are concealed somewhere in the stage-setting. If the writer is not concerned, unlike the chemist, to describe the contents of an extrahuman realm of entities, what is he, or she, up to? The answer we seem to have arrived at is that the business of literature is on the one hand the organisation and elaboration, and on the other hand the critique, of responses to life and the world. Although emotion enters into response, a response is not an "emotional state," a "sentiment" or an "attitude;" not, that is, the bare upwelling of feeling that noncognitivists in ethics like to invoke in support of their theories. A response is a systematic articulation of values, feelings, and beliefs. It outlines, as the term suggests, a way of responding to the human condition, but it does not sketch it as an abstract possibility: it offers it as something that can be inhabited; as a mode of being human. The crucial terms that emerge in such a process, terms such as "Reason," "Nature," or "Sensibility" do not refer to anything that existed prior to the inception of the process of articulating the mode of response, in connection with which they assume the status of crucial terms. The rise of the cult of Sensibility, from *Tristram Shandy* onwards, is not a development in understanding of something that existed before, but a new birth, a bringing into the world of something new: a new mode of response.

Does that mean that such terms merely pick out "phantoms of the mind," or something of the sort? To say that is to suggest that the process of bringing such "phantoms" into being is an entirely arbitrary, strain-free one, subject to no controls arising from the nature of reality. But that is not so. A response is not a pipe-dream, and the business of articulating a serious response to the human condition is not at all isolated from conflict with, and chastening at the hands of, what is the case. A structure of value, feeling and belief that imposes intolerable strains on credulity, relationship, desire or fulfillment, cannot satisfy for long, or at least cannot satisfy many for long. Every new mode of response therefore faces severe tests of adequacy. It must prove capable of representing itself as on the whole truthful and productive. As a novel, *Sense and Sensibility* is interesting, in large part, because it does such a deadly job of exposing ways in which the cult of Sensibility, which in many ways is as influential in our own day as it was in the last quarter of the eighteenth century, may be neither.

The popular but less exacting works grouped by literary historians under the label "the Novel of Sensibility" fail that test because, like much popular literature, they gain too easy a success in evoking from the complaisant reader the responses that their authors wish to evoke: a success gained at the expense of glossing over vast areas of infidelity either to the realities of human life or to any credible estimate of the prospects of organising in practice, on the basis of such responses, a satisfactory life. That is why they are not literature, but kitsch.

So, although we cannot say that either Jane Austen and the Novel of Sensibility are "just wrong" about anything ("the nature of Sensibility," or "the content of the concept – the platonic Form – of Sensibility," say), we nevertheless dispose of types of critical evaluation which mark different levels of engagement on the part of literary writing with reality, in this case the realities of human life. It is just that the mode of engagement with reality exhibited by literature is not that exhibited by the constitutive practices of chemistry, or by those that constitute any form of natural science.

The distinction between these, and other styles of interaction between language and the world, is one that, as we shall see, the views defended here make it easy both to apprehend and to account for. The difference on our view is a matter of the way in which differing practices engage with reality. In terms of Michael Krausz's [29] distinction between singularism and multiplism, singularism being the thesis that only one interpretive response in a given situation can be correct, and multiplism the thesis that many can, it allows us to see why singularism may be appropriate to one field of human activity – inorganic chemistry, say – and multiplism to another – say the articulation and criticism of responses to the human condition – without failure on the part of either activity to meet the demands of a minimal Realism. What makes multiplism appropriate to the conceptual schemes deployed in the discussion of literature, as it is not to the assessment of those successively deployed over the centuries in the development of inorganic chemistry, is simply human difference. The critique of response, sensitive though it may be to failures of truthfulness or plausibility, can never result in the reduction to a single survivor of the range of serious responses to the human condition. The differing conceptual vocabularies appropriate to the articulation, say, of the Augustan and Christian stoicism of Johnson, on the one hand, and the proto-Romantic sentimentalism of Sterne, on the other, are no doubt as richly incompatible as the outlooks within which they take on meaning. But neither is "wrong" or "mistaken" in its assessment of the character and possibilities of a human life. Neither is a merely a tissue of "fanciful" notions deserving to be ranked with such concepts as demonic possession and discarded in favour of the soberly "referential" concepts employed by the other. Both meet the standards of veracity and productivity that the Novel of Sentiment or the works of Georgette Heyer fail. Neither, therefore, can displace the other. Both remain standing as permanent monuments to the power of the literary imagination to fight against the dissolution of human life into darkness and meaninglessness.

Referential Realism, however, with its determination to force the issue of thought and reality into the procrustian bed of a simple choice between the referential and the illusory, makes all such distinctions between the modes of engagement with reality of different human practices not only harder to apprehend, but for many minds impossible to apprehend. The centrality and the prestige it has enjoyed in our intellectual life for the past three centuries constitute, to our minds, one of the main reasons for the gulfs of misunderstanding, and at times mutual hostility, which divide the "Two Cultures" of science and the humanities.

Now for a final postscript. A literary critic of moderately conservative inclinations, reading through the above, might be disposed to reply that the prestige of the referential, in his discipline at least, has long been dissipated by the advance of deconstruction. The revolution that has occurred in literary studies over the past three decades, he will complain, has surely made it otiose to propose, as a new idea, that literature creates its own realities, ungrounded in reality because ungrounded in any pre-existing, extratextual, fabric of meanings, logocentrically conceived. True: but that is not quite what we have been saying.

It is true that we share common ground with deconstruction. The central claim of deconstruction, Derrida's central claim, is that meaning is evolved within language, by shifting the relations of signs to other signs. There is no "logos," no structure of "meanings" given antecedently and externally to language, in which the meanings generated by a given piece of writing, of *écriture*, can be grounded. Something along those lines is also a central thesis of this book. It is, after all, a simple consequence of Wittgenstein's Slogan, of the priority of meaning over truth that the Slogan affirms, that all questions of meaning must be settled internally to language. Doesn't that commit us, then, to the full, radical, implications of Derrida's *Il n'y a pas d'hors-texte?* (aren't Fodor's sights, after all, lined up on us?) Well, no. It depends, as Professor Joad used to say on the radio, what you mean by "grounded." Many readers of Derrida have taken the denial of logocentrism to carry the consequence that the generation of new meaning within language is not only *unconstrained by extralinguistic meaning*, but *unconnected in any way with the extralinguistic per se*. That is to say, the generation of meaning just reels arbitrarily onward, as a function purely of the shifting relations of linguistic signs among themselves, uninfluenced in any way by any consideration arising outside language. We have argued elsewhere at length that Derrida is not committed to the second of these supposed consequences, because it is in fact a nonsequitur. Whether or not Derrida himself supposes it to be entailed by his views is an exegetical question of some complexity: some passages in his writings suggest that he does wish to advance some such view; by contrast, much in his position is formally incompatible with it. We, by contrast, certainly do not wish to find ourselves committed to anything of the sort, and are not. We hold with Derrida (or Saussure, or Merleau-Ponty) that meaning is, roughly speaking, a matter of the relation of linguistic sign to linguistic sign. But we hold also that the relationships in question are relations *across practices*, and that practices, in the required sense, are collectively devised and maintained systems of convention intrinsically involving engagement with the world. Envisaging a new meaning, therefore, involves, at the first level of the two-level model proposed in Part I, envisaging a change in the relationship of a sign to other signs. But at the second level it involves envisaging a change in the mode of operation of a practice, that is to say, a change in our modes of engagement with the world. What this move does for literary studies is, in effect, to reanimate certain ways of thinking about literature long since dismissed by the critical vanguard to the dustbin of history presently occupied by such movements as New Criticism or *Scrutiny*. It allows us to conceive of literature, on the one hand, with Stevens, as one of the main engines through which we continually constitute and reconstitute our nature as human beings, and, on the other, as an engine of continuous rational examination and critique of such constitutions, from whatever source they arise. Such an account, of course, needs much further development. Some of that work has already been done elsewhere.[30] What remains must await another book.

Notes

Introduction

1. Ryle, Gilbert, *Dilemmas*. Cambridge: Cambridge University Press, 1953.
2. And has been objected by Guy Stock, whose comments in this and other ways have proved extremely useful to us.

Chapter One

1. Merleau-Ponty, Maurice, *La Prose du Monde*, Paris, 1969. Translated as *The Prose of the World*, tr. Claude Lefort and John O'Neill. Evanston, IL: Northwestern University Press, 1973, p. 115.
2. Frege, Gottlob, *Logical Investigations*, ed. P. T. Geach, tr. P. T. Geach and R. H. Stoothoff. Oxford: Basil Blackwell, 1977, p. 36.
3. Locke, John, *Essay Concerning Human Understanding*, ed. P. H. Nidditch. Oxford: Clarendon Press, 1975, Book III, Chapter V, §3.
4. Berkeley, George, "Three Dialogues between Hylas and Philonous," in *A New Theory of Vision, and Other Writings*. London: J. M. Dent, Everyman, 1910, p. 244.

Chapter Two

1. Russell, Bertrand, *Logic and Knowledge: Essays 1901–1950*, ed. Robert Charles Marsh. London: George Allen and Unwin, 1956, p. 195.
2. Dummett, Michael, *Truth and Other Enigmas*. London: Duckworth, 1978, p. 157.
3. Russell, Bertrand, *The Problems of Philosophy*. London: Oxford University Press, 1912, p. 48.
4. Russell, *The Problems of Philosophy*, pp. 58–9.
5. Russell, Bertrand, *An Inquiry into Meaning and Truth*. London: George Allen and Unwin, 1940, p. 66.
6. Russell, *Meaning and Truth*, p. 65.
7. Kant, Immanuel, *Critique of Pure Reason*, tr. Norman Kemp Smith. London: Macmillan, 1929. All citations from A51/B75.
8. McDowell, John, *Mind and World*. London and Cambridge, MA: Harvard University Press, 1994, p. 5.

9. Geach, Peter, *Mental Acts*. London: Routledge and Kegan Paul, 1957. See especially §§5–11.
10. McDowell, *Mind and World*, p. 7.
11. Ibid., p. 7.
12. Geach, *Mental Acts*, p. 40.
13. Ibid., p. 40–1.
14. McDowell, *Mind and World*, pp. 4–5.
15. Ibid., p. 5.
16. Ibid., p. 92.
17. Ibid., p. 92–3.
18. Ibid., p. 93.
19. Ibid., p. 95.
20. Zalabardo, José, "Rules, Communities, and Judgments." *Critica* **63** (1989): 33–58.
21. Quine, W. V. O., "Two Dogmas of Empiricism," in *From a Logical Point of View*. Cambridge, MA: Harvard University Press, 1953.
22. Quine, W. V. O., *Ontological Relativity, and Other Essays*. New York and London: Columbia University Press, 1969, p. 75.
23. Quine, W. V. O., *Word and Object*. New York, London, Cambridge, MA: John Wiley and Sons/MIT Press, 1960, pp. 32–3.
24. Ibid., p. 43.
25. Ibid., p. 43.
26. Quine, "Two Dogmas of Empiricism," p. 43.
27. Heal, Jane, *Fact and Meaning: Quine and Wittgenstein on Philosophy of Language*. Oxford: Blackwell, 1989.

Chapter Three

1. Harrison, Bernard, "Wittgenstein and Scepticism," in Klaus Pühl, ed., *Meaning-Scepticism*. Berlin: De Gruyter, 1991, pp. 34–69; "Truth, Yardsticks and Language-Games," *Philosophical Investigations*, **19**: 2 (1996): 105–30; "Criteria and Truth," *Midwest Studies in Philosophy* **20** (1999): 207–35.
2. Wittgenstein, Ludwig, *Philosophical Investigations*, 2nd ed. Oxford: Blackwell, 1953, x^e.
3. Geach, Peter, and Black, Max, *Translations from the Philosophical Writings of Gottlob Frege*. Oxford: Blackwell, 1966, p. 60.
4. Strawson, P. F., Review of L. Wittgenstein, *Philosophical Investigations*. *Mind* **LXIII** (1954): 70–99.
5. Harrison, "Criteria and Truth," *passim*.
6. See Martin, Gottfried, *Leibniz: Logic and Metaphysics*, tr. K. J. Northcott and P. G. Lucas. Manchester: Manchester University Press, 1964, pp. 57–62.
7. Wilkins, John, *An Essay towards a Real Character and a Philosophical Language*. London, 1688.
8. Russell, Bertrand, *Logic and Knowledge: Essays 1901–1950*, ed. Robert Charles Marsh. London: George Allen and Unwin, 1956, pp. 197–8.
9. Bachelard, Gaston, *Le matérialisme rationnel*. Paris: Presses Universitaires de France, 1972. See especially Ch. VII, "Le rationalisme de la couleur," pp. 193–206.

10. On this, see Kovesi, Julius, *Moral Notions*. London and New York: Routledge and Kegan Paul, 1967, Chapter 1 *et seq*.
11. We are grateful to Michael Krausz for making us see the need to extract this topic from the small print and deal with it explicitly at this point in the book.
12. Heal, Jane, *Fact and Meaning: Quine and Wittgenstein on Philosophy of Language*. Oxford: Blackwell, 1989, p. 221.
13. See Dummett, Michael, *The Seas of Language*. Oxford: Clarendon Press, 1993.

> I continue to believe that any knowledge attributed to a speaker as constituting a component of his knowledge of a language must be manifested in his employment of that language, including his reactions to things said in that language to him by others. (p. xii)

Chapter Four

1. Geach, Peter, and Black, Max, *Translations from the Philosophical Writings of Gottlob Frege*. Oxford: Blackwell, 1966, p. 60.
2. Ibid., p. 59.
3. Frege, Gottlob, *Logical Investigations*, ed. P. T. Geach, tr. P. T. Geach and R. H. Stoothoff. Oxford: Basil Blackwell, 1977, p. 33.
4. Ibid., p. 33.
5. Ibid., p. 36.
6. Ibid., p. 26.
7. Ibid., p. 24.
8. Ibid., p. 5.
9. Ibid., p. 5.
10. Ibid., p. 4.
11. Geach and Black, *Translations from Frege*, p. 62.
12. Ibid., p. 63.
13. Ibid., p. 63.
14. A reader questioned whether Frege actually thought this, and demanded chapter and verse. Collating "*Die Gedanke*" with "*Über Sinn und Bedeutung*" offers one route to the required textual backing. In the former essay Frege says, "... the only thing that raises the question of truth ... is the sense of sentences." (Frege, *Logical Investigations*, p. 4). In the latter, he observes that "sentences which contain proper names without reference" will have "a sense and no reference" (Geach and Black, *Translations from Frege*, p. 62). As Frege took the *Bedeutung* of a sentence to be a truth-value, the thought we ascribe to him follows.
15. Russell, Bertrand, "On the Nature of Acquaintance," in *Logic and Knowledge: Essays 1901–1950*, ed. Robert Charles Marsh. London: George Allen and Unwin, 1956, p. 130.
16. Russell, Bertrand, *The Problems of Philosophy*. London: Oxford University Press, 1912, p. 58.
17. Evans, Gareth, *The Varieties of Reference*, McDowell, John, ed. Oxford: Clarendon Press; New York: Oxford University Press, 1982, p. 44.
18. Ibid., p. 64.
19. Ibid., p. 89.
20. Ryle, Gilbert, *The Concept of Mind*. Harmondsworth: Penguin Books, 1963, p. 28ff.

21. Ryle, *Concept of Mind*, p. 29.
22. Russell, Bertrand, "The Philosophy of Logical Atomism," in Marsh, *Logic and Knowledge*, pp. 182–3.
23. Ibid., p. 181.
24. Ibid., p. 182.
25. Ibid., p. 196.
26. Ibid., p. 197.
27. Ibid., pp. 197–8.
28. Ibid., p. 183.
29. Letter to Ottoline Morell, 22.3.12, cited in Ray Monk, *Wittgenstein: the Duty of Genius*. London: Jonathan Cape, 1990, p. 41.
30. Ibid., pp. 81–2.
31. Wittgenstein, Ludwig, *Notebooks 1914–16*, ed. G. H. von Wright and G. E. M. Anscombe, tr. G. E. M. Anscombe. Oxford: Basil Blackwell, 1969, p. v.
32. Ibid., p. 2e.
33. Ibid., p. 3e.
34. Ibid., p. 3e.
35. Russell, Bertrand, *The Problems of Philosophy*, p. 127.
36. Ibid., p. 128.
37. Wittgenstein, *Notebooks*, p. 2e.
38. Ibid, pp. 19e–20e.
39. Ibid., p. 19e.
40. Ibid., p. 2e.

Chapter Five

1. See Davidson, Donald, "A Nice Derangement of Epitaphs," in E. Lepore, ed., *Truth and Interpretation*. Oxford: Blackwell, 1986, pp. 443–6, and the accompanying comments by Michael Dummett and Ian Hacking.
2. According to the OED, "nomothetic" is a rare word that has, since the mid-nineteenth century (following Windelband's distinction between nomothetic [law-seeking] and ideographic [historical] sciences) been used to mean, roughly, "pertaining to the study of laws of nature." There is, however, an earlier body of uses of the term, deriving from "nomothete" = "a lawgiver or legislator," in which the term was used, by Bentham among others, as a variant form of "nomothetical" = "lawgiving; legislative." It is in its older, indeed original, sense that we shall use the term here.
3. It might be objected that the Orthodox View need not require the possessor of an identifying description to be able to "locate" Aristotle, say, in the sense of picking him out from other fourth-century Greeks in a police line-up. But all that shows is that identifying descriptions for different types of individual turn on different types of property. Whatever type of property it appeals to, however, the function of an identifying description on the Orthodox View is to "locate" a given individual in the sense of singling it out from all others individuals of the same kind, whatever form the singling-out may take in a specific case.
4. Dummett, Michael, *Frege: Philosophy of Language*. London: Duckworth, 1973, p. 140.

5. Wittgenstein, Ludwig, *Philosophical Investigations*, 2nd ed. Oxford: Blackwell, 1953, II. xii, p. 230e.
6. Ibid., §31.
7. We owe some of these details to a Scots friend, A. A. H. Inglis.
8. We have in mind the following lines from "The Eolian Harp":

> And what if all of animated nature
> Be but organic harps diversely framed,
> That tremble into thought, as o'er them sweeps
> Plastic and vast, one intellectual breeze,
> At once the Soul of each, and God of all?

Coleridge's thoughts on the interanimation of Mind and Nature, like McDowell's, were chiefly cast in the mould of German Romanticism. Ours are dominated by a certain reading of Wittgenstein. But there are parallels.

9. Wittgenstein, *Philosophical Investigations*, §13.

Chapter Six

1. Mill, John Stuart, *A System of Logic, ratiocinative and inductive*. London: Longmans, 1891, Book I, Chapter 2, §5.
2. Kripke, Saul, *Naming and Necessity*. Oxford: Blackwell, 1980.
3. Ibid., p. 15.
4. Ibid., p. 15.
5. Ibid., p. 16.
6. See Harrison, Bernard, "Description and Identification." *Mind* **91** (1982): 321–38.
7. See Davidson, Donald, *Inquiries into Truth and Interpretation*. Oxford: Clarendon Press, 1984, p. 47.

Chapter Seven

1. Kripke, Saul, *Naming and Necessity*. Oxford: Blackwell, 1980, pp. 91–2.
2. Evans, Gareth, "The Causal Theory of Names." *Aristotelian Society Supplementary Volume* **47** (1973): 187–208.
3. Ibid., p. 187.
4. Ibid., p. 192.
5. Ibid., p. 192.
6. Ibid., p. 203.
7. Ibid., p. 199.
8. Ibid., p. 202.
9. Ibid., pp. 200–1.
10. Ibid., p. 191.
11. Locke, John, *An Essay Concerning Human Understanding*, ed. P. H. Nidditch. Oxford: Clarendon Press, 1975, Book II, Chapter 1, §1.
12. Searle, John, *Speech Acts*, Cambridge: Cambridge University Press, 1969, p. 87.
13. Levi, Primo, *If this is a Man*. Published in America as *Survival in Auschwitz*, tr. Stuart Woolf. New York: Touchstone, 1996, p. 27.
14. Kant, Immanuel, *Critique of Pure Reason*, tr. Norman Kemp Smith. London: Macmillan, 1929, A51/B75.

15. Katz, Jerrold J., "Has the description theory of names been refuted?," in George Boolos, ed., *Meaning and Method: Essays in Honor of Hilary Putnam.* Cambridge and New York: Cambridge University Press, 1990, pp. 31–2.

Chapter Eight

1. Wittgenstein, Ludwig, *On Certainty,* Oxford: Blackwell, 1969, p. 28e.
2. Dummett, Michael, "Wittgenstein's Philosophy of Mathematics," in *Truth and Other Enigmas,* London: Duckworth, 1978. p. 171.
3. Quine, W. V. O., *Word and Object,* London and Cambridge, MA: John Wiley and Sons, MIT Press, 1960, pp. 32–3.
4. Davidson, Donald, "A Nice Derangement of Epitaphs," in E. Lepore, ed., *Truth and Interpretation.* Oxford: Blackwell, 1986, p. 446.
5. Ibid., pp. 445–6.
6. Dummett, Michael, "A Nice Derangement of Epitaphs: Some Comments on Davidson and Hacking," in E. Lepore, ed., *Truth and Interpretation,* p. 473.
7. Ibid., pp. 475–6.
8. Dummett, Michael, "What do I Know when I Know a Language?," in *The Seas of Language.* Oxford: Clarendon Press, 1993, pp. 94–105.
9. Ibid., p. 94.
10. Ibid., p. 95.
11. Ibid., p. 102.
12. Ibid., p. 102.
13. Ibid., pp. 100–1.
14. Ibid., p. 103.
15. Ibid., p. 103.
16. Ibid., p. 104.
17. Ibid., p. 105.
18. Kripke, Saul, *Wittgenstein on Rules and Private Language.* Oxford: Basil Blackwell, 1982.
19. Ibid., p. 17.
20. Wittgenstein, Ludwig, *Philosophical Investigations,* 2nd ed. Oxford: Blackwell, 1953, p. 81e.
21. Kripke, Saul, *Naming and Necessity.* Oxford: Blackwell, 1980, p. 15.
22. Ibid., p. 16.
23. The following two or three sentences paraphrase Kripke, *Naming and Necessity,* pp. 93–4.
24. Ibid., p. 95.
25. See, e.g., Putnam, Hilary, *The Many Faces of Realism: The Paul Carus Lectures.* La Salle, IL: Open Court, 1987, pp. 14–15.
26. Miller, Alexander, *Philosophy of Language.* London: UCL Press, 1998, p. 173.
27. Kripke, *Naming and Necessity,* p. 55.
28. Zalabardo, José, "Rules, Communities, and Judgments." *Critica* **63** (1989): 33–58. Wright, Crispin, "Kripke's Account of the Argument against Private Language." *Journal of Philosophy* **81** (1984): 759–77. See also Blackburn, Simon, "The Individual Strikes Back." *Synthese* **58** (1984): 281–301.
29. Dummett, Michael, "Wittgenstein's Philosophy of Mathematics," in *Truth and Other Enigmas.* London: Duckworth, 1978, p. 170.

30. Ibid, p. 171.
31. See, for example, Baker, G. P., and Hacker, P. M. S., *Scepticism, Rules and Language*, Oxford: Blackwell, 1984; Richard McDonough, "Wittgenstein's Refutation of Meaning-Scepticism," in Pühl, Klaus, ed., *Meaning Scepticism*, Berlin and New York: de Gruyter, 1991, pp. 70–92; and, for a critique of the former, Meredith Williams, "Blind Obedience: Rules, Community and the Individual," in Pühl, *Meaning Scepticism*, pp. 93–125.
32. Goddard, L., "Counting." *Australasian Journal of Philosophy* **XXXIX** (1961): 223–40.
33. Ibid., p. 223.
34. Ibid., p. 224.
35. Ibid., pp. 224–5.
36. Ibid., p. 225.
37. Ibid., p. 226.
38. Ibid., p. 237.
39. Devitt, Michael, and Sterelny, Kim, *Language and Reality*, 2nd ed. Oxford: Blackwell, 1999, p. 187.
40. Ibid., p. 179.
41. Ibid., p. 11.
42. Ibid., p. 188.
43. Robinson, Guy, *Philosophy and Mystification: a reflection on nonsense and clarity*. London and New York: Routledge, 1998. See especially Ch. 2.

Chapter Nine

1. Strawson, P. F., "Truth," in *Logico-Linguistic Papers*. London: Methuen & Co., Ltd., 1971, p. 197.
2. Frege, Gottlob, "Thoughts," *Logical Investigations*, ed. P. T. Geach, tr. P. T. Geach and R. H. Stoothoff. Oxford: Blackwell, 1977, p. 4.
3. Quine, W. V. O., *From a Logical Point of View*. Cambridge, MA: Harvard University Press, 1953, p. 42.
4. Wheeler, Samuel C., III, in correspondence with the authors.
5. This and the preceding quotation are from Davidson, Donald, *Inquiries into Truth and Interpretation*. Oxford: Clarendon Press, 1984, p. 55.
6. Davidson, Donald, "Radical Interpretation," in *Inquiries into Truth and Interpretation*, pp. 125–40.
7. Ibid., p. 127.
8. Ibid., p. 125.
9. Quine, W. V. O., "Epistemology Naturalized," in *Ontological Relativity, and Other Essays*. New York and London: Columbia University Press, 1969, p. 75.
10. Ibid., p. 87.
11. Davidson, "Radical Interpretation," p. 135.
12. Wheeler, Samuel C., III, letter of October 21, 1999, cited earlier. This, and subsequent e-mail correspondence, was a considerable help to us in working out the structure of this chapter.
13. Quine, W. V. O., *Word and Object*. Cambridge, MA: MIT Press, 1960, pp. 29–30.
14. Wittgenstein, Ludwig, *Philosophical Investigations*, 2nd ed. Oxford: Blackwell, 1953, §28, pp. 13e–14e.

15. Ibid., §29.
16. Ibid., §30.

Chapter Ten

1. An earlier version of the argument developed in this and the following four sections appeared in Harrison, Bernard, "Meaning, Truth and Negation." *Proceedings of the Aristotelian Society*, Supplemental Volume l vii (1983): 179–204.
2. Wittgenstein, Ludwig, *Philosophical Remarks*. Oxford: Blackwell, 1975, pp. 110–11.
3. Geach, Peter, *Mental Acts*. London: Routledge and Kegan Paul, 1957. p. 40.
4. Austin, J. L., *Sense and Sensibilia*. Oxford: Clarendon Press, 1962, p. 67.
5. Quine, W. V. O., "Natural Kinds," in *Ontological Relativity and Other Essays*. New York and London: Columbia University Press, 1969, pp. 121–2.
6. Strawson, P. F., *Individuals*. London: Methuen, 1959, p. 208.
7. Ibid., p. 202.
8. Evans, Gareth, "Identity and Predication," in *Collected Papers*. Oxford: Clarendon Press, 1985.
9. Ibid., p. 30.
10. Ibid., p. 31.
11. Ibid., p. 31.
12. Ibid., p. 37.
13. Ibid.,p. 32.
14. Quine, W. V. O., "Epistemology Naturalized," in *Ontological Relativity and Other Essays*, New York and London: Columbia University Press, 1969, p. 75.
15. For an extended attack on this distinction, see Harrison, Bernard, *Form and Content*. Oxford: Blackwell, 1973.
16. Wittgenstein, Ludwig, *Philosophical Grammar*. Oxford: Blackwell, 1974, p. 130.

Chapter Eleven

1. Bell, David, *Frege's Theory of Judgment*. Oxford: Clarendon Press, 1979, p. 109.
2. Frege, Gottlob, *Logical Investigations*. Oxford: Blackwell, 1977, p. 27.
3. Putnam, Hilary, "The meaning of 'meaning'," in *Mind, Language and Reality*. Cambridge, London, New York: Cambridge University Press, 1975, p. 219.
4. Locke, John, *Essay Concerning Human Understanding*, ed. P. H. Nidditch. Oxford: Clarendon Press, 1975, Book III, V, §3.
5. Putnam, "Meaning of 'meaning'," p. 222.
6. For a good selection of the subsequent discussion, see Pessin, Andrew, and Goldberg, Sanford, eds., *The Twin Earth Chronicles: Twenty Years of Reflection on Hilary Putnam's "The Meaning of Meaning."* Armonk, NY, and London: M. E. Sharpe, 1996.
7. Putnam, "Meaning of 'meaning'," p. 224
8. Ibid., p. 224.
9. Ibid,. p. 225.
10. Ibid., p. 231.
11. Ibid., p. 247.

12. Ibid., p. 247.
13. Ibid., p. 257.
14. Ibid., p. 250.
15. Quine, W. V. O., "Natural Kinds" in *Ontological Relativity and Other Essays*. New York and London: Columbia University Press, 1969, pp. 114–38.
16. Putnam, Hilary, *The Many Faces of Realism: The Paul Carus Lectures*. LaSalle, IL: Open Court, 1987, p. 16.
17. Wheeler, Samuel C., III, *Deconstruction as Analytic Philosophy*. Stanford, CA: Stanford University Press, 2000, p. 120.
18. Ibid., p. 124.
19. Chomsky, Noam, *New Horizons in the Study of Language and Mind*, with an introduction by Smith, Neil. Cambridge: Cambridge University Press, 2000. Cited in Fodor, J. A., Review of Chomsky. *Times Literary Supplement* (June 23, 2000), p. 4.
20. Ibid., p. 4.
21. Ancient philosophers are apt to get upset when the work "platonic" is thrown about in this way. Perhaps we had better make it clear, therefore, that in this work "platonism" refers not to Plato's views as determined, insofar as they can be, by accurate scholarship, but to the familiar collection of views that a long tradition of Western thought has, possibly entirely misguidedly, attributed to Plato.
22. Harrison, Bernard, *Form and Content*. Oxford: Blackwell: 1973, p. 13f.
23. Quine, "Natural Kinds," pp. 121–2.
24. This way of developing the account is in fact closer to the version proposed by Harrison in *Form and Content*, in ignorance, at time of writing, of the rather similar suggestion that Quine had published a year or two earlier in "Natural Kinds." The basic principle of the two proposals is identical, however, and priority clearly belongs to Quine.
25. Berlin, Brent, and Kay, Paul, *Basic Color Terms*. Berkeley and Los Angeles: University of California Press, 1969, *passim*.
26. Pedantic though it may be to insist on the point, it is not entirely fair to conscript Frege as a supporter of the Description Theory of Names. In *Über Sinn und Bedeutung*, he indeed speaks as if the senses of such terms as "Hesperus" and "Phosphorus" are descriptions, "the Evening Star" and "the Morning Star"; and elsewhere he says that one function of the sense of an expression is to locate its referent. But for Frege the referent of a predicate expression was not an extension but a concept. And at one point, in "Negation," he makes it perfectly plain that he does not think that knowledge of the sense of a term necessarily enables one to "fix its extension" in Putnam's sense of that expression. There he argues that the sense of a Thought must be accessible in common to all speakers if it is to be possible for them to co-operate in investigating the question of its truth or falsity. The example he chooses is "Bovine tuberculosis is communicable to men." On general Fregean principles, if one knows the sense of a Thought one knows the sense of the names employed in formulating it. So if one knows the sense of "Bovine tuberculosis is communicable . . ." one knows the sense of "bovine tuberculosis." If it followed that, knowing that, one must know how to fix the extension of "bovine tuberculosis" in Putnam's sense, that is, to *recognise, just as a matter of linguistic knowledge, what is a case of bovine tuberculosis and what is not*, there would be nothing left for Frege's medical researchers to investigate!

27. Locke, John, *Essay Concerning Human Understanding*, ed. P. H. Nidditch. Oxford: Clarendon Press, 1975, Book III, §15.

Chapter Twelve

1. Quine, W. V. O., *Philosophy of Logic*. Englewood Cliffs, NJ: Prentice-Hall, 1970, p. 58.
2. Quine, W. V. O., *From a Logical Point of View*. Cambridge, MA: Harvard University Press, 1953, p. 43.
3. Wittgenstein, Ludwig, *Tractatus Logico-Philosophicus*, tr. D. F. Pears and B. F. McGuinness. London: Routledge and Kegan Paul, 1961. All citations from p. 29.
4. Ibid., p. 5.
5. *Tractatus* 5.5563 might be cited as a counterinstance to this claim. But see 4.002 and 3.3223.
6. Diamond, Cora, "Realism and the Realistic Spirit," in *Realism and the Realistic Spirit*. Cambridge, MA, and London: MIT Press, 1991, both citations from p. 54.
7. Quine, W. V. O., *From a Logical Point of View*. Cambridge, MA: Harvard University Press, 1953, p. 34.
8. Grice, H. P., and Strawson, P. F., "In Defense of a Dogma," *Philosophical Review*, **LXV** (1956): 141–58.
9. See, for instance, Cora Diamond's parallel demonstration of how empiricism in its Berkeleyan form can be construed as a (deeply Wittgensteinian) form of Realism, in *Realism and the Realistic Spirit*, pp. 47–58, and *passim*.
10. Wittgenstein, Ludwig, *Philosophical Remarks*. Oxford: Blackwell, 1975, p. 102 (opening of §74).
11. Kripke, Saul, *Naming and Necessity*. Oxford: Blackwell, 1980, p. 34, *et seq.*
12. Mellor, D. H., "Natural Kinds," *British Journal for the Philosophy of Science*, **28** (1977): 219–312; and in Andrew Pessin and Sanford Goldberg, eds., *The Twin Earth Chronicles: Twenty Years of Reflection on Hilary Putnam's "The meaning of 'meaning'."* Amonk, NY, and London: M. E. Sharpe, 1996.
13. Zemach, E., "Putnam's Theory of the Reference of Substance Terms," *The Journal of Philosophy*, **73** (1976): 116–27.
14. Forbes, G. "In Defense of Absolute Essentialism," *Midwest Studies in Philosophy*, **11** (1986): 3–31, *passim*.
15. Robertson, Teresa, "Possibilities and the Arguments for Origin Essentialism." *Mind*, **107** (October 1998): 729–49; Hawthorne, John and Gendler, Tamar Szabo, "Origin Essentialism: The Arguments Reconsidered," *Mind*, **109** (April 2000): 283–98; Robertson, Teresa, "Essentialism: Origin and Order," *Mind*, **109** (April 2000): 299–307.
16. Sterelny, Kim, "Natural-Kind Terms," in Pessin and Goldberg, *Twin Earth Chronicles*, p. 106.
17. Wittgenstein, Ludwig, *Philosophical Investigations*, 2nd edition, Oxford: Blackwell, 1953, §218.
18. Ibid., §373.
19. See the penetrating discussion by Julius Kovesi, in Chapter 1 of *Moral Notions*, London: Routledge; New York: Humanities Press, 1967.

Chapter Thirteen

1. A very early version of some of the points in this chapter appear in Hanna, Patricia, "Translation, Indeterminacy and Triviality," *Philosophia*, **14**, nos. 3–4 (1984): 341–8.

2. Quine, W. V. O., "Indeterminacy of Translation Again," *The Journal of Philosophy*, **84**, no. 1 (January 1987); "On the Reasons for Indeterminacy of Translation," *The Journal of Philosophy*, **67**, no. 6 (1970); "Three Indeterminacies," in *Perspectives on Quine*, ed. R. Barrett, and R. Gibson, Cambridge, MA: Blackwell, 1990: 1–16.

3. Quine, W. V. O., *Word and Object*. Cambridge, MA: M.I.T. Press, 1960.

4. Ibid., p. 27.

5. Ibid., p. 27.

6. Quine, W. V. O., "Ontological Relativity," in *Ontological Relativity and Other Essays*. New York and London: Columbia University Press, 1969, pp. 26–68.

7. Ibid., p. 47.

8. Quine, W. V. O., "Speaking of Objects," in *Ontological Relativity*, p. 20.

9. Wittgenstein, Ludwig, *Philosophical Investigations*, 2nd edition, Oxford: Blackwell, 1953, §206.

10. There is, of course, another alternative: locate the connection between language and the world at the level of the entire language. Quine tends strongly towards this when he writes that meaning is fixed in the theory as a whole; but he doesn't take the next step and argue that the connection between the world and language occurs *only* at this juncture. More important, given the structure of his argument, it is apparent that for Quine if language as a whole (or theory) is to have a connection with the world, it can *only* acquire this connection via observation sentences and stimulus meaning, not via language *tout court.*

   In an important sense, the two-level account of meaning we offer in this book may be seen as a variant of the view that it's language as a whole that engages with the world. However, it is of central importance to the present account that this engagement occurs via the *practices* that make up language, and not via linguistic items themselves, however they might be construed.

11. Quine, *Word and Object*, p. 27.

12. Ibid., p. 27.

13. Quine, W. V. O, "On Empirically Equivalent Systems of the World," *Erkenntnis* **9** (1975): 313–28, p. 316. This remark is, however, rather troubling. Two pages earlier, he writes that observation statements

   > . . . are indeed separately susceptible to tests of observation; and at the same time they do not stand free of theory, for they share much of the vocabulary of the more remotely theoretical statements. They are what link theory to observation, affording theory its empirical content. (p. 314)

   Here Quine seems to waver between linking observation sentences directly to the world and keeping them internal to language. The explanation lies, we contend, in his ultimate view of observation sentences as representing an ideal that is not in fact realisable.

14. Quine, *Ontological Relativity*, p. 49.

15. Wittgenstein, *Philosophical Investigations*, §217.

16. Gareth Evans's analysis of the "Gavagai" case in "Identity and Predication" (in *Collected Papers*, Oxford: Clarendon Press, 1985, pp. 25–48) presents a similar argument.
17. Quine, W.V. O., "Perceiving and Learning," in *The Roots of Reference*, La Salle, IL: Open Court, 1973, pp. 1–32.
18. Ibid., p. 24.
19. Ibid., p. 25.
20. Ibid., p. 25.
21. Wittgenstein, *Philosophical Investigations*, §28.
22. Ibid., §29.
23. This is where devices such as Goddardian counting (see Chapter 8 §xii) come into play in language learning.
24. Quine, W. V. O., "Epistemology Naturalized," in *Ontological Relativity*, p. 89.
25. Quine, *Ontological Relativity*, p. 53
26. Ibid., p. 49.
27. Ibid., pp. 49–50.
28. Ibid., p. 50.

Chapter Fourteen

1. The main arguments in this chapter appear in Hanna, Patricia, "Linguistic Competence and Kripke's Puzzle," *Philosophia: Philosophical Quarterly of Israel*, vol. 28, nos. 1–4 (2001): 171–89. Permission has been granted by the editor for its inclusion here.
2. Kripke, Saul, "A Puzzle About Belief." *Meaning and Use*, ed. A. Margalit Dordrecht: D. Reidel, 1979, pp. 239–83.
3. Kripke states (**DQ**) in English; however he holds that there are analogues of it in every other language: "... an analogous principle, stated in French (German, etc.) will be assumed to hold for French (German, etc.) sentences" (p. 250). This assumption is necessary given that "we ordinarily allow ourselves to draw conclusions, stated in English, about the beliefs of speakers of any language: we infer that Pierre believes that God exists from his sincere reflective assent to '*Dieu existe*'" (p. 250). In what follows, we use (**DQ**) to justify all disquotations, without bothering to give statements of the warrants for every separate language.
4. Kripke, "Puzzle," pp. 248–50.
5. Ibid., p. 249.
6. Ibid., p. 249.
7. Ibid., p. 249.
8. Ibid., p. 254.
9. Ibid., p. 255.
10. Ibid., p. 255.
11. Ibid., p. 256.
12. Ibid., pp. 256–7.
13. Ibid., p. 257.
14. Ibid., p. 257.
15. Ibid., pp. 258–9.
16. Ibid., pp. 259.
17. Ibid., pp. 239.

18. Ibid., pp. 259.
19. In Chapters 6 and 7, we examine some of the problems that arise for this theory of meaning; however, in this chapter, we accept Kripke's contention that the alleged paradox of belief is not a unique consequence of this particular view of meaning.
20. Kripke, "Puzzle," pp. 260–1.
21. Ibid., pp. 260–1.
22. The same holds for objects that are taken in at a glance (e.g., the referents of "Cicero" and "Tully"); but for our purposes this needn't be argued here.
23. Kripke, "Puzzle," pp. 256–7.
24. This can, of course, be generalised for sentences in other languages; such generalisation will be assumed throughout the chapter.
25. This is similar to Kripke's statement on p. 255, cited earlier. However, there are important differences between the two. (i)–(iii) omit all reference to any actual city; thus, the conditions given here make no mention of the world, as Kripke's statement may easily be taken as doing, and are restricted to the purely linguistic.
26. Kripke, "Puzzle," p. 260.
27. Ibid., p. 259. Also see §iv.
28. Strictly, we should say that what Pierre believes is that London is not pretty and that *Londres est jolie*; however, as it is the *name* that is here at issue, we will allow ourselves to speak a bit more loosely than that.
29. Evans, Gareth, *The Varieties of Reference*, ed. John McDowell. Oxford: Clarendon Press, 1982, p. 44.
30. Although in §v we have seen that not even a strong commitment to Russell's Principle will be sufficient to authorise the generation of the paradox.

Chapter Fifteen

1. The main arguments in this chapter are from Hanna, Patricia, "What Kripke's Puzzle Doesn't Tell Us about Language, Meaning or Belief," submitted to *Philosophia: Philosophical Quarterly of Israel* in 2000, to appear in 2003. Permission has been granted by the editor for its inclusion here.
2. Wittgenstein, Ludwig, *Notebooks, 1914–1916*, H. G. von Wright, and G. E. M. Anscombe, ed.; Anscombe, G. E. M., tr. Oxford: Basil Blackwell, 1969, 29.5.15, p. 52e.
3. Kripke, Saul, "A Puzzle About Belief," in *Meaning and Use*, ed. A. Margalit. D. Reidel, 1979, pp. 239–83.
4. Ibid., p. 269.
5. Ibid., pp. 269–70.
6. Ibid., pp. 269–70.
7. Ibid., p. 253.
8. Ibid., p. 253–4.
9. Kripke, Saul, *Naming and Necessity*. Cambridge, MA: Harvard, 1980.
10. The same can, of course, be said about Frege-Russell theories of names; however, all that concerns us here is the relationship to Millian theories.

11. This is a variant of the characterization of "philosophical paradox" as an argument that "entails pairs of propositions one of which must be true, but neither of which can be true," given in Chapter 13 §i.

12. Kripke, "Puzzle," p. 270.

13. Ibid., pp. 249–50.

14. One might suggest placing the restriction on (**T**), but this would be too stringent a measure. In general, translations needn't be as restrictive as this qualification would require; it is only when some principle of disquotation is also used that we need to be this careful with the translation. Therefore, we prefer to attach the restriction to the principle of disquotation.

15. Perhaps this shouldn't come as a surprise, given Kripke's earlier arguments in *Naming and Necessity* for *de re* essentialism; however, at this point in his paper he is committed to neutrality with respect to theories of meaning, and thus to any consequences of these theories. Later in the chapter we shall consider the implications of Kripke's essentialism in the context of his paradox.

16. This is related to the fallacy of confusing theory of meaning with theory of translation discussed by Gareth Evans in "Identity and Predication," *Collected Papers*. Oxford: Clarendon Press, 1985.

> A translation is one thing, a theory of meaning another. A manual of translation aims to provide, for each sentence of the language under study, a way of arriving at a quoted sentence of another language that has the same meaning. A theory of meaning, on the other hand, entails, for each sentence of the language under study, a statement of what it means. A translator states no semantical truths at all, nor has he any need of the concepts of truth, denotation, and satisfaction. (p. 25)

17. The case is more like the identity of Cicero and Tully, the man. Once that identity is discovered, we realise that there always just *one* man; as it were, the "twoness" was an illusion.

18. Heal, Jane, *Fact and Meaning: Quine and Wittgenstein on Philosophy of Language*. Oxford: Blackwell, 1989.

19. Ibid., p. 219.

20. Ibid., pp. 219–20.

21. Robinson, Guy, *Philosophy and Mystification: a reflection on nonsense and clarity*. London and New York: Routledge, 1998.

22. Ibid., p. 202.

23. Ibid., p. 202.

24. Ibid., p. 203.

Epilogue

1. Wittgenstein, Ludwig, *Remarks on the Foundations of Mathematics*, ed. G. H. von Wright *et al.* Cambridge, MA: MIT Press, 1978, p. 325.

2. Merleau-Ponty, Maurice, *La Prose du Monde*. Paris, 1969. Translated as *The Prose of the World*, tr. Claude Lefort and John O'Neill. Evanston, IL: Northwestern University Press, 1973, p. 17.

3. Fodor, J. A., Review of Chomsky. *Times Literary Supplement* (June 23, 2000): 3–4.

4. Heal, Jane, *Fact and Meaning: Quine and Wittgenstein on Philosophy of Language*. Oxford: Blackwell, 1989, pp. 13–21.

5. Ibid., p. 16.

6. Putnam, Hilary, *Meaning and the Moral Sciences*. London and Boston: Routledge and Kegan Paul, 1978, p. 125.

7. See Fales, Evan, "How to be a Metaphysical Realist," in Peter A. French, Theodore Uehling, Jr., and Howard K. Wettstein, *Midwest Studies in Philosophy XII : Realism and Antirealism*, Minneapolis: University of Minnesota Press, 1988, pp. 253–74.

8. Putnam, *Meaning and Moral Sciences*, p. 125.

9. Fales, "Metaphysical Realist," p. 254.

10. Strawson, P. F., "Truth," in *Logico-Linguistic Papers*. London: Methuen, 1971, pp. 190–213.

11. Frassen, Bas van, *The Scientific Image*. Oxford: Oxford University Press, 1980, p. 8. Cited in Lepore, Ernest and Lower, Barry, "A Putnam's Progress," in P. French *et al.*, *Realism and Antirealism*, pp. 459–73. The first few paragraphs of this section owe much to Lepore and Loewer's discussion.

12. Putnam, Hilary, *Reason, Truth and History*. Cambridge: Cambridge University Press, 1981, p. 49.

13. Putnam, *Meaning and the Moral Sciences*, p. 125.

14. Lepore and Loewer, "A Putnam's Progress," p. 461.

15. Merleau-Ponty, *Prose of the World*, p. 4.

16. Spinoza, B., *Ethics* and *On the Improvement of the Understanding*, ed. James Gutman. New York: Hafner, 1949, 1974, p. 83.

17. Frege, Gottlob, "On Sense and Reference," in Peter Geach, and Max Black, eds., *Translations from the Philosophical Writings of Gottlob Frege*. Oxford: Basil Blackwell, 1970, p. 63.

18. Diamond, Cora, *Realism and the Realistic Spirit*. Cambridge, MA, and London: MIT Press, 1991.

19. Our thanks to Elijah Milgram for reminding us of this.

20. Diamond, *Realistic Spirit*, p. 69.

21. Williams, Bernard, *Ethics and the Limits of Philsophy*. London: Fontana/Collins, 1985, pp. 138–9.

22. Ibid., p. 141.

23. Ibid., p. 146.

24. Ibid., p. 147.

25. Ibid., p. 148.

26. Diamond, *Realistic Spirit*, p. 69.

27. Stevens, Wallace, *The Collected Poems of Wallace Stevens*. New York: Alfred A. Knopf, 1954, p. 355.

28. Merleau-Ponty, *Prose of the World*, pp. 11–12.

29. Krausz, Michael, *Rightness and Reasons: Interpretation in Cultural Practices*. Ithaca, NY, and London: Cornell University Press, 1993.

30. Harrison, Bernard, *Inconvenient Fictions: Literature and the Limits of Theory*. New Haven, CT, and London: Yale University Press, 1991.

Index